Juvenile Delinquency

THE UNIVERSITY SERIES IN PSYCHOLOGY

Editor

David C. McClelland
Harvard University

Juvenile Delinquency

RESEARCH AND THEORY

Edited by

HERBERT C. QUAY

University of Illinois

D. VAN NOSTRAND COMPANY, INC.

Princeton, New Jersey

Toronto　　　　　　　　New York　　　　　　　　London

D. VAN NOSTRAND COMPANY, INC.
120 Alexander St., Princeton, New Jersey (*Principal office*)
24 West 40 Street, New York 18, New York

D. VAN NOSTRAND COMPANY, LTD.
358, Kensington High Street, London, W.14, England

D. VAN NOSTRAND COMPANY (CANADA), LTD.
25 Hollinger Road, Toronto 16, Canada

Published simultaneously in Canada by
D. VAN NOSTRAND COMPANY (Canada), LTD.

PRINTED IN THE UNITED STATES OF AMERICA

3/28/66 Bro-Dart 6.95

Preface

A critical survey of theory, research and research method in juvenile delinquency can serve at least two purposes. We hope to provide a handbook of theory and research both for the student and for the practitioner in the field. We also wish to provide research workers in the area with a summing up of the past and guidelines for future investigation. To these ends the editor sought as collaborators individuals active in research or theory or both, and particularly individuals sensitive to the methodological issues which must be faced if reliable knowledge is to be accumulated. While the editor has attempted to provide some features of over-all structure, the organization within chapters has been left to the contributors. This is really as it should be; those seriously involved in a subject are in the best position to develop a conceptual organization relevant to it.

The initial steps toward the development of this book were taken when the editor was at Vanderbilt University. The majority of the editor's efforts were expended during his tenure at Northwestern University. Finally, the work was brought to a close during the first year of his present academic connection at the University of Illinois. To the administrations of all three universities he offers appreciation for their support of the kind of activity represented by this volume.

H.C.Q.

Urbana, Illinois
March 1965

v

The Contributors

HERBERT C. QUAY is Research Director of the Children's Research Center and Associate Professor of Psychology and of Special Education at the University of Illinois.

PETER F. BRIGGS is Associate Professor in the Department of Physical Medicine and Rehabilitation at the University of Minnesota Medical School.

WILLIAM C. RHODES, on leave as Professor of Psychology at George Peabody College, is currently Consultant in Child Mental Health in the Community Research and Services Branch of the National Institute of Mental Health.

ROBERT D. WIRT is Professor of Psychology, Child Development, and Psychiatry at the University of Minnesota.

DONALD R. PETERSON is Professor of Psychology and Director of Clinical Training at the University of Illinois.

WESLEY C. BECKER is Professor of Psychology at the University of Illinois.

J. DOUGLAS GRANT is Chief of Research for the California Department of Corrections.

JOHN R. EICHORN is Professor of Education and Coordinator of the Peripatology Program at Boston College.

DANIEL GLASER is Professor and Chairman of the Department of Sociology at the University of Illinois.

NATHAN S. CAPLAN is Research Director of the Chicago Youth Development Project and Study Director, Research Center for Group Dynamics, Institute for Social Research, University of Michigan.

committed while in high school which, if discovered, would have resulted in their being classified as a delinquent. They were not caught, however. Such data are further evidence of the social class bias in delinquency statistics. Later studies by Murphy *et al.* (1946) and, quite recently, studies by Miller (1962) confirm these findings regarding hidden delinquency. A number of investigators have since done considerable work in developing self-report techniques. In general, they find that most young people do not report serious anti-social behavior, but that the extent of misbehavior among adolescents is certainly much greater than that reflected in official records. Nye and Short (1957) have refined the technique of assessing unofficial delinquency. Their scaling methods utilize data obtained from questionnaires (usually anonymous). There are some obvious problems in such methodology. The extent to which the respondents cooperate is unknown. Errors exist in the data, both because of the fallibility of memory and because of dissimulation. Doubtlessly, some youngsters withhold the truth by omitting to report some offenses which in fact they did commit, while others may falsely report having taken part in delinquencies in which in fact they did not participate. Efforts have been made to estimate the size of these sources of error by interview techniques, comparison of reported crimes with survey data, and the use of identified questionnaires. In summarizing the data on this point, Dentler (1962) states, "There is evidence in the available literature that given . . . [appropriate] . . . conditions . . . [of data collection] . . . , self-report data are sufficiently reliable and valid to make their collection and analysis eminently worthwhile."

The "official" incidence of juvenile delinquency in the United States is usually estimated from data gathered by two federal agencies: the Federal Bureau of Investigation (1962) of the United States Department of Justice and the Children's Bureau of the United States Department of Health, Education and Welfare (1962). The former obtains police statistics from cities of over 2,500 population. These statistics represent the frequency of arrest for certain crimes. The latter obtains current statistics from a representative sample of court jurisdictions throughout the country. These statistics show the annual number of juveniles adjudicated as delinquent. The narrowest measuring of incidence of juvenile crime would be the number of adjudicated delinquents in a given time period. The broadest meaning would include all juveniles who have broken the law whether apprehended or not. Arrest statistics are in between. Among these different ways of viewing the data there is considerable concordance in the rank order of frequency of types of offenses and rates of crime for various age groups. The most frequent juvenile crime is stealing, and such offenses are committed primarily by those in the middle adolescent years. Whether one looks at arrest statistics or court records, the evidence seems clearly to indicate that at least the detection of incidences of delinquency is rising at a rate which is greater than the rate of growth of the population. In the case of adjudicated delinquents the rate during the last decade shows an increase in court appearance about twice as great as the increase in the population of that age.

The official statistics also show a higher incidence of delinquency in urban, industrial centers than in smaller towns or farming communities, although there is an increasing rate in these areas too. The rate for boys is, and has always been, much higher than the rate for girls. The rate for girls appears recently to be accelerating more rapidly than for boys. While delinquency seems highly related to the developmental phenomena of adolescence in the past decade or more, delinquency is rising at a differentially higher rate during early adolescence in contrast with older youth and adults, especially in urban areas.

In reviewing data from national sources, it should be remembered that the many factors suggested earlier in this section contribute some degree of inaccuracy to the statistics quoted below. In addition, a final source of error may occur because both the FBI and the Children's Bureau act merely as collection agencies.[1] Because not all police departments and courts cooperate, their data are based on a sample rather than the entire population. Participation in their programs by local and state law enforcement agencies and by courts is wholly voluntary. Neither the Department of Justice nor the Department of Health, Education and Welfare can or does vouch for the validity of data sent to them. Nevertheless, to paraphrase Perlman (1957), their reports do contain the best available evidence reflecting trends in juvenile delinquency. With the passage of the Juvenile Delinquency and Youth Offenses Control Act by the Congress in 1961, and its extension in 1963 and 1964, substantial research and action programs in several American cities have been established. We may now hope that the next few years will bring enormously improved methods of assessment and treatment. Because of the additional filtering problems and difficulties in reporting systems

---

[1] Robison (1960) points out: "Like the Children's Bureau, the FBI is apt to allege especially at budget time—the end of the fiscal year—an alarming increase in juvenile delinquency."

for court cases, we have chosen to reproduce here arrest statistics as reported to only the FBI.

Figure 1-1 shows the total number of crimes for which persons age 21 and under were arrested, as reported to the FBI between the years 1953 and 1961. These data show a very rapid increase in the

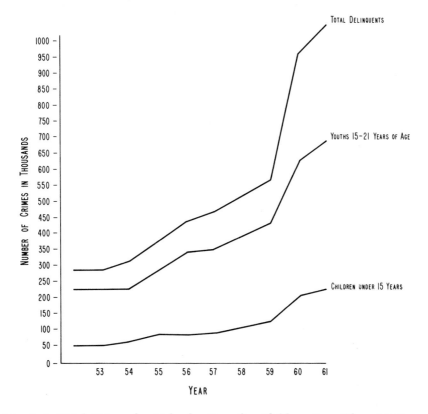

Fig. 1–1. Total Crimes by Calendar Year for Children Less Than 15 Years versus Youths from 18-21 and All Ages Combined.*

absolute number of crimes committed with especially steep gains in the two most recent years for which statistics are available. These figures indicate that there has been more than a tripling of juvenile crime, from about 300,000 to nearly a million arrests, within less than a decade. The data in Fig. 1-1 show number of arrests reported to the FBI. This means that the figure more nearly reflects the number

* Data in this illustration are derived from the Uniform Crime Reports for the United States, 1953-1961, pp. 24-32. Washington FBI, 1954-1962.

of acts which came under official investigation than the number of persons who committed offenses. Some youngsters would have been arrested more than one time during a given year. The extent of such recidivisms cannot be determined from the available records.

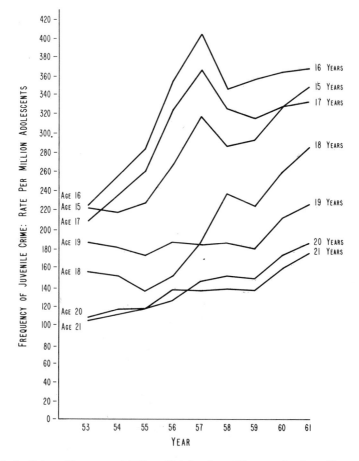

Fig. 1–2. Crime Rate per Million Youths for Offenses Against Property by Year for Each Age Group from 15-21 Years.°

It has been said that there seems to be a trend for increasingly younger members of the society to become delinquent. To assess this trend we prepared the other two curves shown in Fig. 1-1. These show the total crimes committed by persons under 15 years and

° Data in this illustration are derived from the Uniform Crime Reports for the United States, 1953-1961, pp. 24-32. Washington FBI, 1954-1962.

those between 15 and 21 years. This represents approximately equal populations for two seven-year age ranges. The trend here is clearly for a sharp rise in child delinquency, but the increase in the very young is not as marked as that for older adolescents.

Note, however, that these data do *not* reflect the rapid growth of population—especially the adolescent population, during the same

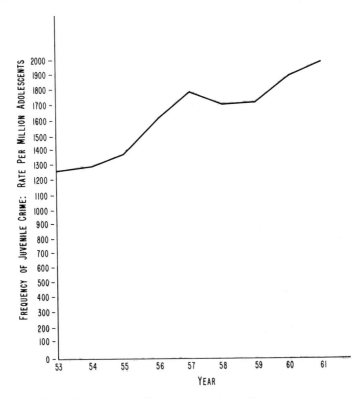

Fig. 1–3. Crime Rate per Million Youths for Offenses Against Property by Year for the Total Adolescent Population.*

period. They are presented only to illustrate the magnitude of the problem; they do not demonstrate an increasing *rate* of delinquency.

In Fig. 1-2, the total crimes for which youngsters were arrested is shown for each age group, and crimes are reported as a *rate* per million of the adolescent population. This figure is corrected for population growth and over-all demonstrates a rise in rate of delin-

* Data in this illustration are derived from the Uniform Crime Reports for the United States, 1953-1961, pp. 24-32. Washington FBI, 1954-1962.

quency greater than can be accounted for by population growth
alone. This figure also roughly indicates the developmental trend in
child delinquency; that is, a rise during early adolescence, up to age
16, and a rapid decline in rate in later years. Figure 1-3 shows the

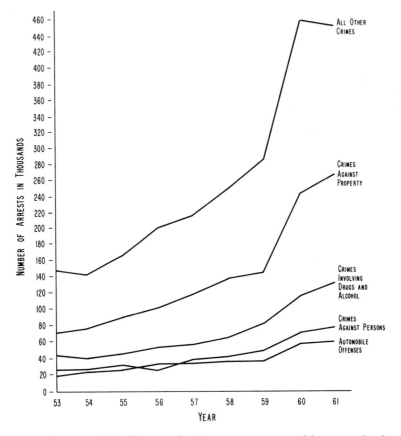

Fig. 1–4. Number of Crimes by Category Committed by Juveniles.*

trend for the total adolescent population from age 15 through 21
years of age. This figure shows a general rise in the frequency with
which offenses have been reported and is also based on rate per million of the adolescent population. As such, it is corrected for population growth.

The FBI statistics may be categorized by type of crime. Table 1

* Data in this illustration are derived from the Uniform Crime Reports for the
United States, 1953-1961, pp. 24-32. Washington FBI, 1954-1962.

gives the major categories, with the titles of offenses included in each. Trends over the past decade of violations within these categories are shown in Fig. 1-4 (again, not corrected for population increase). This figure shows gradual rise in all types of crime, but most markedly in property offenses and the category of "Other Crimes." This last is most heavily contributed to by disorderly conduct and the residual group of "All other offenses."

TABLE 1-1. FBI CLASSIFICATION OF CRIMES

Crimes Against Property:
  Robbery
  Burglary
  Larceny
  Embezzlement
  Stolen property
  Forgery and counterfeiting

Crimes Against Persons:
  Criminal homicide
    Murder and nonnegligent manslaughter
    Manslaughter by negligence
  Forcible rape
  Aggravated assault
  Other assaults
  Prostitution and commercial vice
  Other sex offenses
  Offenses against family and children

Crimes Involving Drugs and Alcohol:
  Narcotic drug law violations
  Liquor law violations
  Drunkenness

Automobile Offenses:
  Automobile theft
  Driving while intoxicated

Other Crimes:
  Violation of laws regulating weapons
  Disorderly conduct
  Vagrancy
  Gambling
  Suspicion
  All other offenses

Thus, on the basis of official statistics, it is apparent that the total number of juvenile offenses is increasing and that it is highly likely, despite the problems associated with estimating incidence, that the rate is also on the rise.

History

While delinquency is a social problem of increasing concern to our society, it is not, by any means, a recent phenomenon. Our current concerns and attempts at prevention and amelioration are not without antecedents and are not independent of earlier thought and action on law, responsibility, and justice. A brief historical review may serve to provide perspective.

Delinquency has existed in all cultures in all epochs of recorded history since there was any semblance of group living. There is not a contemporary society in which misbehavior of young people does not exist and for which provision in law or custom is not made for the socialization of the individual and the management of persons whose social behavior is considered unsatisfactory to the dominant group.

In Western culture, three traditions having ancient roots have become part of contemporary criminal law. In the United States, the most important of these is the *common law* which arose from German tribal law and was greatly modified by British tradition in later centuries. The other two important traditions are those from Judaic-Christian religion and from the Roman law.

Roman law is the primary influence in juridical practice in most of Europe and in Latin-American countries. Beginning with the rule of the Emperor Constantine when Christianity became the state religion of Rome, Christian religious beliefs were more and more finely articulated in common law and ecclesiastical courts. These courts and their influence on secular justice reached their height of power in medieval Europe, after more than a thousand years of significant influence. It was not until much later (the mid-nineteenth century) that even in Great Britain all of the functions of ecclesiastical courts were transferred to secular courts. The guiding principle under which religious jurisprudence is practiced is the aim to understand and apply the Will of God. The most profound effect of this principle finds expression in the American legal tradition of individual responsibility and retributive justice.

The major premise of Roman law was that the individual has no rights except as given by the State. As the power of the Church increased, the tradition became the doctrine that the King rules by Divine Right. Many abuses by European governments can be attributed to the exercise of that doctrine for centuries. Revolt against these developments has limited the Church in most places. In dictatorial states of Europe and Latin America, the political and juridical philosophy of the incontestable validity of state action is maintained. In North America, the tradition of Roman law continues to dominate the legal systems of Quebec, Louisiana, and Mexico. A major difference between the Roman view and the common law, which prevails throughout the rest of the English-speaking world, is that judgment under Roman law is rendered by an official of the state—a judge—while under the common law guilt is determined by the representatives of the citizens—a jury.

In the case of legislation governing judicial proceedings with children, there is also evidence of some Roman law influence. Much juvenile court administration proceeds from a presumption of guilt for acts committed contrary to the general requirement in adult criminal cases of proof by the state beyond reasonable doubt. There is a difficult problem in values in juvenile cases in which a conflict arises between the philosophy of desire to protect (rather than prosecute) children and to dispense justice which is corrective and rehabilitative (rather than punitive) and the philosophy of due process (such as indictment and trial by jury) and protection of individual rights of minors and incompetents (such as the right to counsel).

The special treatment of juveniles under the law began relatively recently. After many years of exploitation subsequent to the Industrial Revolution, children came to be protected by legislation governing child labor. The federal government regulated the type of work and number of hours for which children and adolescents of specified ages were permitted to work. Similarly, state statutes were enacted governing child labor for businesses which were not in interstate commerce. Each of the states also enacted compulsory school attendance laws, typically for children who are educable between the ages of 7 and 16 years. Such laws regarding work and school have been enacted to protect children and to insure their socialization. However, they also, unfortunately, contribute to creating problems for youngsters who adjust poorly to school and for youngsters out of school who are not permitted to work. Such young people seem especially susceptible to delinquency.

The governments in all fifty states also provide special treatment for juveniles in the court system. The first juvenile court was established in Chicago (Cook County) in 1899 after several years of promotion by the great social reformer, Jane Addams. The philosophy of these courts is to remove the delinquent from the class of adult criminals and place him under the protection of the state, just as is done for dependent and neglected children. The courts are human institutions and as such are not always efficient, not always under the leadership of adequately trained or ideally motivated persons, do not always protect the individual's civil rights in their attempt to provide care, and, as a result, do not always render care or justice. However, the philosophy that the purpose of the court is to provide correction and protection and not to assign criminal guilt or extract retributive punishment has led to an enormous advance in human welfare in this century.

With some exceptions, a discussion of which is beyond the scope of this chapter, the criminal code in the United States does not apply to children. It typically provides that children under age 7 are incapable of committing a crime, that children age 7 or over but under age 14 must be placed under the disposition of a juvenile court, that children over 14 but under 18 can only be tried as adults if referred to the appropriate prosecuting authority by the juvenile court (which it rarely does and then only for very serious offenses, such as murder), and that persons 18 and over come under the jurisdiction of district (or other adult) courts. Hearings in children's courts are informal, and disposition of cases is made upon the consideration of the child's best interest.

Thus our society has a specialized legal mechanism for dealing with juvenile delinquency. An extended discussion, in both this chapter and volume, of the operation of the juvenile court and its services would be impractical, but the basic legal structure for dealing with the problem must always be considered in relation to both research and action programs.

THEORIES OF ETIOLOGY

What gives rise to juvenile delinquency? If it is increasing, what are the causes? What can be done? While the later chapters of this book consider these questions and the research related to them in detail, a brief overview may serve to set the stage.

We will sketch in this section some of the major explanations used for the causes of juvenile delinquency with some consideration of the implications of interest in these etiologic theories for appropriate research strategy and for social action. In a later chapter, we make some reference to these theories as they relate to useful predictive systems and comment on the degrees to which they have empirical validity. Other chapters in this volume deal with many of these theories in much greater detail.

Delinquent behavior has been attributed to *spiritual degeneration* or malevolence, to *biological disorders* (including genetic, morphologic, neurologic, and metabolic imbalances), to *experiential deficiencies* (including inappropriate learning, stimulus deprivation, and psychopathogenic factors), and to *social inadequacies* (including cultural, sociological, economic, and political inequities).

Religious Views

The oldest view concerning the causes of delinquency come from religion. Most citizens in the United States are influenced by the Judaic-Christian traditions of Western culture. In the United States, the culture is heavily influenced by the Protestant ethic of individual responsibility. By revelation (for example, the Mosaic Law) and by tradition, there has developed a generally accepted code of conduct which is expected to govern man's relationship to God and to other men. Much of this tradition is reflected in civil statutes. The concept of sin is implicit in this tradition. The consequences of sin and of illegal behavior are punishment. Forgiveness by the state is, for most crimes, contingent upon the expiation of wrongdoing by suffering, and sometimes by restitution and resolution to obey the law. There are differences of theological opinion as to whether the Grace of God is independent of, or follows upon, suffering.

Much of this religious tradition has been codified in the civil law. Often, both citizens and officials of the state express the opinion that the failure of an individual to reform following punishment indicates that the punishment was not sufficiently severe. Correction then involves the extraction of heavier penalties. This principle does not directly derive from religious teaching but rather is said to be "common sense." These ideas were first formally expressed by Beccaria (1804) 200 years ago. He attempted to clarify the meaning of moral philosophy as it related to crime. Beccaria reasoned that in the general exercise of his free will, man will seek pleasure and avoid pain. Thus he proposed that punishment for crime must be appropriate to the severity of the offense and must be greater than the real or expected rewards for continued criminal acts. As we point out later, this simple observation is an important theorem in the contemporary behavior theories which use reinforcement as a fundamental factor in human learning. This point of view, which Robison (1960) calls the classical period in theories of cause, did not sufficiently account for individual differences since it looked at the crime rather than the criminal. To a large degree, and with some merit, this continues to be the philosophy of American law and is related to the precept that all men are equal under a rule of law. However, even beginning with Beccaria, some attention to the individual was recommended. Just as most criminal codes in the United States provide, Beccaria asserted that children are incapable of committing a crime. Law provides punishment for adult offenders, but it also provides for the protection and/or treatment of those individuals judged to be incompetent because of immaturity, mental illness, defective intelligence, and dependent or neglected status.

Religious views, as outlined above, could be taken as a basis for research and action in the treatment and prevention of delinquency. A conceptual scheme based upon the common sense of the people (a not unreasonable approach in a democratic society) would direct research toward refining methods for the detection and apprehension of guilty individuals and toward the development of methods of punishment which would be efficacious in the suppression of criminal behavior and effective in coercing conformity. Social action would involve the implementation of these techniques. The common sense evidence for this approach is obvious: in fact, most burned children do dread the fire. The view derived from religion suggests that a solution will be found when we know how much of which kinds of punishments to apply. However, there is considerable evidence from the psychology of learning which clearly demonstrates that punishment is often a weak method for both suppressing old patterns and establishing new patterns of behavior.

Biological Theories

Medicine, the next oldest of the relevant disciplines, accounts for antisocial behavior as arising from organic or functional pathology of the central nervous system. If such behavior is genetically based and expressed in gross morphology (as Sheldon et al. [1949] would propose), neurologically (as Kallman [1953] would propose), or broadly behaviorally (as Cleckley [1941] would propose), research should be directed toward the anatomical, endocrinological, metabolic, or essentially biochemical processes which result in delinquent behavior of individuals. Any action recommended in consequence of such knowledge would be in the form of eugenic and public health measures, designed to limit transmission of defective genetic constitutional factors and to correct aberrant metabolic processes.

Psychological Theories

Functional psychiatric disorders are also viewed as basic causes of delinquency. The fundamental intrapsychic pathology is often attributed to faulty interpersonal relationships especially between parents and children in the early years (or months) of life. Disturbances in these relationships produce neurotic, psychotic, or character disordered behavior, some of which are antisocial. It becomes antisocial through one of several routes. In some cases the individual, because of neurotic guilt, seeks to be punished; in some cases the individual, because of displaced hostility, seeks revenge on society or symbolic persons or objects; in some cases the individual, because of panic arising from displaced anxiety, thinks that he is protecting his endangered psychic or physical being by attacking others or destroying property he erroneously believes is intent on harming him.

The research task here would be to increase our understanding of the causes of mental illness insofar as they relate to disturbed interpersonal relationships and to increase knowledge of effective methods of psychotherapeutic intervention. Action would require programs designed to alter parent-child relationship, training in and dissemination of mental health material, and applications of psychiatric techniques to those now affected.

Sociological Theories

Sociological theory stresses the contribution of social forces to the occurrence of deviant behavior. According to Durkheim (1897; 1898), serious economic or political stress can lead to a breakdown of power in the social system, whereby cultural norms no longer have inhibiting influence over group and individual behavior. He called this breakdown a condition of normlessness or anomie, that is to say, of lawlessness. Much contemporary sociological thinking concerning delinquency derives from Merton's (1957) extension of Durkheim's nineteenth-century theory of anomie. This theory emphasizes the difficulties which arise when avenues toward, and forms of identification with, the goals and values of the society are not available. The foundation of Cloward and Ohlin's (1960) theory of opportunity rests upon Merton's construction. Delinquency, in their view, is the result of unsuccessful efforts to achieve goals of the society legitimately (especially as they relate to money and power), thereby causing the individual to engage in nonlegal avenues to obtain material wealth and social status, to steal or be a part of assaultive gangs, or to retreat from social participation through drug addiction. Research here would be directed toward the assessment of social goals, the avenues open to their achievement, the opportunity of various groups to use these paths, the development of alternative routes, the methods for making these available, or the methods for altering ambition toward available goals and the inculcation of values for which routes are open. Action would involve modification of the social structure to provide adequate opportunity for achievement.

Other sociological theories, such as those of Veblen (1912) and of Cohen (1955), emphasize other aspects of social structure and individual behavior. Cohen, for example, notes the developmental phenomena involved in destructive behavior of youth. Much of this behavior appears to be senseless in terms of acquiring material advantage or social status. It is the result, Cohen thinks, of the rejection by lower class youth of middle class norms, following what the child perceives to be a rejection of him by middle class authority. As manifest by the lower class group, it is a collective reaction formation. Essentially, such theorists maintain that, given the physical environment in which it occurs, delinquency is not abnormal behavior. Research and action based on this frame of reference would require the delineation of activities which appeal to the adolescent but are not destructive of other people or their property. Improved housing, improved recreation, and appropriate leadership would be necessary.

Conclusion

While, as we mentioned earlier, more complete discussions of many of the factors briefly noted here will come later in this volume, the best judgment appears to be that in a given individual the occurrence of delinquency may be attributable to any one of the determinants suggested but more probably to a concatenation of influences arising from several of these related but distinguishable sources. The prevention of delinquency will, in consequence, require an accurate assessment of the disturbances which cause it in order that these may be corrected. The control of delinquency, in addition, will require the development of remedial and management techniques which ameliorate or arrest the social pathology which is delinquency's symptomatology. And a fully satisfactory diagnostic approach will explicate the relationship among the etiological factors, the preventive measures, the treatment programs, and the occurrence of delinquency in behavior.

Given the above assumptions, there seems to be no alternative in social action research to adopting the hypothesis that delinquency is multiply determined. Furthermore, it seems reasonable to suppose that there are relatively "pure" cases for which one (or a few) causal factors are essential contributors to the outcome of delinquency but that the largest variance among the general delinquent population is attributable to a combination of forces leading to general social pathology, one vector of which is delinquency. It does seem important to note here that delinquency is only one such vector in a pattern of failure which includes among the same populations (mainly urban, industrial), educational underachievement, mental illness, economic underproduction, disintegration of family patterns, mental retardation, disease, social dependency, civil strife, poverty, alcoholism, religious apathy, and adult criminality. All of these are part of the same network and the problem of delinquency cannot be studied or treated in isolation from the more general problems of the individual and society.

DEFINITION OF DELINQUENCY

Earlier in the chapter we alluded to the difficulties which the lack of a universal definition introduced into the process of estimating the extent of delinquency. The definitional problem also has another implication: research into the cause of, and cures for, delinquency will be affected by the definition chosen by the investigator. Because of the importance of the definitional problem, we now return to a discussion of it.

Requirements for a Definition

A definition should serve some purpose and meet some standards. The first requisite of a good definition is that it should, as Feigl (Feigl and Scriven, 1956; Feigl, Scriven, and Maxwell, 1958) says, cut nature at its joints. That is, it should distinguish a given phenomenon from closely allied areas in some *sensible* way. For delinquency we cite two examples of such efforts. First, there is the FBI system of classifying crimes, as shown in Table 1-1. There, delinquency was viewed in terms of delinquent acts which may be separated into classes, such as offenses against property, offenses against persons, and traffic offenses. Such a system of definitions treats the phenomenon in the familiar, legal form of the legislative statutes, the courts, and the law enforcement agencies.

Table 1-2 shows another way to look at delinquency: it contains a system for describing delinquency in terms of the delinquent person. Here, we have attempted to account in a verbal way for different kinds of delinquency at the clinical level.

TABLE 1-2. DIAGNOSTIC TYPES OF DELINQUENCY
(From Wirt & Briggs, 1960) *

1. Diagnostic Category One: Delinquency is primarily due to lack of emotional integration of the family. Such families provide ineffective example setting and disciplining for developing a social conscience. The family is hence an ineffective mediator of positive social values, and the youngster is receptive

* Reproduced by permission of *Minnesota Medicine*.

to the least desirable influences emanating from associates and mass media of communication.

2. Diagnostic Category Two: This includes cases where the antisocial disorder is primarily the result of the child responding to an integrated home, but where the child fulfills the conscious or unconscious antisocial impulses and desires of the parents. Such families have been most intensively studied by Johnson and Szurek (1952).

3. Diagnostic Category Three: This includes those cases where antisocial behavior is primarily the result of disorder within the child. An example would be where the siblings may be making an adequate adjustment but the delinquent youngster suffers from a sociopathic, schizophrenic, neurologic, low intellect, or severe neurotic syndrome promoting antisocial behavior.

4. Diagnostic Category Four: This includes the adolescent without major home or personality disorder whose normal hyperactivity and rebelliousness cannot be constructively integrated by his present environment because of a lack of acceptable outlets.

5. Diagnostic Category Five: This includes those children whose delinquency is largely a result of efforts to seek or maintain status in their peer group.

Which of these two systems of classifying delinquency has the greater utility will depend upon whether one wishes to observe the delinquent or his acts: this is a difference in level of observation between a psychological and a sociological approach. To come to a more nearly complete understanding of delinquency, both of these —or some integration of them—will be needed.

A second requirement of a definition is that it should provide, in its reduction to the statistical language, a concept about which some variability may be associated which in turn may separate a given phenomenon from others in a *useful* way. Thus a good definition provides a method of classification which reliably differentiates individuals or groups or occurrences in a way that is different from the absence of that method of classification with respect to the variables involved; by using the definition, groupings are changed in some meaningful way. At best, there is a regrouping which heightens utility of the concept, say, for improved research methodology or for practical treatment approaches which would have not otherwise been at all obvious or possible or attractive. Finally, as Loevinger (1957) points out, a good statistical reduction of the variance serves to draw together characteristics none of which in itself is distinctive enough to be definitive.

A third requirement of a good definition is that at the conceptual level it is *independent* from, or specifies its dependencies upon, other established variables. This requirement instructs us to be aware of the level of observation of the phenomenon and its relationship to variables at other levels of observation. In our brief discussion of theories in the previous section, we made reference to efforts at etiological accounts for the occurrence of delinquency. If, for example, one takes a sociological level of observation, his definition of delinquency should involve an account of how that definition is dependent upon and affected by his conception of group behavior and social institutions. Cloward and Ohlin (1960) do a reasonably good job of this. On the other hand, if one takes a psychiatric level of observation for his definition of delinquency, then it is necessary to specify the relationship between delinquency, as there defined, and personality theory. Bennett (1960) in her book, *Delinquent and Neurotic Children,* accomplishes this task rather well in explicating the definition of delinquency within the psychoanalytic modal.

Levels of Observation

Now if we think of these requirements as they relate to delinquency, it seems clear that the definitions used may be quite restricted and have little, or no, translatability across disciplines. This may, in part, account for the fact that professional workers in the field have such difficulty in communicating with one another and are so often ignorant of research and practice by others of different training. In the theories which we discussed, delinquency was never explicitly defined. The phenomenon was attributed to genetic factors, metabolic factors, developmental factors, intrapsychic factors, intrafamilial factors, interpersonal factors, group behavior factors, factors in the operation of social institutions, economic factors, political factors, cultural factors, and spiritual factors. But *delinquency* as such was not specified. It is quite possible to meet the three requirements which we have listed for a good definition within any one of these modes without reference to any other, but to do so raises the question of what the implications of the definition might mean when transformed to the language system of different levels of observation.

Problems in Translation

Let us take the broadly psychological frame of reference as an example. Within that framework, delinquency might have a number of definitions which may seem to overlap somewhat but which, even within the structure of a single discipline, are of a separate nature.

1. Delinquency is superego deficiency. This is, perhaps, the most frequently used explanation advanced by clinical psychologists and

psychiatrists for the occurrence of delinquency. Their contention is that the individual fails to incorporate primitive taboos, fails to identify with his parents' values, and seeks pleasure at the sacrifice of principles of reality and morality.

2. Delinquency is "holes" in the superego. This theory, first advanced by Johnson and Szurek (1952) and observed by a number of psychoanalytically oriented investigators since, describes the occurrence of breakthroughs of antisocial behavior in individuals whose ability in most areas to inhibit impulses is adequate. They attribute the acting out to lapses of superego development, metaphorically described as holes in the superego structure, through which id impulses are admitted to overt expression. They attribute this distorted development to the child-rearing practices of neurotic parents who achieve vicarious pleasure from their children's illegal behavior which they would not accept in themselves but are impelled to seek.

3. Delinquency is moral deficiency. Mowrer (1961) takes the position that weak conscience is due to improper teaching. While this point of view has something in common with the first definition, Mowrer's position rests more heavily on learning theory and on religious conviction and less on a psychoanalytic model of behavior than the superego deficiency theories.

4. Delinquency is aggression. Bandura and Walters (1959) take this hypothesis as their premise. They then attempt to relate delinquency to the frustration of dependency needs which cause aggression, and by implication, therefore, that which is the etiology of delinquency.

5. Delinquency is underactivity of the central nervous system. It is Lykken's (1957) belief that there are individuals with genetically based inability, or reduced ability, to learn clear responses to secondary situations. Because of this, such persons cannot associate punishment with the behavior which brought it about and, therefore, do not respond with the sort of anticipatory anxiety which conditions most people from repeating acts for which they are censured.

6. Delinquency is a personality test score. By the use of psychometric devices, such as the Minnesota Multiphasic Personality Inventory (Hathaway & Monachesi, 1953; Wirt & Briggs, 1959; 1960), or projective techniques such as the Rorschach (Finney, 1951; Wirt, 1956) or Thematic Apperception Test (McClelland *et al.*, 1953; Atkinson *et al.*, 1954; Lindzey *et al.*, 1959) scores can be derived which, with variable success, correctly identify persons who

are or will become delinquent. This can be done empirically and does not require a foundation in learning theory or personality dynamics, although such theories may have originally contributed to the selection of the items making up the scales.

7. Delinquency is one aspect of differences in the behavorial history of individuals' social activities. Delinquency as defined by psychologists using this approach amounts to categorizing children's behavior as it is evidenced at school or in other social situations—for example, school dropouts.

8. Delinquency is a police or court record. This is not an explanatory concept—and neither are some of the foregoing definitions—but it is one which many social scientists use. It is a clear and defensible definition.

From these examples it would seem that the difficulty in precise definition is immense even within a single domain of inquiry. There are several reasons for this. Most important is the consideration that there is no psychological theory which has universal acceptance, nor is there any that quite qualifies as a total theory of human behavior. Part of the trouble in attempting to construct a theory of human behavior is that the rational character of such theories becomes confused with the intelligence that is filtered through the relatively short experience of an observer taught to perceive and construe in terms of his own culturally influenced learning history. These historical and individual vicissitudes are quite germane to the point that, in the case of a definition of delinquency, temporal stability is probably not possible. The meaning of delinquency varies with the age of the individuals being considered and the time and place in which his behavior is being assessed.

A Definition of Delinquency

The term *delinquency* is, after all, a legal term. We believe, therefore, that the most sensible, useful, and independent definition of the behavior to which the word refers should maintain a focus upon the legal sense of its meaning, while recognizing the broader social and psychological variables involved. It seems to us that research based on such a conception has greater probability of becoming meaningful across disciplines and among different theoretical orientations and various levels of observation.

To begin with, we point out that nearly everyone would agree that delinquency has something to do with misbehavior. Beyond that, there is considerable disagreement along several lines. The most important of these are in relation to age, psychopathology, and legal *versus* moral transgression. As generally conceived, an act considered as delinquent would partly depend upon the age of the individual whose behavior is under consideration. A given act may be quite acceptable at one age and an indication of antisocial tendencies or psychopathology at a later age. For example, very young children reach for and sometimes destroy pretty objects which attract their attention. We teach them to inhibit these impulses, but it is not until children are older that the failure to inhibit such impulses is interpreted as malicious or disordered behavior. An adequate definition of juvenile delinquency necessarily involves the concept of age appropriateness of the behavior.

Delinquency has something to do with misbehavior, but not all misbehavior is delinquent, even when it might be considered inappropriate behavior for the age of the individual. Both the quality of the behavior and the degree of social deviance are factors in judging an act delinquent or rather trivial, on the one hand, or delinquent or psychopathological, on the other hand. As Redl (1959) points out, the range of acts we consider as delinquent are truncated at either end. Toward one extreme are behaviors indulged in by most people some of the time. They may be silly, they may suggest poor judgment, they may involve a lack of consideration for the welfare of one's self or others, they may involve technical violations of laws, they may be considered of questionable morality, and so on, but to call them delinquent would be to apply the term so generally as to make its meaning useless. Most people have had parking tickets. Nearly everyone gossips some. Neither of these is very commendable, but neither are they usually serious enough to be considered delinquent within a context most people would support as a reasonable use of the word *delinquent*.

Toward the other extreme are behaviors of a bizarre nature which, while perhaps illegal, are symptoms of severe psychopathology. Examples of such behavior make newspaper headlines when a person's delusional thinking leads him to murder. Others, suffering from brain damage, toxicity, or mental defect, also sometimes perform destructive or other illegal acts. To include these groups of individuals in the category of delinquents would confuse the definitional problem by placing in the same class persons whose acts are similar only in a very gross way. The approach to the definition should, we think, properly be through similarity in persons or groups rather than through similarity in acts exclusively. The behavior of the individual rather than the consequences of his behavior should be the focus of the definition, while still keeping in view the essential importance of the term in law.

Some misbehavior is illegal. Some misbehavior is immoral. Not all illegal behavior is immoral (for example, much regulatory legislation governing commerce, industry, and agriculture), and much immoral behavior (as defined in Western religions) has not become a matter of secular legislation (for example, an offense against the First Commandment). The differences are partly practical and partly a matter of cultural relativism. Ellingston (1948) has said that crime is whatever the dominant elements of a particular society believe to be dangerous to the security and solidarity of the society at any particular time. Thus an individual learns from his culture what is delinquent and what is not. If removed suddenly from his own culture into a new society with a very different set of values, an individual might act in ways which are there perceived as strange and as delinquent, though they would constitute behavior quite acceptable at home. Laws change within a society and, to some degree, though more slowly usually, so do concepts of morality. By definition, all societies have codes of conduct, but there are wide differences in time and place among groups as to behaviors which are acceptable and those which are considered immoral. The issue becomes clouded by attempting to fuse jurisprudence and theology in defining delinquency. Despite the high correlation of acts which are immoral and those which are illegal, the differences are important and germane to making as exact a definition as is possible.

If we are to speak of delinquents, the term should refer to kinds of persons whose behavior may be known to be of a defined sort. Such persons should not be categorized as delinquent because of the sometimes capricious behavior of others (for example, a sudden "clean up" campaign because of a change in municipal administration). Following this line of thinking, we find that not all persons contacted by the police, arrested, charged, or even convicted are delinquent. Nor, conversely, are all persons without such a history nondelinquent (there are in most cities notorious persons who for inexplicable reasons avoid prosecution but who seem clearly delinquent as we mean it).

The delinquent, then, would be a person whose misbehavior is a relatively serious legal offense, which is inappropriate to his level of development; is not committed as a result of extremely low intellect, intracranial organic pathology, or severe mental or metabolic dysfunction; and is alien to the culture in which he has been reared.

Whether or not the individual is apprehended or legally adjudicated is not crucial.

This definition is complex. It has not, to our knowledge, been used in either research or theory. However, it is offered in the hope that it may provide some conceptual clarity for future investigators.

References

Atkinson, J. W., Heyns, R. W., & Veroff, J. (1954) The effects of experimental arousal of the affiliative motive on thematic apperception. *J. abnorm. soc. Psychol.,* **49**, 405-410.

Bandura, A., & Walters, R. (1959) *Adolescent aggression.* New York: Ronald Press.

Beccaria, C. B. (1804) *Essays on crime and punishment.* Translated from the Italian of Beccaria; with commentary by Voltaire; translated from the French; 5th ed. rev. and cor. London: Printed by E. Hodson for H. D. Symonds.

Bennett, Ivy (1960) *Delinquent and neurotic children.* New York: Basic books.

Children's Bureau (1962) *Juvenile court statistics.* Washington, D.C.: United States Department of Health, Education, and Welfare.

Cleckley, H. (1941) *Mask of sanity.* St. Louis: Mosby.

Cloward, R., & Ohlin, L. (1960) *Delinquency and opportunity.* Glencoe, Ill: Free Press.

Cohen; A. K. (1955) *Delinquent boys: the culture of the gangs.* Glencoe, Ill.: Free Press.

Dentler, R. A. (1962) Notes on the self-report technique in the study of juvenile delinquency. New York: Teachers College, Columbia University. Mimeo.

Durkeim, E. (1898) Réprésentations individuelles et réprésentations collectives. *Revue de Metaphysique,* **6**, 274-302.

Durkeim, E. (1951) *Le Suicide.* Paris: F. Alcon, 1897. English translation. Glencoe, Ill.: Free Press.

Ellingston, J. R. (1948) *Protecting our children from criminal careers.* New York: Prentice-Hall.

Federal Bureau of Investigation. *Uniform crime reports for the United States, 1953-1962.* Pp. 24-32.

Feigl, H., & Scriven, M. (1956) *Minnesota studies in the philosophy of science. Vol. I: the foundation of science and the concepts of psychology and psychoanalysis.* Minneapolis: Univ. of Minnesota Press.

Feigl, H., Scriven, M., & Maxwell, G. (1958) *Minnesota studies in the philosophy of science. Vol. II: concepts, theories and the mind-body problem.* Minneapolis: Univer. of Minn. Press.

Finney, B. C. (1951) *Instructions for the use of the Palo Alto aggressive content scale.* Palo Alto, Calif.: The Veterans Administration Hospital. Mimeo.

Hathaway, S. R., & Monachesi, E. D. (1953) *Analyzing and predicting juvenile delinquency with the MMPI.* Minneapolis: Univer. Minn. Press.

Johnson, Adelaide M., & Szurek, S. A. (1952) The genesis of antisocial acting out in children and adults. *Psychoanal. Quart.,* 21, 323-343.

Kallman, F. F. (1953) *Heredity in health and mental disorders.* New York: Norton.

Lindzey, G., Bradford, Jean, Tejessy, Charlotte, & Davids, A. (1959) Thematic Apperception Test: an interpretive lexicon for clinician and investigator. *J. clin. Psychol.,* Monogr. supplement, No. 12.

Loevinger, Jane (1957) Objective tests as instruments of psychological theory. *Psychol. Rep.,* 3, 635-694.

Lykken, D. T. (1957) A study of anxiety in the sociopathic personality. *J. abnorm. soc. Psychol.,* 55, 6-10.

McClelland, D., Atkinson, J. W., Clark, R. A., & Lowell, C. L. (1953) *The achievement motive.* New York: Appleton-Century-Crofts.

Merton, R. K. (1957) *Social theory and social structure.* Rev. and enl. ed. Glencoe, Ill.: Free Press.

Miller, W. B. (1962) The impact of a "total community" delinquency control project. *Soc. Prob.,* 10, 168-191.

Mowrer, O. H. (1961) *The crisis in psychiatry and religion.* Princeton, N. J.: Van Nostrand.

Murphy, F. J., Shirley, Mary M., & Witmer, Helen L. (1946) The incidence of hidden delinquency. *Amer. J. Orthopsychiat.,* 16, 686-696.

Nye, F. I., & Short, J. F. (1957) Scaling delinquent behavior. *Amer. sociol. Rev.,* 22, 326-331.

Perlman, I. R. (1957) Reporting juvenile delinquency. *J. Nat. Prob. Parole Assoc.,* 3, 243-249.

Porterfield, A. L. (1946) *Youth in trouble.* Austin, Tex.: Leo Polishman Foundation.

Redl, F. (1959) Who is delinquent? In Eva H. Grant (ed.), *Guiding Children as they grow.* Chicago: Natl. Cong. Parents & Teachers.

Robison, Sophia M. (1960)*Juvenile delinquency.* New York: Holt, Rinehart & Winston.

Sheldon, W. H., Harth, E. M., & McDermott, E. (1949) *Varieties of delinquent behavior.* New York: Harper.

Sutherland, E. H. (1939) *Principles of criminology.* Philadelphia: Lippincott.

Veblen, T. (1912) *The theory of the leisure class: an economic study of
institutions.* New York: Macmillan.

Wirt, R. D. (1956) Ideational expressions of hostile impulses. *J. consult.
Psychol.,* **20,** 185-189.

Wirt, R. D., & Briggs, P. F. (1959) Personality and environmental factors
in the development of delinquency. *Psychol. Monogr.,* **73,** Whole No.
484.

Wirt, R. D., & Briggs, P. F. (1960) Delinquency prone personalities.
Minn. Med., **48,** 718-719.

2

Social Disorganization and Delinquent Subcultures

Daniel Glaser

Social Organization and the Continuity of Cultural Conditioning

Man differs from all other animals because he alone can accumulate learning from one generation to the next. For example, man today can design an automobile, but this is only because the learning of earlier men was repeatedly transmitted to new generations in the thousands of years during which human technology evolved from the first wheel to the most modern automobile. Each generation of animal other than man learns essentially the same things that were learned by all preceding generations in the history of its species. Human knowledge accumulates because men communicate their learning to their descendants by means of language. In no other species of life is there such an efficient means for the transmission of learning as human languages.

Every type of knowledge, belief, or ability which humans learn from other humans can be referred to as "culture." "Culture," in this broad sociological and anthropological sense, includes language, religion, sciences, and the arts, as well as all customs of behavior and of feeling which humans learn from other humans in work, play, child rearing, and other activities. The accumulation of culture depends on communication.

"Social organization" can be operationally defined as the patterns, or networks, of intercommunication between humans. It can be described by noting who communicates to whom, and the quantities and qualities of their communication. The components of social organization generally are called "groups." (In one distinctive sociological idiom, that of Talcott Parsons, the term "collectivity" replaces "group.") Those groups which have an enduring form are usually called "institutions." The school, the church, the state, and the family are examples of institutions.

Since details of culture are continually changing in diverse ways at different times and places, the longer humans in any group communicate with each other more than with humans outside their group, the more likely they are to develop a unique culture. This is because they share new cultural developments with each other, but are not as well informed of new developments communicated in other groups. Since the groups in which one participates determine the communications which one receives, people who differ in the groups in which they have participated are likely to differ in the culture they possess.

The groups with a unique culture vary in size and in the distinctness of their boundaries. Nations and tribes are among the larger groups, generally called "societies," which usually are remarkably unique in the totality of their culture. Within small tribal societies there is relatively little cultural variation. In contrast, modern national societies generally encompass a diversity of religious groups, innumerable occupational groups, and many recreational, regional, economic class, and other more and less sharply defined groups. Each of these, by placing its members in an unusual communication network, makes them recipients of a culture somewhat different from that of members of their society who are in other groups. For this reason it is appropriate to speak of regional, occupational, class, and other "subcultures" within a larger national culture.

One crucial group within any society is the family, which usually serves the major function of transmitting a culture from one generation to the next. As societies become more complex the family is augmented in this culture transmission function by other institutions, especially by the school and the church, as well as by less universal "voluntary" groups, such as the Boy Scouts.

The long period of biological maturation in the human species has always required that children remain in the family, and in other cultural transmission agencies, during most of their prepuberty years. As a culture becomes more extensive, its adequate transmission to new generations requires more and more years beyond puberty. In order to have maximum continuity in this transmission from one generation to the next, the family, the school, the church, and any other social organizations in which children may be involved must coordinate their activities effectively. They must also continually adapt to ongoing changes in the culture, during the new generation's long training period.

Social Disorganization, Discontinuity in Cultural Conditioning, and Delinquency

When the culture transmission and other behavior by members of a society fail to achieve a culturally expected degree of coordination, one can speak of the society as "disorganized." Separate components of a society may also be considered disorganized, such as a family, a school, a government, or a profession. Each of these units is disorganized to the extent that any of its individuals or groups impede the others in work toward organizational goals. The degree of disorganization is relative, and difficult to measure in absolute terms (Merton, 1961; Cohen, 1959).

A certain amount of social disorganization is a normal accompaniment of cultural and social change. Since culture accumulates, and seems to accumulate at a progressively more rapid rate, relatively rapid cultural change has become a normal feature of modern history. Much of this change as well as a variety of other events, such as death and aging, disturb patterns of communication between people. Therefore, some disorganization in cultural transmission and other social behavior always has been a normal feature of human experience.

Discontinuity in cultural transmission is prominent when there is disorganization in those components of a society which encompass more than one generation. This may involve different members of one group working at cross purposes in communicating to a new generation, but it is more often evident as a breakdown in communication between the generations within one institution, such as the family or the school. When this breakdown results in members of a juvenile generation communicating primarily with each other, they may develop a subculture differing in many respects from that of their elders; they may have different customs, different moral standards, and even a somewhat different language. When the behavior promoted in a juvenile subculture seriously offends the expectations of adults, it is referred to as a "delinquent subculture."

Sociological theory and research on juvenile delinquency have focused on three aspects of social disorganization which are believed to impede the inculcation of conventional adult behavior standards in juveniles, and to promote delinquent subcultures. These aspects of social disorganization may be designated as ecological, class-structural, and intergenerational. All three are interrelated, but it is convenient to discuss each separately.

ECOLOGICAL ASPECTS

Ecological analysis in the behavorial sciences seeks to relate human behavior to its physical environment, and is particularly concerned with the distribution of behavior in physical space. Since spatial arrangements may impair or facilitate communication between humans, they can affect patterns of social organization and disorganization. Perhaps the most conclusive early research on juvenile delinquency was concerned with its spatial distribution in large cities, and with the relationship of this spatial distribution to various city conditions.

Outstanding in ecological research on juvenile delinquency is the work of the late Clifford R. Shaw and his colleague, Henry D. McKay. Concentrating most of their study in Chicago, they employed a variety of simple research techniques, including tabulations of the percentage distribution of juvenile court cases for different sections of the city, spotting the separate cases on maps to show their distribution graphically, and analyzing individual life histories of urban delinquents (Shaw et al., 1929, 1930, 1931a, 1931b, 1938, 1942). Their work was coordinated with a flurry of other ecological research in American cities in the period between World Wars I and II (Park et al., 1925; Thrasher, 1927). These investigations yielded a set of interrelated major conclusions on juvenile delinquency and social disorganization, which can be summarized under three headings: spatial arrangement, population movement, and neighborhood-rooted delinquent subcultures.

Spatial Arrangement

Delinquency, as identified by juvenile court cases or by police arrest records, was shown to be concentrated in the most physically dilapidated areas of the city—the *slums*. These are predominantly "interstitial" segments of the city, for they are the remainders of areas once primarily designed for residential use, but now squeezed between commercial districts, factories, warehouses, railroad yards, stockyards, and the main arteries of automotive traffic. Since these types of construction made the older residential areas no longer desirable for investment in residential construction, the average age of the housing in slums is high, and its physical condition has deteriorated (although its value may remain high because of the potential value of the land for industrial and commercial use).

Population Movement

Because these high delinquency slum areas are the least desirable for residence, they are the areas where the newest and least-skilled immigrants to the city, who have the lowest social status, have been able to make their first settlements with the least resistance. Frequently they overcrowd these areas far beyond normal room-space-per-person ratios.

In United States cities, the new low status immigrants who populated the slums in the nineteenth century were predominantly peasants and laborers from Ireland, Scandinavia, and Germany. In the first two decades of the twentieth century, this influx was primarily from Poland, Italy, and other parts of eastern and southern Europe. The immigration quota system in 1921 reduced migration from Europe to a trickle. When the slum residents from Europe were able to move to better sections of the city, they were replaced in the slums by poor farm families moving to urban areas from within the United States, primarily from the South, and they were mainly Negro. A mid-twentieth-century development, for some United States cities, was the influx to the slums of impoverished Spanish-speaking migrants, especially from Puerto Rico.

Perhaps the most striking finding of the Shaw and McKay research was that the same slum areas had the highest delinquency rates in the city even after the predominant national or racial identity of their residents changed completely. Furthermore, for each national or racial group taken separately, delinquency rates declined as place of residence became more distant from the central business district of the city.

Neighborhood-Rooted Delinquent Subcultures

Shaw and McKay showed that the delinquency which comes to the attention of official agencies, from its onset, usually is group behavior, and becomes increasingly group behavior as youths become more advanced in delinquency. For example, they found that there were two or more associates involved in 88 per cent of the stealing cases. Their case studies augmented such statistics by showing that delinquent gangs are traditional in the high delinquency areas. The children of poor immigrant parents in overcrowded houses lived on the street to a greater extent than would be expected in other neighborhoods. In this situation, a boy's normal experience in growing up involved participation in street gangs, thus acquiring and transmitting the delinquent subculture traditional to the gangs.

Shaw and McKay's data indicated that poverty, commercial vice, broken homes, graft, and other evidence of disorganization of economic, political, and family institutions were distributed in the same spatial pattern in the city as the official delinquency cases. They also demonstrated that delinquents from these high delinquency areas had higher rates of recidivism than delinquents from other parts of the city.

Thrasher's study of 1313 boys' gangs in Chicago portrayed the progressive development of casual play groups on the streets of the slums into unified and aggressive gangs. The integration of these groups and the development of mutual loyalty among their members were ascribed to their experience of conflict as a group, in opposition to the police and to other gangs (Thrasher, 1927). The case studies of Shaw, McKay, Thrasher and others indicated that gangs in the high delinquency areas gave youth affection, recognition, respect, and other emotional need fulfillments at a time when absence of the parents from the home, or the parent's nonassimilation in American culture, prevented the satisfaction of these needs in the home. In an area of less social disorganization, such services to youth would be provided more extensively by the family and other traditional institutions.

The foregoing conclusions have stood the test of time remarkably well. Post-World War II research on the ecology of delinquency has yielded.findings which supplement, but do not seriously contradict, them. If these conclusions become less accurate or useful, it is likely not to be from their error or omission when made, but from major changes since then in conditions of urban life for the most delinquency-prone segments of the population. These changes are a consequence of large-scale public housing, "urban renewal," industrial suburbs, and freeway transportation through metropolitan areas, not in existence or not extensive when the earlier studies were done.

One allegation directed at ecological studies of delinquency charges that their data are invalid because delinquency rates cannot be measured. It is contended that most juvenile behavior that could be considered delinquent under the law is never even brought into court; the family or the community takes care of it out of court (Robison, 1936). Certainly, such incompleteness in available statistics on delinquency is undeniable. Yet there are two reasons for relying on research based on the operational definition of delinquency as that juvenile misconduct which elicits police, court, or other government action. First of all, these acts are of special significance as problems to the community and to the juveniles who commit them, simply because the people or places they involve, if not the acts themselves, render these juveniles subject to official police or court action. Secondly, only delinquent behavior that is officially recognized is measurable; any hypotheses as to trends or correlates of all delinquency, known or unknown, can be tested only on the assumption that the rates of delinquency not officially known are highly correlated with the rates of officially recorded delinquency.

Some critics have made much of the fact that there are many exceptions to the concentric circle model of city spatial arrangements presented by early ecologists (Lander, 1954; Jonassen, 1949). In this model, a central business district circle was surrounded by a ring known as the "zone of transition" (changing from residence to commerce and light industry) where delinquency was expected to be highest; from this second ring outward, through increasingly better residential rings, delinquency was expected to decline. The concentric circle conception, however, was an ideal-typical model for representing the effects of invasion and succession processes in the growth of a city from its point of origin. Even the ecologists who first applied this model pointed out major sources of deviation from a concentric circle pattern, notably (1) natural barriers, such as lakes and mountains, which prevent uniform rates of city growth in all directions; (2) expansion of commerce and industry into residential areas mainly along the arteries of automotive, rail, and water transport, rather than in a perfectly circular pattern; (3) the merging of expanding central cities with their satellite cities, including industrial suburbs, each of which generates a separate approximately concentric circle pattern; (4) and islands of cultural resistance to social disorganization, for example, "Chinatowns" and Japanese neighborhoods, with their own stable institutions, which maintain low delinquency rates even in slum areas (Shaw and McKay, 1949; Toby, 1950).

The first outstanding methodological advance beyond Shaw and McKay in the ecological study of delinquency was the work of Bernard Lander. He interrelated 1939-1942 juvenile delinquency information with seven items from the 1940 census on all 155 census tracts of the city of Baltimore, employing zero order, partial and multiple correlation, both linear and curvilinear, as well as factor analysis. The strongest relationship which this revealed was an inverse correlation between home ownership and delinquency for census tracts in which from zero to about 60 per cent of the homes were owner-occupied; a slight positive relationship of delinquency with home ownership existed for the few tracts in which housing was more than 60 per cent owner-occupied. Percentage of nonwhites in a census tract was positively related to delinquency, but this relationship also was curvilinear, since higher delinquency was found in racially mixed tracts than in those either entirely white or entirely nonwhite. As in earlier research, he also found a progressive decrease in delinquency rates moving outward from the center of the city (Lander, 1954).

Lander saw the Shaw and McKay findings as contradicted by the fact that zones of transition exist in all segments of Baltimore, including areas with low delinquency rates. However, he did find delinquency most concentrated in the zones of transition from residential to commercial use; his findings only were inconsistent with those of Shaw and McKay on zones of transition from residential to industrial use. The commercial zones of transition are the oldest, located near the center of the city, settled by the lowest status migrants to the city (and thus most like the Chicago zones of transition at the time of Shaw and McKay's work). New zones of transition, mainly from residence to industry, frequently are in outlying parts of a city and are less consistently associated with high delinquency rates than the older zones of transition.

Lander argues that his findings are most adequately interpreted by ascribing delinquency to anomie, rather than to social disorganization. However, he equates "anomie" with "instability" and, as Albert K. Cohen observes, he contributes little to the clarification of the concept anomie, or to its independent definition in a manner which would permit one to test its explanatory validity independently from that of social disorganization (Cohen, 1955).

Bordua repeated Lander's operation in the city of Detroit, using 1950 census data and 1948-1952 court delinquency rates for 366 census tracts (Bordua, 1959). He found an inverse relationship between home ownership and delinquency similar to that found by Lander, but Detroit showed a continuously direct relationship between delinquency rates and percentage of nonwhite, unlike the curvilinear relationship found in Baltimore. In addition, in Detroit, overcrowding remained directly related to delinquency and education inversely related, despite all types of partial and multiple correlation, whereas in Baltimore their zero order relationship disappeared when other variables were held constant. Factor analysis in Detroit suggested that the primary factors associated with high delinquency rates of city neighborhoods are ethnicity (indicated by high proportions nonwhites and low proportions foreign born), social status (low education and low income), and what might be called a "slum rooming house" factor (low proportion owner-occupied, high proportion of "unrelated individuals" in households, high overcrowding, and low income). Both anomie and social disorganization, as ordinarily conceived, are applicable to the interpretation of these data.

Radically new ecological aspects of delinquency may be developing from recent changes in our cities. Vast sections of slum residence have been torn up and replaced by other types of construction. Meanwhile, persons who would normally find homes in slum areas have been domiciled in new housing projects erected in huge developments at arbitrarily scattered locations. Here each resident is a stranger to all, there are no traditions either of crime or of noncrime, and the long-established vice and gambling syndicates and the political machines of the slum are not present. As will be pointed out, Cloward and Ohlin (1960) suggest that in these new housing situations delinquent subcultures acquire unique characteristics, stressing intergang conflict rather than crime.

Another feature of much modern city life is an increased geographical mobility of the residents within the metropolitan area. Even impoverished segments of the population may travel many miles to work and return, or to contact friends. Freeways and expressways make such travel less time-consuming than it formerly was, and gross inadequacy of public transportation makes an auto a necessity even for poor persons. This probably is best illustrated in Los Angeles. Here, it is claimed, many older delinquents have cars. Their gangs recruit members living many miles apart, so that gang activities are conducted in convoys of old cars. When they rendezvous, or when they move collectively to another destination, they create a minor traffic jam.

CLASS-STRUCTURAL ASPECTS

Differences in the prestige or rank of members of a group or a society are an aspect of social organization, for they determine the manner in which people communicate to each other. Where a seg-

ment of a society is distinguishable as receiving less deference, respect, or other indices of rank or prestige than another segment,
these segments are referred to as social classes. While differences in
prestige exist within every society, the readiness with which a number of people can be discerned as forming a distinct class varies
greatly from one society to the next. In feudal Europe, for example,
it was quite clear that the nobility were distinctly above peasantry,
servants, and artisans in wealth, in power, in the respect they received, and in other indices of rank. Also, there was little doubt or
disagreement in classifying people into these categories. As the
middle class of free entrepreneurs grew, and the nobility lost some
of their status attributes, these European class differences became
increasingly less clear-cut. In the United States, where there was no
clear and unitary feudal heritage, class lines have been especially
fluid.

Nevertheless, Americans are familiar with differences of rank, or
social status, in their communities. For example, the prestige and
deference given to members of so-called "high society" or "the 400"
contrast with the scorn and disdain with which the skid-row derelicts
or the newest minority group migrants to the slums generally are
regarded. Between these extremes, the "white collar" workers commonly see themselves, and are seen by others, as of higher status than
the "blue collar" manual workers, regardless of actual income. Despite some consensus in these status rankings, the criteria of class
are vague, numerous, and imperfectly correlated, and labels for
classes vary. This is evident in the fact that different procedures for
trying to distinguish classes in the United States yield different results.

If asked to which class they belong, or whether they belong to
"upper, middle, or *lower* class," three-fourths of Americans say "middle class." On the other hand, if asked whether they belong to the
"upper, middle or *working* class," slightly over half say "working
class," over 40 per cent say "middle class," and less than 10 per cent
say "upper class." This is very close to the distribution of "lower,"
"middle," and "upper" class, respectively, procured by W. L. Warner
in several small cities when he asked old residents to rank those
whom they knew in a sample from the city directory. In addition, he
divided each of these three classes into an upper and a lower, yield-
ing "lower upper," "upper middle," and so forth. Many students of
social class in America have simply divided people into classes by
objective indices, such as income, education, or occupation (Morris, 1963).

The middle class is generally regarded, in American sociological literature, as the main protagonist of the dominant morality of our culture. This morality, often designated after Weber as "the Protestant ethic" (Weber, 1930), emphasizes hard work, frugality, study, ambition, and deferment of immediate impulse gratification for the sake of accumulating wealth and vocational capacity, hence greater gratification later. Also, emphasis on "good manners" and language —the "ritual of class"—is especially linked with middle and upper class status. The schools and the churches, and many youth organizations, such as the Boy Scouts, devote a major portion of their effort to the propagation of these values. They are part of the dominant injunction to succeed, to view low status as not necessarily permanent, which has been called "the American dream" (Chinoy, 1955).

Disorganization in the class structural aspect of American communities is suggested by the fact that people tend to rank themselves higher in social class than others rate them, and by the fact that so many institutions enjoin Americans to try to raise their status to a greater extent than is possible for most of them. Disorganization in the sense of uncoordinated action, or action in violation of common expectations, is indicated by the fact that the deference which people can command on the basis of their class status varies with the criteria of class on which attention is focused, and is thus inconsistent for many individuals. Such imperfectly correlated criteria include manners, income, education, and performance of clean "white collar" work. These disorganized aspects of American class structure have provided the basis for several interesting theories of delinquency.

A major landmark in post-World War II theorizing on delinquency in the United States is the work of Albert K. Cohen, *Delinquent Boys: The Culture of the Gang* (1955). Its primary concern is to explain the development of delinquent subcultures distinctive of working class male juveniles. Cohen rejects the notion that cultural transmission alone accounts for the distribution of subcultures, since the prevalence of the subculture values is not always a function of the amount of exposure to them. Similarly, he rejects the explanation that the delinquent subculture merely expresses the psychogenic problems of the individual delinquents, since many youth with such problems, especially in low delinquency areas, do not manifest the values of the delinquent subculture; they express personality disturbances in other ways. His alternative solution is that psychogenic and subcultural processes blend in a single causal process when youth with similar personal problems are thrown together.

All subcultures, Cohen reminds us, are acquired by interaction with those who already share and embody the subculture in their beliefs and actions. A subculture owes its existence to the fact that it provides a solution to certain problems shared by those who align themselves with the subculture. These problems are produced by a conflict between an actor's frame of reference and the situations which he confronts. The problems are solved by a change in the frame of reference. However, a solution, to be satisfactory to an individual actor, must be one in which he feels some social support and, therefore, legitimation. Our values must be acceptable to those on whose cooperation and good will we are dependent, and, reciprocally, consensus in values leads to acceptance, recognition, and respect.

The working class child, Cohen points out, is exposed to pressures from many adults to conform to standards of the middle class. These adults include school teachers, ministers, and recreation center directors. A working class background, however, hinders a child in conforming to these standards. For example, planning and foresight are not as habitual in the working class family as middle class standards demand. Thus working class youth have a common core of status discontent.

A typical solution to loss of status in a group to whose values we cannot conform well, Cohen suggests, is to devalue the good will and respect of that group. This is consistent with the psychiatric observation that inadequacy leads to rebellion (Plant, 1937). Thus people tend to redefine criteria of status so that their present attributes become sources of status. Working class boys with similar difficulties in meeting middle class standards band together and make their very nonconformity to middle class standards a source of status. Delinquency thus becomes a solution to the individual's problems in meeting middle class standards. Gangs fiercely try to assert their autonomy by being intolerant of middle class values.

Delinquent gangs, Cohen reminds us, consist of boys who individually possess many different kinds of problems and different personality traits. Indeed, it is reasonable to infer that personality differences are necessary for there to be complementary roles within the gang, such as the leaders and the led. However, the fact of their common rejection by bearers of middle class values and their experience of a common conflict with authority force gang members to identify with each other, and to cultivate activities which enhance their sense of independence from middle class demands. Their delinquency, according to Cohen, is more expressive than instrumental;

it is a reaction formation, in Freud's sense, but a collective one. Cohen cites in support of this contention the extent to which delinquents are nonutilitarian (e.g., turning to vandalism, and stealing items for which the thief has no use). He points out also the extent to which delinquents are versatile, rather than specialized, in their delinquent acts. He also notes the negativistic and malicious quality of their expressive acts and their remarks toward middle class persons, as evidence of this reaction formation in working class male delinquents.]

Delinquency in the *middle* classes, Cohen suggests, is most often an attempt to exhibit masculine behavior. Because the father in the middle class home is absent long hours, he therefore exhibits little masculine authority at home, where the mother must manage things. According to Cohen and others, the son, in this middle class situation, feels the need to enhance his conception of his own masculinity, if not through legitimate means (e.g., athletic prowess), then through delinquent violence and independence. Cohen points out that in all classes, female delinquency is primarily sexual, and he suggests that this is because the main source of female status in our society is attractiveness to men.

Sykes and Matza, in a 1957 paper, object to Cohen's notion that delinquency is based on a set of norms opposed to those of the dominant culture, and developed as a reaction against dominant class expectations. Instead, these authors contend, the delinquent is committed to the values of the dominant culture, and cannot pursue delinquency until he develops "techniques of neutralization" to cope with the shame and guilt which are aroused when he contemplates committing a delinquent act. These techniques, essentially, are processes of rationalization *before* the act, rather than the rationalizations with which Freud was concerned, those which occur *after* the act. The techniques of neutralization, which the delinquent addresses to himself as well as others, include the denial of responsibility for any damage or injury which his delinquent acts involve, the denial that serious injury is done, the denial that there is a victim (the victim is a wrongdoer whom the delinquency properly punished), the condemnation of the condemners ("They're all mean and crooked themselves"), and the appeal to higher loyalties ("It would be wrong not to help one's friends") (Sykes and Matza, 1957). This view of such rationalizations before the act resembles the view of motivation as a verbal process implied by diverse writers, from C. Wright Mills (1940) to George A. Kelly (1955).

Cohen and Short, commenting on the Sykes and Matza essay, deny that it contradicts Cohen's *Delinquent Boys* formulation. They suggest, indeed, that reaction formation and the development of a delinquent subculture are themselves techniques for neutralizing middle class values (Cohen and Short, 1958). One might add that the techniques which Sykes and Matza cite are a familiar part of the content of delinquent subculture which boys transmit in delinquent groups, and which they strengthen by repeated affirmation to each other.

The anthropologist Walter B. Miller, after several years of working with gangs in a high delinquency section of Boston, contends that lower class delinquency is derived directly from the distinctive attributes of lower class culture, rather than its being a reaction against middle class expectations. He suggests that the poor families in American slums, among which delinquency is especially concentrated, are characterized by a distinctive way of life patterned on certain unique focal concerns. While "achievement" is a generally recognized concern of most members of the middle class, the lower class thinking is portrayed by Miller as patterned especially around concern with:

Trouble. Miller suggests that not "right and wrong" so much as avoiding difficult consequences, all indiscriminately labeled "trouble" in lower class speech, are the primary considerations in lower class evaluation of such diverse acts as entering into premarital sexual intercourse, stealing, being truant from school, becoming drunk, or getting into a gang fight. Furthermore, in the relatively deprived situation of "the youngster born and bred in this cultural milieu," Miller says, "the total dynamics underlying choice of alternative forms of behavior, including the individual's perception of potential gains to himself, frequently throws the weight of decision on the side of norm-violating behavior" (Kvaraceus and Miller, 1959, Vol. 1, p. 65; see also Miller, 1959).

Toughness. Masculinity, physical strength, and endurance, all are seen as unusually important to lower class adolescents. Their heroes are the "tough" males, whether they be tough criminals or tough policemen or teachers—they will be even proud of their father's having given them a "good" beating up, according to Miller's portrayal. This emphasis, he suggests, may be related to the predominance of females in all parental functions for lower class children, due to the frequency of illegitimacy, desertion, and divorce or simply to the father's indifference to child-care problems. These conditions of female domination have been interpreted as giving male youth in these homes an unusual need to establish and assert their masculine identity.

Smartness. Skill in duplicity, rather than academic wisdom, is connoted by "smartness" in the lower class culture described by Miller. Prestige comes to a boy who "cons" money or assistance out of those who are "suckers," or who "beats the rap" for his misdeeds by prevarication to teachers or policemen. "Although the 'IQ' of the lower-class adolescent—as measured by school administered intelligence tests, which entail certain types of verbal and academic aptitudes—is almost invariably low, his 'duplicity' quotient must be high if he is to operate effectively in the world of the street corner" (Kvaraceus and Miller, 1959, p. 66).

Excitement. "The search for thrill and stimulation is a major concern in the lower-class community, where life often involves monotonous and dull routines in the home, on the job, and in just 'hanging around.' . . . The desire for excitement is reflected in prevalent patterns involving drinking, gambling and playing the numbers, goading('testing') official authorities such as teachers and policmen . . . destroying public property, stealing a car, and joy-riding. . . . Much of the delinquency related to this cultural concern involves the quality of high adventure. Although aggression against persons and property may figure in many of these acts . . . the aggressive component is one by-product of complex motives which includes the quest for 'excitement'" (Kvaraceus and Miller, 1959, pp. 66-67).

Unusual concern with "luck," a fatalistic component in thinking about one's behavior, and stress on autonomy ("Nobody is going to boss me around") are also identified by Miller as distinctive features of the culture transmitted in the lower class. These concerns are seen by Miller as particularly adaptive to the adult life of the approximately 50 per cent of the population who remain in unskilled or semiskilled jobs, and who are likely not to finish high school. The large group that has internalized such values is what Miller calls the "stable" lower class, who eventually become predominantly law-abiding adult members of the lower class. Those youths who aspire to higher status may become either what Miller calls the "aspiring but conflicted" lower class, many of whom turn to delinquency and crime when they fail at legitimate pursuits, or the "successfully aspiring" lower class, who enter the middle class.

The middle class is seen by Miller as having concerns somewhat different from those of the lower class, due to the middle class pattern of deferring immediate gratification for the sake of long-run achievement. The existence of some delinquency in the middle

class is ascribed by Miller largely to the diffusion of some of the
lower class values to the middle class. Such diffusion is illustrated
by the spread of jazz and rock-and-roll music from the Negro slums
through the white slums to the white middle and upper classes. He
also notes the spread of lower class styles of dress to middle class
youth, including blue jeans, tight skirts, leather jackets, and duck-
tailed haircuts. Because these styles are opposed by middle class
parents, Miller asserts, they are valued by middle class youth as
devices for the expression of independence from parents.

Bohlke ascribes middle class delinquency to the diffusion of lower
class cultural patterns through quite a different process. He suggests
that such delinquency has increased as an indirect result of the
economic enrichment of many manual workers reared in a lower
class culture but employed in strongly unionized industries where
the income of workers equals or exceeds that of traditionally middle
class people. This income shift in the mid-twentieth century creates
a widespread condition of "status inconsistency" in the United
States, he argues, especially when these newly middle income families move into middle class neighborhoods. Their children are likely
to develop delinquent subcultures because they suffer "marginality,"
according to Bohlke, from failure to be accepted in the "old middle
class" circles. They are poorly prepared by their home life with
relatively uneducated parents for competition in conventional pursuits, especially in the school, with children of the "old middle class"
(Bohlke, 1961). Alternatively, it has been speculated, many children of the "old middle class" may engage in delinquency because
they lack the income to keep up with the consumption patterns of
the "new middle class."

It must be evident that the theory on class-structural aspects of
social disorganization and delinquency is not buttressed by statistical
data nearly as much as was theory on the ecological aspects of this
problem. Of course, Cohen and Miller designations of delinquency
as largely a lower class phenomenon appear to be partially supported
by the fact that lower class children overwhelmingly predominate
in those adjudicated delinquent and, especially, in the population of
institutions for delinquents. However, there is reason to believe that
when middle and lower class children behave in a particular delinquent manner, the middle class juveniles are much less likely to be
brought to the juvenile court than are the lower class children. Even
when they are brought to court, the middle class juveniles are much
less likely to be sent to state institutions for delinquents than are
lower class children, for there appears to be more prospect of the

family's providing private assistance. Whether a consequent class bias in official statistics makes the apparent predominance of delinquency in the lower class purely an artifact, or whether it merely exaggerates a genuine class difference in rates of juvenile misbehavior, has long been a moot issue. A few researchers, however, have provided some systematic evidence on this matter.

James F. Short and F. Ivan Nye developed a Guttman scale for the measurement of delinquency in terms of the acts admitted on anonymous questionnaires. In administering these questionnaires to high school students in several small cities in the state of Washington, they asked the respondents to state the occupation of their father. No significant differences were found in the admitted delinquency of children classified in socioeconomic levels on the basis of the occupation of their fathers (Nye, Short, and Olson, 1958).

In a much more extensive investigation in Nashville, Tennessee, Reiss and Rhodes procured both the court delinquency record of 9238 juveniles and interview data for a random sample of 158 of these juveniles. Their results indicate a somewhat complex relationship between status and delinquency. More frequent and more serious delinquency was admitted in the lower than in the middle stratum, but this contrast was greatest in comparing juveniles from school areas in which the inhabitants were highly homogeneous in occupational status. Areas in which residents were mixed in status had less differentiation of delinquency rates by social status of parents than was found in comparing homogeneous districts of different social class predominance (Reiss and Rhodes, 1961).

The Reiss and Rhodes finding of relatively homogeneous delinquency rates within school districts may account for the failure of Short and Nye to find close relationships of delinquency to social status within small towns. Reiss and Rhodes also interpret this finding as a contradiction of Cohen's theories on delinquent subculture formation as a lower class reaction to failure in competing with the middle class. They reason that lower class youth would confront more of the middle class, against which to react, in areas where parents are most heterogeneous in status, but they note that here these class differences in delinquency rates are minimal. The tendency for delinquency to be relatively uniform across class lines within school areas supports the Shaw and McKay view of delinquency as primarily acquired by cultural transmission. This also supports Sutherland's differential association theory for the explanation of individual delinquent and criminal careers.

The Reiss and Rhodes interview data suggest that very few delin-

quents are oriented to careers as criminals. Most simply conform to
peer expectations. In the high delinquency areas, those who do not
conform to delinquent patterns are likely to be social isolates. In
fact, most lower class youth were found to be conforming to conventional work and study expectations, and a majority were not involved in serious delinquency, despite greater relative rates of their
areas compared to others.

Clark and Wenninger have largely validated the Reiss and Rhodes
findings, although they measured delinquency by its being admitted
on anonymous questionnaires, as Short and Nye did, instead of using
juvenile court records. Comparing a lower class urban school district
within a Chicago slum area with an upper class Chicago suburb,
they found markedly less delinquency in the suburb. In a small, industrial, predominantly lower class city of northern Illinois, delinquency was admitted by the students almost as frequently as in
the Chicago slum, but in a clearly low income rural area of northern
Illinois, delinquency rates were almost as low as in the suburb.
Within each of the four separate communities, however, admitted
delinquency was not significantly differentiated by the social status
of a youth's father, as indicated by his occupation (Clark and Wenninger, 1962).

In summary, that delinquency rates vary inversely with the predominant social class level of a school district, but do not vary significantly with the social status variations of parents within separate
school districts, has been found with Nashville court records by
Reiss and Rhodes, and by questionnaire admissions of Chicago students through the work of Clark and Wenninger. The latter finding
was also supported by the research of Short and Nye in the state
of Washington. These findings have been interpreted as supporting
Miller's theory of delinquency as expressing lower class culture, as
well as Shaw, McKay, and Sutherland theories of delinquency as a
product of social transmission, but contradicting Cohen's theory that
delinquency is a lower class reaction on encountering middle class
expectations.

AGE GROUP CLEAVAGES AND DELINQUENCY

Bloch and Niederhoffer (1958) assert that there is a similar "gang-
ing process" among adolescents at all class levels in our society, and
in other societies as well, including diverse primitive tribes. In all
societies they see the gang as a social device whereby a youth,
struggling for the power which goes with adulthood, can "prove he

is a man" before an audience of his age peers. While societies vary in the extent to which they structure the transition from childhood to adulthood, and the adolescent groups vary in the violence of their activities and in their conflict with adults, these groups are all seen as having the common function of providing "ego support" and "courage" for youth in this adolescent period.

In areas that are not highly urbanized and industrialized, the family or extended kinship group is a more basic unit in the social division of labor than it is in the large cities of the United States and Europe. In family activities persons are allocated different roles according to age and sex, but they all function as an integrated group in those tasks and pleasures which are family enterprises. The problem of delinquency may arise, in large part, from the fact that family functions now have diminished. S. N. Eisenstadt has documented the extent to which age-homogeneous groups "tend to arise in those societies in which the family or kinship unit cannot ensure, or even impedes, the attainment of full social status by its members" (Eisenstadt, 1956, p. 54).

Numerous sources of decline in the extent and intimacy of social enterprises by youth with parents could be cited. These include the transfer of education functions from the family to the school, the growth of the school and of youth organizations as centers of leisure time pursuits for juveniles, the radical decrease in family businesses, the increase in the extent to which married women are employed away from home, and the fact that workers move from one house to another about once every four years, scattering youth far from grandparents, aunts, uncles, and other non-parent kin. All of these trends increase the extent to which adolescents live in a social world in which their most direct and intimate relationships are others of their own age level.

Augmenting all of the foregoing in separating generations within American society is the disparity, for many youth, between the age when they leave school and the age when they can procure employment. For those youth not strongly committed to school attendance and achievement, the age 16 maximum of compulsory education in most areas has not been an age of ready access to the world of employment. This is because education itself is a major requirement for much employment. For example, a U. S. Census survey in 1959 indicated that, for males of age 16 to 24, rates of unemployment were about twice as high for those not graduated from high school as for high school graduates, for both whites and nonwhites (U. S. Census, 1961, Table 19).

In the age grade, or intergenerational disorganization, one readily discerns the interaction of many social and cultural factors operating through several different institutions, such as the family, the school, and the state. Delinquency rates have generally been high among children of immigrants to the city from rural poverty-stricken areas where schooling is not extensive. This was exemplified by the children of Italian and Polish peasant immigrants in the first quarter of the twentieth century, the children of Negro migrants from the rural South to the urban centers of the North in the second quarter of this century, and the children of Puerto Rican and Mexican migrants in the third quarter of this century. The low crime rates of the immigrant adults probably reflected the rigid moral indoctrination they acquired in the cohesive rural communities in which they were reared. However, the low education of the parents, their poverty, their language handicaps, and their tradition of employment at an early age made their ability to aid and inspire their children to schooling relatively low.

These children from new lower class migrants particularly, and from the lower class generally, have, as a whole, been unable to reach the school achievement standards of middle class children. This lesser achievement in schooling is cumulative, since poor reading and other poor learning skills in the early grades impede progress later. Consequent low grades or retardation in school reduces interest in school beyond the minimum age required by law and promotes truancy before the legal drop-out age. Concentration of these youth in slum areas of the city facilitates their finding widespread peer support for resistance to schooling. This spatial concentration, plus the reduction of employability from dropping out of school, all augment the extent to which these youth live in a social world isolated from adults.

Inverse evidence of the significance of age group hiatuses in the development of delinquent subcultures is provided by findings that family cohesion is the major variable "insulating" some juveniles in high delinquency areas from serious involvement in delinquency. The Gluecks, in their famous comparison of 500 delinquents and 500 nondelinquents matched by neighborhood, age, intelligence, and national descent, found that a close and affectionate relationship with their parents was one of the features most often distinguishing nondelinquents from delinquents. The nondelinquents also had parental discipline which was "firm but kindly," rather than lax, over-strict, or erratic. The McCords' follow-up of predelinquents yielded findings of family relationships correlated with delinquency similar to those of the Gluecks; quarreling or rejecting parents, not broken homes or criminal parents, were associated with delinquency (McCord, 1959). The "Glueck Social Prediction Scale," based on family relationship variables, has had some success in differentiating children of high delinquency areas into groups with diverse probability of future delinquency (Glueck, 1959). The Reckless studies indicate that the mechanism of this family influence is the parental ability to instill in their children a conception of themselves as "good"; they apparently then avoid engaging in activity that would seriously jeopardize such a self-conception (Reckless *et al.*, 1956; Lively *et al.*, 1962).

Female delinquency, less frequent in police and court records and less researched than male delinquency, seems to involve intergenerational conflict within the family to a much greater extent than does male delinquency. Girls comprise only about 15 per cent of arrestees under 18, and not quite 20 per cent of juvenile court delinquency cases. A major portion of these court cases involve "incorrigibility," which generally means conflict of the girl with her parents over her hours away from home and her male associates. However, arrests for larceny and other conventional offenses by girls under 18 have increased in the 1960's, according to the FBI's *Uniform Crime Reports*.

Elaborate analyses of court statistics by Monahan (1957) and Toby (1957) show broken homes to be markedly more associated with female delinquency than with male delinquency, but this correlation varies inversely with the age of the delinquent. Monahan found that female delinquents recidivate less than male delinquents, but, for both sexes, those from broken homes recidivate more often than do those from homes in which both parents are present.

Differences in the delinquency rates of various ethnic groups show the interaction of the family with other institutions in promoting or reducing intergenerational disorganization as a factor in delinquency. For example, the south Italian peasant immigrants retained a tradition of distrusting school as a threat to family influence on children, their children left school early, and the delinquency rate of these children was about twice the average for other white children in the same cities (Toby, 1958, p. 549). The family was relatively intact and influential among Italian migrants, and, as Whyte (1937) observed, the Italian youth soon differentiated into a few "college boys" who rose out of the lower class by means of education, a few delinquents who eventually became young adult criminals, and a large number of ex-delinquent frequently unemployed "corner boys."

The latter remained in considerable idleness as out-of-school advanced adolescents, although most eventually found employment, often in the gambling syndicates. The cohesive family and the political machine facilitated movement from youth to adult conventional or criminal worlds, but it tended to make the school ineffective as a delinquency prevention agency.

Jewish immigrants from eastern Europe had little formal education and took unskilled jobs on an economic level comparable to that of the Italian immigrants, but the children of the Jewish immigrants had an extremely low official delinquency record. Also the children of lower class Jewish immigrants acquired middle class occupations in one generation at perhaps the most rapid rate in the history of immigrant groups. Among the Jewish immigrants, however, a cohesive family like that of the Italians was supplemented by an extremely high valuation of education, particularly for boys, a valuation rooted in cultural traditions and derived from their religion. Due to this regard for schooling, the school served as a major aid to the family in facilitating the transition of these youth to adulthood without involvement in delinquency and, indeed, with relatively little frustration of aspirations to economic mobility (Toby, 1958). Low delinquency rates of Chinese and Japanese children of poor immigrants also were facilitated by a combination of cohesive families and a high valuation of education.

Children and grandchildren of Negro migrants from the rural South to large American cities, particularly in the North, encounter the most extreme concentration of barriers to the achievement of conventional adult roles. Not only do they come from poor homes in which the level of parental education generally is low, but also a high proportion of the youth lack consistent parental influences. This reflects a mother-centered household tradition which goes back to slavery, has been aggravated by extreme poverty conditions, and is manifested today in high rates of illegitimacy, desertion, and divorce. Further, Negroes confront the problem of race prejudice in obtaining employment, in addition to the usual employment handicaps of out-of-school youth; unemployment rates for nonwhites age 16-25 are twice those for whites (U. S. Census, 1961, Table 18). Because of these sources of greater isolation from conventional adults than other youth experience, it is not remarkable that Negroes are conspicuous among juveniles developing subcultures which are among the most deviant from those of adults. Negroes are particularly prominent as conveyors of the culture of the "bopping" or conflict gangs in large Northern cities, and of the "cat culture" of narcotic users (Finestone, 1957). But this leads to a separate research issue: the varieties of delinquent subculture and their correlates.

THE CONTENT OF DELINQUENT SUBCULTURES

Since its publication in 1960, Cloward and Ohlin's *Delinquency and Opportunity* has been a major influence on sociological research on delinquency, and on delinquency prevention programs. These authors assert that delinquent subcultures tend to be differentiated into three major types—criminal, conflict, and retreatist—according to: (1) the "opportunity structure" which delinquent youth encounter for the pursuit of conventional goals, and (2) their degree of integration with persons of older age levels.

In the traditional slums described by Thrasher, Shaw, and McKay, youth involved in delinquency were in communication with illicit liquor dealers, gambling operators, stolen goods dealers, and other adults in organized crime, as well as with some adult professional thieves and burglars. These provided models for the development of a criminal delinquent subculture oriented toward crime as a means of obtaining conventional material success goals, and as a path to an adult career in illegitimate pursuits. Since the illegal businesses recruited their staff from older delinquents, considerable continuity of cultural conditioning bridged the generations in the deviant population of these areas. Indeed, ward and precinct politicians, who worked closely with heads of gambling and other criminal syndicates, and dispensed patronage and other aid to cooperating residents, provided considerable leadership and social organization in these neighborhoods. Social disorganization was a factor in this delinquency mainly in the sense that the adult world centered in this area was in partial opposition to the larger society, in their evaluation of illegitimate means (Whyte, 1937).

This coordination of juvenile delinquent and adult criminal social worlds has declined, Cloward and Ohlin point out, because lower class youth are increasingly on their own. Isolation of delinquent youth from adults expands as government housing projects replace slum dwellings, for families are assigned quarters among strangers, impersonal government offices replace politicians in dispensing assistance, and even organized crime moves its chieftains to suburbs and its operations to other areas. Indeed, the priority given to families on relief in low-cost public housing makes for extreme concentration there of broken and other problem-ridden families receiving Aid to Dependent Children.

In these urban areas, where youth not in school are "on their own" to an extreme degree, Cloward and Ohlin report the greatest concentration of what they call the "conflict" subculture. This is primarily devoted to intergang conflict rather than to adult types of crime. Achievement in terms of conflict values—"rep" and "heart"— replace wealth as primary goals in delinquent activity. Although stealing occurs, there is little opportunity to pursue it "as a calling" with adult models.

The "retreatist" subculture, Cloward and Ohlin assert, attracts youth who are "double failures," being unsuccessful in both delinquent and conventional groups. An alternative sense of achievement is available to them in the pursuit of distinctive experience—"kicks" —with narcotics or alcohol. Of course, in this as in all other types of delinquent subculture, the goals specified may not be as motivating in themselves, as the approbation which youth with common needs give each other for their distinctive achievements. Social approval, a generalized secondary reinforcer in most social situations, may well be primary in much delinquency.

In one of the first tests of the Cloward and Ohlin theory, Spergel (1961) located areas of New York where each type of delinquent subculture prevailed, but he found it appropriate to divide the criminal culture into a rackets and a theft type. Interview and official record data were collected systematically to permit analysis of the goals inculcated in delinquent youth, their opportunity structure, and their integration with persons of other age levels.

Spergel found the rackets subculture in a neighborhood where the population was predominantly of Italian descent, and in which loan shark, policy gambling, and other rackets were centered. The racket leaders had a paternalistic relationship to street youth, occasionally employing the older ones, and assisting them in evading difficulties with the law. They also were able to exercise leadership to keep intergang conflicts from reaching extremes, and to limit the spread of drug use. These youth were distinguished by their emphasis on "connections" as a means of attaining conventional monetary success goals ("It's not what you know, but who you know"). They were extremely hostile to police and other conventional authorities, but integrated with other adults in the neighborhood.

The conflict culture was found by Spergel in an extremely deteriorated and congested slum neighborhood, of predominantly Puerto Rican population, although the delinquents were not from the most impoverished families there. These were youth on the street, with no close integration across age levels, and with frequent intragroup conflict. Indeed, the delinquent gangs often split into factions which fought each other and sometimes became separate gangs. There was also extensive intergang conflict. Some theft occurred, but with little orientation to long-run monetary gain from crime; these youth were in an isolated social world and oriented to their own unique goals.

The distinctive theft culture was found in an area of mixed nationality, including Italian, Irish, German, and Czech families. A mixture of class levels also existed there, but the average family income was lower there than in the Italian neighborhood. These delinquent youth had a high emphasis on material acquisition goals, such as automobiles, record players, fancy clothes, and money to spend. There was close integration across age levels, but only within a youthful age range; the older delinquents gave leadership to the younger ones in shoplifting, burglary, and other crimes, and in disposing of loot. These youth exceeded delinquents of other areas in the extent of their conflict with their parents. However, they had some ties with adult operators of radio and television stores, auto parts shops, and restaurants to whom they sold stolen merchandise.

Some drug use was found in all three of the areas, but was most extensive in the conflict area. The drug users were predominantly youth who had grown too old for the delinquent groups, but had not assimilated into the rackets or into conventional employment. They also had some associates who were rejected by the delinquent groups at an earlier age, for personality reasons. Drug users in the theft area included some who were most proficient at crime, and those elsewhere also had illegal income "hustles" or rackets. But drug users in each of the three areas had little contact with users outside their own neighborhood, and had separate channels of drug procurement.

As a more rigorous test of theories of delinquent subculture differentiation, Short and associates had YMCA "detached workers" long acquainted with 16 Chicago gangs rate the participation of 598 members of these gangs in 37 types of delinquent and nondelinquent behavior. When these ratings were factor-analyzed, the largest amount of common variance was accounted for by a "Conflict" factor, clearly concerned with fighting. On a second factor, which they labeled "Stable Corner Activities," the highest loadings were for items dealing with athletics, social activities, and gambling. Their third factor, called "Stable Sex Maturity," gave highest loadings to sexual intercourse, petting, and "signifying" (verbal teasing, usually with a sexual theme). For their "Retreatist" factor, highest loadings were for use of narcotics and "pot" (marijuana), but also high on this fourth factor were homosexuality and common-law marriage. This indicates that the latter experiences frequently occur in careers involving narcotics use. On the fifth factor, labeled "Authority Protest," highest loadings were for stealing cars, driving without a license, and running away.

Use of alcohol loaded fairly high on all of the five factors described above except Stable Corner Activities. Theft had moderate loadings on the Conflict, Stable Corner, and Authority Protest factors. The 16 gangs studied varied considerably in average score on these five factors. In summary, fairly independent conflict and retreatist subcultures were identified empirically, but criminality (other than auto theft and narcotics offenses) seemed to be distributed among gangs diverse in other interest, rather than being the dominant theme of a distinct criminal subculture. This finding could stem from failure to sample the most criminally oriented gangs, but the researchers claim that they and others were unsuccessful in extensive efforts to locate gangs in Chicago more concerned with crime than those studied (Short, *et al.*, 1963).

The pervasiveness in these Chicago gangs of some crime, use of alcohol, "hanging on street corners," and "being a public nuisance" suggests the evolution of specialized delinquent subcultures from a more common pattern. The factor analysis brings out these common features, and also serves as a heuristic procedure, in revealing the independence of patterns not distinguished in theoretical analyses. The Authority Protest pattern is notable here. Replication of such statistical typing is needed for data from other samples, to indicate the generality of the types which Short and his associates found.

A more urgent research need is for longitudinal studies of delinquent careers. If delinquency is a tangential development during adolescence, temporarily diverting most youngsters from socialization for adulthood, what sequence of events is involved in entrance into delinquency, and what are the paths of departure from it? There is reason to believe that cessation of delinquency by some youth occurs at each stage through which others progress, from initiation or "predelinquency," through early delinquency, and even in the most advanced and specialized delinquency. Hints for delinquency prevention might be gained from knowledge of the processes of change at each stage. While we have tabulations and case studies on delinquent careers antecedent to adult criminality, and some data on admitted delinquency of cross sections of adult populations, we have little systematic tabulation of types of behavior following particular kinds of delinquency.

From a few clues that are available, some surmises can be made as to the probable findings of such longitudinal research. It appears that the earliest delinquency is the most expressive and nonspecialized. It is closest to the nonutilitarian and versatile model of delinquency which Cohen presented in his pioneer work (1955), and which Cohen and Short later called the "parent" delinquent subculture (1958).

In early stages of delinquency especially, and to a large extent thereafter, while youth are oriented to the expectations of their delinquent subculture, they also clearly maintain much reference to the dominant culture, and some identification with conventional adults. This is indicated by the evidence that most conventional adults engaged in some delinquency during adolescence (Porterfield, 1943; Wallenstein and Wyle, 1947). It has been contended further that delinquency, radicalism, and Bohemianism are part of a "subterranean tradition of youth" which pervades our entire culture, shared by young and old, but accepted more ambivalently by adults than by youth (Matza, 1961). Perhaps this aspect of intergenerational disorganization in our society is indicated by the intensity of much effort by adults to impede or hide their normal aging, or to indulge in institutionalized juvenile escapades in certain clubs, lodges, and parties.

Departure from "parent" nonspecialized delinquency, we can surmise, is a function of efforts to pursue behavior that is increasingly instrumental, rather than just expressive. As teen-age juveniles mature, they seem to become more oriented to achieving specific goals, rather than merely expressing spontaneous feelings and gratifying immediate impulses. This was indicated when Reiss and Rhodes (1963) measured relative deprivation with the question: "Would you say that most of the students in your school have better clothes and a better home to live in than you have?" The extent to which youth responded positively to this inquiry increased with age, and this response was more closely related to delinquency with increasing age.

Television, movies, and other mass media, as well as direct observation in urban areas, expose American youth of all backgrounds and circumstances to similar ideals of consumption. They aspire to drive their own automobiles, to be customers at shows, amusement parks, ball games, and other public recreational establishments, to wear "sharp" or "fancy" clothing, and to visit night clubs and dance halls with attractive members of the opposite sex. Ralph England (1960) compiled statistics indicating extremely rapid growth, between 1945 and 1960, in special media to stimulate teen-age consumption goals. These media include special magazines, radio and television programs, and other commercial enterprises catering to adolescent interests in "hot-rods," sex, and in the life of show business celebrities. Dansereau (1961) suggested that the progressive reduction of the work week and of household tasks for adults may make this teen-age culture a prototype of future adult culture.

Responses by Nashville children to inquiry on how they thought their home and clothes compared with those of their classmates indicated that feelings of relative deprivation were greatest in the lower class, and more extensive among children from school districts homogeneous in class than from districts mixed in class (Reiss and Rhodes, 1963). Apparently lower and upper class youth do not differ greatly in consumption aspirations. As a consequence, Toby points out, modern increases in the average standard of living simply augment lower class youth perceptions of their relative deprivation (Toby, 1962). The significance of this for delinquency was suggested when Gordon, Short, Cartwright, and Strodtbeck used the semantic differential technique to compare evaluations of presumed class and delinquent subculture themes by lower class gang boys, lower class non-gang boys, and middle class boys. The gang boys evaluated a steady job more favorably than did the middle class boys. However, in evaluation of illegitimate means, such as knowing how to sell stolen goods, and pandering, the gang boys were more favorable than the lower class non-gang boys, who in turn were more favorable than were middle class boys. Apparently, the gang boys see both legitimate and illegitimate means as acceptable, hence interchangeable (Gordon et al., 1963). It would follow that, as Cloward and Ohlin argue, their delinquency is shaped by variations in their opportunities.

THE SOCIAL STRUCTURE OF GANGS

One controversy in sociological literature concerns the stability and unity of delinquent gangs. Yablonsky (1959) coined the term "near-group" to locate gangs in the middle range of a continuum between completely amorphous mobs and organizations with definite membership and stability. In a notorious New York conflict gang he found only a small core persistently identified with the gang, but in times of excitement this core attracted a large following from other idle youth in the area. The added "marginal members" did not maintain a gang identity at other times. However, to meet their own personality needs, the core members persistently deluded themselves and each other with fantasies on the immensity of their following.

Pfautz (1961) argued that Yablonsky's observations can more fruitfully be interpreted in terms of established theory on collective behavior, particularly the theory of social movements. Other critics have questioned the sampling basis for Yablonsky's generalizations; they report a wide variety in the cohesiveness and the definition of membership in different gangs. Yablonsky (1962) restricts his conception of the gang as "near-group" primarily to what he calls "the violent gang," but others report highly formal membership in some conflict groups. Yablonsky also recognizes the existence of more close-knit boys' groups which he calls "social gangs," but he describes these as only mildly delinquent.

The core members of violent gangs are seen by Yablonsky (1962) as paranoid psychopaths. He compares their myths of huge membership to what Cameron (1943), in a notable essay, called "the paranoid pseudo-community." Such delusions of social support were seen by Cameron as an integral part of paranoid syndromes. Further research on the different functions which gangs may have for different personalities, and on the relevance of these functions to role differentiation within gangs, is highly desirable. This may well be a by-product of extensive research under way to evaluate the effectiveness of "detached workers."

The latter, sometimes called "street workers," are employed by various agencies to contact gang members on the street, and gain their confidence, then lead them in constructive activities. We already have cited the utilization of Chicago YMCA detached workers by Short to procure ratings on individual gang member activity, based on direct observation. Unusual rapport with delinquents, gained by streetworker relationships, permitted the Schwendingers (1963) in Los Angeles to elicit a striking amount of cooperation in role-playing games ingeniously designed to measure delinquent values. Caplan et al., (1964), in research with Chicago Boy's Club streetworkers, note the extent to which leaders who achieve dominance in gangs mainly by physical prowess maintain their control largely by "veto power." They dismiss activities at which they are not sure of excelling as "too square" or "kid stuff"; in this way they conserve the illusions of their omnicompetence which they have instilled in their followers. Such leadership, of course, may reduce the gang members primarily to hanging on street corners, and may keep them from trying available conventional activities at which they might discover much gratification, including greater ability in comparison with that of the leader than they realized. Change in group activities may also erode control by a delinquent leader and result in his aggressively promoting group delinquency, in order to regain power. When these as yet unpublished impressions are more systematically assessed and reported, both theory on delinquent sub-cultures and practice in altering these subcultures should benefit greatly.

Summary and Conclusion

Social organization and the continuity of cultural conditioning re-sult from man's unique ability to transmit his learning from one generation to the next. Social disorganization occurs when there is a breakdown in this communication, and the actions of different components of a society fail to achieve a culturally expected degree of coordination. Some disorganization is normally concomitant to social and cultural change. Sociological research has stressed the relationship between juvenile delinquency and three aspects of this disorganization: ecological, class-structural, and intergenerational.

The pioneer studies of Shaw, McKay, and others demonstrated the concentration of delinquency in slum areas. They also offered an ecological competition and social disorganization explanation for the predominant location of these high delinquency areas, and a cultural diffusion interpretation of the concentration of a delinquent subcul-ture there. Some later studies suggest qualifications for the earlier ecological observations and theories, but do not drastically contradict them. However, more recent theory and research stimulated by Cloward and Ohlin suggest that large-scale alteration in the housing of slum residents, as a consequence of government action, may alter the types of social disorganization related to delinquency, and the consequent character of delinquent subcultures.

Although class differences in the United States are not clear-cut, it is evident that some difference in way of life is associated with rela-tive rank in a status hierarchy. Most identified with the middle class is a higher valuation than that given on other class levels to the de-ferment of immediate pleasures for the sake of long-run benefits. Major social institutions, such as school and church, endeavor to pro-mote this morality in all classes. The consequent inconsistencies between lower class aspirations and achievements are an aspect of social stratification which have inspired much theorizing on delin-quency.

The dominant class-linked theories of delinquency stress the inability of youth in the lower class to achieve the middle class standards. Cohen interpreted lower class male delinquency as primarily a reaction formation to this frustration, and oriented mainly to expressive revolt against all conventional values and authorities. He views gang organization among delinquents as necessary to provide group support for values which counter those which the school, the church, and other adult institutions attempt to inculcate. Sykes and Matza assert that all delinquent youth carry a multiplicity of value commitments, and must rationalize delinquent acts in terms of middle class values. Alternatively, Miller sees lower class delinquents as merely expressing thinking which pervades the lower classes. Delinquency within the middle class is ascribed by Bohlke to the frustrations encountered by former members of the lower class when new wealth gives them a middle class residence and standard of living, without the habits necessary for successful competition in middle class educational and social activities.

Recent statistical studies of the class distribution of delinquency suggest that within any single school district there is little difference between delinquency rates of children from diverse class backgrounds, but that there is much more delinquency in predominantly lower class school districts than in more middle class districts. This can be interpreted as indicating that delinquency is acquired primarily by diffusion, as a subculture pervading a neighborhood, rather than emerging as a reaction of lower class youth to their difficulties in meeting middle class standards. However, the research of Reckless, the Gluecks, and others suggests that within these neighborhoods families provide the major cultural influence insulating some youth from serious involvement in delinquency.

The age group disorganization view of delinquency notably identified with Bloch and Niederhoffer stresses the discontinuity between childhood and adulthood in all classes and societies as a major stimulus to delinquent gang formation. Eisenstadt documents the view that this problem is greatest in industrialized countries.

The juvenile-adult separation is particularly acute among lower class immigrant groups, except where a distinctive ethnic subculture promotes unusually strong influence by the family or the school or both. The post-World War II period has also seen in the United States a tremendous commercial exploitation of distinctively juvenile consumption interests, which have served further to isolate the adolescent from the adult world, and to create special problems of relative economic deprivation for those who cannot meet the new standards of consumption.

Cloward and Ohlin ascribe the differentiation of delinquent subcultures to variation in the economic and status opportunities of juveniles in criminal and conventional worlds. Youth with limited access to legitimate and illegitimate goals and alienated from adults are seen as adopting conflict-developing subcultures which stress conflict goals. The conflict delinquent subculture is viewed as particularly amenable to change through adult intervention, especially in the provision of work opportunities for youth.

Progressive industrialization of an economy, requiring a longer period in the training of children for adult roles, and greater concentration of the population in urbanized areas, together with urban renewal and relocation, and increased geographical mobility of adults, are likely to increase the separation of juvenile from adult society. Increase in the prevailing standard of living, and increase in rates of status mobility, will probably augment the relative deprivation of those youth who lag in preparation for economic self-sufficiency in conventional middle class pursuits. These changes accompanying industrialization seem to be in progress all over the world, including both capitalist and communist countries (Field 1955; Geiger, 1962).

The growing number of youth who are both out of school and out of work are the hard core of America's delinquency problem, regardless of the type of delinquent subculture in which they are involved. Education and employment, which this group lacks, have been the major institutionalized adjuncts to the family in providing communication between youth and conventional older persons, and in creating continuity in our population's cultural conditioning. Therefore, the largest current investment of government and foundation funds for delinquency reduction have been directed to this group. Efforts to expand the access of such youth to work or schooling, and to non-delinquent types of recreation, are indicated by the titles of two of the largest projects, "Mobilization for Youth" in New York, and "Opening Opportunities" in New Haven. Fortunately, research programs are an integral part of these massive efforts to enlist employers, schools, and others in the community to provide juveniles with job opportunities and with satisfying social relationships with non-criminal adults.

To further test current interpretations of the relationship between various aspects of disorganization and delinquency, there is a critical need for more longitudinal research. This should determine the processes, and the rates of change, in both development and termination of delinquency. Current experimental research in delinquency treatment or prevention, by indicating the effectiveness of intervention in different types of delinquency, or by using diverse intervention techniques, may also contribute much to theoretical understanding of etiological processes in delinquency.

References

Bloch, H., & Niederhoffer, A. (1958) *The gang*. New York: Philosophical Press.

Bohlke, R. (1961) Social mobility, stratification inconsistency and middle class delinquency. *Soc. Prob.*, **8**, 351-363.

Bordua, D. (1959) Juvenile delinquency and "anomie": an attempt at replication. *Soc. Prob.*, **6**, 230-238.

Bordua, D. (1962) Some comments on theories of group delinquency. *Sociol. Inquiry*, **32**, 245-260.

Cameron, N. (1943) The paranoid pseudo-community. *Amer. J. Sociol.*, **49**, 32-38.

Caplan, N. S., Suttles, G., Deshaies, D. J., & Mattick, H. W. (1964) Factors affecting the process and outcome of street club work. *Sociol. & so. Res.*, **48**, 207-219.

Chinoy, E. (1955) *Automobile workers and the American dream*. New York: Random House.

Clark, J., & Wenninger, E. (1962) Social class, area, sex and age as correlates of illegal behavior among juveniles. *Amer. sociol. Rev.*, **27**, 826-834.

Cloward, R., & Ohlin, L. (1960) *Delinquency and opportunity*. Glencoe, Ill.: Free Press.

Cohen, A. (1955) *Delinquent boys*. Glencoe, Ill.: Free Press.

Cohen, A. (1955) Review of Lander. Towards an understanding of juvenile delinquency. *Amer. J. Sociol.*, **60**, 419.

Cohen, A. (1959) The study of social disorganization and deviant behavior. In R. K. Merton, L. Broom, & L. S. Cottrell (eds.), *Sociology today*. New York: Basic Books, 461-484.

Cohen, A., & Short, J., Jr. (1958) Research in delinquent subcultures. *J. soc. Issues*, **14**, 20-37.

Dansereau, H. (1961) Work and the teen-ager. *Ann. Amer. Acad. Pol. Soc. Sci.*, **338**, 44-52.

Eisenstadt, S. (1956) *From generation to generation: age groups and social structure.* Glencoe, Ill.: Free Press.

England, R., Jr. (1960) A theory of middle class delinquency. *J. crim. law, Criminol. & police Sci.*, **50**, 535-540.

Field, M. (1955) Alcoholism, crime and delinquency in Soviet society. *Soc. Prob.*, **3**, 100-109.

Finestone, H. (1957) Cats, kicks and color. *Soc. Prob.*, **5**, 3-13.

Geiger, K. (1962) Juvenile delinquency in Soviet Russia. Report prepared for the Youth Development Program, The Ford Foundation.

Glueck, S., & Glueck, Eleanor (1959) *Predicting delinquency and crime.* Cambridge, Mass.: Harvard Univer. Press.

Gordon, R., Short, J., Jr., Cartwright, D., & Strodtbeck, F. (1963) Values and gang delinquency: a study of street corner groups. *Amer. J. sociol.*, **69**, 109-128.

Kelly, G. (1955) *The psychology of personal constructs.* 2 vols. New York: Norton.

Kvaraceus, W., & Miller, W. (1959) *Delinquent behavior: culture and the individual.* Washington, D.C., National Education Association.

Jonassen, C. (1949) A re-evaluation and critique of the logic and some methods of Shaw and McKay. *Amer. sociol. Rev.*, **14**, 608-614.

Lander, B. (1954) *Towards an understanding of juvenile delinquency.* New York: Columbia Univer. Press.

Lively, E., Dinitz, S., & Reckless, W. (1962) Self-concept as a predictor of juvenile delinquency. *Amer. J. Orthopsychiat.*, **32**, 159-168.

Matza, D. (1961) Subterranean traditions of youth. *Ann. Amer. Acad. Pol. Soc. Sci.*, **338**, 102-118.

McCord, W., & McCord, Joan (1959) *Origins of Crime.* New York: Columbia Univer. Press.

Merton, R. (1961) Social problems and sociological theory. In R. K. Merton & R. A. Nisbet (eds.), *Contemporary social problems.* New York: Harcourt, Brace & World.

Miller, W. (1959) Lower class culture as a generating milieu of gang delinquency. *J. soc. Issues*, **14**, 5-19.

Mills, C. W. (1940) Situated actions and vocabularies of motive. *Amer. sociol. Rev.*, **5**, 904-913.

Monahan, T. (1957) Family status and the delinquent child. *Soc. Forces*, **35**, 250-258.

Morris, R. (1963) Social stratification. In L. Broom & P. Selznick (eds.), *Sociology.* 3rd ed. Evanston, Ill.: Row, Peterson.

Nye, R., Short, J., & Olson, V. (1958) Socio-economic status and delinquent behavior. *Amer. J. sociol.*, **63**, 381-389.

Park, R., Burgess, E., & McKenzie, R. (1925) *The city.* Chicago: Univer. of Chicago Press.

Pfautz, H. (1961) Near-group theory and collective behavior: a critical reformulation. *Soc. Probl.*, 9, 167-174.

Plant, J. (1937) *Personality and the cultural pattern.* New York: Commonwealth Fund.

Porterfield, A. (1943) Delinquency and its outcome in court and college. *Amer. J. sociol.*, 49, 199-208.

Reckless, W., Dinitz, S., & Murray, Ellen (1956) Self-concept as an insulator against delinquency. *Amer. sociol. Rev.*, 21, 744-746.

Reiss, H., Jr., & Rhodes, A. (1961) The distribution of juvenile delinquency in the class structure. *Amer. sociol. Rev.*, 26, 720-732.

Reiss, A., Jr., & Rhodes, A. (1963) Status deprivation and delinquent behavior. *Sociol. Quart.*, 4, 135-149.

Robison, Sophia (1936) *Can delinquency be measured?* New York: Columbia Univer. Press.

Schwendinger, Julia, & Schwendinger, H. (May 1963) The illegal marketplace among adolescents. Paper presented at the Pacific Sociol. Conference.

Shaw, C. (1929) *Delinquency areas.* Chicago: Univer. of Chicago Press.

Shaw, C. (1930) *The jack roller.* Chicago: Univer. of Chicago Press.

Shaw, C. (1931) *The natural history of a delinquent career.* Chicago: Univer. of Chicago Press.

Shaw, C., & McKay, H. (1931) Social factors in juvenile delinquency. In *Report on the causes of crime.* National Commission on Law Observance and Law Enforcement, Vol. 2.

Shaw, C., & McKay, H. (1942) *Juvenile delinquency and urban areas.* Chicago: Univer. of Chicago Press.

Shaw, C., & McKay, H. (1949) Rejoinder to Jonassen. *Amer. sociol Rev.*, 14, 614-617.

Shaw, C., McKay, H., & McDonald, J. (1938) *Brothers in crime.* Chicago: Univer. of Chicago Press.

Short, J., Jr., Tennyson, R., & Howard, K. (1963) Behavior dimensions of gang delinquency. *Amer. sociol. Rev.*, 28, 411-428.

Spergel, I. (1961) An exploratory research in delinquent subcultures. *Soc. serv. Rev.*, 35, 33-49.

Spergel, I. (1962) A multidimensional model for social work practice: the youth worker example. *Soc. serv. Rev.*, 36, 62-71.

Sykes, G., & Matza, D. (1957) Techniques of neutralization. *Amer. sociol. Rev.*, 22, 664-670.

Thrasher, F. (1927) *The gang.* Chicago: Univer. of Chicago Press.

Toby, J. (1950) Comment on the Jonassen-Shaw and McKay controversy. *Amer. sociol. Rev.*, 15, 107-108.

Toby, J. (1957) The differential impact of family disorganization. *Amer. sociol. Rev.*, 22, 505-512.

Toby, J. (1958) Hoodlum or business man: an American dilemma. In M. Sklare (ed.), *The Jews: social patterns of an American group.* Glencoe, Ill.: Free Press.

Toby, J. (1962) Criminal motivation. *Brit. J. Criminol.*, **2**, 317-336.

U.S. Bureau of Census and U.S. Department of Agriculture. Educational status, college plans, and occupational status of farm and non-farm youths: October 1959. *Farm population*, August 1961, Series Census ERS, No. 30, 27.

Wallerstein, J., & Wylie, C. (1947) Our law-abiding law-breakers. *Probation*, **25**, 107-112.

Weber, M. (1930) *The protestant ethic and the spirit of capitalism.* London: George Allen and Unwin.

Whyte, W. (1937) *Street corner society.* Chicago: Univer. of Chicago Press.

Yablonsky, L. (1954) The delinquent gang as a near-group. *Soc. Probl.*, **7**, 108-117.

Yablonsky, L. (1962) *The violent gang.* New York: Macmillan.

3

Family Interaction and Delinquency

Donald R. Peterson and Wesley C. Becker

This is a review of literature on family interaction and delinquency, and a statement of some generalizations which emerge from the review. We assume that tendencies toward delinquency, like most other behaviors of social importance, are learned mainly through experience with other people, and that the execution of delinquent behavior ordinarily has reference to the prior stimulation or expected reaction of somebody else. Parents and other family members are not by any means the only agents involved in determining delinquency. They may not even be the most important agents. But as the following survey will show, mothers and fathers, and the various ways they treat their children, have much to do with developing dispositions to delinquency.

The review will focus on studies in which family characteristics and delinquency have been statistically related, usually by comparing the families of delinquent and nondelinquent adolescents. Where appropriate, however, we will extend discussion to other characteristics, e.g., aggression, lack of self-restraint, and psychopathic trends, which have some reasonable relationship to delinquent behavior. Because of the lack of behavioral specificity in the legal concept of delinquency, the examination of such a variable as aggression is frequently more revealing than study of delinquency itself. But most of the pertinent available research has dealt with delinquency as a dependent variable, and consideration of this work may

63

at least direct future study toward examination of variables with more definite psychological and sociological meaning.

THE FAMILY AS A TRANSMITTER OF SUBCULTURAL VALUES

Within a society like that of the United States, delinquency rates vary widely from one part to another. One of the most striking differences is found in comparing delinquency rates for rural areas with those in large cities. Data show that the rates are substantially higher in big cities than they are in the country (Watt, 1931; Lottier, 1938; Clinard, 1942). While rural delinquency is less apt to be detected than delinquency in the city, it seems likely that some difference remains in actual delinquent activity. Efforts to tie the discrepancy to differences in family attitude (a puritanical, close-to-the-soil orientation versus a more worldly, sinful outlook) have not been very successful. The most compelling interpretations are those which emphasize the greater opportunity and inducement for delinquent behavior in the city, the greater mobility and anonymity of people there, and the greater likelihood of differential association with criminal or criminally inclined others. But whatever the reasons for the fact, delinquency rates appear to be higher in urban than in rural areas.

Within any large city there are wide sectional differences in delinquency rate. In general, delinquency is more common near the center of a large city and less frequent toward the periphery (Shaw and McKay, 1942; Lander, 1954). Following the lead of Burgess and Shaw, analysts attempting to account for this trend have most often emphasized the social disorganization prevalent in interstitial districts between the expanding industrial-commercial city centers and the residential zones farther out. But urban delinquency rates covary with many conditions. General educational level, average rental costs, rate of population change, concentration of Negroes, percentage of owner-occupied homes, and frequency of substandard housing are all significantly and sometimes very closely related to the incidence of delinquency (Lander, 1954; Morris, 1958).

A complex of determining conditions is suggested with economic deprivation at the center. According to some lines of thought, residents of slum areas are as vulnerable as anyone else to the status appeals which pervade our culture. They want "the good life," but are deprived of opportunities to gain the social advantages and material possessions they seek. Lacking legitimate means to the ends of material well-being and social status, many choose whatever means are available to them, and some of the latter may be illegitimate by legal standards (Cloward and Ohlin, 1960). Whatever guilt may arise as a consequence of the generality of middle class ethics in our culture is effectively neutralized by devaluing the unattainable "honest" means and "worthy" ends, coupled with complementary acceptance of accessible if illicit ways to gratification (Sykes and Matza, 1957).

When numbers of people share a similar problem, subcultures tend to form, and the members of groups who share the subcultures tend jointly to solve the problems they mutually face. Thus the juvenile gang reinforces an opposition to middle class norms its members cannot meet, and encourages a more easily available and immediately more satisfying pattern of behavior. Such behavior is usually delinquent in at least some of its aspects (Cohen, 1955).

Not only adolescents but also their parents may adopt such subcultural solutions to the problems which lower class living imposes upon them. According to Miller's (1958, 1959) analysis of the values prevalent in lower class American society, "toughness" (whether of pugilist or criminal), "smartness" (the worldly smartness of the "con" man rather than the academic knowledge of the scholar), and "autonomy" ("Nobody is going to push *me* around"), are held in considerably higher esteem than responsibility, frugality, and the other qualities prized by people in the middle class. The search is more for excitement than for long-term achievement, and outcomes are thought to be more in the hands of fate and circumstance than at the command of the doer. Lower class parents, possessing such values themselves, transmit them to their children, partly in realistic preparation for the harsh and rugged life their children are likely to lead.

According to Jephcott and Carter (1954), who examined life in the slums of an English city, high delinquency rates and a "rough" family life go hand in hand. Where delinquency rates were highest, behavior standards were grossly different from those in the middle class where laws are defined, and from the standards of "respectable" families at the same lower economic level. Quarrels were open and frequent, language was coarse; money, when there was some, was spent with little planning; sexual relationships were casual; the children were released or thrust from family ties as soon as they were physically able to fend for themselves, and sometimes before. The meaning of the family and the meaning of law were simply different from meanings assumed by members of the middle class.

Certain differences in the child-rearing practices of lower and middle class parents have been known for some time. While there is evidence that the gap is narrowing, and the pattern changing (Bronfenbrenner, 1958), there is still substance to the belief that lower class parents place less emphasis on achievement, consideration for others, and self-control than do the parents of middle class children (Kohn, 1959). Lower class parents have also appeared to be more permissive than middle class parents in regard to certain forms of sexual and aggressive behavior which may lead to delinquency (Davis and Havighurst, 1948). Concerns for "morality" among lower class parents tend to center on immediate obedience and short-term respectability (Kohn, 1959).

In the framework of cultural transmission theory, the values, attitudes, and child-rearing practices of parents reflect the norms of the particular subculture in which they have been reared and in which they are preparing their children to survive. The occurrence of delinquent behavior is largely incidental to the transmission of a larger complex of values, in which crime is not discouraged with any particular force and the reinforcement system actually mobilizes and maintains the kinds of behavior a court may define as delinquent.

The role of the family as a system within larger social systems must thus be recognized if delinquent and other socially oriented behaviors are to be understood. It is a mistake to assume, as so many psychologists and psychiatrists do, that the behavior of a child can be explained solely through reference to the internal structure of the family, without reference to the larger social system in which the family is embedded.

But it is equally fallacious to assume that the family serves *only* to transmit subcultural values from one generation to another and from the society "outside" to the family members within. The family, more specifically the people in the family, cast their own impressions on the norms they have learned from their parents and from the others around them. The family adds variance of its own. Theories of cultural transmission which ascribe basic identity to people who live in low class, high delinquency areas fail to account for the fact that most children in the worst slum areas do not become delinquent (Kobrin, 1951). Those theorists who assume that lower class parents generally transmit "delinquent" ideals to their offspring fail to note that the quality esteemed most highly by parents of all classes is honesty (Kohn, 1959). The research of Reckless and his colleagues (Reckless *et al.*, 1957; Scarpitti *et al.*, 1960) has shown the extent to which identification with a stable cohesive family and the development of a "good" self-concept can insulate youth from crime-inducing influences of high potency. According to the reports of Jephcott and Carter (1954) wide differences in delinquency rate occur from one street to another in the areas of highest general delinquency rate, and in fact wide differences are found between individual families on the same street. To ignore the independent influence of the family is just as serious an error as to ignore the fact that no family nor any of its members can ever be entirely independent of other social influences.

The Physical Characteristics of the Home

The homes in which delinquents live tend to be dirty and run down. The parents of delinquents examined in the Gluecks' research (Glueck and Glueck, 1950) paid just as much for housing as the heads of nondelinquent families, but facilities for sanitation (bathtubs, flush toilets, and so on) were poorer. The homes of delinquents are often disorderly and cluttered; preset routines are weakly fixed. Physical space is at a premium, and privacy can best be had by leaving the house. There is little recreation in the home (Nye, 1958; Glueck and Glueck, 1950), and whatever enjoyment a child may seek must usually be found outside.

To develop self-control and a tendency to behave in accordance with middle class standards of achievement, self-sacrifice, and responsibility, a child has to expect some gratifications for such behavior. If he is to expect gratifications, some gratifications must exist, and these are few and far between in most delinquent homes. Stability, system, and order in sequences of events help make acculturation a feasible task. There is little order in the modal delinquent home. As a physical-social stimulus, the typical delinquent home acts mainly as a repellent, driving people out. As a setting for socialization, it is considerably less than adequate.

The Presence and Absence of Socializing Agents in the Family

But socialization depends mainly on the people who do the socializing. And some of the major questions which must be considered in an examination of family interaction and delinquency relate to the make-up of the family—what people are there to rear the children? Put another way, are some of the people who normally contribute to socialization (such as parents) missing from the families of delinquents?

Investigations of this question have concentrated on study of the "broken home." We will review these findings first, and then a smaller literature on other conditions which have the general effect of limiting the number of socializing agents in the family, or the amount of time they can spend in active involvement with the rearing of children.

Broken Homes and Delinquency

The gross relationship is well established—the families of delinquents have been disrupted by death, desertion, divorce, separation, or prolonged parental absence much more frequently than the families of nondelinquents. Major findings of some tolerably well-controlled studies are presented in Table 3-1. The direction of the difference is the same in all comparisons. Even the magnitude of the difference is fairly uniform; broken homes are one and one-half to two times more frequent among delinquents than among nondelinquents. The impact of family disruption varies with certain characteristics of the child (Toby, 1959; Monahan, 1957, 1960),

TABLE 3-1. INCIDENCE OF BROKEN HOMES

| | | Broken Homes | | | |
| | | Delinquents | | Controls | |
Investigator	Sex	N	%	N	%
Burt, 1929	Both	197	57.9	400	25.7
Shaw and McKay, 1932	Boys	1675	42.5	7278	36.1
Hodgkiss, 1933	Girls	362	66.8	362	44.8
Weeks and Smith, 1939	Boys	330	41.4	2119	26.7
Carr-Saunders et al., 1944	Boys	1955	28.5	1970	15.8
Gardner and Goldman, 1945	Men	500	58.6	200	32.0
Merrill, 1947	Both	300	50.7	300	26.7
Glueck and Glueck, 1950	Boys	500	60.4	500	32.4
Oltman et al., 1952	Both	90	47.7	230	32.2
Nye, 1958	Boys	368	23.6	792	17.6
	Girls	231	36.4	931	16.9
Monahan, 1958	White Boys	11236	27.7*		7.0
	White Girls	1984	52.0		
	Negro Boys	8706	53.0		33.0
	Negro Girls	2736	73.2		

* Monahan's figures for "controls" are those for nonhusband-wife families in the 1950 census. The broken home percentages for delinquents are based on the usual definition of broken home, which is not quite the same. If comparability is improved by counting only nonhusband-wife families among delinquents, the adjusted figures for the four groups are 22 per cent, 42 per cent, 49 per cent, and 68 per cent, respectively.

notably age (preadolescents are more strongly affected than older children) and sex (girls are affected more than boys), but the substantial relationship between delinquency and broken homes remains as one of the overriding facts any conception of delinquency must take into account.

Demonstration of the statistical relationship between family disruption and crime is only a starting point for causal analysis. It is not particularly illuminating to regard the broken home as a direct cause of delinquency. Family disruption probably operates indirectly, through the neutralization of influences which ordinarily impede delinquency, or the exaggeration of influences which promote it. Better comprehension of the meaning of a broken home begins to develop when the reasons for the break are considered.

In general, death of a parent is less damaging than disruption from marital discord, though this proposition needs to be qualified. Burt (1929) found no difference between delinquent and nondelinquent groups in regard to death of the father, but the groups differed widely in the incidence of divorce, separation, and desertion. Absence of the mother, however, was related to delinquency regardless of the reason for absence, and the effect of maternal absence was especially severe for delinquent girls. Twenty-seven per cent of the Navy brig inmates studied by Gardner and Goldman (1945) came from homes broken by divorce, separation, or desertion, contrasted to only 10 per cent of the controls. There were no differences in the proportions of homes broken by death. Oltman, McGarry, and Friedman (1952) found nearly half (48.8 per cent) of the broken homes of a group of alleged psychopaths to have been disrupted by marital discord, but marital discord was the cause of disruption in only 18 per cent of a group of control families. With the exception of the Gluecks' study (1950), where all forms of disruption were more common among delinquents than among controls,[1] major investigations uniformly support the proposition that the cause of the breach must be taken into account along with the fact of disruption itself. A most damaging condition is one in which family strife has led, on the one hand, to separation or divorce of the parents and, on the other, to the instigation of delinquent tendencies among the

[1] The Gluecks fround some tendency for the *first* breach in the homes of delinquents to occur from abandonment, desertion, or temporary separation, while death or permanent dissolution of the home through separation or divorce were more common factors in the first breach for nondelinquents, but their general results, while not contradictory to those of the other studies cited above, are still discrepant in failing to support the hypothesis under discussion.

children. Not only is there a lack of continuity in the influences which contribute to socialization; the effectiveness of such influence is limited or nullified by the stress within the family.

The high incidence of foster home placement among delinquents (Burt, 1929; Wittman and Huffman, 1945; Bennett, 1960) further reflects the fact that the primary homes of delinquents tend to be unstable and disharmonious. For one reason or another, conditions in the home have required that the child be placed somewhere else.

The effects of broken homes have been interpreted by Bowlby (1944) in terms of his well-known, widely criticized concept of the "affectless character." The trouble with delinquents, according to Bowlby, is that they have failed to develop adequate emotional-motivational bases for socialized behavior, and this is due to a lack of affection in the early years. Bowlby compared forty-four juvenile thieves with forty-four children referred to a guidance clinic for various other reasons, and found a history of separation from the mother in only two of the latter cases, but for seventeen of the forty-four delinquents. He distinguished further between thieves who were "affectless" and those who were not, and found early separation from the mother to be much more common in the lives of the affectless children. Methodological subjectivity in the isolation of the "affectless" group leaves conclusions about that group open to some question, but the gross disparity between delinquents and other disturbed children in the historical fact of separation from the mother is still of great interest. Oltman and his colleagues (Oltman, McGarry, and Friedman, 1952) also made comparisons between various disturbed groups and found the frequency of broken homes to be significantly high for psychopaths and neurotics, but not for manic-depressives, schizophrenics, or alcoholics. A history of family disruption is hardly specific to delinquency, but it does act as an important precondition to crime, and it seems to have more to do with the formation of character disorders than with the etiology of some other equally serious forms of disturbance.

Working Mothers and Delinquency

If adequate socialization requires the fairly continuous presence of parents and other people who do the socializing, then not only major and lasting changes in family composition, as in a broken home, but also periodic or short-term absences of parents should be related to failures in socialization. Among the latter conditions, most has been made of the role of the "working mother" in the etiology of delinquency. If she is at work, the reasoning goes, she cannot be home rearing her children, and her children should therefore be somewhat more prone to antisocial behavior than those from families where the mother is home taking care of the children.

A clear-cut test of this proposition is difficult to obtain. Nye (1958) found very slightly stronger tendencies toward delinquency where the mothers worked. The effect was greater for girls than for boys, and Nye attributed the small relationship he found to a loss of direct control associated with absence of the mother. Andry (1960), in a study in England, found no significant relationship between delinquency and the work status of the mother, but the fathers' work schedules did have a bearing on delinquency among the children in his sample. The fathers of delinquents were on shift work more than the fathers of nondelinquents. Also, they more often reported that they were absent frequently from the home for reasons of work when the child was 6 to 15 years old. Andry suggests that it may be the lack of a close relationship with the father—the fathers always seemed to have some reason for staying away from their sons—that mattered more than the fact of absence itself.

The Gluecks (1950) found no deleterious effect to come from regular employment on the part of the mother, but the mothers of delinquents engaged in occasional outside employment more often than the mothers of nondelinquents (26.6 per cent versus 14.7 per cent), and less often listed their occupation simply as "housewife." Two-thirds of the mothers of nondelinquents were full-time housewives (and parents); only a little more than half of the mothers of delinquents (53 per cent) were listed as housewives.

Occupation outside the home would thus seem to bear some relationship to delinquency, but the association is slight, and it is complicated by a number of other factors. The extent to which working mothers provide for the supervision of their children during the work period matters, and so does the temperament of the child. Glueck and Glueck (1957) found mothers' occupation to interact significantly with a number of child characteristics. The effect of the working mother was most damaging when the child was physically ectomorphic and, according to the Sheldon-Glueck interpretation, cerebrotonically sensitive and prone to worry.

Outside employment by the mother is not so important a contributor to delinquency as some observers have suggested. It may be deleterious for mothers to work, but not very. Children can apparently mature psychosocially and avoid delinquency even if the mother is gone from time to time, just as they can endure the death of a parent when the basic relationships in the family are adequate.

THE PARENTS AS INDIVIDUALS AND
RELATIONSHIPS BETWEEN THEM

There is a good deal of evidence to suggest that the parents of delinquents tend to be discontented, short-tempered people, whose qualities affect not only their attitudes toward their children, but also toward each other. On some questions relating to cheerfulness, "hot-headedness," and so on, the most delinquent group in Nye's study (Nye, 1958) tended to see the dispositions of both parents as "unfavorable" or "intermediate." Among those who said their parents had "favorable" dispositions, 80 per cent were in the least delinquent group. The children in the high delinquency sample also tended to say their parents were unhappy in marriage. Andry (1960) failed to find a significant difference between delinquents and nondelinquents in the amount of quarreling which went on between parents, but a number of other studies have suggested such a difference. In the Gluecks' research, 65 per cent of the parents of nondelinquents, but only 37 per cent of parents of delinquents, were said to have good conjugal relationships (reasonable compatibility, freedom from undue quarreling, and so on). Disturbed relationships between father and mother were more common among the delinquent families studied by Bennett (1960) than among families where the child had some kind of neurosis. McCord, McCord, and Gudeman (1960) found relationships to be "affectionate" in only 12 per cent of seventy-eight criminal families examined. The attitudes between parents tended instead to be antagonistic or, still more often, indifferent.

The parents of delinquents do not appear to provide their offspring with the models of socially appropriate behavior children require. Subjects in Nye's study who said their parents never lied, were always honest, and were of strong moral character in other ways tended to be among the least delinquent (Nye, 1958). The situation is worse, understandably, if the parents themselves have known criminal histories, and the general association between criminality among parents and delinquency in children is well established. The relationship is complicated, however, by some interactions with the way the child is treated. In the study of McCord, McCord, and Zola (1959), it was found that delinquency was quite uncommon, even among the sons of criminals, so long as the fathers were consistent in discipline of the children. The pertinent relationships are shown in Table 3-2, where it can be seen that crime rates become enor-

TABLE 3-2. RELATION OF PARENTAL DISCIPLINE AND
FATHER'S ROLE MODEL TO CRIME RATE
(From McCord, McCord, and Zola, 1959)

	Percentage of Boys Convicted of Later Crimes	
Type of Discipline	Criminal Father	Nondeviant Father
Consistently punitive	0	18
Consistently love-oriented	18	29
Erratically love-oriented	67	26
Erratically punitive	76	44
Lax	75	50

mously high when a criminal father treats his child in an erratic or neglectful way but remain low when consistent discipline is applied. Similar interactions were found on examination of mothers. See Table 3-3.

TABLE 3-3. RELATION OF PARENTAL DISCIPLINE AND
MOTHER'S ROLE MODEL TO CRIME RATE
(From McCord, McCord, and Zola, 1959)

	Percentage of Boys Convicted of Later Crimes	
Type of Discipline	Criminal Mother	Nondeviant Mother
Consistently punitive	0	23
Consistently love-oriented	29	26
Erratically love-oriented	40	33
Erratically punitive	94	66
Lax	67	44

The interdependence between role model and parental attitude extends not only to the disciplinary mode of parents but also to the affectional relationships between parents and children. Where fathers are cruel or neglecting *and* criminal, the chances of delinquency are very great. The McCords found that 85 per cent of the Cambridge-Somerville subjects reared under those conditions had been convicted of at least one crime. Where mothers were deviant and nonloving, the crime rate was nearly as high—81 per cent (McCord, McCord, and Zola, 1959). We are led to consider some more direct relationships between parents and children, for it seems that these relationships—affectional bonds, disciplinary treatment, and the like

—pervade all the others in forming predispositions to delinquent behavior.

Parent-Child Relationships in Delinquency

Authority Relationships

Popular writers (e.g., Liebowitz, 1957) often lay great emphasis on the weak role of men in contemporary American families. Father has lost his place as head of the family, they say; his dignity is gone, his authority weakened. And if the delinquency problem is ever to be attacked at its roots, fathers are going to have to reaffirm their rights and reassume their obligations at the head of the household.

Like most propositions with high popular appeal, this one appears to have an element of truth in it, but the problem is not as simple as all that, and the statement needs qualifying. There is no clear evidence that mothers have "taken over" in the homes of delinquents, or that the family histories involve a power struggle in which weak, meek husbands have been subjugated to the more assertive wills of their wives. When the Gluecks (1950) attempted to determine which parent was dominant in the families they examined, they emerged with the figures in Table 3-4, which show that a dominance

TABLE 3-4. Dominance Patterns in the Families
of Delinquents and Nondelinquents
(From Glueck and Glueck, 1950)

Dominant Parent	Percentage of Families	
	Delinquents	Nondelinquents
Father	49.6	49.7
Mother	48.1	46.0
Neither	2.3	4.3

pattern is ordinarily established in the American home, that the mother is dominant in about half the families and the father dominant in the other half, but that delinquents do not come from homes where "mother is boss" any more often than nondelinquents. When the McCords (1960) compared dominance configurations in the homes of criminals with those in the homes of alcoholics, they found dominance assigned to the father *more* often in the homes of criminals. When Andry (1960) asked his subjects which parent had the "final say" in family decisions, the father had more authority in both delinquent and nondelinquent families, but the differences between groups were not significant. Questions pertaining directly to obedience and punishment, however, did reveal some differences. Both parents, or the father alone, did most of the punishing in less than two-thirds (64 per cent) of the families of delinquents, but in three-fourths (76 per cent) of the families of nondelinquents. Responsibility for punishment was relegated solely to the mother in 36 per cent of the delinquent families, but in only 24 per cent of the families of nondelinquents.

It seems likely that these differences are not so much a matter of feminine dominance as of masculine neglect and indifference. Delinquency is very common in the "female based households" described by Miller (1958, 1959). In most of these families the father has either deserted or has never been a permanent member of the family. Italian-American families tend to be dominated by the father, the more so a generation ago, but these families contributed more than their share of criminals in Chicago, say, in the twenties and thirties. There is, in short, little or no evidence for a common belief that delinquency arises from a domination of American husbands by their wives, or for the proposal that delinquency can be stopped by restoring father to his traditional place at the head of the home.

Affectional Relationships

The importance of parental love is ordinarily assumed by clinicians concerned with the adjustment of children. The basic defect in delinquency, as in most other forms of disturbance, is thought to lie somewhere in the feelings parents and childen have for each other. Systematic studies of affectional relationships in delinquency, however, are rather rare, and most of them are fairly recent. Burt's early analysis (Burt, 1929) of "defective family relationships" focused mainly on broken homes. When he looked to the way parents and children got along together, the major emphasis was on matters of discipline, not affection. Healy and Bronner (1926) made much of the rejection and deprivation of love which seemed to distinguish delinquent from nondelinquent siblings. Bowlby (1944) emphasized lack of affection even more, but his judgments, like those of Healy and Bronner, were sufficiently vulnerable to bias to cast some doubt on the dependability of the findings. Some direct but limited information on parental affection was gained in Merrill's research on delinquents (Merrill, 1947). About half the parents of delinquents and most of the parents of controls were compared by placement on an "affection" scale, with sympathy and kindness at one end and definite hostility at the other. Only 3 per cent of the controls, but 22 per cent of the delinquents were said to come from "definitely hostile" homes. No distinction was made between the attitudes of mothers and fathers.

More refined studies of affectional relationships, recognizing possible differences between parents, examining interactions between affection and other variables, and allowing for differential effects of various patterns of parental behavior, did not begin to appear until fairly recently. One of the first reports to offer any of the needed refinements was that of Hewitt and Jenkins (1946). While not focally addressed to the study of delinquency, their analysis of the differential effects of differing parental attitudes have some implications for the understanding of delinquency. After distinguishing three major patterns of maladjustment, viz., unsocialized aggression, socialized delinquency, and overinhibition, the authors related certain parental attitudes to the behavior syndromes of the children. Results are given in Table 3-5, where findings about unsocialized aggression and

TABLE 3-5. CORRELATIONS * BETWEEN PARENTAL ATTITUDES
AND BEHAVIOR OF CHILDREN
(From Hewitt and Jenkins, 1946)

Parental Attitude	Unsocialized Aggression	Socialized Delinquency	Over-inhibition
Rejection	.48	.02	−.20
Negligence and exposure	.12	.63	−.17
Repression	.10	−.12	.52

* Tetrachoric r's.

socialized delinquency are most pertinent to this discussion. While the garden variety delinquency of city gangs would appear to be related mainly to parental neglect, unsocialized aggression is evidently related to active rejection on the part of parents.

The confidence which can be placed in these results is unfortunately limited by a mode of analysis which capitalized on chance. The syndromes of parental treatment were defined by selecting those variables which were positively correlated with one of the child behavior syndromes, and then selecting a small number of those situational items which were logically interrelated.

Selective analyses of this kind can lead to spuriously positive results, and indeed a related investigation by Horwitz (1944) found no statistically significant differences in family background between a group of unsocialized-aggressive and a group of overinhibited children defined by the methods Hewitt and Jenkins had developed.

Biases generated by the Hewitt-Jenkins data selection method, however, would tend to be in the nature of an over-all exaggeration of the strength of association, rather than a forcing of the pattern of relationships. It is of interest to note that Lewis (1954), studying the family backgrounds of children at a diagnostic placement center, found a pattern result similar to that reported by Hewitt and Jenkins. Unsocialized aggressive delinquents had more parental rejection in their backgrounds, socialized delinquents showed histories of neglect and bad company, while the inhibited-neurotic children tended to have experienced excessive constraint. This study is also subject to criticism on the grounds that the same person made judgments of both child behavior and family. In addition, as Lewis notes, the definition of socialized delinquency is contaminated with the background pattern of negligence and exposure. Both definitions require *exposure to delinquents* for placement in the categories. It is of considerable interest that specific ratings of *neglect by mother* and *neglect by father* did not significantly differentiate among the problem groups in Lewis' study. These data and difficulties thus raise a question concerning the specific relation between neglect and socialized delinquency. However, Lewis' results with a different sample and different methodological flaws from those in the Hewitt-Jenkins study do tend to support Hewitt and Jenkins' findings on the association of rejection with unsocialized aggression and repressive family backgrounds with overinhibited behavior.

Refinement along other parameters was offered by the Gluecks' (1950) study. Some of the more relevant findings appear in Table 3-6. Indifference, rejection, and outright hostility were very com-

TABLE 3-6. AFFECTION OF PARENTS FOR DELINQUENT
AND NONDELINQUENT BOYS
(From Glueck and Glueck, 1950)

	Percentage of Parents Showing Attitude			
	Father *		Mother *	
Parental Attitude	Delinquent	Non-delinquent	Delinquent	Non-delinquent
Warm	40.2	80.7	72.1	95.6
Indifferent	42.9	16.0	21.2	3.4
Hostile, rejecting	16.9	3.3	6.7	1.0

* x^2 values are significant well beyond the .01 level for both mothers and fathers.

monly displayed by the parents of delinquents, especially by the fathers, in contrast with the warmth and affection which the vast majority of "normal" parents gave their children. Bandura and Walters (1959), in their study of aggression, obtained similar results, as shown in Table 3-7. From interviews with fathers and mothers

TABLE 3-7. PARENTAL AFFECTION FOR AGGRESSIVE AND NONAGGRESSIVE BOYS
(From Bandura and Walters, 1959)

| | Group Means | | | | | |
| | Fathers | | | Mothers | | |
Parental Attitude	Aggressive Group	Control Group	p	Aggressive Group	Control Group	p
Data from Father Interviews:						
Warmth	6.94	8.40	.001	7.83	8.44	.10
Rejection by father	4.63	3.04	.001			
Affectionate interaction in early childhood	6.00	7.04	.10	8.69	8.98	—
Data from Mother Interviews:						
Warmth	6.38	7.60	.05	7.44	8.02	.10
Rejection by mother				4.50	3.00	.001
Affectionate interaction in early childhood	5.77	6.85	.05	8.44	8.96	.10
Data from Child Interviews:						
Rejection by father	4.48	2.59	.01			
Rejection by mother				3.61	2.64	.02

alike, it was clear that the aggressive boys were loved less and rejected more than the nonaggressive children. Again, the differences were greatest in regard to the attitudes of fathers.

Andry (1960) places heavy emphasis on defects in the father-child relationship as a leading factor in delinquency. This is not to say that the relationship between mothers and sons are unimportant. In a comparison between 80 court-committed repeat offenders and a rather carefully matched sample of nondelinquents, Andry found both mothers and fathers of delinquents to differ sharply from control parents in adequacy of affection. But the fathers differed more, and, in the affectional aspect of the parent-child relationship, as well as in other facets of the relationship, it was the attitude of the father which appeared to have the stronger influence in forming emotional predispositions to delinquency.

Alone among the more sophisticated studies, the McCords' research (1959) attributed greater significance to the mother, though relationships between crime and fathers' attitudes were also found.

Classifying fathers as warm, passive, cruel, or neglecting (as well as dead or absent), they found the greatest incidence of criminality where fathers were neglectful, unconcerned, and indifferent. Crime rates were lowest when fathers were "warm" or "passive." The latter finding surprised the authors a little, considering other findings on the deleterious effects of paternal passivity, but the generally damaging effect of a lack of affection from fathers seems clear enough.

The McCords' classification system for mothers was more complex. Instead of just deciding whether mothers were "warm" or not, a four-place categorization into "loving-normal," "overprotective," "loving-anxious," and "loving-neurotic" was considered necessary. When the findings emerged, all the "loving" categories were related to the lowest crime rates, though it was less criminogenic for a mother to be "normally" affectionate than to be "neurotically" so. As with fathers, the highest delinquency rates were associated with neglect, but in contrast with the finding for fathers, maternal "passivity" was the next most damaging attitude.

In a rather lengthy interpretation of this discrepancy, the authors suggest that boys are less upset by passivity from fathers than from mothers, because fathers are expected to be somewhat disengaged from the home, while passivity on the part of a mother is interpreted as rejection. This is one possibility, but others should be considered. As the McCords suggest, passive fathers offer a model for the boy which is antithetical to status in a delinquent group. But most obviously, it is important to note that the definition of "passivity" for fathers is not the same as that for mothers. For fathers, the definition naturally connotes some disavowal of responsibility for child rearing, but it also stipulates a positive affection for the child. "Passive fathers," according to the McCords' definition, "in their way love their child." The definition of passivity for mothers contains no such statement. Mothers judged to love their children were placed in one of the several "loving" categories. The "passive" ones were supposed to fit the following description: "Weak and ineffectual. Phlegmatic in manner. Play a minor role in the family, leaving direction and discipline to others in the home." That sounds very much like a weak neglect, and it is hardly surprising that "passive" and "neglecting" attitudes appear together, at the opposite end from "loving" attitudes, closely related to crime on the part of the sons.

Conclusions reached in this study about the relative significance of a mother's and father's love come mainly from a study of some interactions between attitudes of the two parents. Pertinent findings are given in Table 3-8. As expected, crime was most frequent when

TABLE 3-8. RELATION OF PARENTAL AFFECTION TO CRIME RATE
(From McCord, McCord and Zola, 1959)

	Percentage of Boys Convicted of Later Crimes	
	Attitude of Father	
Attitude of Mother	Loving	Rejecting
Loving	32	36
Rejecting	46	70

both parents were rejecting, and least when they were both affectionate, but, the McCords say, the contribution of mothers' attitudes to variance in crime was greater than that for fathers. If mother was rejecting, fewer who had loving fathers than those with rejecting fathers became criminals; but the difference was not significant. However, if father was rejecting, the affectional status of mother significantly affected crime rates. In view of their failure to test the significance of the difference between differences (70 per cent to 36 per cent versus 70 per cent to 46 per cent, which is obviously insignificant), their conclusion that "maternal rejection appeared to be more criminogenic than paternal rejection" (McCord, McCord and Zola, 1959, p. 108) is not fully justified. But even if it were, no denial of the importance of paternal affection was intended. From other analyses by the McCords, and from those in the investigations cited above, it is perfectly obvious that fathers' attitudes, as neglected as they have been in past research and theory, are very important in determining proneness to crime.

The Child's Response to Affection (or Lack of it)

A dyadic relationship is a two-directional affair, and researchers have lately begun to examine not only the attitudes parents express toward their children, but also the reciprocal feelings children hold toward their parents. Most inquiries to date have centered rather narrowly on the child's-attitudes-about-the-parents'-attitudes-toward-the-child, but that, at least, is a step in the direction of recognizing the interactional nature of parent-child relationships.

Not unrealistically, delinquent boys tend to think their parents do not love them very much. Andry's inquiry about the adequacy of parental love showed 78 per cent of the nondelinquents to say that both parents were "very satisfactory" in this regard. Only 11 per cent of the delinquents described their parents as "very satisfactory," and three-fourths of them said one or both of their parents were "very

bad" in regard to the love they showed their children (Andry, 1960).
The delinquents in the Glueck study did not think their parents were
honestly concerned about their welfare (Glueck and Glueck, 1950).
Displays of affection seem to be either so rare or so insincere in the
homes of delinquents that both parties are embarrassed by them
(Andry, 1960).

In an atmosphere like this, the emotional reaction of the child
tends toward indifference (Bach and Bremer, 1947), counterrejec-
tion of the parents (Nye, 1956, 1958), or at least some attitude other
than normal, close attachment. The Gluecks' examination of emotional ties between parents and children yielded the results in Table
3-9. If a "noncommittal" response is taken to imply, at best, ambivalence in the parent-child relationship, it is obvious that the feelings
delinquents have toward their parents, and especially toward their
fathers, tend to be something other than warm affection.

The lack of a strong affectional relationship has many consequences. Bandura and Walters (1959) found aggressive boys to be
more reluctant to ask for help from their fathers, to be less inclined
to seek the company of their parents, to show less warmth of feeling
for either parent, and to display weaker identification with parents
than the nonaggressive boys. The Gluecks' delinquents likewise
found their fathers rather unsuitable objects for emulation, a finding
which takes on considerable meaning in the context of identification
theory. Using a story completion technique, Zucker (1943) inferred
that delinquent boys in need of help seek the assistance of peers
rather than parents. Similar results are reported by Kagan (1958)
for a comparison of aggressive and nonaggressive boys. Using stories
told to nine pictures, Kagan found that aggressive boys were less
likely to seek help from an adult when faced with a problem, were
less likely to see a parent as providing nurture than other adults, and
were more likely to tell stories depicting parental anger toward a

TABLE 3-9. EMOTIONAL ATTITUDES OF BOYS TOWARD PARENTS
(From Glueck and Glueck, 1950)

	Percentage of Boys Displaying Attitude			
	Fathers [*]		Mothers [*]	
Attitude	Delinquent	Nondelinquent	Delinquent	Nondelinquent
Attached	32.5	65.1	64.9	89.8
Indifferent	16.5	5.6	4.6	0.2
Hostile	11.8	2.8	2.2	0.6
Noncommittal	39.2	26.5	28.3	9.4

[*] x^2 values are significant beyond the .01 level for both mothers and fathers.

child. Of the many repercussions parental rejection can have on a child, driving him into emotional dependence on his peers is probably not the least important.

The reactions discussed in this section are not unique responses to isolated affectional stimuli. The love of a parent has many correlates, and the affectional aspect of the parent-child relationship is only one of those which require examination.

Discipline

If one endorses the common assumption that capacities for internal control are complexly but closely related to previously imposed external restraints, then parental discipline assumes focal significance as a factor in delinquency. One of the earliest studies to stress the importance of discipline was that by Healy and Bronner (1926), who found 40 per cent of a sample of 4000 delinquents in Chicago and Boston to have come from homes where parents failed to exert even a minimum of "good discipline." In the lack of control data, this figure is difficult to interpret, but such labels as "below a minimum of good discipline" carry implicit standards with them. In Burt's (1929) more carefully controlled investigation, "defective discipline" emerged as *the* most important background determinant of delinquent behavior. The "defects" were defined with such breadth as to include laxity, indifference, disagreement, or excessive strictness, but some combination of these faults was found seven times as often among the parents of delinquents as among the parents of nondelinquents. Merrill (1947) found three-fourths of her group of delinquents to come from homes where parents were too lax, too severe, or erratic. The findings in the Gluecks' research are shown in Table 3-10. Most parents of nondelinquents evidently treat their children in a "firm but kindly" way. The parents of delinquents

TABLE 3-10. DISCIPLINARY ATTITUDES OF PARENTS
(From Glueck and Glueck, 1950)

	Percentage of Parents Showing Attitude			
	Fathers [*]		Mothers [*]	
Attitude	Delinquent	Nondelinquent	Delinquent	Nondelinquent
Lax	26.6	17.9	56.8	11.7
Overstrict	26.1	8.7	4.4	1.6
Erratic	41.6	17.9	34.6	21.1
Firm but kindly	5.7	55.5	4.2	65.6

[*] x^2 values are highly significant.

tend to be too harsh or too "soft," or are inclined to alternate unpredictably between severity and license. From these other studies, the notion that *something* is wrong with the discipline of delinquents is well established. The nature of the fault is not quite so clear, but the literature still permits certain generalizations. Some findings in regard to leniency and strictness are presented in Table 3-11. The investigations were carried out in different countries, and rating standards varied somewhat from one study to the other, but the results are still highly consistent. It is the mothers of delinquents, mainly, who are guilty of extreme laxity, though the fathers of delinquents also appeared lax significantly more often than the fathers of nondelinquents. Excessively strict discipline, on the other hand, was primarily directed by fathers toward sons. Strict mothers were rare in all groups. Similar findings are reported by Bandura and Walters (1959), who found the mothers of aggressive boys to be less demanding of obedience than the mothers of controls, to place fewer restrictions on the boys in the home, and to make fewer demands for school achievements. Both parents were inclined to use physical punishment and deprivation of privileges, but it was the fathers who were seen as the very strict ones.

TABLE 3-11. STRICTNESS AND LAXITY IN DISCIPLINE

| | | Percentage of Parents Showing Attitude | | | |
| | | Fathers | | Mothers | |
Attitude	Sex of Child	Delinquent	Non-delinquent	Delinquent	Non-delinquent
Lax Discipline:					
Gluecks, 1950	Boys	26.6	17.9	56.8	11.7
Burt, 1929	Boys	17.1	1.0	68.0	8.0
	Girls	11.0	0.5	32.2	5.5
Overstrict Discipline:					
Gluecks, 1950	Boys	26.1	8.7	4.4	1.6
Burt, 1929	Boys	14.6	2.5	1.6	0.5
	Girls	1.4	3.0	5.4	2.0

Laxity and severity of discipline, however extreme they may be, and whichever parent offers the treatment, seem less damaging than an erratic approach to training. McCord, McCord, and Zola (1959) classified disciplinary attitudes under the following heads:

1. Love-oriented. Both parents consistently used methods based on withholding love, rewards, or privileges in combination with "reasoning."

2. Punitive discipline. Both parents consistently used beatings, physical isolation, violent anger, or aggressive threats.
3. Lax discipline. Neither parent exerted control.
4. Erratic discipline A (love-oriented and lax). One parent used love-oriented methods, and the other was lax, or they varied inconsistently between the two types.
5. Erratic discipline B (love-oriented, lax, and punitive). One or both parents wavered inconsistently in using these methods, so that all three were combined.
6. Erratic discipline C (punitive and lax). One parent used punitive methods and the other was lax, or they varied inconsistently between the two methods.

The results of their analyses are given in Table 3-12, where the destructive effects of inconsistent discipline are plainly shown.

TABLE 3-12. RELATION OF PARENTAL DISCIPLINE TO CRIME
AND INCARCERATION
(From McCord, McCord and Zola, 1959)

Type of Discipline	Percentage of Boys Convicted of Later Crimes	Percentage of Boys Sentenced to Penal Institutions
Punitive	21	7
Love-oriented	27	5
Erratic A (love-lax)	35	5
Erratic B (love-lax-punitive)	49	19
Lax	50	19
Erratic C (punitive-lax)	56	30

Bennett's (1960) comparison of disciplinary attitudes among parents of delinquent and neurotic children (see Table 3-13) offers additional support for contention that erratic discipline is a very important factor in determining delinquent predispositions.

TABLE 3-13. PARENTAL DISCIPLINE IN FAMILIES OF DELINQUENT
AND NEUROTIC CHILDREN
(From Bennett, 1960)

Type of Discipline	Number of Families Delinquent	Neurotic
Normal	4	14
Overstrict	7	19
Overlenient	3	3
Inconsistent	36	14
Total N	50	50

In apparent contradiction to many previous findings, punitive discipline was associated with the lowest crime rate of all in the McCords' analysis, but one must note that their definition of "punitiveness" specifies a consistent use of beatings and other methods by both parents. It seems reasonable to suppose that children in homes like that would simply be afraid to do anything which would surely incur the wrath of their parents. Bennett's findings that consistently overstrict discipline is more associated with neurotic problems than delinquency supports this interpretation. Most of the "punitive" parents in the studies which have shown a positive relationship between punitiveness and delinquency (Burt, 1929; Glueck and Glueck, 1950; Bandura and Walters, 1959) would probably be classed as "erratic" (punitive-lax; or love-oriented, lax, punitive) in the classification system used by the McCords. In any case, punitive discipline, by itself, consistently administered by both parents, does not seem to promote delinquency. It probably helps control delinquency, though one may wonder about the cost in regard to other aspects of behavior and development.

Studies of disciplinary techniques have tended to yield the conclusion that the parents of delinquent children are quicker to inflict corporal punishment than the parents of nondelinquents, and less inclined to use such moderate means as praise and reasoning (Glueck and Glueck, 1950; Bandura and Walters, 1959). But it is difficult to say whether cause or effect is represented in this fact. In clinical interviews, the parents of delinquents often complain that reasoning "just doesn't work" with their obstreperous children, and indeed it is possible that the parents have resorted to physical discipline in an effort to control otherwise uncontrollable children whose tendencies have developed from other determinants. An argument of this sort, however, could not account for the findings of McCord et al., where the discipline of the parents was assessed many years prior to the delinquent acts. The truth of the matter probably lies somewhere in between. Parents are more likely to shift to stronger disciplinary procedures when they see less intense procedures fail, and at the same time there are reasons to believe that physical punishment can actually increase aggressive behavior through frustration effects (Dollard et al., 1939) and modeling effects (Bandura, 1962).

A particularly difficult problem arises in attempting to separate the effect of type of discipline from affectional relations, since praise and reasons tend to be used by warm parents and physical punishment by hostile parents (Bandura and Walters, 1959; Becker et al., 1962; Sears et al., 1957; Unger, 1960, 1962). A further complication arises from the fact that hostile-punitive parents may also directly encourage and reward aggression. For example, Bandura (1960) found that mothers of aggressive boys, while quite punitive when aggression was expressed toward them, were more permissive than mothers of inhibited boys when the aggression was expressed toward peers or siblings. Becker *et al.* (1962) found that when the mother was high in the use of physical punishment, she was also likely to insist that her children fight for their rights with other children. In view of the complex coexistence of several parental variables, it is not possible at this time to determine with precision the meaning of the obtained associations of physical punishment and delinquency. On the basis of the present evidence, the most appropriate generalization would be that, in a *hostile context,* high use of physical punishment tends to promote aggression in children (Becker, 1964).

Some time ago, Whiting and Child (1953) proposed that certain aspects of superego development (e.g., responsibility, guilt proneness) are fostered by love-oriented discipline and hindered by the use of physical-material incentives. The evidence for this proposition is conflicting and, when it is supportive of the proposition, is open to alternative interpretations. As noted in Table 3-12, McCord *et al.* found *both* consistently love-oriented and punitive discipline associated with low crime rates. Bandura and Walters (1959) did not find any compelling support for the postulated relationship in their study of aggressive children. The parents of the aggressive boys were prone to use physical punishment, to deprive their sons of privileges, and to nag and scold, but they were also more strongly inclined than parents of less aggressive controls to withdraw love and to ridicule. There were no significant differences with respect to the use of material rewards and praise as positive incentives. Nye's study (1958), based on the perceptions of the "most delinquent" and "least delinquent" children in a high school sample, did not support the Whiting-Child hypothesis.

Most of the positive evidence for the hypothesis has come from the study of "normal" children and from cross-cultural studies. In a recent review of this evidence, Becker (1964) first points out a need to distinguish between positive love-oriented methods (praise, reasoning) and negative love-oriented methods (withdrawal of love, expressions of disappointment, and so on). The evidence indicates that negative love-oriented techniques are associated with internalized reactions to transgression in the form of guilt or acceptance of self-responsibility only when the parent is high in warmth. Positive love-oriented techniques are used primarily by warm parents and, *in this context,* are associated with greater internalized reactions to transgression. These qualifications, and those discussed earlier with respect to physical punishment, suggest the reasons for the presumably inconsistent findings by McCord *et al.,* Bandura and Walters, and Nye in their studies of delinquents. In the McCord's study consistently punitive discipline (or consistent discipline of any kind) was not likely to occur in a hostile context. Bandura and Walter's findings of more use of withdrawal of love and ridicule in parents of aggressive boys was associated with a hostile context. The research on normal children suggests that Whiting and Child's hypothesis should hold only under special conditions which were not present in the studies of delinquents.

The possible bases for the relations between love-oriented techniques and greater self-responsibility and internalized reactions to transgression are summarized by Becker (1964) as: (1) warmth, which makes the parent important to the child and obviates the need for more severe forms of discipline to gain compliance, (2) the presence of a model of controlled behavior, (3) the provision of verbal cues (reasons) which facilitate understanding of what is expected and aid the child's anticipation of consequences, and (4) the fact that punishment is likely to continue until the child shows a restitutive reaction, thus directly reinforcing such reactions by the termination of punishment.

A number of generalizations are justified by available research on discipline and delinquency. The unhappy consequences of erratic discipline are clear to see. Failure to strike a moderate balance between harshness and leniency is harmful. Over all, a situation in which hostility is aroused but not controlled would seem most certain to create delinquent dispositions. Bandura and Walters (1957) especially stress the viciousness of a pattern in which the father is hostile (thus evoking counterhostility) and the mother is lax. Following examination of some "conduct problems" referred to a guidance clinic, Becker *et al.* (1959) put it the other way around—the mother appeared thwarting and the father lax. It probably doesn't matter which parent does which. More generally it appears that the primary situation in which delinquency is generated, as a function of parent behavior, is that home where hostility is generated and no controls are demanded from the child when he rebels.

The Child's Response to Discipline (or Lack of it)

When delinquent or delinquency-prone youngsters are asked about the disciplinary attitudes of their parents, they are apt to emphasize the unfairness and unfavorable partiality of the treatment they have received (Nye, 1958; Andry, 1960). Like other observers, delinquents themselves say their parents fail to attain a proper balance between strictness and leniency (Andry, 1960). They are resentful of restrictions and resist controls imposed upon them (Bandura and Walters, 1959; Nye, 1958).

One should not place too much confidence in the literal accuracy of a delinquent's appraisal of his parents. We deal in reports of perceptions. But whether the statements are interpreted as undistorted descriptions, rationalizations for misbehavior, or whatever else, delinquents *say* their parents' disciplinary attitudes leave much to be desired. And that itself is an attitudinal fact which can contribute to delinquency.

Rewards for Delinquency

A number of psychoanalytically oriented writers have suggested that delinquent behavior is permitted, indeed encouraged, by many parents, who thereby gain some vicarious gratification of their own shoddy impulses. Lippman (1954) cites some individual histories purporting to show this, and suggests that collaborative therapy is indicated in cases of this kind. Johnson and Burke (1955) propose that delinquency, especially in "respectable" families, may often result from specific stimulation of a child's antisocial behavior by the unconscious (sometimes conscious) sanction of the parents.

There are unfortunately few acceptable data which bear on this provocative thought. Bandura and Walters (1959) found both fathers and mothers of aggressive boys to be fairly active in encouraging aggression. The children were taught aggression, one might say, as a way of solving adjustive problems. Certainly the role of parents, not only in the direct arousal of aggression and the failure to control it, but also in the subtle encouragement of aggressive behavior, could bear more careful study.

THE DYNAMIC EFFECTS OF PARENTAL TREATMENT

Any serious effort to examine the origins of delinquency must go beyond study of social influences in direct relation to delinquency.

The delinquent response pattern is mediated by the delinquent person, and study of the interactions between the person and his environment must be examined before his behavior tendencies can be understood. As one approach, the personality characteristics which participate in delinquency proneness can be isolated, and those characteristics related systematically to the influences which have molded them.

The Gluecks have pursued this goal more ambitiously than any other investigators. In the latest report of their massive research (Glueck and Glueck, 1962), the analyses which led to *Unraveling Juvenile Delinquency* (1950) and then *Physique and Delinquency* (1956) are extended to the *Family Environment and Delinquency* (1962). In the last, an effort is made to place the traits previously shown to distinguish between delinquents and nondelinquents on a biosocial continuum. Characteristics related to body type and unrelated to social influences are placed at the "constitutional" end of the scale. Characteristics related to social influences but not to body type are said to have a "psychosocial" orientation. Results of the analysis are given in Table 3-14, which speaks for itself and is worth some careful study. Among the more interesting findings is the designation of emotional instability and emotional conflicts, traditionally related to social experience, as constitutional traits, and the placement of intellectual functions at the socially conditioned end of the scale (cf. Hunt, 1961).

Unfortunately, some basic design limitations restrict the confidence which can be attached to the findings the Gluecks' report. Associational data are used as the basis for cause-effect propositions, though this is so common a practice it scarcely seems worth criticizing. More serious is the fact that constitutionality of traits is defined solely by a body-typing operation. This admits the possibility that genuinely constitutional traits which happen to be unrelated to body type will be placed at the psychosocial end of the scale. The authors are aware of this possibility, but, considering the nature of the traits analyzed in their work, regard the possibility as remote. The dependability of results is open to strong question. In the course of relating sixty-six traits to forty-four determinants, the Gluecks gave themselves a chance for 2904 significant effects to emerge. In the pertinent appendix, a total of 255 relationships are listed as "significant" at the .10 level. Two hundred and ninety should occur by chance.

Difficulties in interpretation are even more formidable in the second part of the report, where the authors attempt to establish interactive relationships between factors in the family environment and

TABLE 3-14. BIOSOCIAL ORIENTATION OF TRAITS
RELATED TO DELINQUENCY
(From Gleuck and Glueck, 1962)

Constitutional Traits	Probably Constitutional Traits
Cyanosis	Poor health in infancy
Tremors	Enuresis in early childhood
Genital underdevelopment	Irregular reflexes
Strength of hand grip	Dermographia
Social assertiveness	Intuition
Submissiveness to authority	Unmethodical approach to problems
Fear of failure and defeat	Capacity for objective interests
Vivacity	Defiance
Sensitivity	Ambivalence to authority
Emotional instability	Poor surface contact with others
Aestheticism	Emotional liability
Sensuousness	Lack of self-control
Emotional conflicts	Stubbornness
	Adventurousness
	Psychopathy

Constitutional and Socially Conditioned Traits	Socially Conditioned Traits
Tendency to phantasy	Low verbal intelligence
Destructiveness	High performance intelligence
Dependence on others	Originality
Masochistic trends	Poor power of observation
Destructive-sadistic trends	Common sense
Feeling of inadequacy	Enhanced feeling of insecurity
Uninhibited motor responses to stimuli	Feeling of not being wanted or loved
Acquisitiveness	Feeling of not being taken care of
Unconventionality	Feeling of not being taken seriously
Impracticality	Feeling of helplessness
	Feeling of resentment
	Hostility
	Suspiciousness
	Feeling of isolation
	Feeling of being able to manage own life
	Receptive trends
	Compulsory trends
	Preponderance of extroversive trends
	Preponderance of introversive trends
	Lack of self-criticism
	Conscientiousness
	Neuroticism

the mediating traits which predispose youngsters to delinquency. Using a method of multiple comparisons developed by Tukey, they compare the proportional incidence of delinquents and nondelinquents displaying each of the sixty-six traits under consideration, in reference to each of the forty-four environmental factors they examined. This type of analysis, like the other, involves 2904 possible significance tests, but a count of relevant tables in the appendix shows that only ninety-eight of the interactions were "significant" at the .10 level. Some selectivity in reporting may possibly have been imposed. In the light of these methodological shortcomings, the final section of the book, containing "implications for the management of delinquency" must be read with caution.

The Gluecks' latest findings badly need replication. In constructing tests, indices developed by picking "significant" elements from a very large pool are routinely crossvalidated *before* they are reported as reliable. A similar practice should be instituted in research of the kind the Gluecks have done. Until then, propositions based on their findings are hypotheses and no more.

A clear distinction, however, should be made between the somewhat dubious "facts" in the Gluecks' latest book, and the methods and guiding principles they have employed. The model they use in examining person-environment relationships, unlike most models, provides for the differential impact of various external influences as a function of the receptive characteristics of the person exposed to the influences. Some factors which are not generally related to delinquency may assume criminogenic importance when they act on people who are particularly vulnerable to the influence. The factors serve a "catalytic" function. Conversely, certain factors which are related to crime in a general way may have no deleterious effect on people who are relatively impervious to the stress. "In other words, it is differential *contamination*, rather than differential *association*, that is at the core of the etiologic process; and contamination depends not merely on exposure but also on susceptibility as opposed to immunity" (Glueck and Glueck, 1962, p. 155). This is a useful idea, and the concept of a biosocial continuum seems equally powerful, if not indispensable, to development of a rational eclecticism in regard to the origins of crime. The concepts are worth developing whether or not the Gluecks' empirical findings support the particular substantive propositions they have offered in their writings to date.

SUMMARY

Let us now summarize some of the major findings on family interactions and delinquency and attempt, in a necessarily limited way, to
interpret them within the framework of general behavior theory.

The family functions, in part, to transmit cultural values from one
generation to another and from the larger social systems outside the
family to the members of the family itself. Delinquency is concentrated in certain strata of the social structure, notably among members of the lower socioeconomic classes. The values which are
attached to human acts by members of these classes are sometimes
different from those attached by people in the middle class, where
laws are defined, and designations of delinquency are imposed. Em-
phases on toughness, worldly smartness, and independence from
authority are sometimes coupled with a de-emphasis of achievement,
consideration for others, and self-control among members of the
lower class. In the terms of behavior theory, this means that models
for behavior of the kind that are "tough," "smart," and so on are
plentifully available, and social reinforcement for such behavior is
frequent, immediate, and strong. When peer gangs as well as parents encourage behavior of this kind, occasional conflict with middle
class law is not surprising.

Most lower class children, however, do not become chronically
delinquent, and there is evidence that individual families are powerful determiners of proneness to delinquency.

The home offers a physical-social background for many of the
critical interactions which influence the course of social-motivational
development. To promote such development, a home must be sufficiently attractive to keep the children inside it for fairly long periods
of time, and it must be managed with some degree of order. Events
must occur in predictable sequences, and day-to-day routines must
not be so chaotic that the energies of everyone in the household are
exhausted meeting one crisis after another.

The homes of many delinquents tend to be cluttered, overcrowded,
hectic, noisy, and strife-torn. As soon as a predelinquent child is
mobile enough to exercise some choice in the matter, he may well
choose to stay out of the home whenever he can. This deprives the
parents of many opportunities to exercise socializing influence, and
places the child more strongly in the influence of any other social
groups which happen to be available. In some sections of many
cities, the most easily available groups are unsupervised peer gangs.

In the home, parents do most of the socializing. To fulfill this task, they must first of all be present. Broken homes are very common in the histories of delinquents, but the circumstances impelling the breach must be considered along with the fact itself. Given adequate relationships with others, children can survive the death of a parent. They can even tolerate separation or divorce between the parents. But all too often relationships with others are not adequate in a broken home, and even if the relationship with one parent is satisfactory, the influence of the other is denied. Temporary absences, as occur when mothers work, seldom have much ill effect, provided arrangements for adequate supervision are made. In the latter case, the fact of employment reflects a more basic fault in the emotional climate of the family.

To serve well in the socialization of his children, a parent must possess characteristics which merit at least some measure of admiration and respect. If he is neither admirable nor respectable, he offers an inadequate model for the behavior of his children, and his effect as a disciplinarian is limited. The parents of delinquents tend to be short-tempered, often discontented people themselves. They are not uncommonly in difficulty with the law, and are seldom said to have clear and vigorous moral values. It is entirely possible for a once-criminal parent to produce noncriminal children. But he must take a strong enough interest in his children to be a consistent and concerned disciplinarian if he is to manage that. If he is cruel, neglecting, *and* criminal himself, the chances are overwhelming that his children will be delinquent.

The decision of whether or not to commit a delinquent act depends in large part on anticipated emotional consequences of the behavior of other people who might respond to the act. The expectancies are formed through a history of emotionally toned experiences with others, so that their approval and disapproval take on some regulatory meaning. That is to say, dependence and anxiety in reference to the responsive actions of others depend on the prior occurrence of pleasure and pain in reference to those others. The affective character of the parent-child relationship is therefore of prime significance in determining the social motives which participate in the determination of delinquency. Delinquents say their parents care little for them, and they are probably correct. To single out this consideration for the exclusive emphasis assigned to it by Bowlby and some others is probably overstating the point, but the importance of parental affection, and the serious consequences of its lack, cannot be denied. It is becoming ever more clear that the affectional and other attitudes of both parents are important, not just those of the mother, no matter what prevailing theory might suggest or how convenient it may be to study housewives.

The development of stable behavior tendencies depends on the intensity and consistency with which emotionally effective rewards and punishments are administered. Excessively harsh treatment, especially if unaccompanied by generally affectionate acceptance, ordinarily arouses resentment, and this reduces the effectiveness of discipline. Excessive leniency is tantamount to neglect. The regulatory emotional expectancies are never established. There is ample empirical support for the predictable specific in the families of delinquents: the parents are indeed prone to extremes of severity and laxity, or to erratic alternation between the two. Vigorously punitive discipline, if consistently applied by both parents, is associated with a low crime rate, though it may be associated with some other less desirable characteristics as well.

The role of particular techniques of discipline in contributing to delinquency-proneness is not entirely clear. The parents of delinquents are somewhat more disposed to use more physical punishment and less praise and reasoning, but this could be an effect as much as a cause, or an incidental concomitant of associated variables, such as hostility and encouragement of aggression. There is some reason to believe, however, that the use of physically aggressive forms of discipline contributes to the development of aggression in the child through frustration effects and/or modeling. Whiting and Child's hypothesis concerning love-oriented and physical-material-oriented discipline has not been supported in studies of delinquents. However, studies of normal children suggest that positive love-oriented methods (praise and reasoning), which are typically accompanied by a warm relation to the child, are rather consistently associated with signs of conscience development, whereas the negative love-oriented methods (withdrawal of love, disapproval) are effective only when used by warm parents. Thus, there is reason to believe that with a better differentiation of classes of discipline, and with greater attention to their interaction with other parent variables, techniques of discipline may yet be demonstrated to play a role in the development of delinquent-prone children.

Directions for Research

Some of the most pressing needs for further study are perfectly clear. There is a great need, first, for prospective research. It is much more convenient and a good deal cheaper to examine delinquent backgrounds retrospectively, but retrospective accounts are inevitably subject to distortion, and their interpretation must be made with more than the usual amount of caution. When the years have passed and delinquents have been formally identified, the chances for distortion become enormous. Whether or not serious distortions actually occur is of less methodological importance than the fact that they can occur, and neither the investigator nor the reader of his report has any way of telling.

Surely the best prospective study in the literature is that done by McCord, McCord, and Zola (1959). But this was pure gratuity from a project addressed originally to other issues. If the yield of causal information from a study designed as an experiment in treatment can be as rich as all that, it seems reasonable to suppose that a prospective study specifically and planfully directed to the investigation of family interaction and delinquency would be still more fruitful.

A second need is for research of expanded scope. Delinquency is a complex phenomenon, complexly determined, and some of the questions about it cannot be answered in narrow investigations. Only through very comprehensive multivariate research can the critical interactions be explored and the organization of determinative influences examined. The Guecks' latest report (1962) represents a step in this direction, but not even the Gluecks took a very large number of possibly relevant variables into account, and there is a need for continual expansion of scope as research proceeds.

A third clear need is for refinement of the concept of delinquency. Election to study so heterogeneous a variable as "delinquency" does not constitute a methodological error. In principle, behavior can be abstracted and examined at any level. It is a question of fruitfulness. And it becomes continually more obvious that the study of so diffuse a variable as delinquency is offering rather limited return. We must know more than we do of the functional and situational characteristics involved in delinquency before we can understand delinquency itself. Bandura and Walters (1959) chose to study aggression rather than delinquency. This was wise. Aggression can be defined behaviorally with fair precision; delinquency cannot. But delinquency, of course, involves more than aggression. There is need for parallel study of family influences on such intrapersonal tendencies as guilt-proneness, such interpersonal variables as parent and peer affiliations, and such other parameters as theory and empirical data may implicate. And we do have an increasing amount of evidence that both delinquency and delinquents can be subdivided along dimensional lines. It is beginning to appear, in fact, that the most rapid improvement in our understanding of delinquency will come to pass if we de-emphasize the frontal assault on delinquency itself, and deploy more energy skill and money to the study of various processes related to delinquency—characteristics like aggression, for instance, and such processes as socialization. Once we have refined the concept of delinquency, and further examined some of its elements, it may be possible to return in greater depth and breadth to an improved comprehension of delinquency itself, and the influence of the family in producing or preventing it.

These are our prejudices for further study. But delinquency is a problem of great social and political importance, support for its investigation is bountiful now, and investigators will no doubt continue to study it in many ways, at many levels, from many points of view. That is as it should be.

References

Andry, R. G. (1960) *Delinquency and parental pathology.* London: Metheun.

Bach, G. R., & Bremer, G. (1947) Projective father fantasies of pre-adolescent, delinquent children. *J. Psychol.,* **24**, 3-17.

Bandura, A. (1960) Relationship of family patterns to child behavior disorders. NIMH Progress Report (M-1734), Stanford Univer.

Bandura, A. (1962) Social learning through imitation. In M. R. Jones (ed.), Nebraska Symposium on motivation. Lincoln, Neb.: Univer. of Neb. Press.

Bandura, A., & Walters, R. H. (1959) *Adolescent aggression.* New York: Ronald.

Becker, W. C. (1964) Consequences of different kinds of parent discipline. In M. L. Hoffman & Lois Hoffman (eds.), *Review of child development research.* Lafayette, Ind.: Society for Research in Child Development.

Becker, W. C., Peterson, D. R., Hellmer, L. A., Shoemaker, D. J., & Quay, H. C. (1959) Factors in parental behavior and personality as related to problem behavior in children. *J. consult. Psychol.,* **23**, 107-118.

Becker, W. C., Peterson, D. R., Luria, Zella, Shoemaker, D. J., & Hellmer, L. A. (1962) Relations of factors derived from parent-interview ratings to behavior problems of five-year olds. *Child Develpm.*, 33, 509-535.

Bennett, Ivy (1960) *Delinquent and neurotic children.* New York: Basic Books.

Bowlby, J. (1944) Forty-four juvenile thieves: their characters and home life. (I). *Int. J. Psychoanal.*, 25, 19-53.

Bronfenbrenner, U. (1958) Socialization and social class through time and space. In Eleanor Maccoby, T. M. Newcomb, & E. L. Hartley (eds.), *Readings in social psychology.* 3rd ed. New York: Holt.

Burt, C. (1929) *The young delinquent.* New York: Appleton.

Carr-Saunders, A. M., Mannheim, H., & Rhodes, E. (1944) *Young offenders.* New York: Macmillan.

Clinard, M. B. (1942) The process of urbanization and criminal behavior. *Amer. J. Sociol.*, 48, 202-213.

Cloward, R. A., & Ohlin, L. E. (1960) *Delinquency and opportunity.* Glencoe, Ill.: Free Press.

Cohen, A. K. (1955) *Delinquent boys: the culture of the gang.* Glencoe, Ill.: Free Press.

Davis, Allison, & Havighurst, R. J. (1948) Social class and color differences in child rearing. *Amer. sociol. Rev.*, 11, 698-710.

Dollard, J., Miller, N. E., Doob, L. W., Mowrer, O. H., & Sears, R. (1939) *Frustration and aggression.* New Haven: Yale Univer. Press.

Gardner, G. E., & Goldman, N. (1945) Childhood and adolescent adjustment of Naval successes and failures. *Amer. J. Orthopsychiat.*, 15, 584-596.

Glueck, S., & Glueck, Eleanor T. (1950) *Unraveling juvenile delinquency.* New York: Commonwealth Fund.

Glueck, S., & Glueck, Eleanor T. (1956) *Physique and delinquency.* New York: Harper.

Glueck, S., & Glueck, Eleanor T. (1957) Working mothers and delinquency. *Ment. Hyg.*, 41, 327-352.

Glueck, S., & Glueck, Eleanor T. (1962) *Family environment and delinquency.* London: Routledge and Kegan Paul.

Healy, W., & Bronner, A. L. (1926) *Delinquents and criminals: their making and unmaking.* New York: Macmillan.

Hewitt, L. F., & Jenkins, R. L. (1946) *Fundamental patterns of maladjustment, the dynamics of their origin.* Springfield, Ill.: State of Illinois.

Hodgkiss, Margaret. (1932-1933) The influence of broken homes and working mothers. *Smith Coll. stud. soc. Wk.*, 3, 259-274.

Horwitz, Ellen (1944) A study of overinhibited and unsocialized aggressive children. Part I: A quantitative analysis of background factors. *Smith Coll. stud. soc. Wk.*, 15, 121-122.

Hunt, J. McV. (1961) *Intelligence and experience.* New York: Ronald.

Jephcott, A. P., & Carter, M. P. The social background of delinquency. Privately printed. Cited by Sophia M. Robison (1960) in *Juvenile delinquency.* New York: Holt.

Johnson, Adelaide M., & Burke, E. C. (1955) Parental permissiveness and fostering in child rearing and their relationship to juvenile delinquency. *Proc. Staff Meetings, Mayo Clinic,* **30,** 557-565.

Kagan, J. (1958) Socialization of aggression and the perception of parents in fantasy. *Child Develpm.,* **29,** 311-320.

Kobrin, S. (1951) The conflict of values in delinquency areas. *Amer. sociol. Rev.,* **16,** 653-661.

Kohn, M. L. (1959) Social class and parental values. *Amer. J. Sociol.,* **64,** 337-351.

Lander, B. (1954) *Towards an understanding of juvenile delinquency.* New York: Columbia Univer. Press.

Lewis, Hilda (1954) *Deprived children.* London: Oxford Univer. Press.

Liebowitz, S. S. (Dec. 15, 1957) Nine words that can stop juvenile delinquency. *This week.*

Lippman, H. S. (1954) Antisocial acting out. Symposium, 1954. *Amer. J. Orthopsychiat.,* **24,** 667-696.

Lottier, S. (1938) Distribution of criminal offenses in metropolitan regions. *J. crim. Law Criminol.,* **29,** 37-50.

McCord, W., McCord, Joan, & Zola, I. K. (1959) *Origins of crime.* New York: Columbia Univer. Press.

McCord, W., McCord, Joan, & Gudeman, J. (1960) *Origins of alcoholism.* Palo Alto: Stanford Univer. Press.

McKinnon, D. W. (1938) Violation of prohibitions. In H. A. Murray *et al., Explorations in personality.* New York: Oxford Univer. Press.

Merrill, Maud A. (1947) *Problems of child delinquency.* Boston: Houghton Mifflin.

Miller, W. B. (1958) Lower class culture as a generating milieu of gang delinquency. *J. soc. Issues,* **14,** 5-19.

Miller, W. B. (1959) Implications of urban lower class culture for social work. *Soc. serv. Rev.,* **33,** 219-236.

Monahan, T. P. (1957) Family status and the delinquent child: a reappraisal and some new findings. *Soc. Forces,* **35,** 250-258.

Monahan, T. P. (1960) Broken homes by age of delinquent children. *J. soc. Psychol.,* **51,** 387-397.

Morris, T. (1958) *The criminal area.* London: Routledge and Kegan Paul.

Nye, F. I. (1956) The rejected parent and delinquency. *Marriage Fam. Living,* **18,** 291-296.

Nye, F. I. (1958) *Family relationships and delinquent behavior.* New York: Wiley.

Oltman, Jane, McGarry, J. J., & Friedman, S. (1951-1952) Parental deprivation and the "broken home" in dementia praecox and other mental disorders. *Amer. J. Orthopsychiat.,* **108,** 685-694.

Reckless, W. C., Dinitz, S., & Murray, Ellen (1957) The "good" boy in a high delinquency area. *J. crim. Law Criminol.*, **48**, 18-26.

Scarpitti, F. R., Murray, Ellen, Dinitz, S., & Reckless, W. C. (1960) The "good" boy in a high delinquency area: four years later. *Amer. sociol. Rev.*, **25**, 555-558.

Sears, R. R., Maccoby, Eleanor E., & Levin, H. (1957) *Patterns of child rearing.* Evanston, Ill.: Row, Peterson.

Shaw, C. R., & McKay, H. D. (1932) Are broken homes a causative factor in juvenile delinquency? *Soc. Forces*, **10**, 514-524.

Shaw, C. R., & McKay, H. D. (1942) *Juvenile delinquency and urban areas.* Chicago: Univer. of Chicago Press.

Sykes, G. M., & Matza, D. (1957) Techniques of neutralization: a theory of delinquency. *Amer. sociol. Rev.*, **22**, 664-670.

Toby, J. (1957) The differential impact of family disorganization. *Amer. sociol. Rev.*, **22**, 505-512.

Unger, S. M. (1960) On the development of guilt-response systems. Unpublished doctoral dissertation, Cornell Univer.

Unger, S. M. (1962) Antecedents of personality differences in guilt responsivity. *Psychol. Rep.*, **10**, 357-358.

Watts, R. E. (1931) The influence of population density on crime. *J. Amer. Statist. Ass.*, **26**, 11-20.

Weeks, H. A., & Smith, Margaret G. (1939-1940) Juvenile delinquency and broken homes in Spokane, Washington. *Soc. Forces*, **18**, 48-59.

Whiting, J. W. M., & Child, I. L. (1953) *Child training and personality.* New Haven: Yale Univer. Press.

Wittman, M. Phyllis, & Huffman, A. V. (1945) A comparative study of developmental, adjustment, and personality characteristics of psychotic, psychoneurotic, delinquent, and normally adjusted teen-aged youths. *J. genet. Psychol.*, **66**, 167-182.

Zucker, H. J. (1943) Affectional identification and delinquency. *Arch. Psychol., N. Y.*, No. 286.

4

Intellectual Functioning

Nathan S. Caplan

INTRODUCTION

The question of the relationship between juvenile crime and intellectual characteristics of the offender has a long and controversial history. The role attributed to various intellectual traits in the causation of crime has been the focus of serious concern among criminologists and students of social deviance since long before the advent of tests to measure intelligence. The introduction of intelligence tests in the early part of this century generated even more interest in this issue, and within a few short years as many as 200 studies reported findings on the intelligence of delinquents. Almost all of these studies indicated an abnormally high incidence of mental deficiency among juvenile offenders, and, in consequence, many investigators subscribed to the predominant belief that low intelligence played the prime criminogenic role in the etiology of juvenile delinquency. Some even went so far as to maintain that the very presence of mental deficiency could be considered a direct "incitement" to juvenile crime. In the course of subsequent studies, however, it became clear that the early investigations had seriously underestimated the intelligence of juvenile delinquents, and it became necessary to revise previous conceptions of the connection between these two phenomena. Intelligence, as an index to social adjustment, or, more specifically, the ability to behave in accord with prevailing legal standards, was, by no means, as simple and clear an issue as had been stated earlier.

The relationship of intelligence and delinquency is still the subject of some dispute, but the issues of controversy today differ from those prevailing prior to and shortly after the first scientific investigations into the subject. The developments which have led to the gradual acceptance of the present views are inextricably bound to an improved understanding of juvenile delinquency, better instruments to test intelligence, and advances in the methodology of social science research. It is the purpose of this chapter (1) to review the various lines of evidence in past and current research on intellectual functioning of juvenile delinquents, (2) to critically appraise this body of knowledge in terms of methodological and other considerations, and (3) to discuss the implications of this appraisal in terms of theoretical concerns and future research.

HISTORICAL BACKGROUND

Because of its importance in past theories of criminal behavior, a discussion of intelligence in juvenile crime requires at least some comment on the historical origin of the issues involved. During the eighteenth century, the classical school of criminology held that man was a free moral agent capable of behaving as he rationally chose to behave, regardless of his past experience and present circumstance. Failure to behave within legal expectations was viewed as the consequence of a defect in man's rational abilities which prevented him from distinguishing right from wrong. In this sense, the power of rationality was viewed as the primary source of moral discrimination and behavioral control required for social comformity.

The neoclassic school of criminology of the latter half of the nineteenth century broke with the tradition of the classic school by maintaining that man was not entirely a free moral agent but was largely a product of heredity. Those holding this view, nevertheless, showed a similar disregard for the consequences of adverse environmental circumstances upon those aspects of mental development that we now know to have serious social implications. This biological, noninteractional point of view, growing out of the discoveries of Darwin and Mendel, represented the view that the criminal offender was a throwback to man's beginnings—an atavistic moral idiot born into a society in which he was biologically unequipped to function responsibly. Lombroso (1890), the leading exponent of this position, devoted his attention to the identification of physical correlates of these inborn and unalterable criminal traits, and, while he did not go into great detail in describing genotypic characteristics, it appears rather certain that he considered low mentality of fundamental importance in the atavistic syndrome. Somewhat later, Goring (1913) largely disproved that recognizable physical "stigmata" were distributed differentially in the criminal and nonincarcerated populations. He did, however, concur with Lombroso that inborn mental defects were the prime determinants of criminal behavior and specifically recognized mental deficiency as its chief cause. The born criminal was thought to lack the necessary mental capacity to grasp the social values of his culture, and was unable to see either the consequences of his actions or to learn from corrective past experience. Goring based this belief on the finding of prison physicians who, using a medical diagnosis of mental deficiency, found that 10 per cent of the incarcerated offenders were mentally deficient in contrast to a 4.6 per cent estimate for the general population. The social irresponsibility expressed by juvenile and adult offenders was believed to be the consequence of a mental defect due entirely to heredity.

Those holding this rather fatalistic view of the constitutionally defective offender were unequipped to verify their assumptions empirically until scientific means were developed for assessing intelligence. Thus, when Goddard became aware of Binet's attempts in France to test intelligence, he welcomed the opportunity to undertake a study of delinquents' performance on intelligence tests in an attempt to resolve the issue. Using his own literal translation of Binet's limited and crude instruments, Goddard tested incarcerated delinquents around 1912 and found results that suited his hopes and expectations. Finding 50 per cent of the delinquents tested to be feeble-minded, Goddard (1912) was led to assert dogmatically that mental deficiency was the chief cause of antisocial behavior. Goddard became the foremost proponent of the psychological school of criminology, maintaining that low intelligence was the major cause of unlawful behavior, and, like his predecessors, he believed that intelligence was genetically determined and not subject to the influence of social inequalities or environmental adversities.

Since the time of Goddard's investigations, approximately 450 separate studies on the intelligence of juvenile delinquents have been published. It seems probable that no other single characteristic of the juvenile delinquent has been so thoroughly studied. Still, these investigations have not provided conclusive evidence of the role intelligence plays in juvenile delinquency.

It would be impossible and beyond the immediate purposes of this chapter to discuss all the studies bearing directly on the relation of intelligence to delinquency. Further source material, however, is available for extended reading. An extensive summary of early research, published up to the year 1929 on the relationship between morality and intelligence, is presented in a major monograph on the subject by Clara Chassell (1935). The section of this work more directly concerned with delinquency and intelligence has been published recently by the Psychological Service Center (Cook, 1961). Numerous accounts of other research can be found in an annotated bibliography by Cabot (1946) which covers 970 articles on delinquency appearing between 1914 and 1944. In addition to the work already cited, general surveys of the issues and findings on this subject as well as extensive bibliographies are provided in Metfessel and Lovell (1942), Shulman (1951), and Woodward (1955).

Many aspects of the relationship between intelligence and juvenile delinquency have been discussed in the scientific literature. In the present discussion, however, special attention will be addressed to the quantitative and qualitative intellectual characteristics of the juvenile delinquent. The relationship of intelligence to such issues as the choice of offense and recidivism will be treated only in passing. It is felt that while these aspects of the problem are important in their own right, it is also true that the nature of the conclusions to be drawn from an examination of the larger issues apply equally well to these more special concerns.

Juvenile Delinquency and General Level of Intelligence

Early research on the intelligence of delinquents, although varying to some extent, generally yielded a mean IQ score of the delinquent that was from 15 to 20 points below that of the general population. Also, the incidence of delinquents classified as mentally deficient was five to ten times greater than that for the general population. Thus, it appeared that the delinquents were significantly duller than the general population.

Chassell (1935) reported twenty-four separate instances of comparisons of feeble-mindedness in delinquent and nondelinquent samples for the period of 1913 to 1926. In twenty-two of these instances the percentage of feeble-minded cases was higher in the delinquent sample. Sutherland (1931) surveyed 340 separate reports of 150,000 delinquent and adult offender IQ's from 1910 through 1928 and similarly reported an unusually high percentage of juvenile delinquents classified as feeble-minded. He noted, however, that the percentages of delinquents classified as feeble-minded were not uniform over the years. During the period from 1910 to 1914, in keeping with Goddard's findings, Sutherland noted that approximately 50 per cent of the delinquents were classified as mentally deficient in contrast to an average of 20 per cent for the period from 1925 to 1928. Better sampling and testing procedures are offered as explanations for this decreased percentage of delinquents falling in the feeble-minded classification.

The following mean IQ's were typical for early studies of delinquent samples: Snyder (1931), 71; Bean (1931), 82; and McClure (1933), 80. The following were typical of the percentage of mental defectives in such samples: Merrill (1925), 23 per cent; Rogers and Austin (1934), 13 per cent; and Glueck (1934), 13.1 per cent. The samples studied in these reports were either from court or correctional school populations and were tested with the 1916 Stanford-Binet Intelligence Scale. Lane and Witty (1935), however, using group rather than individually administered tests of intelligence, found somewhat higher IQ's. These authors reported that 700 male delinquents examined with the Otis Test of Mental Abilities achieved a mean IQ of 88 with only 10 per cent of the cases falling in the mentally deficient range.

More recent studies have repeatedly shown a higher mean IQ for delinquent samples than was true in the past. Merrill (1947) reported the mean IQ of 500 court cases tested with the 1937 Revised Binet as 92.5. The Gluecks (1950), using the Wechsler-Bellevue Intelligence Scale, found a mean IQ of 92.4 for 500 institutionalized males. Siebert (1962) reported the Otis IQ (all forms) of 8003 court cases at 91.4. Therefore, it appears that the most recent evidence, based on a variety of intelligence tests, consistently reveals a difference of about 8 points between the mean IQ's of delinquent and general population samples.

This 8-point difference does not, however, mean that delinquents are significantly inferior in intelligence to nondelinquents. It simply means that the delinquent samples under investigation tested lower than the random samples used in standardizing the test norms. Comparatively speaking, the standardization samples represent a relatively high socioeconomic group in comparison with the low socioeconomic status groups from which delinquent samples are derived. Since cultural factors are known to play a significant role in determining intelligence test performance (Neff, 1938; Jones, 1946), it would seem essential that local norms be used before accepting what might appear to be a first class relationship between delinquency and intelligence.

Two studies in particular underline the importance of taking cultural factors into consideration when making comparative analyses of intelligence between delinquent samples and nondelinquent controls. Maller (1937) examined the intelligence test results from New York City schools and compared these data for each school with the delinquency rate for the area in which the school was situated. The findings indicated that intelligence test results and delinquency rates were negatively related throughout the various areas of the city. On the basis of these findings, Maller concluded that cultural and social conditions that characterized the high delinquency areas had an adverse effect upon the intellectual development of not only the delinquents, but also of all children residing in such areas. Similarly, Lichtenstein and Brown (1938), in a study of 658 grade school children living in a high delinquency area of Chicago, found a mean Kuhlman-Anderson IQ of 90.6 with slightly less than 10 per cent of the sample falling below an IQ of 70. These authors concluded that a high percentage of lower IQ children is typical in the areas from which delinquents come; they also warned of the dangers in drawing conclusions that delinquents are excessively low in intelligence unless such data were based upon comparative studies of children with similar socioeconomic backgrounds.

In this connection, some early investigators had already begun to employ matching procedures to control for cultural factors. Burt (1929) matched delinquent and nondelinquent controls for both age and social class and reported a higher incidence of mental deficiency among the delinquents (7.8 per cent and 1.2 per cent). Backer, Decker, and Hill (1929) matched delinquents and nondelinquents for age, nationality, and neighborhood and found intelligence scores on an unnamed test revealed only a small difference between groups. Glueck (1935) compared the Stanford-Binet findings of 100 juvenile court clinic cases and 3638 school children from roughly approximated social backgrounds. The results from this study revealed that, while the school children deviated somewhat lower than the expected norms based on the general population sample, the delinquents still trailed even farther behind. Similar results were reported by Charles (1936), who attempted to control for both race and socioeconomic level in a study of 176 Negro and 352 white reform school boys. Charles matched his delinquent subjects with two groups of 172 public school boys for race, age, and approximate social economic status. For both races, the public school boys were found to be superior to the reform school boys in intelligence as measured by the Kuhlman-Anderson Intelligence Scale.

In a number of other studies, even more precise attempts were made to control those external conditions not necessarily provided for by neighborhood matching alone. Shulman (1931), using twenty-eight sibling pairs, found a mean difference of 11 IQ points in favor of the nondelinquents. Ackerly (1933), however, tested a sample of thirty matched pairs of delinquent and nondelinquent siblings and found no appreciable difference between the two groups. Healy and Bronner (1936), in a well-planned and controlled study, reported the 1916 Stanford-Binet intelligence results of 105 pairs of delinquent and nondelinquent siblings as follows: 110 IQ and above, 13 per cent and 17 per cent; 90-110 IQ, 52 per cent and 57 per cent; 72-90 IQ, 31 per cent and 23 per cent; 71 IQ and below, 3 per cent for both groups. These children were matched for age and sex, but known mental deficients were excluded from the delinquent group. Thus, the 3 per cent of delinquents reported in the 71 IQ and below category may be an underestimation of mentally deficient children who were apprehended for juvenile offenses.

Despite conflicting evidence on quantitative differences in mental capacity between delinquents and nondelinquents, those who have examined the research in the field generally tend to agree on the implication of the findings. The general conclusion reached is that, once proper care is taken to consider the various sources of bias, there is either no difference or that the difference in favor of the control groups is so small as to be of theoretical interest only. Rouke (1950) maintained that the plotted intelligence distributions of delinquents and nondelinquents were superimposed. Woodward (1955) comments that studies carried out in both the United States and England generally yielded about an 8-point difference which could be explained on the basis of sampling errors. Woodward concludes that ". . . low intelligence plays little or no part in delinquency" (p. 300). Bloch and Flynn (1956) state that ". . . delinquents, by and large, do not differ radically in intellectual capacity from nondelinquent children coming from the same social and economic environments . . ." (p. 115). Others have suggested a significant but slight difference (Tappan, 1949; Reckless, 1950; Shulman, 1950). In their review, Metfessel and Lovell (1942) found the data to be inconclusive.

QUALITATIVE DIFFERENCES

The intelligence test most extensively used to study the quantitative differences between delinquents and nondelinquents was the 1916 Stanford-Binet. However, this test provided no means of independently assessing the various mental functions which the test items were presumed to measure. The test yielded a single index of relative intellectual rank on the basis of a composite of test items welded together into a single instrument. Yet, the need to isolate specific intellectual abilities for study, in addition to the organization of these abilities, was evident for at least two reasons: (1) a single index of intelligence, such as an IQ, obscures the individual component abilities which are combined in the index score. Thus, two individuals having the same relative IQ status may differ radically in terms of their individual strengths and weaknesses on specific mental abilities. (2) Psychological research, after the appearance of the first intelligence tests, revealed that specific intellectual abilities were differentially related to certain personality traits.

The Wechsler-Bellevue Intelligence Scale

The Wechsler-Bellevue Intelligence Scale was introduced in 1939 and provided a means of assessing a subject's "global" intelligence as well as component abilities and their relationships. The test was designed to examine the relative strengths and weaknesses of the various intellectual abilities and to provide diagnostic signs of particular clinical characteristics as manifested in the different patterns of intellectual functioning. Since much of the research on qualitative intellectual functioning among juvenile delinquents has been carried out with the Wechsler test, the following description may be helpful in interpreting the results from these investigations.

The scale is composed of eleven subtests and was constructed so that each subtest yielded a score which, when combined with certain other subtest scores, provided a Verbal IQ, a Performance IQ, and a Full Scale IQ. The set of subtests used in deriving the Verbal IQ is composed of Information, Comprehension, Digit Span, Arithmetic Reasoning, Similarities, and Vocabulary. The subtests making up the Performance subdivision are Picture Arrangement, Picture Completion, Block Design, Object Assembly, and Digit Symbol. The sum of the scores of all subtests, weighted for the subject's age, yields the Full Scale IQ which indicates a relative rank on the over-all test performance.

In brief, the Information subtest measures "the range of a man's knowledge" (Wechsler, 1944, p. 78). Successful handling of the items in this subtest depends upon the extent of learned facts the person has acquired and, to a large extent, is dependent upon formal education. The Comprehension subtest is essentially a series of common-sense items. Practical situations are presented, and the subject is asked what he would do if faced with such a situation. The

Similarities subtest involved handling verbal analogy-type items and measures the subject's ability to conceptualize relationships and to verbalize the qualities of these abstract relationships. Digit Span requires the subject to repeat a series of from 2 to 6 digits and is primarily a test of immediate recall or attention span. The Arithmetic Reasoning subtest contains problems requiring a progression from simple to more complex arithmetic manipulation for their solution. The Vocabulary subtest requires the subject to define the meaning of words graded from rather easy to the more difficult. The Picture Arrangement subtest requires the subject to arrange a series of cartoon-like pictures into a logical sequential order and is, to some degree, a measure of the subject's ability to deal with simulated social situations. The Picture Completion subtest requires the subject to relate "what is missing" in a series of separate pictures and, according to Wechsler, measures the ability "to differentiate essential from nonessential details" (p. 91). The Block Design subtest requires the subject to organize a series of randomly presented blocks into an abstract design pictured for him on a card. The handling of this subtest requires visual-motor coordination and perceptual skills. Wechsler (p. 92) states that this subtest measures the subject's ability to synthesize and analyze problems. The Object Assembly subtest requires the ordering together of jigsaw-type puzzles and, according to Wechsler, tests the subject's ability to order a series of separated parts into unified and familiar configuration. The Digit Symbol subtest is a visual-motor test which requires the subject to relate a series of symbols to corresponding numbers and is generally considered to be a measure of flexibility in a new learning task.

Subsequent factor analytic studies of the Wechsler Intelligence Scale have shown that it measures types of intellectual abilities somewhat different from those assumed by Wechsler. Also, these factorially separated mental abilities are not exactly congruent with the subtest divisions as ordered by Wechsler. Nevertheless, the Wechsler-Bellevue Intelligence Scale, and its subsequent forms, have proved to be reliable and remain exceedingly useful clinical tools for studying intelligence and related personality factors.

Wechsler (1944) used clinical groups as well as a general population sample to test the diagnostic value of his instrument and found that certain types of clinically classed subjects, in fact, did have distinguishable subtest patterns. Other investigators corroborated these findings in general, and have extended and adapted the use of the subtest scatter analysis for widespread diagnostic purposes. One of the clinical groups studied by Wechsler was adolescent psychopaths, a group roughly fitting the more stereotypic image of delinquent-type youth. These adolescents were found to have three outstanding subtest scatter diagnostic signs which distinguished them from normal adolescents.

The first and most outstanding sign noted by Wechsler was that these subjects, in almost all cases, obtained a Performance IQ superior to their Verbal IQ. This finding is not surprising, however. It had been known for some time prior to Wechsler's study that delinquents suffered from a retardation in those verbal skills dependent upon academic achievement but evidenced a reasonable mastery of psychomotor or mechanical skills, e.g., Slawson (1926), Babcock (1932), Glanville (1937), and Bijou (1942). According to Shulman (1951), such findings gave early impetus to the vocational and trade school movement in this country.

A second diagnostic sign noted by Wechsler was that in nearly all cases the sum of the Object Assembly plus the Picture Arrangement subtests was greater than the sum of the Block Design plus the Picture Completion subtests. Thus, within the battery of Performance subtests, the subjects tended to do better on items requiring visual-motor coordination and social understanding than on subtests involving perceptual and analytical abilities in addition to visual-motor coordination.

The third sign noted by Wechsler was a subtest scatter pattern peculiar to the psychopathic adolescents. That is, the pattern of relative strength and weakness among the subtest scores of adolescent psychopaths revealed an intellectual organization or configuration of abilities which significantly differed from that of normal adolescents. The scatter pattern position of each subtest is measured by its standard score deviation, with the Full Scale IQ as a reference point. The particular pattern of scatter which characterized the adolescent psychopaths, in effect, includes the subtest differences already noted, but also takes into account the more subtle differences in the rank order position of all subtest scores.

The Gluecks (1950) focused directly on the qualitative aspects of intelligence by matching 500 delinquents and 500 nondelinquents on the basis of socioeconomic status, race, age, anthropomorphic measurement, and the Wechsler Full Scale IQ scores. Thus, by matching for Full Scale IQ, the investigators maximized the opportunity for isolating qualitative differences between the two samples. The Performance IQ's were about equal for the two groups, but the Verbal IQ was significantly less for the delinquent group (88.56 and 92). The most notable difference resulted from the significantly poorer performance by delinquents on the Information and Digit Symbol subtests. The nondelinquents were slightly superior on the Comprehension and Vocabulary subtests, but fell below the delinquents on Block Design and Object Assembly. The two groups were equal on the Similarities subtest. The results obtained from the Wechsler analysis, in addition to certain Rorschach responses, led the Gluecks to the following conclusions regarding the intelligence of delinquents: (1) they more often failed to approach problems methodically, (2) they were more concrete and direct in their approach to intellectual tasks, and (3) they showed greater variability in their intelligence.

Although this investigation represents one of the most extensive and direct attempts to study the question of qualitative intellectual differences between delinquents and nondelinquents, it is still open to serious criticism. At least two comments seem appropriate at this point aside from the broader methodological considerations to be discussed later in this chapter. First, by equating the over-all level of general intelligence for both groups, the investigators necessarily limit the generalizations that can be made about intratest differences between delinquents and nondelinquents outside of the intellectual range to which this study was restricted. Performance items are more heavily weighted at the lower intellectual levels and Verbal items more heavily weighted at the upper intellectual levels on the Wechsler Scale. Therefore, a study of the ratio of Verbal to Performance IQ's at each intelligence level, extending from the lower through the upper levels, would be necessary to determine if the findings in this study can be applied to delinquents in general. Second, because the two groups were matched for Full Scale IQ, it would seem that if significant differences were found between groups with respect to the Verbal IQ's, then the Performance IQ's could not be equal. That is to say, the Verbal and Performance IQ's cannot vary independently of each other because the two groups were matched on Full Scale IQ's which represent a weighted score derived exclusively from summing the Verbal and Performance subtest scores. One possible explanation for this result is that the Full Scale IQ's were not matched closely enough to rule out the possibility that errors in matching are, to some degree, responsible for the differences attributed to the Verbal and Performance subdivision variance. The "matched" Full Scale IQ's for the nondelinquent and delinquent groups were 94.2 and 92.3. The corresponding Verbal and Performance IQ's were 92 and 98 for the nondelinquents and 88.7 and 97 for the delinquents. Although the small difference of less than 4 IQ points on the Performance scale is slightly larger than the difference between the two groups on the Verbal scale, the fact remains that the difference in Performance scores is only about 1.5 IQ points greater than the discrepancy between the "matched" Full Scale IQ's. It seems highly improbable that statistically significant differences in qualitative intellectual performance would have been obtained had Full Scale IQ's of the subjects been more closely equated.

Diller (1952), in a study of delinquent and nondelinquent girls, found Performance scores higher than the Verbal scores in fifty-six out of eighty cases of the delinquents, but found no significant differences between these parts of the scale for the nondelinquents. Also the Object Assembly plus Picture Arrangement results were greater than the Block Design plus Picture Completion totals in greater proportion among the delinquents. The subtest scatters were also found to distinguish the two samples, thereby substantiating all three Wechsler signs.

The inferences drawn from this study should, however, be tempered by several facts which suggest the possibility that the variation between Diller's delinquent and nondelinquent groups could have arisen as the result of failure to hold certain relevant factors constant. The mean Full Scale IQ of the nondelinquents was significantly higher than that of the delinquents (107.1 and 83.6). Therefore, the obtained qualitative differences may have been simply a function of the quantitative discrepancies between the samples studied since there is a differential weighting of Verbal and Performance items at the various IQ levels. But, even more serious, Diller's controls were nursing school applicants who were older, better educated, and, undoubtedly, different from the institutionalized delinquent girls in many personality respects. Therefore, quite apart from the question of delinquency, these two groups differed in a number of important ways which could have accounted for the obtained differences in test performance. Nevertheless, the performance of the delinquent girls on the Wechsler-Bellevue Intelligence Scale was substantially in accord with Wechsler's predictions.

Richardson and Surko (1956), using the Wechsler Intelligence Scale for Children (WISC) in a study of 105 court cases, found agreement with Wechsler regarding the differences between Performance and Verbal Scale IQ's, but did not corroborate his findings on scatter characteristics and proportionality on particular subtest ratios. The Full Scale IQ was found to be 88.4. Verbal and Performance Scale IQ's were 87.0 and 92.4. These authors interpreted their findings as indicating that delinquents tend to perform less satisfactorily on tasks which are most dependent on school learning or which require concentration and consistency of effort. They conclude that ". . . the delinquent is not so much deficient in intellectual ability as in the utilization of his ability in school tasks" (p. 260).

In an attempt to explain differences in Verbal and Performance IQ's among delinquents on other than intellectual grounds, Bernstein and Corsini (1953) tested the hypothesis that the particular test scatter pattern found among delinquent samples was a function of their adjustment to the test setting. They point out that delinquents are ordinarily tested in an atmosphere of greater stress than that in which normal youth are tested. Delinquents, therefore, tend to perform poorly on the initial test items because of the stress-producing conditions under which they are tested. As the test continues, however, their adjustment to the tasks and requirements at hand increases, and, in consequence, they are increasingly more able to perform satisfactorily on subsequent test items. Because the Verbal items of the Wechsler Scale are presented before the Performance items, it was hypothesized that differences commonly found between these two subtest divisions among delinquents are a product of the adjustment pattern to the testing situation and the order of subtest presentation.

Bernstein and Corsini tested two groups of institutionalized delinquent girls of 100 each, presenting the test to the control group in the standard subtest sequence and to the experimental group in reverse order. The test results of these two groups were compared and found to be almost identical.

Eighty-three per cent of the control and 82 per cent of the experimental groups obtained Performance IQ's greater than Verbal IQ's. The sum of the Object Assembly plus the Picture Arrangement subtests was higher than the sum of the Block Design plus the Picture Completion subtests in 60 per cent of the control and 47 per cent of the experimental cases. The rank order correlation of the subtests between the two groups was .99. The obtained subtest rankings correlated .70 with Wechsler's predicted pattern. These results substantiate Wechsler's findings and rule out the possibility that the delinquents' scatter pattern is an artifact due to the order of subtest presentation.

A number of other studies have been undertaken to compare subtest scatter patterns among delinquent samples and have yielded additional confirmatory evidence consistent with the differences noted by Wechsler, e.g., Franklin (1945), Altus and Clark (1949), and Blank (1958). Other researchers have either failed to substantiate Wechsler's predicted diagnostic signs, or have found differences between delinquents and nondelinquents too small for practical purposes, e.g., Sloan and Cutts (1945), Strother (1944), and Foster (1959).

While the results are not entirely conclusive with respect to some of the more subtle differences in subtest achievement among delinquents, it appears that the tendency for delinquents to obtain higher Performance than Verbal IQ's is recurrent even in those studies failing to corroborate other diagnostic signs. This does not, however, necessarily mean that certain children possess a particular configuration of intellectual strengths and weaknesses which would predispose them toward unlawful behavior. Not only juvenile delinquents but also most children in the lower socioeconomic class generally have been shown to perform rather poorly on verbal tests. Verbal skill, as measured by standard intelligence tests, tends to be highest among children in the upper socioeconomic classes (Eells *et al.*, 1951; Janke and Havighurst, 1945). It is likely, therefore, that factors related to class differences could account, at least in part, for the weak Verbal IQ's generally found among delinquent samples.

The Porteus Maze Test

Analogous in some respects to the investigations of differential qualitative analysis of intelligence using the Wechsler tests has been similar research using the Porteus Maze Test. This test consists of a series of printed line mazes of increasing degrees of difficulty through which the subject is required to negotiate using a pencil. It has the advantage of being a nonlanguage performance test and, consequently, is less culture-bound than most other tests of intelligence. Test performance can be scored for both quantitative (T score) and qualitative (Q score) aspects of intellectual functioning (Porteus, 1942, 1945a). The Q score is computed from certain errors a subject makes in performing the test and has generally been found to be negatively related to the degree of quantitative achievement (i.e., T score). That is, as the number of errors contributing to the Q score increases, the T score tends to decrease. Further, a high Q score usually is indicative of higher performance (i.e., psychomotor) than verbal abilities.

Although various approaches are used in computing the Q score, the items included are almost always "errors" which do not figure into the computation of the T score, e.g., lifting the pencil, the quality of the pencil line (waviness, heaviness), and permissible self-corrections. Porteus (1945b) explains the performance of delinquent subjects as follows:

The typical delinquent response is marked by careless, haphazard work, persistent disregard of instructions, and satisfaction with an inferior grade of execution of poor workmanship in the task. He does not, of course, know that his effort is being scored in these particulars, and concentrates all his attention on finding his way through the maze; thus, in many cases he gains a good quantitative score. It is when the delinquent is off guard that his habitual reactions are exhibited without check. It should be emphasized, however, that this is not true of all delinquents, some of whom are as meticulous in performance as any nondelinquent (p. 269).

The following table from Gibbens (1958, p. 211) is a summary of earlier work as well as the results of his own investigation ("Present study") on the Q score characteristics of delinquents and nondelinquents:

TABLE 4-1. MEAN Q SCORES

	Delinquents			Nondelinquents		
	N	Mean	S.D.	N	Mean	S.D.
Porteus	100	49	25	100	22	13
Wright	54	49	28	—	—	—
Grajales	60	56	29	—	—	—
Porteus	50	48	22	179	19	13
Docter and Winder	60	47	26	60	25	20
Present study	191	35	22	52	14	11

Table 4-1 reveals that the Q scores of delinquents is consistently high—about double that of the nondelinquents when such comparisons were made. Relatively similar findings have been reported by Fooks and Thomas (1957), who found a Q score difference significant beyond the .001 level of confidence between fifty delinquent and fifty nondelinquent subjects.

In the study by Gibbens (1958), 200 delinquents, aged 16-21, committed to Borstal training by English courts were compared on Porteus Maze Q Test scores with a control group composed of fifty-two boys from similar backgrounds, aged 16-18. The controls were considered to be either nondelinquent or at least "unlikely to be seriously delinquent." Actually twenty-two members of the control group admitted having had experienced at least some trouble with the law, and eighteen admitted having engaged in "petty thieving."

The delinquent and control groups differed significantly on Q scores based upon nine separate qualitative errors. This difference remained significant at the same level even after thirty-eight of the Borstal boys were dropped from the delinquent sample so as to equalize the T scores of the two groups under study. The average Q scores of the remaining 162 delinquent and fifty-two controls were 36.6 and 14. This difference was found significant beyond the .01 level of confidence using the Critical Ratio statistic.

The studies employing the Q score of the Porteus Maze Test have consistently revealed highly reliable differences between delinquents and nondelinquents. In the case of Gibbens' study, wide differences were found even between a mildly delinquent control group and a group of more serious offenders. In short, the Q score does appear to distinguish delinquents from nondelinquents, but whether or not this implies a difference in the purely qualitative aspects of intellectual functioning is indeterminant on the basis of available research. It appears more likely that the Q score is indicative of emotional factors that affect specific intellectual abilities rather than of intellectual skills per se.

Basic Methodological Considerations

In order to properly evaluate the research carried out on delinquency and intelligence, it is necessary to examine some of the more basic methodological assumptions underlying most of the studies addressed to this problem and to determine if the requisites necessary for accurate interpretation have been met. Both intelligence and juvenile delinquency are highly complex phenomena requiring serious methodological consideration if they are to be studied properly. The investigation of the relationship between these phenomena poses an even more complex problem. In addition to a thorough understanding of each phenomenon, a carefully planned research procedure is needed that will permit the emergence of their relationship free of bias and contamination which may otherwise yield spurious results; this is of special importance if, as in the present instance, an assumption of causality is involved.

The elementary methodological requirements in research of the type reported on here is to define the major variables and then to select samples that would permit opportunity to measure the effects and relationship of these variables. The major variables under consideration here are "delinquency" (criterion variable) and intelligence (test variable). Ideally, we would like to have two groups of subjects under study who do not resemble each other with respect to the criterion variable, but who are otherwise alike. If, under these conditions, concomitant variation is found to exist between the principal variables, then a basis would exist for presuming a relationship between their conceptual counterparts. Otherwise, differences in the intelligence of delinquent and nondelinquent groups may be due to the unequal distribution between the two samples on factors whose relation to "delinquency" may not be under investigation. Such ideal conditions, however, seldom are achieved in social research. Nevertheless, statistical procedures are available which can determine concomitance between variables under even less than ideal conditions if the distribution and values of all pertinent variables are at least known for both the delinquent (experimental) and nondelinquent (control) samples. This is really a question of sampling—the problem of obtaining representative samples of delinquents and nondelinquents while all other critical factors are held constant.

The Use of Test Norms as Comparison Controls

The early studies of quantitative difference between delinquents and nondelinquents involved comparing the IQ's of a delinquent sample with the distribution of IQ's derived from a general population sample presented in the form of test norms. When the IQ achievements of a delinquent sample were found to be recognizably lower than that of the test standardization group, this difference was often interpreted as indicating that low intelligence was an exclusive or predominant characteristic of youth with a predilection for behavior.

There appears to be a peculiar circularity in the logic which investigators apply to establish a relationship between low intelligence and delinquency when test norms are used as a basis for such proof. Under such conditions, the distribution of the test variable or IQ is known for both the experimental and the control groups. The delinquents' IQ's generally are found to cluster at the lower end of the scale representing the total distribution or relative ordering of IQ's in the general population. However, the empirical value for the criterion variable, "delinquency," is known only for the delinquent group. Yet, when a high percentage of the delinquents do poorly on the IQ tests, investigators imply a causal relationship between the criterion and test variables. The implicit assumption behind such an interpretation is that those cases in the test standardization sample which are dissimilar in intelligence to the delinquents are also dissimilar in "delinquency." In turn, this assumption is used as if it were an inductive fact to substantiate a relationship between intelligence and delinquency.

Furthermore, even if it were possible to demonstrate conclusively that all delinquents were categorically mentally deficient, such a finding would be striking, but not as informative as it might appear; it would have only limited etiological or predictive significance. Knowing a child was delinquent, we could predict his intelligence, but knowing a child was mentally deficient would not necessarily mean he was also delinquent. Predicting A from B may be a very different matter from predicting B from A, unless the relationship between A and B is known to be symmetric. If, for example, all delinquents were mentally deficient and all mentally deficients were delinquents, then it would appear that mental deficiency may well be a necessary and sufficient condition for delinquency. If, on the other hand, all delinquents were found to be mentally deficient and only a small percentage of mentally deficients were delinquent, then it would appear that mental deficiency was a necessary but not a sufficient condition in the causal determination of delinquency.

The main point to be made is that a comparison control sample having an empirically known criterion value is indispensable if generalizations are to be made to children other than those in the experimental sample under immediate study. The delinquent samples employed in almost all studies constitute nonrandom, specific samples, and any generalization of the attributes of such samples to a larger and general population sample would be exceedingly risky business.

Another source of ambiguity closely allied to the use of test norms is found in the procedure involved in deriving a test score criterion for designating mental deficiency. During the years shortly after the introduction of intelligence tests, one means commonly employed was to derive empirically a criterion score by testing subjects already committed to institutions for the mentally defective and then to use their top scores to designate the upper limit for the mental deficiency classification. Any score below the criterion status of the best performing institutionalized defectives was considered to be indicative of mental deficiency.

In this connection, Zeleny (1933) re-examined 163 of the papers reported by Sutherland and concluded that the reported percentages of mental defectives varied with the individual standards for mental deficiency of the various investigators. When a common standard was applied to these study data, Zeleny found the ratio of mental deficients in delinquent samples to that of the general population as only 1.26 to 1.00.

Matched Controls

The primary purpose of using matched controls is to isolate the major variables related to a hypothesis being tested while holding all other variables of probable relevance constant. This is done through the use of a selective sampling procedure that controls for the "randomness" of those variables other than the criterion variable used to distinguish the experimental and control samples. In many investigations control groups were used to reduce systematic biases which might exert an inimical influence on intelligence test performance of the particular delinquent samples studied. Generally, this was done by selecting pairs of children who, presumably, resembled each other closely with respect to personal and situational characteristics, but who differed with respect to delinquent behavior. Thus, systematic and known variation of all pertinent factors other than "delinquency" was assumed to be similar for both samples. Under such conditions any observed differences in intelligence between these samples could be attributed to the one factor permitted to vary, i.e., "delinquency."

The matching of samples for controls confronts the investigator with great practical difficulties that complicated the advantages of this approach in most social research. Selection of matching variables must be determined by factors which have a known or potential effect upon intellectual development. Such a host of contingencies involves not only the comprehensiveness of the researcher's knowledge, but also his skill in balancing the number and relative importance of such items within practical limitations. This is especially problematic in the case of the more broadly focused empirical "grab-bag" studies in which the same controls are used for a series of comparisons on a variety of factors.

A great many things can influence intelligence test performance, and, in most studies, residual differences between delinquent and nondelinquent controls are often sufficient to account for obtained differences in intelligence scores. The results of such research have generally been disappointing even when the most conscientious attempts are made to control bias through matching. Despite the elaborate and careful precautions used by the Gluecks (1950), several reviewers of this study have concluded that the obtained results are all but vitiated because of failures in their matching procedure and, in particular, those items other than the Full Scale IQ's (Kahn, 1952; Rubin, 1958). In regard to the intellectual differences noted by the Gluecks, Rubin comments that "... *there is a greater difference between the delinquents and the nondelinquents in the quality of their social background than in their intelligence scores*" (p. 223). The percentage of delinquents from blighted tenement areas, "poor homes," disturbing family, social, psychological, and physical home situations, and other related factors is pointed out by Rubin as being in greater disproportion than the obtained differences in Verbal and Performance IQ's.

Another problem in control group research grows out of the serious misinterpretation of results due to a posteriori matching procedures. Matching generally takes place only after a juvenile offender has been detected and some official agency has remanded him to a correctional school for a period of time. These events seriously interrupt a child's normal development and have a profound developmental effect in their own right. Yet, in a posteriori matching, the incorporated consequences of events subsequent to detection are often treated as having been present prior to detection. Thus, *post hoc* findings, such as a somewhat lower than average IQ, or slight retardation on subtests dependent upon continuity in formal academic training, may easily be due to the effects of the same variable whose cause is under study. Certainly the entire process accompanying official apprehension, court handling, and adjustment to a correctional school living can hardly be considered conducive to intellectual growth and development. This last point will be elaborated shortly.

Moreover, even if perfect matching were possible, it is doubtful that a single experiment could conclusively prove the relationship of juvenile delinquency and intelligence without subsequent investigation. First, simply because a child is not delinquent at one point in time is no assurance that the same boy would not eventually indulge in such activities; therefore, a follow-up of the controls is necessary. Second, studies in which a number of different variables are held constant preclude the possibility of revealing significant information about the factors that have been controlled. To understand the interaction and role of all the factors associated with differences in intelligence between delinquents and nondelinquents, a second study would be necessary to investigate the factors controlled for in the first instance. Third, replication of *post hoc* studies on fresh samples is essential before the generalization value of such findings can be established.

"Delinquency" as a Criterion Variable

"Nondelinquents"

To a large extent, the accuracy of the interpretations found in the studies discussed so far is dependent upon the assumption that the distinction between delinquent and control groups connotes a real difference in unlawful conduct. Therefore, it would seem important to examine this assumption: is official "delinquency" a reliable criterion variable to use as an index of unlawful activity, and, secondly, if "delinquent" and "nondelinquent" are not sharply differentiated classifications with respect to unlawful behavior, how can the obtained differences in intellectual performance be explained?

There have been several investigations of undetected delinquent behavior among youths with no official record of delinquent activity. The general conclusion that can be reached from these investigations is that any presupposition that groups characterized by official detection have a higher incidence of unlawful behavior than those who have not been officially detected is subject to serious question. Short and Nye (1957) found few significant differences in admitted delinquencies between high school children of different socioeconomic levels, as indicated by "buried" items in a self-report questionnaire. Thus, the familiar observation that "delinquency" is primarily a lower class phenomenon does not hold when nonadjudicated cases are studied for "delinquent" behavior. Similar studies by Murphy (1946), Wallerstein (1947), and Porterfield (1946) have also indicated that unlawful activity is not unique to official delinquents, but also can be found in an unknown but high proportion of children in the general population without official delinquency records. All of these studies point to the serious limitations of using official records as a criterion of assignment to dichotomize samples of children into delinquent and nondelinquent groups. While official records may be indicative of delinquent acts among children who are known delinquents, the absence of such records apparently does not mean that confidence can be placed in a corresponding absence of unlawful behavior among nonadjudicated children.

Properly speaking, unless subjects are randomly chosen from the sample of all children committing delinquent acts, regardless of their official delinquency status, it may be argued that the official delinquents are specific, nonrandom samples and are possibly different in some important respects from all children engaged in unlawful behavior. If, for example, brighter children have personal and family resources at their disposal which enable them to escape detection or to deal with its consequences, then it may be that any opinion as to the role of intelligence in delinquency, based upon the fraction of cases which are apprehended, would not apply to the brighter, socially advantaged, unapprehended "delinquents." Furthermore, if delinquent behavior is as pervasive as some studies indicate, then there is every reason to believe that it is a general phenomenon characteristic of most children irrespective of their intelligence.

DELINQUENT SAMPLES

Court Cases

The juvenile delinquents studied in most investigations of intelligence represent either court, court clinic, or correctional school cases, all of which yield samples biased along different dimensions. The court cases represent the broadest sample and possibly the most nearly representative delinquent sample available but are also the most limited in terms of available data for research purposes. Both clinic and correctional school cases are more accessible for intensive study. A sizable amount of previously collected case record material in contrast with the more routine and limited court case data also make these cases more attractive for study. However, these cases also present serious research limitations.

The selective factors that might operate to bring a child to court attention must, of course, be related to (1) detection and (2) the decision of authorities to take official action against a known offender. In the absence of systematic research on undetected offenders we can only speculate that intelligence is directly or indirectly related to the factors that eventuate in court action. Quite apart from factors in the legal process which might favor the brighter child, in avoiding apprehension and court action, is the fact that the intelligence testing of those taken into custody is likely to be unfavorably affected by the official handling process. Thus, a given delinquent would likely test higher prior to detection than at the time he is tested by a court psychologist.

Intelligence data on court cases are generally obtained shortly after arraignment and prior to the appearance before a juvenile court judge or referee. A subject's test response is affected by prior emotional stress, and, considering the stress under which a court tested case must perform, there is every likelihood that intellectual performance will be adversely affected. McCarthy (1944), for example, demonstrated that the same children tested on a nonverbal intelligence test after writing an essay on "The Best Thing That Ever Happened to Me" averaged 4 to 5 IQ points higher than when tested after writing an essay on "The Worst Thing That Ever Happened to Me." The effects of official handling of delinquent offenders and the conditions under which they are tested are probably far more profound and more detrimental to test performance than the essays used by McCarthy. Similarly, Wechsler (1950) has emphasized the role of nonintellectual, largely motivational factors in test performance. It would seem, therefore, that the court case is not tested for intelligence at a point in time where he is likely to be functioning at an optimum test level. Any test results under these conditions would, to some degree, be an underestimation of intellectual level of activity prior to detection. These remarks apply to both quantitative and qualitative aspects of intelligence and would also hold for any children tested after detection, court hearing, clinic referral, or correctional school placement. Intelligence test performance is not fixed by heredity; many things can cause test performance to vary and, in the case of delinquent subjects, cause them to reflect far less than their intellectual potential.

Court Clinic Referrals

Court clinics often serve many latent functions that have little or nothing to do with the examination of either the more delinquent or the more emotionally disturbed cases that come to the attention of the court. In the main, clinics examine the children who are the most disturbing to the court rather than those who are the most disturbed. If a child represents a problem to the placement officer he will be referred for psychological and psychiatric examination. If, for any number of reasons, the judicial authorities are puzzled or uncertain over a case disposition, they, as well as other court workers, usually find it convenient to order a child examined or re-examined so as to delay the official hearing. In short, the criteria of selection for clinic study generally suit purposes other than those for which the clinic was intended, and these selection criteria are far too broad to warrant the use of such cases as representatives of delinquents in general.

Institutionalized Delinquents

Although convenient in terms of accessibility and ready-made case history data, institutionalized delinquents present a variety of problems which may limit their research value. There is reason to believe that the official delinquent who is selected out for special treatment is not chosen purely on bases related to the persistence or severity of his delinquent history. In a study of institutional commitments from several large western cities, Short and Nye (1957) found the proportion of children from broken homes and lower socioeconomic status was considerably higher among institutionalized delinquents in comparison with the general high school population from the same areas. Yet, these authors found that the high school children from homes which were intact and of higher socioeconomic status admitted committing delinquencies almost as frequently as those from broken homes and lower economic status. Thus, the authors conclude that children from broken homes and/or lower socioeconomic standing were much more likely to be arraigned and committed to correctional institutions than children without these associative factors even when committing the very same offense. Therefore, it would not be surprising if such official delinquents performed poorly on standard IQ tests since they constitute that portion of juvenile law breakers whose intellectual development is likely to be affected adversely because of the limited opportunities of the underprivileged neighborhoods and the emotional stress resulting from broken homes.

There is the further likelihood that a child's IQ may itself be a factor in selecting that child for correctional school placement. Shulman (1951), reviewing the differences in IQ between court and institutionalized delinquents, concluded that duller children tended to be placed in correctional schools. Similarly, McCord, McCord and Zola (1959), in their follow-up of the Cambridge-Sommerville study, concluded that brighter children do not go to correctional schools.

Effects of Institutionalization

One of the common fallacies in interpretation associated with a posteriori matching arises from treating changes occurring subsequent to an event as causes of the event. This is the type of fallacy in the logic of causal proof that is the familiar "*post hoc, ergo, propter hoc*" (i.e., after this, therefore, because of this) or, in the vernacular, "pigs are well named because they are so dirty." The use of institutionalized samples provides one of the best examples of failing to make this important distinction between the effects of prior and subsequent events. The effects of institutionalization on IQ have been known to be detrimental for a long time. Sarason

(1949), for example, discovered that children already mentally retarded repeatedly dropped in IQ with each succeeding year of
institutionalization after custodial placement. Thus, the experience
of institutional life can generate changes in test-measured intelligence. Similarly, and quite apart from the motional effects of stig-
matization and other damaging consequences of legal processing and
detention (cf. Mattick, 1959), the interruption of relatively unre-
stricted way of life by replacement with another which uniformly
controls and structures the subject's behavior surely must have a
pronounced effect on intellectual functioning.

There is some substantiation of this possibility in Gibbens (1958),
who reported finding that the Porteus Maze Q score increased in
magnitude as a positive function of the amount of time spent in
Borstal placement. This would mean that the longer a child experienced correctional school placement, the lower his T score or general
intelligence could be expected to fall, and the greater the likelihood
of his performance skills surpassing his verbal abilities.

"Delinquency" as a Homogeneous Classification

Another feature common to most studies is the use of "delinquency" as a blanket term when, in fact, there is good reason to
believe that there is substantial variability among the children included in any delinquent sample. Simply because children are
officially adjudicated delinquent or are known to have committed a
particular type of offense is no reason to assume that they are geno-
typically similar or represent any particular empirical uniformity.
In this connection, Barron has stated that ". . . probably the only
thing that is alike in all delinquents is that there are violations of
law" (1954, p. 83).

There is good reason to believe that generalized statements based
upon research in which delinquents are studied as a unitary class are
not necessarily true for the entire population of children who commit delinquent acts, officially or unofficially. Some findings may be
common in degree and quality to all cases. On the other hand, some
variables may be positively related to some segments of the delinquent population and negatively related to other segments. In the
case of the latter, a finding reported as a single value will mask what
could be a series of different degrees of relationships. Under such
conditions it is also impossible to know which findings may represent
common values among all delinquents and which may represent an
average of several different subsample relationships.

A number of investigators using factor analytic and related techniques have been able to identify fairly distinct delinquent subtypes on the basis of background and personality factors, e.g., Hewitt and Jenkins (1946); Peterson, Quay, and Cameron (1959); and Wirt and Briggs (1959). So far, however, there is no report in the literature of specific attempts to use such refined statistical operations to identify delinquent subtypes on the basis of intelligence factors. Yet, in many of the studies reported, the variability of intelligence scores among delinquent subjects has been considerably greater than among controls. Glueck and Glueck (1950) and Diller (1952) have specifically commented on this, and it is also evident among the Q score results reported in the table by Gibbens (1958). The relatively high variance of IQ performance among the delinquents may suggest a heterogeneity of intellectual activity not characteristic of nondelinquents. If so, a refined statistical approach may provide a clearer view of the nature of intellectual differences between delinquents and nondelinquents.

At least two studies have separated intelligence out as one factor in the causation of juvenile crime and have studied its interrelationship with an extensive assortment of personal and environmental characteristics of juvenile offenders by employing differences in intellectual level as a means of subdividing samples. The general outcome of these studies has been to demonstrate that more precision can be exercised in the investigation of the role of intelligence in juvenile crime by such procedures. From these studies it appears that the association of intelligence and other characteristics of the offender may not be a fixed relationship but changes as intelligence changes.

Glueck (1935) undertook to compare delinquent children having IQ's below 80 with those having IQ's above 80. The lower IQ children seemed to exhibit all of the background adversities and disadvantages of the children with higher IQ's, but usually in greater measure, plus some additional disadvantages peculiar to the lower IQ sample. The lower IQ children were characterized by poorer home, family, housing, economic status, and school adjustment. These differences were not calculated for statistical significance.

Caplan (1961) carried out a similar study with higher IQ level children separated by a 10-point IQ gap to reduce overlap due to errors of measurement. Using a broader array of variables than those included in Glueck's study, he compared 100 average IQ (90-100) delinquents with an equal number of superior IQ (120 and above) children drawn from the same court population. The IQ's were based upon results obtained on the various forms of either the Otis or Wechsler Test. The highest IQ found among the superior group was 143. Comparisons were made on the basis of background factors, personal characteristics, and a series of delinquency related measures, such as prior delinquency, court disposition, and recidivism. Significant differences between the two groups were found on many of the factors studied. In general, it appeared that among the lower IQ children maladjustment was present in many of the child's life activities. On the other hand, among the brighter children delinquent behavior seemed to be directed at specific sources of discontent and did not disrupt their general life patterns. There was some indication that the lower IQ children had a poorer level of over-all adjustment, whereas the higher IQ children channelized their frustrations by overcompensating with outstanding success in some activities. For example, whereas the average IQ children were extremely poor in school adjustment (grade point average, grade standing in relation to chronological age, and school citizenship), the brighter children were successful in these areas to a greater degree than could be explained on the basis of IQ differences alone. The higher IQ group held a large number of elected school positions, and 10 per cent had an all "A" or highest possible grade point average. It would appear, therefore, that the widely accepted belief that delinquents adjust poorly to school or that school is a constant source of frustration that can lead to delinquency is not true for all delinquents. In fact, for the higher IQ children, the converse appears to be true.

In addition to the studies mentioned above, which attempt to relate intelligence to a variety of factors, attempts have also been made to relate a single factor to differences in intelligence. For example, age and intelligence were studied among 1731 juvenile delinquents by Mann and Mann (1939), who found that boys over 14 years of age had higher IQ's on the Revised Binet than boys under 14 years of age. This difference was small but statistically significant. Zeleny (1933) specifically examined the evidence for sex differences and intelligence among delinquents from data reported in 163 studies. He found that more girls (39 per cent) than boys (25.6 per cent) had been classified as mentally deficient. These data, however, were drawn from very early studies; the more recent evidence has consistently shown that both quantitative and qualitative findings apply equally to delinquents of both sexes.

Most of the research devoted to relating a single aspect of juvenile delinquency to intelligence has dealt with recidivism and offense.

The research on recidivism has been contradictory, and, as yet, no study has conclusively shown it to be a product of low intelligence. If intelligence played an important role in the determination of delinquent behavior, one logically would expect recidivism to be more common among the intellectually duller children. The absence of such evidence, however, appears to contravene the possibility of a close relation of delinquency and intelligence.

Studies of offense have yielded some correlates with IQ scores, particularly with respect to female sex offenders who repeatedly have been shown to be of low intelligence. Usually studies of offense have been carried out using samples too small to provide sufficient numbers in the various offense categories necessary for either adequate statistical application or for full coverage of the variety of offenses. Table 4-2 represents the results of an investigation in which 100 cases drawn from the major offense categories for each sex were compared on IQ (Caplan and Gligor, 1964).

TABLE 4-2. MEANS AND STANDARD DEVIATIONS OF IQ's
FOR OFFENSE GROUPS
(N = 100 for Each Group)

	Mean	Standard Deviation
Runaway–girls	95.6	13.3
Runaway–boys	93.7	15.0
Sexual offenses–girls	88.1	16.5
Sexual offenses–boys	92.8	15.5
Incorrigible–girls	92.6	13.4
Incorrigible–boys	92.8	14.7
Truancy–girls	91.6	12.3
Truancy–boys	91.8	14.2
Auto theft–boys	93.6	13.5
Assault–boys	87.9	11.1
Unlawful entry, stealing–boys	91.5	12.4

The t statistic was used to compare the IQ means of the offense groups for each sex and yielded the following differences as significant at the .05 level of confidence or better: among the boys, assault was significantly lower than all other categories of offenses studied. Among the girls, runaway was higher than truancy, and both runaway and incorrigible were higher than sex offenders.

Perhaps the main significance that can be drawn from these rather exploratory studies is that there may be many aspects to the relation between intelligence and delinquent behavior; any general statement with respect to this relationship may be seriously misleading.

It should also be mentioned that it is now recognized that intelligence is not a single entity but is composed of numerous classes of interrelated mental functions, not all of which are purely intellectual. Therefore, the variety and extent of the interrelations of intellectual functioning and juvenile delinquency may vary also with the different phases of social development leading to and growing out of social misbehavior.

TEST VALIDITY

Some of the personal and environmental sources of influence that may affect performance on intelligence tests have already been pointed out in other sections of this chapter. Leaving aside errors of measurement, a number of other common sources of invalidity and bias could be mentioned; the linquistic handicaps of foreign-born delinquents with highly verbal test items would be only one example. Even more important is the ability of a test to discriminate accurately the relative standing among children of different intelligence. This is what validity means in its simplest sense.

If a test has discriminatory value, accurate, reliable, and unambiguous findings can be obtained to the extent that other factors affecting an individual's test performance are controlled. If, on the other hand, a test has little or no discriminatory value, then no amount of ingenuity in manipulating experimental operations can improve the correspondence between scores on the test and the variable it is designed to predict. There is evidence that the increased validity of intelligence tests used to examine juvenile delinquents played a significant role in bringing about the changing and improved status of the juvenile delinquent.

Merrill (1947) compared 300 delinquents and an equal number of "nondelinquents," matched for age, sex, and neighborhood, and found no statistically significant difference in IQ's between the two groups as measured by the 1916 Stanford-Binet. The mean IQ's of the delinquent and nondelinquent subjects were 86.7 and 89.7, respectively. However, when these children were retested later with the 1937 revision of the Stanford-Binet, a statistically significant difference of 8.9 IQ points between the two groups was found. The corresponding delinquent and nondelinquent mean IQ's at the time of the second testing were 98.4 and 107.3. Merrill concluded that the 1916 Binet failed to reveal the "true" intellectual differences between these subjects due to its "ceiling effect." A caution, however, should be sounded with respect to the confidence that can be placed in assuming that differences obtained on the second testing are in-

dicative of inferior mentality on the part of the delinquents. Woodward (1955) has used this same study to point out the limitations
of neighborhood matching in equalizing environmental influences.
Merrill's delinquents and nondelinquents differed on a number of
such intelligence-related factors (e.g., the occupational status of the
father), which could account for the obtained differences in IQ
between her subjects.

Changes in IQ scores among delinquents as a consequence of
variations in test repertoire is even more dramatically demonstrated
in a study by Caplan and Siebert (1964). These investigators concerned themselves with changes in the IQ status of 51,808 routinely
tested first-offender court cases over a thirty-four-year period. The
purpose of the study was, first, to determine any changes in IQ status
of children appearing before a large metropolitan juvenile court
(Cleveland, Ohio) and, secondly, to relate any detected fluctuations
in IQ status to their probable causes.

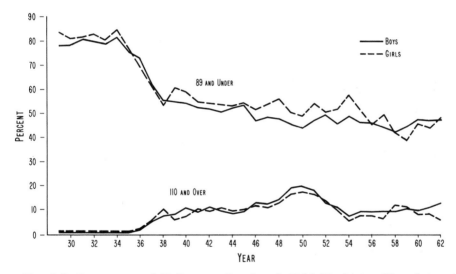

Fig. 4–1. Percentages of Delinquent Boys' and Girls' IQ Scores Classed as
Dull-normal or Below and as Above-average or Above from 1929-1962
(N = 51,808).

As can be seen in Fig. 4-1, the percentage of cases achieving less
than average IQ's for the years 1929 through 1934 was consistently
around 80 per cent, and the mean percentages of above average
IQ's was less than 2 per cent. The only test used to measure intelligence for these years was the 1916 Stanford-Binet. These results

were in keeping with the early findings reported by other investigators. The mean IQ for this six-year period was 80 (N = 10,164).

There is a sharp decrease in the percentage of less than average
IQ cases and an increase in the above average IQ cases for the period
1935 through 1938. After this time there appears to be a slight, but
fairly consistent, downward trend in the percentage of below average
cases and, conversely, a rise in the percentage of above average
cases. During the period of accelerated rise in IQ (1935-1938), the
1916 Binet was steadily replaced by the Otis Test of Mental Abilities
and, later, by the Otis Test in conjunction with the 1937 Revision of
the Stanford-Binet. By 1938 the 1916 Binet was no longer used at
the court. From 1957 through 1962 approximately 95 per cent of
all tests used were the Otis, with the remaining 5 per cent consisting
almost entirely of various forms of the Wechsler. The mean IQ for
these years was 92.1 (N = 9579). The most pronounced change in
IQ status during the years studied, i.e., the rise in IQ level from 1935
through 1938, is interpreted as a function of the replacement of the
1916 Binet by more sensitive tests with higher ceilings.

Another example of the close association between IQ level of
delinquents and the choice of intelligence tests is evident in the
unusual rise and fall in the above average percentages during the
years 1946-1953. For several years before 1946 and after 1953, the
percentage of cases achieving IQ's of 110 or over was consistently
around 10 per cent. During the years 1946-1953, however, the percentages of above average cases is higher, averaging 15.1 per cent
and reaching a peak level of approximately 18 per cent for the years
1949, 1950, and 1951. The Healy Picture Completion Test, a nonverbal performance intelligence test, was used as one of the routine
test instruments to measure the intelligence of a substantial number
of children during the years 1946-1953 by the court clinic staff. Over
these years, 30.1 per cent of the children tested with this instrument
attained above average IQ status. The fluctuation of higher than
average IQ cases for the total court sample during these years was
found to be in direct proportion to the percentage of children examined with the Healy Picture Completion Test. When the Healy
Test was eliminated from the routine test battery in 1953, the percentage of above average IQ cases returned to the same level that it
had been prior to the introduction of this test.

The authors conclude that there have been two major sources of
influence responsible for the change from a fairly retarded to a fairly
normal IQ status among apprehended delinquents. First, and most
significant, has been the change due to the use of more sensitive in-

struments to measure intelligence. The replacement of the 1916 alone resulted in an increase of over 10 points in mean IQ performance. Secondly, there appears to be a slight, but steady, rise in IQ status that occurs independently of changes in the test repertoire. It is suggested that this latter, and more gradual, rise, most noticeable during the period 1938-1962, may be due to the appearance of children before the court who were progressively and genuinely better able to handle intelligence test items. Such factors as improved educational opportunities and special protective care and treatment for the mentally retarded at a precourt level are cited as probable reasons for this gradual improvement in test achievement on the part of the delinquents.

CONCLUSIONS

It is now several decades since attempts first were made to test scientifically the hypothesis that low intelligence was an index of social inadequacy and, therefore, the major explanation of juvenile delinquency. It is difficult to appraise this past research because of a variety of fallacies in basic research procedure and because of the techniques employed to measure intelligence. Despite these fertile sources for error, the weight of the research evidence is sufficiently clear to permit certain conclusions to be drawn.

1. The early assertion that low intelligence was causally related to delinquency appears to have been based upon erroneous assumptions about the nature of both intelligence and juvenile delinquency. Critical examination of existing research on the subject suggests that the obtained differences in intelligence scores between known delinquents and "nondelinquent" controls may be mainly, if not entirely, accounted for on the basis of differences between such samples on variables other than delinquency. The test scores of delinquent samples tend to be about 8 IQ points less than that of the general population, but appear comparable to that which would be expected from nondelinquents of similar backgrounds if tested under similar circumstances. Furthermore, even if this 8-point difference represented a true difference in intelligence, it would be foolish to attribute importance to it since only apprehended and nonofficial "delinquents" are represented in such samples.

2. The more recent interest of investigators in differential qualitative intellectual functioning between delinquents and nondelinquents has revealed differences of two types, each with different implications. The characteristic patterns of the intelligence of delinquents,

obtained by means of the Wechsler-Bellevue Scales, can be explained largely on the basis of differences arising out of schooling, social background, and the effects of legal-correctional processing and institutional confinement. Furthermore, these discrepancies are relatively small and tend to diminish as greater care is shown in the matching of delinquent and nondelinquent samples.

The conspicuous difference between delinquents and controls on the Porteus Maze IQ score, however, is not easily interpreted. The Q score is a gross index of functions which appear to be intricately related to intellectual performance, but whose origin may be entirely in the area of personality. While attempts on the part of investigators to explain the Q score seem genuine enough, its meaning and significance remains vague and seemingly uncommunicable. It would be particularly important to determine if the functions tapped by the Q score reflect enduring personality characteristics or if they reflect the more immediate and direct consequences of training and experience on intellectual development. If the functions involved are determined by basic personality characteristics that affect intellectual behavior, then the very promising predictive potential of the Q score may be a consequence of a particular precondition for the development of antisocial behavior rather than the consequences of poor social adaptation, as reflected in the subsequent inefficient utilization of normal intellectual endowment. Future research may afford some understanding of the Q score and thus provide a basis for critically evaluating its significance in delinquent behavior. At present only a series of complicated assumptions are available for interpreting the significance and meaning of findings involving the Q score.

3. Early research emphasis on the relationship between delinquency and intelligence was begun on a false start, and, as a result, subsequent research has most frequently been addressed to the clarification of earlier misconceptions. This does not, however, rule out the problem as an area of fruitful study in the future, nor does it preclude the possibility that a close interdependence between intellectual functioning and juvenile delinquency exists. If intellectual functioning does operate in some way to cause juvenile delinquency, however, it cannot be discovered or empirically verified by continuing to use the traditional approaches to the problem. In order to gain new insight into this problem, it is necessary that the problem be redefined and that different investigative procedures be used. More of the traditional IQ and delinquency data are not needed; what is needed is a reformulation of the problem to allow for the use of

research procedures free from both the obvious limitations of official police statistics and of "intelligence" as assessed by IQ-type tests.

One means of improving research operations would be to adopt the convention of defining delinquency by a common measure with stable dimensions—preferably some means other than official records. At present it is difficult to define accurately what juvenile delinquency means. If we mean children after they have been known officially to have committed an unlawful act, then, for the variety of reasons already discussed, it is highly improbable that any causal connections between the act and its antecedent causes can be established. If our concern is unlawful conduct apart from the limited scope of police attention and official processing, then dichotomous groupings based entirely upon the criterion of official records may fail to distinguish between subjects. Some means of measuring social conformity irrespective of official records should be considered. The possibility should be entertained that research on the determining causes of unlawful behavior can be carried out most fruitfully between "delinquent" and "nondelinquent" subjects drawn entirely from undetected populations.

Another means of improving such investigations would be to extend the study of intelligence beyond the traditional concerns. The tendency has been to study the elementary units and association patterns of various intellectual abilities in relation to delinquency or some of its aspects, such as offense and recidivism. Conspicuously absent from the literature thus far have been the investigation using factor analytically derived measures of intelligence (cf. Jenkins and Paterson, 1961). Also, with the exception of one study (Baker and Sarbin, 1956), there has been an absence of investigations in this field addressed to determine the cognitive structure of the larger mental framework which correlates with conceptualization, learning, perceptions, and other areas of mental activity that affect patterns of social adjustment.

In the Baker and Sarbin study the emphasis was entirely upon the higher order cognitive functioning of delinquents. These investigators obtained results suggesting that delinquents generally were unable to predict the behavior of others because of limited cognitive categories which made it impossible for them to adequately perceive the role of the others. They, therefore, were unable to tolerate ambiguities and were less able to deal with social incongruities than nondelinquents because of ". . . undifferentiated cognitive structures in the interpersonal region" (p. 69). In short, then, delinquent subjects used only a limited number of higher order perceptual-cognitive categories by which they made social judgments. In consequence of this failure to make new differentiations, especially between themselves and others, they tended to react to all social objects as if they were, more or less, mirror images of themselves. This failure to perceive dissimilarity between themselves and other social objects was viewed by the authors as a source of social retardation growing out of a fixated "maturational-enculturation" sequence. The authors pointed out that while psychologists have been preoccupied with one form of mental retardation, they have failed to investigate (a) the effects of mental retardation due to arrested perceptual-cognitive development, and (b) the effects of such retardation upon social adjustment.

Another important feature of this study is that it was carried out to test hypothetical assumptions based upon a particular theoretical framework. Most studies on delinquency and intelligence evidence no explicit recognition of any theoretical orientation which might otherwise provide a planful and more orderly approach for subsequent investigations.

4. It would be naive to assert that there is no relationship between intellectual functioning and juvenile delinquency behavior. Intelligence operates as a life-shaping force in all human behavior and must enter into the final crystallization of delinquent activity however we choose to define it. It is the view of this author that intellectual functioning is intimately involved in the development of the general cognitive framework which guides social adaptation. This involvement may be not only structural in the sense of Baker and Sarbin's findings, but also functionally involved with ongoing personality processes. Intellectual activity probably has a dual function: (a) serving as a basis of reality testing for the familial and social preachments which constitute the publicly condoned prescription and rationale for social conformity; and (b) serving as a form of impulse control to prevent the acting out of tensions arising from discrepancies between the externally set forth rationale for social conformity, vis-à-vis the youth's own independent reality testing of these external dictates as a basis for social sufficiency as he knows it.

Detected discrepancies in the social exhortations laid upon a child and the absence of opportunities within the culturally prescribed "maze-ways" for him to express his own disagreements are possibly mediated by intervening cognitive processes in the final determination of his social behavior. Although this last view is presently more speculative and somewhat different in theoretical orientation than that of Baker and Sarbin, it is in accord with their approach and, similarly, underlines the possible importance for investigating higher order intellectual functioning as a means of understanding the determinants of delinquent behavior.

References

Ackerley, S. (1933) Rebellion and its relation to delinquency and neurosis in sixty adolescents. *Amer. J. Orthopsychiat.*, 3, 146-158.

Altus, W. D., & Clark, H. J. (1949) Subtest variation on the Wechsler-Bellevue for two institutionalized behavior problem groups. *J. consult. Psychol.*, 13, 444-447.

Babcock, M. E. (1932) *A comparison of delinquent and nondelinquent boys by objective measurements of personality.* New York: Columbia Univer. Press.

Baker, B. O., & Sarbin, T. R. (1956) Differential mediation of social perception as a correlate of social adjustment. *Sociometry*, 19, 69-83.

Baker, H. J., Decker, F. H., & Hill, A. S. (1929) A study of juvenile theft. *J. educ. Res.*, 20, 81-87.

Barron, M. L. (1954) *The juvenile in delinquent society.* New York: Knopf.

Beane, J. C. (1931) A survey of 300 delinquent girls. *J. juv. Res.*, 15, 198-208.

Bernstein, Rachel, & Corsini, R. J. (1953) Wechsler-Bellevue patterns of female delinquents. *J. clin. Psychol.*, 9, 176-179.

Bijou, S. (1942) Psychometric pattern approach as an aid to clinical analysis. *Amer. J. ment. Defic.*, 46, 354-362.

Blank, L. (1958) The intellectual functioning of delinquents. *J. soc. Psychol.*, 47, 9-14.

Bloch, H. A., & Flynn, F. T. (1956) *Delinquency.* New York: Random House.

Burt, C. (1925) *The young delinquent.* London: Univer. Press of London.

Cabot, P. S. De Q. (1946) *Juvenile delinquency.* New York: Wilson.

Caplan, N. S. (1961) A comparative analysis of average and superior IQ delinquents. Unpublished doctorial dissertation, Western Reserve University.

Caplan, N. S., & Gligor, A. M. (1964) A study of the relationship between intelligence and offense among juvenile delinquents. Unpublished paper.

Caplan, N. S. & Siebert, L. A. (1964) The distribution of juvenile delinquent intelligence test scores over a thirty-four year period (N= 51,808). *J. clin. Psychol.*, **20**, 242-247.

Charles, C. M. (1936) A comparison of the intelligence quotients of incarcerated delinquent white and American Negro boys and of groups of St. Louis public school boys. *J. appl. Psychol.*, **20**, 499-510.

Chassell, Clara F. (1935) *The relation between morality and intellect.* New York: Columbia Univer. Press.

Cooper, Clara C. (1961) A comparative study of delinquents and non-delinquents. *Psychol. Serv. Cent. J.*, **10**.

Diller, L. (1952) A comparison of the test performance of delinquent and non-delinquent girls. *J. genet. Psychol.*, **81**, 167-183.

Eells, K. (1951) *Intelligence and cultural differences.* Chicago: Univer. of Chicago Press.

Fooks, G., & Thomas, R. R. (1957) Differential qualitative performance of delinquents on the Porteus Maze. *J. consult. Psychol.*, **21**, 351-353.

Foster, A. L. (1959) A note concerning the intelligence of delinquents. *J. clin. Psychol.*, **15**, 78-79.

Franklin, J. C. (1945) Discriminative value and patterns of the Wechsler-Bellevue Scales in the examination of delinquent Negro boys. *Educ. Psychol. Measmt.*, **5**, 71-85.

Gibbens, T. C. N. (1958) The Porteus Maze Test and delinquency. *Brit. J. educ. Psychol.*, **28**, 209-216.

Glanville, A. D. (1937) Psychometric patterns of industrial school boys. *Del. State med. J.*, **9**, 91-94.

Glueck, Eleanor T. (1935) Mental retardation and juvenile delinquency. *Ment. Hyg.*, **19**, 549-573.

Glueck, S., & Glueck, Eleanor T. (1934) *One thousand juvenile delinquents.* Cambridge: Harvard Univer. Press.

Glueck, S., & Glueck, Eleanor T. (1950) *Unraveling juvenile delinquency.* New York: Commonwealth Fund.

Goddard, H. H. (1921) *Juvenile delinquency.* New York: Dodd, Mead.

Goring, C. S. (1913) *The English convict.* London: HM's Stationery Office.

Healy, W., & Bronner, Augusta F. (1936) *New light on delinquency and its treatment.* New Haven: Yale Univer. Press.

Hewitt, L. S., & Jenkins, R. L. (1946) *Fundamental patterns of maladjustment: the dynamics of their origin.* Springfield, Ill.: State of Illinois.

Janke, L. L., & Havighurst, R. J. (1945) Relation between ability and social status in a midwestern community: II. Sixteen-year-old boys and girls. *J. educ. Psychol.*, **36**, 499-509.

Jenkins, J. J., & Paterson, D. G. (eds.) (1961) *Studies in individual differences: the search for intelligence.* New York: Appleton-Century-Crofts.

Jones, H. E. (1946) Environmental influences on mental development. In L. Carmichael (ed.), *Manual of child psychology.* New York: Wiley.

Kahn, A. J. (1952) Analysis of methodology of unraveling delinquency. In D. G. French (ed.), *An approach to measuring results in social work.* New York: Columbia Univer. Press.

Lane, H. S., & Witty, P. A. (1935) The mental ability of delinquent boys. *J. juv. Res.,* **19,** 1-12.

Lichtenstein, M., & Brown, A. W. (1938) Intelligence and achievement of children in a delinquency area. *J. juv. Res.,* **22,** 1-25.

Lombroso, C. (1912) *Crime: its causes and remedies.* New York: Little, Brown.

Maller, J. B. (1937) Juvenile delinquency in New York: A summary of a comprehensive report. *J. Psychol.,* **3,** 1-25.

Mann, C. W., & Mann, H. P. (1939) Age and intelligence of a group of juvenile delinquents. *J. abnorm. soc. Psychol.,* **34,** 351-360.

Mattick, H. W. (1959) Some latent functions of imprisonment. *J. crim. Law Crimol. pol. Sci.,* **50,** 237-244.

McCarthy, Dorothea. (1944) A study of the reliability of the Goodenough drawing test of intelligence. *J. Psychol.,* **18,** 201-216.

McClure, W. E. (1933) Intelligence of 600 juvenile delinquents. *J. juv. Res.,* **17,** 35-43.

McCord, W., McCord, Joan & Zola, I. K. (1959) *Origins of crime.* New York: Columbia Univer. Press.

Merrill, Maude (1926) Mental differences among juvenile delinquents. *J. Delinq.,* **10,** 415-427.

Merrill, Maude (1947) *Problems of child delinquency.* Boston: Houghton Mifflin.

Metfessel, M. F., & Lovell, Constance (1942) Recent literature on individual correlates of crime. *Psychol. Bull.,* **34,** 133-164.

Murphy, F. J., Shirley, Mary M., & Witmer, Helen L. (1946) The incidence of hidden delinquency. *Amer. J. Orthopsychiat.,* **16,** 686-696.

Neff, W. S. (1938) Socio-economic status and intelligence. A critical survey. *Psychol. Bull.,* **35,** 727-737.

Peterson, D. R., Quay, H. C., & Cameron, G. R. (1959) Personality and background factors in juvenile delinquency as inferred from questionnaire responses. *J. consult. Psychol.,* **23,** 395-399.

Porterfield, A. L. (1946) *Youth in trouble.* Fort Worth: Leo Potishman Foundation.

Porteus, S. D. (1942) *Qualitative performance in the Maze Test.* New York: Psychological Corporation.

Porteus, S. D. (1945a) Q-scores, temperament, and delinquency. *J. soc. Psychol.,* **21,** 81-103.

Porteus, S. D. (1945b) Porteus Maze tests: application in medical and allied field. *Brit. J. med. Psychol.,* **20,** 267-270.

Reckless, W. C. (1950) *The crime problem.* New York: Appleton-Century-Crofts.

Richardson, H. M., & Surko, E. F. (1956) WISC scores and status in reading and arithmetic of delinquent children. *J. genet. Psychol.*, **89**, 251-262.

Rogers, K. H., & Austin, O. L. (1934) Intelligence quotients of juvenile delinquents. *J. juv. Res.*, **18**, 103-106.

Rouke, F. L. (1950) Recent contributions of psychology to the study of criminogenesis. In *Proceedings of the 2nd international congress on criminology.* Paris.

Rubin, S. (1958) *Crime and juvenile delinquency.* New York: Oceana Publications.

Sarason, S. (1949) *Psychological problems in mental deficiency.* New York: Harper.

Short, J. F., Jr., & Nye, F. I. (1957) Reported behavior as a criterion of deviant behavior. *Soc. Probl.*, **5**, 207-213.

Shulman, H. M. (1929) *A study of problem boys and their brothers.* Albany: New York State Crime Commission.

Shulman, H. M. (1951) Intelligence and juvenile delinquency. *J. crim. Law Criminol.*, **41**, 763-781.

Siebert, L. A. (1962) Otis IQ scores of delinquents. *J. clin. Psychol.*, **18**, 517.

Slawson, J. B. (1926) *The delinquent boy.* Boston: Badger.

Sloan, W., & Cutts, R. A. (1945) Test patterns for defective delinquents on the Wechsler-Bellevue test. *Amer. J. ment. Defic.*, **50**, 95-97.

Snyder, M. A. (1931) A comparison of mental traits and attitudes of delinquent boys and girls. *J. juv. Res.*, **15**, 181-191.

Strother, C. R. (1944) The performance of psychopaths on the Wechsler-Bellevue test. *Proc. Ia. Acad. Sci.*, **51**, 397-400.

Sutherland, E. H. (1931) Mental deficiency and crime. In K. Young (ed.), *Social attitudes.* New York: Holt.

Tappan, P. W. (1949) *Juvenile delinquency.* New York: McGraw-Hill.

Wallerstein, J. S., & Wyle, C. (1947) Our law-abiding lawbreakers. *Probation*, **25**, 107-112.

Wechsler, D. (1943) Non-intellective factors in general intelligence. *J. abnorm. soc. Psychol.*, **38**, 101-103.

Wechsler, D. (1944) *The measurement of adult intelligence.* Baltimore: Williams and Wilkens.

Wirt, R. E., & Briggs, P. F. (1959) Personality and environmental factors in the development of delinquency. *Psychol. Monogr.*, **73** (whole No. 485).

Woodward, Mary (1955) The role of low intelligence in delinquency. *Brit. J. Delinq.*, **5**, 281-303.

Zeleny, L. D. (1933) Feeble-mindedness and criminal conduct. *Amer. J. Sociol.*, **38**, 564-578.

5

Personality and Delinquency

HERBERT C. QUAY

THE NOTION that there are personality characteristics which set delinquents and criminals apart from normals has a long history. The first assumption about the nature of these characteristics was that they had to do with morality or righteousness. However, as the psychology of personality began to develop, it appeared that other personality variables might be related to delinquent tendencies. Much of the early research, however, was inconclusive. In 1950 Schuessler and Cressey reviewed the results of 113 investigations and concluded that the combined results did not support the hypothesis that criminality and personality elements were associated. This conclusion now appears to warrant re-examination. Of the thirty different tests used in the studies which they reviewed, only four are presently considered valid enough to remain in current use in personality assessment. These four tests (Rorschach, MMPI, Guilford-Martin, and Porteus Mazes) had been employed in only twelve of the studies, and in half of these they had shown an ability to differentiate statistically the criminal group from whatever group had been used as a control. This suggests that the use of more valid tests coupled with greater sophistication in design and analysis might succeed where earlier work failed.

There is another and potentially even more important facet of the problem. This is the possibility of demonstrating, in a consistent and systematic way, differences in personality between subgroups *within* the total delinquent group. This problem has received increasing attention, and its successful solution could provide the basis for more scientifically oriented studies of both etiology and treatment.

This chapter will review the more recent studies attempting to demonstrate differences in personality between delinquents and controls. Then special consideration will be given to an analysis of studies attempting to develop subcategories of delinquents based on personality characteristics.

STUDIES OF "UNSELECTED" DELINQUENTS

Time Orientation

In view of the frequently expressed notion that delinquents are more impulsive and less concerned with the future consequences of their behavior than are nondelinquents, it seems reasonable to assume that some differences might be demonstrated in the area of temporal experience. At least three published studies have dealt with the question of time orientation and its relationship to delinquency.

Barndt and Johnson (1955) compared twenty-six institutionalized delinquents with twenty-six high school boys selected to approximate the experimental groups on age, intelligence, school achievement, and socioeconomic status. Subjects were instructed to tell a story in response to a stimulus situation provided by the experimenter. The stories were recorded and subsequently analyzed in terms of the time span which they encompassed. Results indicated that the stories produced by the delinquents occurred during shorter time periods than did the stories of the controls.

Using a procedure identical to that of the above study, Davids, Kidder, and Reich (1962) tested a sample of twenty-four institutionalized boys and thirty institutionalized girls. Their findings indicated identical time-period scores for the boys and the girls. Although they had no control groups of their own, they compared the scores of their *Ss* with scores obtained by other *Ss* in previous research. Comparisons indicated their delinquent boys were similar to emotionally disturbed boys of a younger age group and to the delinquent sample of Barndt and Johnson (1955). The delinquent boys of this study were, as expected, more "present-oriented" than Barndt and Johnson's nondelinquent controls. Finally, Siegman (1960) found that young offenders in a prison in Israel had significantly shorter future time perspectives than did a control group of young army inductees. He also found that in estimating the length of intervals of time the delinquents consistently underestimated, whereas the controls tended toward overestimation.

Taken together, these studies certainly suggest that the delinquent is more present-oriented than the normal when both groups are predominantly from the lower and lower middle classes. If one can extrapolate from the concept of future time orientation to the concept of an attenuated gradient of reinforcement, then these findings suggest a mechanism by which the self-defeating behavior of the delinquent may be understood; the delinquent behaves so as to maximize immediate reward failing to be influenced by the possibility of later punishment. Mowrer and Ullman (1945) have used this notion in explanation of the self-punishing behavior of the psychoneurotic and the criminal, and it seems equally applicable here. It would now seem profitable to study this variable in the more impulsive or psychopathic groups of delinquents. The results of these studies are also relevant to a theory of delinquency which ascribes the problem to the nature of lower class values per se (Miller, 1959). One of the cardinal assumptions of this theory is that lower class culture places more emphasis on immediate gratification than on the anticipation of longer range rewards. While it may be that lower class children are more present-oriented than those of the middle class (Le Shan, 1952), it also appears that this orientation exists in even greater magnitude in those guilty of delinquency. Thus, the notion that a direct transmission of this particular orientation in equal strength to all lower class children is a primary causative agent in delinquency is certainly questionable: individual differences must be considered.

Cognitive and Perceptual-Motor Functions

In recent literature there has appeared a number of studies dealing with the perceptual-motor functioning of delinquents. In this research it is assumed that if intellectual ability and gross motor skills are controlled, then differences in perceptual motor functioning can be attributed to aspects of psychological functioning generally classed as personality variables.

Zolik (1958) compared forty-three delinquents with forty-three nondelinquents who were residing in a high delinquency area on their performance on the Bender-Gestalt Test. The groups had been matched for age, intelligence, and absence of motor defects. Employing the Pascal and Suttell (1951) method of analyzing the Bender figures, a number of significant differences were found between the two groups. Using the median over-all deviation scores as the point for dichotomizing the groups, a tetrachoric correlation of .77 was obtained between delinquency and size of deviation score.

Differences in the deviation scores could not be accounted for by either age or intelligence. Differences found between the groups in more detailed aspects of the scoring system were interpreted by Zolik as indicating that the delinquents are either less mature or more regressive, and that they suffer a higher degree of neuro-muscular incoordination under conditions of tension.

Unfortunately, Zolik's paper fails to provide information in regard to the reliability of scoring, nor does he indicate whether or not the records were scored without knowledge of group membership. While Pascal and Suttell themselves provide data indicating adequate reliability of their scoring systems, the possibility of systematic bias due to the scorer's knowledge of group membership cannot be completely ignored.

As it stands, this study lends support to the findings of studies relating delinquency to Porteus Maze Q scores. It does seem that inferior Bender reproductions that cannot be accounted for by age, IQ, or sensory motor defect are likely the result of the same factors of impulsiveness and lack of control that would relate to poor Porteus qualitative performance.

Jones, Livson, and Sarbin (1955) have provided a study of cognitive functioning as it is manifested in perceptual completion. They utilized the Street Gestalt Completion Test (Street, 1931) in which familiar objects are represented by only partially complete drawings, the task of the S being to name the object in as short a time as possible. As a rationale for the employment of this instrument these investigators theorized that "the class of delinquent behavior which is loosely designated 'psychopathic' (e.g., impulsive, unpremeditated, repetitive) has its origin in part in a retardation of perceptual-cognitive development." Thus they hypothesized that psychopathic delinquents would exhibit greater difficulty in the recognition of the incomplete pictures than nondelinquents.

The experimental group consisted of forty-one boys, aged 14-18, who had committed at least three acts of legal delinquency and who were incarcerated at the time of the study. In order to maximize the number of "psychopathic" boys only those who had been convicted of serious offenses, such as assault, auto theft, armed robbery, and malicious mischief, were selected. The control sample was of a comparable age range and was made up of boys with no known behavior problems. Results indicated that during the 60 seconds in which the incomplete drawings were exposed, significantly fewer of the delinquents arrived at the solution. When the data were analyzed in terms of the number of correct solutions in the first 10 sec-

onds of exposure, thereby introducing a speed element, the delinquents were even less efficient in their performance.

In evaluating the results in terms of possible sources of differences
between the groups other than those associated with "psychopathic"
delinquency, a number of factors must be considered. The experimenters considered and ruled out differences in task motivation.
Intelligence presents somewhat more of a problem even though the
Street has been shown to be unrelated to verbal intelligence. Since
there were no intelligence data on the Ss of this study the influence
of differential intelligence between the two groups remains a possibility. The contribution of "psychopathy" as opposed to other intrapersonal factors associated with delinquency is perhaps least well
documented. The selection did produce Ss who were repeaters and
who were guilty of the more serious offenses, but serious offenses
and recidivism do not belong solely to the "psychopathic" delinquent.
On the other hand, there is evidence that institutional recidivism
and the tendency to be guilty of crimes against the person are associated with "psychopathic" delinquency (Quay, Peterson, and
Consalvi, 1960). Certainly this research warrants replication and
extension to larger samples of delinquents representative of both
the psychopathic and other subgroups.

A problem common to the interpretation of all studies of perceptual motor function is that of deciding what specific personality
variable is responsible for observed differences. Does inferior cogni-
tive-perceptual functioning reflect impulsivity, lack of ego-strength,
immaturity, regression, or some other attribute? There is also the
problem of what is cause and what is effect. Does poor perceptual-
motor control give rise to behavioral impulsivity or is poor perceptual-motor control a manifestation of a more general lack of
impulse control? While satisfactory solutions to these problems must
await further research, the studies of perceptual-motor functioning
nevertheless are of interest and may shed light, if only by inference,
on some personality characteristic associated with delinquency.

Since there is considerable evidence (Gough and Peterson, 1952;
Gough, 1960; Peterson, Quay, and Anderson, 1958) that at least a
sizable portion of the delinquent population is lacking in socialization either in terms of the values embraced by the larger culture or
even in terms of the norms of any segment of the population, the
relative effectiveness of social rewards and punishments has received
some attention.

McDavid and Schroeder (1957) have investigated the process by
which a given event might function at the same time as blame to

one individual and as praise to another. It was assumed that the delinquent boys, having evidenced by their behavior a failure of "proper" response to environmental events of praise and punishment, would not discriminate between such positive (rewarding) and negative (punishing) events as clearly or as consistently as the control Ss. A further assumption was that within the delinquent group those poorest on such discrimination would be more likely to be recidivists.

The experimental task consisted of a series of situations, presented in story form, for which the S had to choose between two possible interpretations: one indicating a positive and the other a negative state of self-evaluation. Results indicated first of all that interpretations were unrelated to age or measured intelligence in a normative sample of 750 adolescent males. In a sample of 160 delinquents, scores indicated that the delinquents less frequently interpreted positive events as self-positive while at the same time interpreting positive events as more self-negative. It was also demonstrated that the delinquents were much less able, as a group, to discriminate positive from negative events. The hypothesis in regard to recidivism was, however, unsupported. The investigators interpreted their results as demonstrating a lack of discriminal ability among adolescent delinquents with respect to positive and negative interpersonal or situational events. They theorized that developmental antecedents of this undifferentiated interpretation might be found in inconsistency of discipline and failure of identification with authority figures. Further, they noted that the high incidence of undifferentiated interpretation suggests a lack of ability to change as a function of situational input. Along similar lines Pesetsky (1961) found that delinquent's judgments as to the meaning of various antisocial acts were less influenced by the context in which the act was set than were the judgments of a group of controls.

Added support for the notion of the decreased effectiveness of situational and interpersonal reinforcers in certain kinds of delinquents is provided in a study by Johns and Quay (1962). Using young adults (mean age of 20) who were confined to a military stockade, they found those categorized as psychopathic were less responsive to the verbal reward than those classified as neurotic. This study has recently been replicated in a sample of more serious offenders in the same age group with similar results (Quay and Hunt, 1965).

Studies of Multiple Attributes

In a series of studies (Hathaway and Monachesi, 1953; Hathaway, Monachesi, and Young, 1960; Wirt and Briggs, 1959), a group of psychologists and sociologists at the University of Minnesota have studied the relationship of personality characteristics as measured by the MMPI to the rate of juvenile delinquency in large samples of both urban and rural children. The children were tested when they were in the ninth grade, and follow-up data in regard to delinquent activity have been collected after lapses of two, four, and five years. All of these studies have demonstrated that high scores on certain combinations of the MMPI scales measuring tendencies toward psychopathic deviate, schizophrenia, and hypomania are associated with a rate of later delinquency higher than that for the entire population while high scores on scales for social introversion, depression, and masculinity-femininity presage a lower rate of delinquency than that for the entire sample. These consistent findings over large samples certainly provide evidence that some aspects of personality are associated with later delinquency.

Interpretations going beyond the simple (but useful) actuarial level require considerations of the meaning of scores on the various MMPI scales. Except for the Psychopathic Deviate scale, where many of the Ss in the clinical validation groups were actually adolescents or young adults already in difficulty with the law, the scales predictive of later delinquency were developed by contrasting groups of adults with certain psychiatric diagnoses with other adults without such diagnoses. There is a vast literature (see Dahlstrom and Welsh, 1961) on the interpretation of the MMPI, not all of which is in agreement as to what basic attributes the various scales measure. A further problem in interpretation was pointed out by Hathaway and Monachesi (1960) when they noted that test items directly related to delinquent activity were frequently answered in obviously invalid ways by both delinquents and nondelinquents. More subtle problems of interpretation notwithstanding, the Minnesota studies have shown that personality variables of aggression, hostility, overactivity, and individualistic thinking are, when found in children, predictive of delinquent activity. However, other personality characteristics felt to reflect withdrawal, repression, physical symptom-formation, and a tendency toward opposite sex identification in interests and attitudes have an inhibitory effect in regard to delinquent behavior in children. Further, it has been demonstrated (Wirt and Briggs, 1959) that while certain of the personality traits have environmental correlates, others seem independent of obvious environmental influence.

The Minnesota studies are all well done methodologically and have the decided advantage of having measured the personality characteristics of the subjects before they became delinquent, thus assuring that observed differences between delinquents and non-delinquents are not produced by the process of arrest, adjudication, and incarceration. Since, as is the case with all exploratory studies, many comparisons were made, those of statistical significance need cross validation before they can be fully accepted as fact. The results as they stand certainly suggest that emotional maladjustment is related to some delinquency, but certainly not all. Further, the finding that certain patterns of emotional maladjustment are inversely related to later delinquency is of considerable importance and should not be overlooked by those who ascribe delinquency to emotional maladjustment irrespective of its pattern.

Reckless and his associates have provided a number of studies in which various personality measures have been applied to groups of boys judged to be delinquency-prone and control groups judged to be relatively delinquency-immune. All of the subjects resided in an urban area where the delinquency rate was high. In the initial study (Reckless, Dinitz, and Kay, 1957), 101 sixth-grade white boys thought by their teachers to be potential delinquents and 125 sixth-grade white boys judged by their teachers to be insulated against delinquency were administered (1) the Socialization and Responsibility scales of the California Psychological Inventory (Gough, 1956), (2) a scale designed to measure some aspects of the self-concept, and (3) four items from an occupational preference scale previously shown to relate to delinquency. In addition, mothers were interviewed and data on social background characteristics were obtained. Results indicated that the groups were similar on the social factors as might have been expected due to the method of selection. However, fewer of the insulated boys came from broken homes. On the Socialization scale the potentially delinquent boys scored significantly lower than did the "good" boys; the same was true for the Responsibility scale. The results of the self-concept measure indicated that a more socialized self-image had been developed in the insulated group.

A second paper (Dinitz, Reckless, and Kay, 1958) reported additional data on the potentially delinquent group. Twenty-four of these boys were found to already have had police contact for some delinquent act. When these twenty-four were compared with the remaining seventy-seven, it was found that they scored significantly lower on socialization and responsibility and perceived themselves to be more likely to get into more trouble and less likely to finish high school.

Four years later a follow-up of the good boys (Scarpitti, Murray, Dinitz, and Reckless, 1960) succeeded in locating and restudying 103 of the original 125. For the ninety-nine still in school, the home-room teacher was asked to indicate whether the boy was (1) one who would not experience difficulty with the law, (2) one who would get in trouble, or (3) one about whom she was unsure. Each of 103 was also cleared through the police and juvenile court files for official or unofficial delinquency in the intervening four years. The boys were again administered the Socialization scale along with especially developed scales to measure attitudes toward involvement with the law, rejection of and by the mother and father, and a measure of the boys' concept of friends, school, and self.

Teacher nominations placed ninety-five of the ninety-nine in school in the "good" category. Court records revealed that only four of the 103 had become known to the police. Thus, the incidence of recorded delinquency in this group which had been predicted non-delinquent four years earlier was only 4 per cent. The retest mean on the Socialization scale was not significantly different from the mean that this group had earned in the original testing, indicating a continuing tendency for this group to score positively on socialization. As was also the case previously, the boys regard themselves as being able to stay out of trouble and to have favorable attitudes toward the law and law enforcement officials. Their orientation to school remained favorable, and they expressed favorable attitudes toward parents and friends.

The follow-up of the vulnerable boys (Dinitz, Scarpitti, and Reckless, 1962) was successful in restudying seventy of the original 101. Twenty-seven of these had had "serious and frequent contact with the court during the four year interlude between the initial assessment at 12 years of age and the assessment at 16 years of age" (p. 516). These twenty-seven boys averaged three plus contacts for separate complaints of delinquency. Both the self-concept inventory and the socialization scale indicated a continuing tendency to poorer socialization and self-regard with respect to legal difficulties. While it is likely that the missing thirty-one boys would be as (or possibly more) delinquent than those restudied, this loss of one-third of the original group does pose interpretive problems and illustrates one of the practical difficulties in longitudinal research.

The Reckless studies are unique in examining those exposed to un-usual social influences who do not become delinquent. Here again the personality characteristics of impulsivity, aggressiveness, and lack of responsibility were found to occur in those who do become delinquent. While these investigators feel that the self-concept, as influenced by either favorable or unfavorable socialization, is a cru-cial variable in either vulnerability or resistance, one can question the need for this intervening construct (self-concept) between past experience (socialization), present stimuli (the social setting), and current behavior (delinquent or nondelinquent). Wylie (1961) has provided an excellent review of the difficulties inherent in the use of such phenomenological constructs.

STUDIES OF SELECTED GROUPS

Solitary Delinquents versus Gang Members

Wattenberg and Balistrieri (1950) have provided data based on a comparison of boys known to be members of gangs with a sample of boys who were not gang participants. Using samples of over 2000 boys in each group who had had police contact in a metropolitan area, they found that gang members appeared to have come from less well-organized homes which were located in socioeconomically low neighborhoods. However, while the non-gang boys came from "better" homes in the socioeconomic and organizational sense, they were more likely to have been living in homes in which there were disturbed family relationships. The gang boys also tended to come from more racially mixed neighborhoods. In predicting repeated de-linquency, socioeconomic indices were more valid for the non-gang members.

This study is, of course, plagued by the ever-present problem of the reliability of official records, especially since these records relate to less easily observable variables. The data are, however, consonant with general expectations; the gang delinquents' greater prevalency in economically disadvantaged areas has been the common observa-tion.

A more recent study comparing the personality characteristic of boys known to have always been either social or solitary in their de-linquencies has been provided by Randolph, Richardson, and John-son (1961). These investigators administered the Wechsler Adult Intelligence Scale, the MMPI, and a modification of the Warner Index to a sample of thirty-nine social and eighteen solitary delinquent males. Age range was reported as 14-18; no information was given as to race.

Results indicated that the solitary group was significantly brighter. The mean IQ of the solitary boys (105.00) was exceeded by only 15 per cent of the social group (93.23). More of the "lone wolf" group came from the upper middle and lower middle socioeconomic groups, whereas more of the social group came from the upper lower and lower lower strata. On the MMPI there were no differences on the validity scales (L, F, K), and clinical profiles were very similar in shape. However, the solitary group had significantly higher mean scores on all clinical scales except that for hypomania. As the authors noted, the data indicate clearly that the two groups differ; the solitary delinquent is more intelligent, more emotionally disturbed, and more apt to have come from better socioeconomic circumstance. The results of this study confirm the earlier conclusion of Wattenberg and Balistrieri (1950), especially in regard to the difference in socioeconomic level.

Auto Thieves

Wattenberg and Balistrieri (1952) have also studied the characteristics of boys charged with automobile theft as opposed to delinquents charged with other offenses. They compared these two groups of offenders (230 auto thieves versus 2544 others) on a total of fifty variables obtained from police records with statistically significant differences emerging for fourteen. The automobile violators were more likely to have come from a better socioeconomic background as indicated by a number of specific variables. They were also judged to have significantly better relations with their peers, i.e., to be less withdrawn and/or suffering fewer disturbed interpersonal relations. The authors interpreted their results as indicative of the importance of personality structure in delinquency since a significant proportion of those guilty of auto theft were free from the damaging influence of social disorganization.

It does seem likely that the study of delinquents guilty of specified offenses taken singly or of multiple offenses forming unitary dimensions of delinquent activity (see Nye and Short, 1957; Scott, 1959; Quay and Blumen, 1963) might be fruitfully pursued. It is possible, and it is certainly suggested by the results of the above study, that there might be meaningful relationships between certain kinds of delinquent activity and the personality characteristics of the delinquent engaged in these activities.

A word of caution should be expressed. Even in those studies in which the difference between the delinquents and normals are highly statistically significant, there is always overlap between the groups. While some of this overlap can be attributed to unreliability of measuring both the independent and dependent variables, one should not be misled into thinking that, for example, all delinquents are more present-oriented than all controls. Thus, while a given personality characteristic may occur more frequently or in greater magnitude, in a delinquent group it cannot be argued that this characteristic is pathognomic of delinquency.

Research in the Empirical Development of Subgroup Classifications

Analyses Based on Case History Data

A pioneering investigation in the development of a classification system for problem children by statistical methods was that of Hewitt and Jenkins (1946). These investigators hypothesized that children who demonstrated fundamentally different patterns of behavior maladjustment could be shown to have experienced different patterns of environmental influences. Since the relationship of the behavior syndromes to the family background variables has been considered in Chapter 3, only the development of the behavior syndromes will be discussed here.

Hewitt and Jenkins began with a pool of 500 case records of children who had been referred to a child guidance clinic for some behavior problem. Ninety-four descriptive phrases about behavior were rated as to their presence or absence in each case record. Elimination of items infrequently noted and items thought not to be theoretically important resulted in the retention of forty-five items. These forty-five items were then intercorrelated with further analysis focusing on the clusters of interrelated traits within this matrix. According to the authors, a group of traits was judged to form a cluster or syndrome if the traits within it intercorrelated at least .30 and were logically consistent with experienced clinical judgment.

Their procedures resulted in the delineation of three behavioral syndromes, which are presented in Table 5-1. Inspection of this table will reveal that the statistical criterion requiring no trait interrelationships of less than .30 was not strictly adhered to, although in the three matrices only eight coefficients fall below this value. The next step involved locating children who, on the basis of the requirement

TABLE 5-1. INTERCORRELATION AMONG THE TRAIT INDICATION
FOR THE THREE SYNDROMES

From Hewitt and Jenkins (1946)

Unsocialized Aggressive

	1	2	3	4	5	6
1. Assaultive tendencies		.37	.66	.39	.44	.39
2. Initiatory fighting	.37		.48	.47	.24	.33
3. Cruelty	.66	.48		.39	.47	.22
4. Defiance of authority	.39	.47	.39		.52	.39
5. Malicious mischief	.44	.24	.47	.52		.39
6. Inadequate guilt feelings	.39	.33	.22	.39	.14	

Socialized Delinquent

	1	2	3	4	5	6	7
1. Bad companions		.27	.57	.56	.53	.41	.53
2. Gang activities	.27		.49	.44	.41	.33	.29
3. Cooperative stealing	.57	.49		.72	.42	.31	.10
4. Furtive stealing	.56	.44	.72		.45	.57	.29
5. Habitual school truancy	.53	.41	.42	.45		.57	.60
6. Truancy from home	.41	.33	.31	.57	.57		.45
7. Staying out late nights	.53	.29	.10	.29	.60	.45	

Overinhibited

	1	2	3	4	5	6
1. Seclusiveness		.67	.33	.53	.40	.33
2. Shyness	.67		.42	.49	.48	.33
3. Apathy	.33	.43		.36	.41	.36
4. Worrying	.53	.49	.36		.57	.24
5. Sensitiveness	.40	.48	.41	.57		.37
6. Submissiveness	.33	.36	.36	.24	.37	

of possession of at least three of the traits in a syndrome, could be said to illustrate the syndrome. Fifty-two children were classified as "unsocialized aggressive," seventy as "socialized delinquent," and seventy-three as "overinhibited." The number of children who could be multiply classified was small: eight cases fit both the "unsocialized" and "socialized" syndromes, five could be included in both the "socialized" and "overinhibited," while none could be doubly classified on "unsocialized" or "overinhibited."

Additional analysis provided information relative to the relationship of other behavioral traits to the three behavior patterns. In general, these relationships were in keeping with expectations based upon consideration of the psychology of the syndromes.

A number of issues relative to the design of this study must be considered. The sample was in no way representative of the urban child population from which the majority of legally delinquent children is drawn in that 97 per cent of the cases studied were white, 94 per cent had American-born parents, and the average age was only 11.5. Only 9.2 per cent of their cases were court referred. The fact that their population was not representative of the population of legally delinquent children was, of course, not central to their concerns but is a factor which must be considered when interpreting this study as bearing on the classification of delinquents.

Other methodological points are perhaps more crucial. No data were presented in regard to the reliability of either the material in the case records or the ratings made from these records. It is well known that case histories themselves tend toward unreliability, and that judgments about case material may suffer from a similar lack of agreement.

The procedure whereby a trait must have met the criteria of clinical relevance for inclusion obviously opens the door to biases which could have serious results for the validity of the classification scheme. Such clinical biases have no place in an empirical statistical analysis, and their explicit presence in this study is a potent argument for the use of factor analytic rather than inspectional procedures for arriving at structural concepts. However, the results do make conceptual sense, and the trait clusters have been independently replicated in later researches. Hewitt and Jenkins have made a major contribution, methodological weaknesses notwithstanding.

Further research by Jenkins and Glickman (1947) extended the original study to a group of adjudicated delinquents. Working with a sample of 300 institutionalized males, they selected cases to represent the unsocialized aggressive and the socialized delinquent syndromes on the basis of the presence of the traits contained in these categories in behavior ratings. To be classified as unsocialized, a boy must have been rated as exhibiting at least three of the following: assaultive tendencies, cruelty, defiance, destructiveness, quarrelsomeness, revengefulness, and shamelessness. Fifty-six cases met the criteria. To be called socialized, a boy must have been rated as manifesting all of the following: gang activity, aggressive stealing, and cooperative stealing. Seventy-eight boys were so classified. The authors apparently did not anticipate that the overinhibited syndrome would occur in an all-delinquent group. However, sixty-three of the boys were rated as showing at least four of the following: apathy, daydreaming, depression, inferiority feelings, seclusiveness, sensitiveness, submissiveness, and timidity. Subjects comprising this group were labeled as "disturbed." Overlap among categories was appreciably greater than in the earlier study. Eighteen of the "unsocialized" were also "socialized," fourteen of the "unsocialized" were also "disturbed," twenty of the "socialized" were also "disturbed," and six cases fell into all three categories.

After categorizing the Ss, Jenkins and Glickman then investigated the relationship of other rated traits to the three categories. Table 5-2 presents those traits found related above .30 to the three categories. As in the earlier study the relationships of the additional traits are generally consonant with expectations.

TABLE 5-2. BEHAVIOR TRAITS CORRELATED WITH THE
THREE CATEGORIES OF DELINQUENTS
(From Jenkins and Glickman, 1947)

	Unsocialized Aggressive	Socialized	Disturbed
Impudence	.64		
Bullying	.58		
Irritability	.52		
Obscenity	.50		
Feels persecuted	.48		.42
Temper tantrums	.48		
Disobedience	.47		
Projection	.37		.34
Craftiness	.35		.35
Overaggressiveness	.35		
Sullenness	.33		
Sex manifestations	.31		
Active homosexuality	.30		
Undesirable companions		.38	
Extreme untidiness			.45
Feeding difficulties			.43
Lonesomeness	.30		.42
Emotional immaturity			.42
Self-consciousness			.42
Carelessness			.40
Overdependence			.40
Fears and phobias			.38
Emotional instability	.30		.36
Oddities of behavior			.33
Nostalgia			.30

Demographic analysis revealed that of the "unsocialized aggressive" group, 66 per cent were Negro; of the "socialized" group, 46 per cent were Negro, and of the "disturbed" group, 51 per cent were Negro. (The proportion of Negroes in the entire 300 cases or in the training school as a whole was not stated.) The median age for all groups was 14, and the median IQ was about 80, with no significant differences among the groups for either variable.

This study indicated that at least two-thirds of a sample of male delinquents could be arbitrarily classified as belonging to one or more of the three categories. While one-third of the 300 cases did not fit any of the categories, had the case records been more complete or more reliable, it might have been possible to classify an additional number of cases.

A replication and extension of these two studies has recently been provided by the writer (Quay, 1964). The case histories of 115 institutionalized adolescent delinquents were rated on a check list containing, among others, the Jenkins and Glickman traits. Factor analysis revealed (see Table 5-3) that three factors, labeled "unsocialized-psychopathic," "neurotic-disturbed," and "sub-cultural-socialized," accounted for most of the variance. A fourth factor, called "incompetent-immature," was also found although it accounted for relatively little of the variance.

Hart, Jenkins, Axelrod, and Sperling (1943) studied a sample (58 per cent Negro, 42 per cent white) of 300 institutionalized males ranging in age from 12 to 15 for whom extensive case records had been prepared by mental health personnel and other institution staff. After preliminary study, twenty-five traits and behaviors were selected for analysis and Ss histories searched so that the presence or absence of each of the twenty-five variables could be rated for each boy.

The first factorial analysis was made by a method which the authors refer to as a "directed analysis" (p. 195). This analysis resulted first in the identification of a factor labeled "group stealing" which was composed of the variables of cooperative stealing, aggressive stealing, gang activity, and, to a lesser extent, the traits of submissiveness and destructiveness. A second factor was then extracted which was labeled "temper-assault" and was composed of temper tantrums, assaultive tendencies, emotional instability, negativism, inferiority feeling, overaggressiveness, and, to a lesser degree, leadership distractiveness, and attention-getting behavior.

At this point both the directed analysis and the more well-known centroid method were applied in extracting additional factors. At the same time rotation procedures, which result in correlated factors, were employed. Needless to say, interpretation at this point becomes difficult since alternative factors with different compositions are possible. Factor three, now correlated with the temper-assault factor as

TABLE 5-3. ROTATED FACTOR MATRIX
From Quay (1964)

Variable	Factor				
	I	II	III	IV	h²
1. Assaultive *	.14	.54	−.16	−.03	.34
2. Has bad companions **	.59	.06	−.02	−.08	.36
3. Seclusive ***	−.38	−.14	.07	.08	.17
4. Engages in gang activities **	.58	−.04	−.16	−.13	.33
5. Shy ***	−.33	−.11	.46	.04	.33
6. Engages in cooperative stealing **	.15	−.06	−.02	.41	.19
7. Quarrelsome	−.09	.43	−.12	−.20	.25
8. Loses interest quickly	−.05	−.05	−.08	.13	.03
9. Defies authority *	.14	.47	−.26	.06	.31
10. Engages in furtive stealing **	−.25	.18	−.15	.02	.12
11. Worries ***	−.13	−.07	.67	.04	.47
12. Engages in malicious mischief *	.00	.01	−.21	.06	.05
13. Habitually truant from school **	.23	.17	.04	.11	.09
14. Sensitive ***	−.04	.13	.70	−.01	.51
15. Unable to cope with complex world	.02	.04	.06	.55	.30
16. Timid	−.17	−.09	.59	.15	.41
17. Inadequate guilt feelings *	−.10	.14	−.27	−.14	.12
18. Habitually truant from home **	.27	−.27	−.21	.42	.37
19. Stays out late at night **	.48	−.05	−.26	.25	.36
20. Irritable	.03	.61	.10	.00	.32
21. Accepted by delinquent subgroup	.63	−.15	−.09	−.32	.53
22. Verbally aggressive, impudent	−.04	.56	−.19	.00	.35
23. Strong allegiance to selected peers	.36	.13	−.07	−.29	.24
24. Incompetent, immature	−.20	.08	.02	.36	.17
25. Feels persecuted, others unfair	.16	.49	.00	.15	.29
26. Has anxiety over own behavior	−.23	−.07	.42	.01	.23
27. Callous, little concern for others	.16	.16	−.26	−.06	.12
28. Unable to profit by praise or punishment	−.28	.31	−.31	−.03	.27
29. Suspicious	−.12	.00	−.19	−.12	.06

* Appears in Hewitt and Jenkin's Unsocialized Aggressive cluster.
** Appears in Hewitt and Jenkin's Socialized Delinquent cluster.
*** Appears in Hewitt and Jenkin's Overinhibited cluster.

a function of the oblique rotation, was called "ego-compensation" and was composed of attention-getting behavior, overaggressiveness, bravado, passive homosexuality, inferiority feelings, active homosexuality, enuresis, and negativism. A fourth factor, named "street gang," was made up of staying out late at night, gang activity, truancy, and furtive stealing. In regard to this factor the authors report that "it is distinct from the delinquent gang activity reflected in group stealing, and inspection of the original matrix indicates it would have appeared as a distinct factor had the centroid method been used throughout" (p. 197). The fifth factor was labeled "aggressiveness" and was composed of the presence of aggressiveness but the absence of passive homosexuality and furtive stealing if one interprets the solution provided by the directed analysis. If the centroid results are preferred, this factor is composed of the presence of aggressive stealing, active homosexuality, furtive stealing, and inferiority feelings. A final factor was labeled "leadership" and was composed of the traits of leadership on the positive pole and seclusiveness and destructiveness on the negative.

Unfortunately, this study does not represent the best use of the factor analytic method. As it stands it would appear that the clusters of "unsocialized," "socialized," and "disturbed" defined in the previous studies have their counterparts in "temper assault," "group stealing," and "ego-compensation." The additional three factors are less easily interpreted, but they might well have been collapsed into these first three had a centroid or principal axis method been used throughout. It seems legitimate to conclude, however, that this study is generally confirmatory of the earlier studies if one assumes comparability of factors on the basis of seeming similarity of their component variables.

Reiss (1952) has approached the problem of the isolation of subtypes and the discovery of the correlates of these subtypes in a different way. From the analysis of case history records, psychiatrists and social workers classified subjects into one of three categories, the categories apparently having been chosen a priori. Category one was that of the relatively integrated delinquent who was described as an "adolescent with relatively integrated personal controls who in all probability will become a mature adult." The second subtype was labeled the delinquent with markedly weak ego controls who was viewed as having low self-esteem and manifesting insecurity or as being highly aggressive and hostile. Group three was referred to as the delinquent with relatively defective superego controls and was described as failing to internalize the social controls of middle class society, and as experiencing little guilt over their delinquent acts. Following the classification of Ss, various social indices were examined for their possible differential relationships with the three subtypes.

Over 100 comparisons were made, and many significant relationships emerged which tended to further characterize the subtypes. Weak ego delinquents were found to reside less frequently in the high delinquency areas as compared to the other two groups; to be more apt to still be in school, to be less likely to have foreign-born fathers, to be more withdrawn from social participation, and to be more likely to be solitary offenders. This pattern of associated variables suggests that the weak ego or emotionally disturbed delinquent is more likely to come from an area of less social disorganization and to be less of a participant in the delinquent peer culture; in short, his delinquencies seem likely to be a function of personality maladjustment which is being manifested in acting-out behavior.

On the other hand, the defective superego delinquent was found less often in the settled residential areas, was less likely than the defective ego type to still be in school, was more apt to have a foreign-born father, more likely to have come from a home in which the father was absent but siblings present, and was more frequently a gang member. This group then seemed to typify the lower class delinquent whose delinquencies reflect either the lack of identification with middle class standards, or the direct participation in a culture with values opposed to those of the middle class, or both.

Finally, the well-integrated delinquent was more likely to have achieved some high school education, more likely than the weak ego to be employed if school had been terminated, less likely to be from a home broken by separation, desertion, or divorce, and less likely to be from a home characterized by marked conflicts. This group also appeared more likely to be older (15-16) at first court contact and to be less often a recidivist.

This study, like that of Hewitt and Jenkins, suffers from the unknown reliability of both the case history data and the judgments made from them. While the subtypes evolved bear considerable resemblance to those isolated statistically in previous research, it is, of course, quite possible that knowledge of just this previous research may have influenced the judges in their category definitions. Then, too, as Reiss himself points out (p. 711), the relationships between the social indices and the psychological types may have been inflated because of the possible use of these very indices by the judges in assigning Ss to the categories. Methodological considerations notwithstanding, this study represents another contribution to our understanding of the differences between delinquents and is another link in the chain of evidence suggesting that a meaningful analysis of the delinquency phenomena must take into account the presence of subgroups within the population of delinquents.

Analysis of responses to questionnaire

Another approach to the problem has been taken by Peterson and Quay and their collaborators (Peterson, Quay, and Cameron, 1959; Quay, Peterson, and Consalvi, 1960; Tiffany, Peterson, and Quay, 1961; Peterson, Quay, and Tiffany, 1961). Concerned with the unreliability of case history data, they have sought to discover personality and behavioral dimensions associated with delinquency through the analysis of the responses of delinquents to questionnaires whose component items have been empirically shown to be related to delinquency.

In the first study (Peterson, Quay, and Cameron, 1959), two questionnaires (Gough and Peterson, 1956; Quay and Peterson, 1958) were administered to 116 institutionalized delinquents and 115 high school students who had been equated for age and area of residence. The items were intercorrelated, and fifteen factors were extracted by the complete centroid method. Judgments based on Tucker's function and relative contributions to total variance led to the exclusion of ten of the factors. Two rotations were performed: an orthogonal and an oblique. Comparison of the results indicates that the orthogonal rotation, accomplished according to the quartimax program for the electronic computer, was essentially identical to the oblique solution which was, in part, visually directed. Because of the simplicity and unbiased nature of the orthogonal solution, it was presented in their results.

The first factor was composed of items implying the presence of a tough, amoral, rebellious attitude coupled with an impulsivity and an open distrust of both social institutions and other people. This factor was labeled "psychopathic delinquency." The elements of the second factor also implied impulsive acting-out, but these elements were accompanied by items suggesting the presence of remorse, tension, guilt, and depression. This factor was considered a manifestation of neurotic acting-out. A third factor consisted entirely of items relating to a history of dissension in the family. The fourth factor was much less easy to interpret; however, the items did suggest a feeling of incompetence and pervasive failure, and this factor was tentatively entitled "inadequacy." Factor five was also less straightforward, but appeared to be related most closely to a history of scholastic maladjustment.

A follow-up study (Quay, Peterson, and Consalvi, 1960) sought to further explore the meaning of the three personality factors by relating scores on them to other variable thought to be associated. In a sample of 170 consecutive admissions to a training school, the psychopathy factor was found to have low but significant positive relationships with commitment for crime against the person, recidivism, problem behavior while incarcerated, and longer institutionalization. In another sample of ninety-three boys in a different institution, the neurotic delinquency factor related only to the children's form of the manifest anxiety scale while the psychopathy factor was unrelated to this variable. While neither psychopathy nor neuroticism was related to intelligence, the factor which has been tentatively labeled "inadequacy" showed a low (−.23) but statistically significant negative relationship. The results of this study were interpreted as confirmatory of the interpretation which had been given the factors and gave impetus to a more ambitious study.

The larger study (Peterson, Quay, and Tiffany, 1961) involved the analysis of additional questionnaire items with demonstrated relationships to delinquency. Four hundred six subjects were used, about equally divided between institutionalized delinquency and high school students, and also approximately equally divided between the Midwest and middle South. Items selected for analysis came from a number of sources: the fifty-nine items comprising the factors identified previously with nine additional items hypothesized to measure the inadequacy dimension; the items comprising the Personal Index (Loofbourow and Keys, 1933); a selected group of items from the KD Proneness Scale (Kvaraceus, 1950); thirty-three items from the MMPI related to delinquency (Hathaway and Monachesi, 1957); and 121 items developed in a program of research with young offenders in the U.S. Navy (Hanley, 1954).

These items were organized into four separate "tests" and were administered to the sample noted previously. Since it was not possible to factor a matrix as large as would have been provided by the intercorrelations of the entire set of items, each test was first factored independently. Then these factors were rotated and interpreted, factor scores were calculated for these first order factors, these factor scores were intercorrelated over the entire subject sample, and this matrix of intercorrelations was factor-analyzed.

Results were surprisingly straightforward and consistent. Most of the "tests" contained factors independently labeled "neuroticism" and "psychopathy," as well as those factors appearing to relate to a background of delinquent activity. In the higher order analysis the factors in the individual "tests" aligned themselves, without exception, in accordance with their independently assigned labels. This second factor study indicated that most of the variance in a wide

TABLE 5-4. ROTATED FACTOR LOADINGS WITH LOADINGS FROM OTHER STUDIES FOR COMPARISON *

From Quay & Quay (1965)

Factors

Peterson's 5th and 6th Grades — Variable	Quay's Adolescent Delinquents I	II	h²	Quay's Preadolescent Delinquents I	II	III	h²	Peterson's 5th and 6th Grades I	II	7th Grade I	II	III	8th Grade I	II	III
Restless	12	63	40	15	70	-04	51	20	70	14	46	37	03	44	04
Attention seeking	22	48	28	19	61	-08	42	02	76	-07	70	20	01	49	-09
Inability to have fun	19	-27	11	03	-15	31	12	48	-09	60	23	22	39	-12	10
Self-conscious	55	-22	35	-11	00	54	30	63	16	48	-05	39	59	-08	00
Disruptive	14	64	43	21	70	-12	56	11	76	-05	77	11	00	67	15
Feelings of inferiority	66	01	43	17	-07	57	36	62	17	47	05	29	65	06	05
Boisterousness	07	60	36	15	60	-03	39	-09	68	-14	71	18	00	69	08
Preoccupation	52	13	29	62	-04	21	43	41	37	60	14	28	18	-21	48
Shyness	42	-35	31	00	-42	38	31	51	-13	54	-28	13	59	-27	08
Withdrawal	55	-11	31	12	-18	15	07	60	05	67	-06	04	41	-34	27
Short attention span	25	59	41	56	44	11	51	29	60	11	59	28	19	37	55
Lack of confidence	59	-13	36	22	-17	63	47	58	16	66	12	30	57	03	22
Inattentive	21	64	45	58	46	-08	54	28	69	24	64	18	22	50	52
Easily flustered	41	04	16	02	14	34	13	58	24	55	19	46	60	21	25
Lack of interest	47	44	42	48	-02	-02	23	28	51	49	49	-02	29	-03	47
Reticence				08	-23	18	09	41	14				14	-04	25
Laziness in school	33	57	42	59	22	-15	41	31	37	20	55	00	09	24	66
Irresponsibility	38	67	58	51	29	00	34	20	65	34	75	00			
Daydreaming	48	32	34	57	13	20	38	47	49	70	08	26	-07	41	50
Disobedience	01	58	34	22	62	00	43	11	86	11	74	00	-03	64	06
Uncooperativeness				25	36	-07	19	21	71	15	74	01	-04	59	13
Aloofness	13	-27	09	20	-32	22	18	31	05	29	-01	02	20	-30	27
Passive, suggestible	12	47	23	38	13	14	18	30	52	21	47	30	28	12	27
Hyperactivity	-16	48	25	-01	54	08	29	03	49	03	37	53	-05	60	09
Distractibility	09	62	40	36	59	-11	48	26	72	30	34	62	03	46	53
Impertinence	13	47	24	11	33	07	12	08	76	21	62	29	-16	57	02
Lethargy	47	06	22	27	-17	02	10	43	31	62	22	-05	29	-16	58
Nervous, jittery	11	26	07	-14	28	35	22	26	50	42	22	43	40	39	17

variety of questionnaire items could be understood on a function of three underlying dimensions: the psychopathic or basically asocial, the neurotic or disturbed, and the dimension called "delinquent background," suggesting the acceptance of delinquent mores without personality maladjustment. Needless to say, parallels between these dimensions and those elucidated in the research utilizing case history analysis are evident.

Analysis of Behavior Ratings

In two recent studies (Quay, 1964a, 1966), behavior ratings of institutionalized male delinquents have been subjected to factor analysis. In both studies a check list of problem behavior was filled out on each subject by cottage officers and/or academic teachers. Together, these Ss covered an age range of 11 through 18. In both studies three factors clearly emerged: psychopathy, neuroticism or emotional disturbance, and inadequacy-immaturity. It should be noted that the problem check list, first analyzed by Peterson (1961), does not contain items relevant to subcultural or gang delinquency.

Since the same behavioral check list has been studied in samples of public school students (Peterson, 1961; Quay and Quay, 1965), it is possible to compare the factor structure between delinquent samples

TABLE 5-5. COEFFICIENTS OF FACTOR SIMILARITY FOR LOADINGS IN TABLE 5-4 ("Validity" values italicized) From Quay & Quay (1965)

	Seventh Grade		Eighth Grade		
	I	II	I	II	III
	Person-ality	Con-duct	Imma-turity	Con-duct	Person-ality
Eighth Grade:					
Immaturity (I)	.67	.70			
Conduct (II)	.09	.83			
Personality (III)	.70	−.15			
Peterson's Fifth and Sixth Grades:					
Personality (I)	.91	.23	.61	.13	.80
Conduct (II)	.50	.91	.75	.88	.12
Quay's Adolescent Delinquents:					
Neurotic (I)	.91	.20	.60	.02	.75
Psychopathic (II)	.42	.93	.72	.84	.00
Immature (III)	.55	.58	.44	.55	.58
Quay's Preadolescent Delinquents:					
Neurotic (I)	.84	.08	.27	−.09	.72
Psychopathic (II)	.10	.88	.45	.93	−.06
Immature (III)	.70	.56	.89	.29	.26

and "normal" grammar and junior high school pupils. Tables 5-4 and 5-5, taken from Quay and Quay (1965), indicate the high degree of similarity which is present. Certainly these basic dimensions of problem behavior are not the exclusive property of institutionalized delinquents. Rather, the evidence is that the average scores on the dimensions are simply higher when adjudicated delinquents are sampled. This fact should be considered before delinquents are thought of as a group apart from "problem" children not actually afoul of the law.

Personality Dimensions versus Personality Types

Miller (1958) has emphasized the need to distinguish between the concept of a pattern of traits and a typology of persons who possess a given pattern of traits. He has noted that the existence of such a given pattern of traits as might be discovered through factor analysis does not mean that there has to be a group of individuals who can be characterized as being of a given "type" because of their possession of this one particular pattern of traits and no other. Thus, the existence of such a cluster of traits as Hewitt and Jenkins (1946) labeled "unsocialized aggressive" does not necessarily mean that there can be found a group of delinquents who possess all or a majority of the traits in the pattern and none or only a small minority of those traits characterizing other patterns.

Miller's experimental work centered on an analysis of specific traits which had been either explicitly or implicitly hypothesized to differentiate the three "types" of delinquents (unsocialized aggressive, socialized delinquent, and emotionally disturbed) elucidated by Jenkins' researches already noted above. Hypotheses were as follows: the "socialized" delinquent would be impulsive, but not hostile or lacking a sense of guilt and would show a need for exhibition, have poor reality contact, and deny interpersonal problems; the unsocialized aggressive will be impulsive, hostile, and lacking a sense of guilt, will show need for exhibition, have poor reality contact, and deny interpersonal problems; the "emotionally disturbed" would show strong underlying hostility, would not be impulsive, would have poor reality contact, deny interpersonal problems, and have no exhibitionistic needs.

Subjects were selected by the use of a behavioral rating scale made up of twelve items representing each of the three behavioral types. Three hundred forty-three institutionalized delinquents were rated by their cottage officers or counselors. Multiple ratings of subsamples were obtained to check the rater's reliability; coefficents averaged .76. A boy was selected if his rating score for a single type was in the upper 27 per cent of the entire group while at the same time his score for the other two patterns was below the median. In addition to thirty-two "socialized," thirty-one "emotionally disturbed," and nineteen "unsocialized aggressive" selected by this procedure, seventeen boys having scores in the upper 27 per cent for both "socialized" and "unsocialized aggressive" traits were used as an additional group and labeled "socialized-aggressive." The four groups appeared to be equated for age and IQ although no significance tests for the differences were provided by Miller.

In order to test his hypothesis, Miller administered a number of personality measures including a group TAT, the Sc and F scales of the MMPI, a story-completion test designed to measure guilt, the Edwards Personal Preference Schedule, and the Impulsivity Scale of Gough's California Psychological Inventory.

For an initial analysis, groups were compared on all variables by means of an analysis of variance with subsequent "t" tests. Significant F ratios (.05 level) were found for the variables of hostility, impulsivity, reality contact (Sc and F scales), and Need Aggression. In amount of hostility, the "unsocialized aggressive" were significantly higher than both the "socialized" and "socialized aggressive" but failed to exceed the emotionally disturbed group. The latter exceeded the "socialized" but not the "socialized aggressive." In impulsivity the "unsocialized" exceeded the "socialized" but not the other two groups, while the disturbed also exceeded the "socialized." For the MMPI Sc scale the "unsocialized" exceeded all but the disturbed while the disturbed themselves exceeded the "socialized." On MMPI F the "unsocialized" exceeded the "socialized" and the "socialized aggressive." In measured Need Aggression the "unsocialized" exceeded the "socialized" and the "disturbed" with no other comparisons significant. Thus, as Miller points out, the "unsocialized aggressive" is the most divergent group in manifesting a pattern of hostility, impulsivity, poor reality contact, and Need Aggression. However, with the exception of Need Aggression, the disturbed group shows the same patterns of elevation of these variables when compared to the two socialized groups. Only on Need Aggression was the unsocialized group differentiated from the disturbed. The results, to this point, suggest the relative independence of the unsocialized and unsocialized groups but fail to provide support for hypothesized differences between the unsocialized and the disturbed.

In an additional analysis Miller investigated the interrelationships among the personality variables themselves in order to investigate the possibility that they might all be measures of a single factor. Applying a method of analysis which Miller (p. 16) refers to as ". . . cluster analysis, a technique based on Thurston's (sic) group method." Three oblique factors were obtained. The first factor was characterized primarily by impulsivity, Sc, and F; the second factor by hostility, absence of neurotic guilt, lack of expressed guilt, and lack of need achievement; while factor three loaded most highly on insecurity and admission of problems. Information relative to the amount of obliqueness, i.e., the correlations between the three factors, was not presented.

Miller interpreted his results as generally failing to confirm his hypothesis relative to the expected differences between the three types. He also concluded (p. 19) that the "only two distinct personality patterns are needed to account for the four groups." The first pattern is the "socialized" personality pattern which shows good reality contact, low impulsivity, little hostility or Need Agression. The second pattern Miller labels "disturbed-aggressive" and "emphasizes poor reality contact, strong underlying hostility, impulsivity, and some need aggression."

Actually Miller's results have little bearing on the existence or nonexistence of Jenkins' three "types," and his preliminary consideration of the traits versus types problem was disregarded in his discussion of his results. Rather, his results indicate only that groups of subjects selected on the basis of extreme scores on certain sets of traits are not differentiated from one another on the basis of other measures of personality. The fact that groups considered representative of trait syndromes do not differ from one another on three other measured attributes does not disprove the existence of a "type." To disprove the existence of a "type" it is necessary to show that people, in sufficient number to be useful, cannot be found who are like one another by virtue of their possession of the traits said to characterize the type. Research specifically relevant to this problem will be discussed below. In fact, Miller's ability to find boys characterized by traits representing one of Hewitt and Jenkins' three clusters and not the others is actually evidence for the partial validity of the scheme.

The problem of how delinquents might be grouped in terms of an empirically derived trait system was first considered experimentally by Tiffany, Peterson, and Quay (1961). In this study 103 institutionalized males were presented with a set of items which were known on the basis of prior research (Peterson, Quay, and Cameron, 1959) to be measures of three personality factors related to delinquency and were asked to Q-sort these items; this procedure allows correlations to be computed between Ss rather than between items or tests. A factor analysis of this type matrix results in factors composed of Ss similar by virtue of having responded similarly to the items on the Q-sort.

Results were on the whole unrevealing. "Ss did not coalesce into types. They distributed themselves diffusely and normally over the four-dimension space defined by the vectors. However useful a typology might be, the behavior of these delinquents did not permit non-arbitrary classification" (p. 21). In essence, it was not possible to locate enough Ss who loaded highly enough on only one factor to permit a meaningful interpretation in terms of types.

A similar analysis was made by Bowen (1960). His Ss were ninety-four men confined to a military stockade whose mean age was just over 21. The method was identical to that of the Tiffany et al. (1961) study. The results were also identical: the presence of a typology sufficient to account for an appreciable number of subjects in the delinquent population was not demonstrated.

The results of these studies suggest that it is imperative that such constructs as unsocialized aggressive, neurotic delinquent, and weak ego be considered as dimensions of personality associated with delinquency rather than as types of delinquents. It is true that individuals can be found whose characteristics are quite predominately those of a single dimension. But these individuals will be the exception and should be recognized as such.

Various research approaches in the development of dimensions of behavior related to delinquency have apparently produced results of considerable comparability. It seems likely that delinquent males can now be most meaningfully studied within a four-dimensional framework. The first dimension is comprised of a constellation of attitudes, opinions, and behavior tendencies which reflect a basic lack of socialization and emotional rapport with others. The second dimension also involves overtly hostile behavior, but here this behavior is accompanied by feelings of guilt, anxiety, unhappiness, and concern. This dimension seems closely akin to what has been referred to in adults as alloplastic neuroticism. The third dimension involves the acceptance of standards, values, and ways of behaving which are at variance with the legal code and with the mores of the larger community but quite in keeping with the subculture in which many delinquents find themselves. This dimension does not represent a true lack of socialization—only a deficiency in socialization from the reference point of the middle class culture. Neither does it appear that emotional disturbance, either subjective or objective, is involved. Finally, there is a dimension of inadequacy, immaturity, and general inability to cope with complex situations. This constellation of characteristics is less well documented and certainly accounts for a much smaller portion of the variance in the personalities of delinquents than do the other three dimensions.

While we have assumed that research based on the ratings of behavior as inferred from case histories and research based on the analysis of questionnaire data had produced equivalent results, some caution must be voiced. As the literature so well reveals (Becker, 1960; Cattell, 1961), comparability of factor structure across data media can only be assumed until factor scores across these media have been empirically related.

CONCLUSIONS

While some studies of heterogeneous groups of delinquents have produced interesting and conceptually meaningful results, it now appears that greater rewards will come from the detailed study of more homogeneous subgroups as these may be isolated by statistical means. The research in primary personality dimensions has now provided us with meaningful ways to order or to group delinquents, and it appears that seeking the causes and correlates of these dimensions will be more fruitful than attempting to study *the* "delinquent." In fact, many promising leads, such as are reflected in the studies of time orientation, responsivity to social reward, and perceptual-motor functioning, may become even more meaningful when the sample of delinquents being studied can be more precisely selected. Certainly it is time to stop considering delinquents as anything like psychologically homogeneous.

References

Barndt, R. J., & Johnson, D. M. (1955) Time orientation in delinquents. *J. abnorm. soc. Psychol.*, **51**, 343-345.

Becker, W. C. (1960) The matching of behavior rating and questionnaire personality factors. *Psychol. Bull.*, **57**, 201-212.

Bowen, T. W. (1960) A typological analysis of conduct disorders. Unpublished master's thesis, Vanderbilt Univer.

Cattell, R. B. (1961) Theory of situational, instruments, second order, and refraction factors in personality structure research. *Psychol. Bull.*, **58**, 160-174.

Dahlstrom, W. G., & Welsh, G. S. (1960) *An MMPI Handbook.* Minneapolis: Univer. of Minn. Press.

Davids, A., Kidder, Catherine, & Reich, M. (1962) Time orientation in male and female juvenile delinquents. *J. abnorm. soc. Psychol.*, **64**, 239-240.

Dinitz, S., Reckless, W. C., & Kay, Barbara (1958) A self gradient among potential delinquents. *J. crim. Law Criminol. police Sci.*, **49**, 230-233.

Dinitz, S., Scarpitti, F. R., & Reckless, W. C. (1962) Delinquency vulnerability: a cross group and longitudinal analysis. *Amer. sociol. Rev.*, **27**, 515-517.

Gough, H. G. (1956) *Manual for the California Psychological Inventory.* Palo Alto, Calif.: Consult. Psychol. Press.

Gough, H. G. (1960) Theory and measurement of socialization. *J. consult. Psychol.*, **24**, 23-30.

Gough, H. G., & Peterson, D. R. (1954) The identification and measurement of predispositional factors in crime and delinquency. *J. consult. Psychol.*, **16**, 207-212.

Hanley, C. H. (1954) *An inventory of personal opinions.* First Technical Report, Rehab. Research, U. S. Naval Retraining Command, Camp Elliott, San Diego, Calif.

Hart, H. H., Jenkins, R. L., Axelrod, S., & Sperling, P. I. (1943) Multiple factor analysis of traits of delinquent boys. *J. soc. Psychol.*, **17**, 191-201.

Hathaway, S. R., & Monachesi, E. D. (1953) *Analyzing and predicting juvenile delinquency with the MMPI.* Minneapolis: Univer. of Minn. Press.

Hathaway, S. R., & Monachesi, E. D. (1957) The personalities of predelinquent boys. *J. crim. Law Criminol. police Sci.*, **48**, 149-163.

Hathaway, S. R., Monachesi, E. D., & Young, L. A. (1960) Delinquency rates and personality. *J. crim. Law Criminol. police Sci.*, **50**, 433-440.

Hewitt, L. E., & Jenkins, R. L. (1946) *Fundamental patterns of maladjustment: the dynamics of their origin.* Springfield: State of Illinois, 1946.

Jenkins, R. L., & Glickman, Sylvia (1947) Patterns of personality organization among delinquents. *Nerv. Child*, **6**, 329-339.

Jones, D. D., Livson, N. H., & Sarbin, T. R. (1955) Perceptual completion behavior in juvenile delinquents. *Percept. mot. Skills*, **5**, 141-146.

Kvaraceus, W. C. (1956) *Forecasting juvenile delinquency.* New York: World Book.

LeShan, L. I. (1952) Time orientation and social class. *J. abnorm. soc. Psychol.*, **47**, 589-592.

Loofbourow, G. C., & Keys, N. (1933) *The personal index.* Minneapolis: Educational Testing Bureau.

McDavid, J., & Schroeder, H. M. (1957) The interpretation of approval and disapproval by delinquent and non-delinquent adolescents. *J. Pers.*, **25**, 539-549.

Miller, R. C. (1958) *Personality patterns among delinquent behavioral types.* Washington, D. C.: Catholic Univer. Amer. Press.

Miller, W. B. (1959) Lower class culture as a generating milieu of going delinquency. *J. soc. Issues*, **14**, 5-19.

Mowrer, O. H., & Ullman, A. D. (1945) Time as a determinant in integrative learning. *Psychol. Rev.*, **52**, 61-90.

Nye, F. I., & Short, J. F., Jr. (1957) Scaling delinquent behavior. *Amer. sociol. Rev.*, **22**, 327-331

Pascal, G., & Suttell, Barbara (1951) *The Bender-Gestalt Test.* New York: Grune and Stratton.

Pesetsky, F. J. (1961) Variability in the meaning of delinquent behavior. Unpubl. Ph.D. Thesis, Vanderbilt University.

Peterson, D. R. (1961) Behavior problems of middle childhood. *J. consult. Psychol.*, **25**, 205-209.

Peterson, D. R., Quay, H. C., & Anderson, A. C. (1958) Extending the construct validity of a socialization scale. *J. consult. Psychol.*, **23**, 182.

Peterson, D. R., Quay, H. C., & Cameron, G. R. (1959) Personality and background factors in juvenile delinquency as inferred from questionnaire responses. *J. consult. Psychol.*, **23**, 395-399.

Peterson, D. R., Quay, H. C., & Tiffany, T. L. (1961) Personality factors related to juvenile delinquency. *Child Develpm.*, **32**, 355-372.

Quay, H. C., & Blumen, L. (1963) Factor dimensions of delinquent behavior. *J. soc. Psychol.*, **61**, 273-277.

Quay, H. C., & Hunt, W. A. (1965) Psychopathy, neuroticism and verbal conditioning: a replication and extension. *J. consult. Psychol.* In press; will appear in 1965.

Quay, H. C., & Peterson, D. R. (1958) A brief scale for juvenile delinquency. *J. clin. Psychol.*, **14**, 139-142.

Quay, H. C., Peterson, D. R., & Consalvi, C. (1960) The interpretation of three personality factors in juvenile delinquency. *J. consult. Psychol.,* **24,** 555.

Quay, H. C., & Quay, Lorene C. (1965) Behavior problems in early adolescence. *Child developm.* In press.

Quay, H. C. (1964) Dimensions of personality in delinquent boys as inferred from the factor analysis of case history data. *Child Developm.,* **35,** 479-484.

Quay, H. C. (1964a) Personality dimensions in delinquent males as inferred from the factor analysis of behavior ratings. *J. res. crime & del.,* **1,** 33-37.

Quay, H. C. (1966) Personality dimensions in preadolescent delinquent boys. *Educ. Psychol. Measmt.* In press, will appear in 1966.

Randolph, Mary H., Richardson, H., & Johnson, R. C. (1961) A comparison of social and solitary male delinquents. *J. consult. Psychol.,* **2,** 293-295.

Reckless, W. C., Dinitz, S., & Kay, Barbara (1957) The self-component in potential delinquency and potential nondelinquency. *Amer. sociol. Rev.,* **22,** 566-570.

Reiss, A. J. (1952) Social correlates of psychological types of delinquency. *Amer. sociol. Rev.,* **17,** 710-718.

Scarpitti, F. R., Murray, Ellen, Dinitz, S., & Reckless, W. C. (1960) The "good" boy in a high delinquency area: four years later. *Amer. sociol. Rev.,* **25,** 555-558.

Schuessler, K. F., & Cressey, D. R. (1950) Personality characteristics of criminals. *Amer. J. Sociol.,* **55,** 476-484.

Scott, J. F. (1959) Two dimensions of delinquent behavior. *Amer. sociol. Rev.,* **24,** 240-243.

Siegman, A. W. (1960) The relationship between future time perspective, time estimation, and impulse control in a group of young offenders and in a control group. *J. consult. Psychol.,* **25,** 470-475.

Street, R. F. (1931) A. Gestalt Completion Test. *Teach. Coll. Contr. Educ.,* No. 481.

Tiffany, T. L., Peterson, D. R., & Quay, H. C. (1961) Types and traits in the study of juvenile delinquency. *J. clin. Psychol.,* **17,** 19-24.

Wattenberg, W. W., & Balistrieri, J. J. (1950) Gang membership and juvenile misconduct. *Amer. sociol. Rev.,* **15,** 744-752.

Wattenberg, W. W., & Balistrieri, J. J. (1952) Automobile theft: a "favored group" delinquency. *Amer. J. sociol.,* **57,** 569-574.

Wirt, R. D., & Briggs, P. F. (1959) Personality and environmental factors in the development of delinquency. *Psychol. Monogr.,* **73** (Whole No. 485).

Wylie, Ruth C. (1961) *The self concept.* Lincoln, Neb.: Univer. of Neb. Press.

Zolik, E. S. (1958) A comparison of the Bender-Gestalt reproductions of delinquents and nondelinquents. *J. clin. Psychol.,* **14,** 24-26.

6

Prediction

Peter F. Briggs and Robert D. Wirt

Introduction

The prediction of delinquency can be seen as the first step in gaining control of juvenile delinquency. While there has been a trend in recent research and action programs to approach delinquency control without reference to prediction, the earlier studies emphasized the prediction and then the control measures. Prediction is viewed as an urgently needed first step toward delinquency control.

The emphasis on delinquency control comes from the desire at all levels of society to change the behavior patterns of nonconforming individuals in order to further general standards of conduct. Business groups of the past emphasized the work ethic and are presently echoing the importance of school achievement. The educators of the past emphasized the importance of citizenship and now, along with the business groups, emphasize achievement. Citizens' organizations press for opportunities which will enable youth to maximize their poential, to free themselves from adverse influences, and, at times, to rescue themselves from the past. All of these interested groups have taken strong action to eradicate grossly nonconforming behavior, much of which is conveniently designated antisocial. Parents as members of a social class are, within their own class, concerned with the preservation of their ideals. Static class groups resent the intrusion of other, generally lower, social class values. Upwardly mobile groups desire greater social flexibility and the expression of the dominant class values in their children. Parental concern for their children and the availability of certain goals should not be confused with the possibly conflicting nature of these goals.

170

History and political theory both emphasize the importance of youth and the importance that societies have attached to the preservation of their own values. Since Socrates was executed for the corruption of youth, insightful political theorists have never needed to further emphasize the vulnerability that society feels about tampering with the values of the younger generation.

While Plato and the early traditional philosophers attempted to stabilize and better society through the assignment of younger members to useful if not prescribed roles, other philosophers, developing their ideas in the context of social reform, have suggested the importance of the basic nature of man, such as in Rousseau's concept of the natural man. In the latter, perspective society is seen as the corruptor.

Without doubt, much of the impetus for predicting and controlling juvenile delinquency stems from the political forces that counter nonconformity in all established societies. The zealous revolutionaries of the early Bolshevik movement were the young members of Russian society. Indeed, many of their most heroic acts were performed by teen-agers. Even more dramatic, because of its visibility, was the importance of the youth group in the development of political power within Nazi Germany. The likeness of these early Brownshirts to the present-day street gangs is appalling.

Thus, delinquency control is really an age-old institution now clothed in the newest scientific garb. Delinquency control, or youth control, is joined in this position by the fight against the extreme nonconformity of "mental illness" and the more positive attempt to further "adjustment" that we see in the mental hygiene movement.

We are not suggesting that delinquency control or the other movements stemming from the needs in society for social conformity are, in fact, the same in their result as witch burning, political persecution, or confinement to the infamous Bedlam insane asylum of the last century. Indeed not, for although society may have less tolerance for deviation and there may be greater resources to produce conformity, the new, if not revolutionary, balance in the arguments for social control of delinquency partakes of a new refrain which, like the Christian ethic, suggests that it is best for both youth and society to be preserved from delinquency. Although there is a suggestion that society knows best, this is really in line with the reward-oriented culture into which we have entered. Our society offers *less* in reward to those who follow grossly antisocial paths. The revolution in direction then stems from the fact that greater social reward does follow nondelinquent behavior, and that youth following such paths are confirmed in their expectation that it generally "pays off" to prefer socially acceptable behavior.

To have forsaken the early political and philosophical theories of the origins of delinquency (or sin) and to undertake a scientific enterprise in understanding, predicting, and controlling youthful behavior is, indeed, a social revolution. The revolutionary aspect is in the belief that rewards offered for behavior will, in fact, both justify and preserve the system. Orwell in *1984* (1949) and Huxley in *Brave New World* (1932) have exploited and exposed the innocence of this argument. Rogers and Skinner (1956) have attracted considerable attention in their attempts to resolve differences concerning the ethical issue of behavior control. In the meantime, we should not overlook the fact that science is the agent of the culture: a great percentage of behavioral research is actually sponsored by government.

If prediction and control of juvenile delinquency are successful, then delinquency may be a phenomenon that, but for present scientific attention, may be just a passing social pest. On the other hand, it is possible that juvenile delinquency is only the name for the yet uncontrolled behavior of youth which will change only in form and cause, as societies and parents differently affect their youngsters.

Factors Relating to Delinquency

Prediction, in the sophisticated sense, can be distinguished from prediction in the sense of "hunch," of "wise observation," of "common sense," and of "rule by thumb" that is often—sometimes of necessity—used in administrative decision-making. These gross observations, as Robison (1960) points out, sometimes fit one or another particular theory of etiology and then are assumed to be explanations of delinquency. These causal theories vary in their levels of observation and in the degree to which interaction effects are taken into account. Some examples of theories and observations which are quasi-predictive are discussed below:

The Individual

Observations concerning the individual range from speculation about the contribution of hereditary factors to delinquency (McCord and McCord [1956], Cleckley [1941], Mullins [1945]) and gross morphology (Lombroso [1918], Goring [1919], Hooton [1939], Sheldon [1949]) through more careful physiological studies (Lindner

[1942-1943], Lykken [1956], Stafford-Clark and Ponds [1951]) and studies of neurological functioning (Knott & Gottlieb [1943], Ostrow and Ostrow [1946]) to those of individual differences in intelligence (Merrill [1947], Metfessel and Lovell [1942], Goldfarb [1945]) and personality (Friedlander [1945], Bettleheim [1950], Johnson and Szurek [1952], Aichorn [1935], and Bennett [1960]).

Each of these and many other studies have come up with relationships, sometimes of statistical significance, which show an association between one or more personal physical or psychological characteristics and antisocial behavior. Thus, while Mullins (1945) can argue that families with a history of criminal behavior tend to produce more than their share of delinquent offspring, McCord and McCord (1956) point out that these tendencies do not follow the line of closest blood kinship. In the earliest anthropometric studies of criminals, Lombroso (1918) found a high rate of stigmata, but Goring (1919) found no difference when he used a control group. Instead, he attributed the delinquent tendencies to defective intelligence. But Goldfarb (1945) asserts that the lower average intelligence is due to early deprivation, and Merrill (1947) reminds us that the range of intellect in delinquents overlaps the range of the general population and that we have more opportunity to observe the delinquency of those with low intellect. Sheldon *et al.* (1949) have related the mesomorphic body type to delinquent behavior, and Glueck and Glueck (1950) did indeed find more mesomorphs than any other type in their large sample. Yet, 40 per cent of their sample represented other varieties of physique, and we know that most muscular men are not in prison. There are studies by Lindner (1942) and by Lykken (1957) which suggest that some delinquents, especially those psychiatrically diagnosed as psychopathic, are physiologically underreactive to painful or anxiety-arousing stimuli. These findings and those by Stafford-Clark (1951) showing developmental anomalies and dysplasias at the morphological level have led some investigators to posit a theory of physiological immaturity as the etiologic basis for delinquency. In addition, the electroencephalographic studies of delinquents by Knott and Gottlieb (1943) and of Ostrow and Ostrow (1946) and others show patterns which Stafford-Clark (1951) believes are evidence of neurological immaturity. The data from all such studies come from highly select groups and do not account for the substantial incidence of similar findings in nondelinquent populations or substantial absence of such findings in the general delinquent population.

The Family

The parent-child relationship is viewed by most psychiatrists as *the* critical factor in the development of personality, including those who become delinquent. Friedlander (1945) emphasizes the failure of superego development in some (those who become delinquent) and its overdevelopment in others (those who become neurotic). Bennett's (1960) study of those differences contains findings which generally support Friedlander's position. Johnson and Szurek (1952) delimit the superego problem involved. Their construction provides for the development of holes in the superego which permit anti-social behavior to become manifest as a result of the parents' encouraging the child to act out their own unconscious rebellious attitudes. Aichorn (1935) emphasizes that the failure within the family resides in inappropriate affectional ties, rejection, or smothering love; Bettleheim (1950) notes that "love is not enough" to prevent nonconformity. Most of these theorists center their observations on mother-child relationships (e.g., Parsons, 1947), although Andry (1960) reminds us of the important role of fathers. All such clinical and statistical surveys of delinquent and delinquogenic families give important interpersonal data which appear to relate to the emergence of child delinquency. However, neither is there a general theory of the phenomenon nor does any one adequately explicate the behavior to be observed. They are more useful in planning individual treatment programs than in building useful indices of prediction. The more extended net of social influences in the development of delinquency is emphasized by some sociologists and anthropologists who take into account the force of culture as a determinant of nonconformity.

The Culture

When the focus of attention is upon the acts of an individual, Eissler (1949), for example, rightly points out that the values of the society in which they occur determine the interpretation of the behavior. Miller (1959) saw lower class delinquency as normal and a consequence of lower class training for life in that class. In explaining gang behavior, Cohen (1955) builds upon the observation that most delinquency is a lower class phenomenon. He sees the gang as providing the status that lower class adolescents cannot find in our middle class dominated society. They may add to each other's morale by adopting similarities of dress, for example, varying from the oversized "zoot" suit popular in the 1940's to the too-tight "ivy league" attire fancied by some gang members in the 1960's. But empirical studies (e.g., Wirt and Briggs, 1959) suggest that these fads reflect the mode of the general adolescent culture more clearly than any particular segments within it. Cloward and Ohlin (1960), building on Merton's (1957) theory, provide an understanding of delinquent behavior resulting from the barriers to opportunity for wealth and power among culturally deprived youth. These sociological explanations of delinquency are weakened by the occurrence of many nondelinquents in the same areas. Early efforts to measure delinquency (Robison, 1936) and recent efforts, such as those of Nye (1948), to detect the "unofficial" delinquent by self-report methods may make tests of these theories more practicable. As it stands, the fact seems to be that some conflict of generations becomes manifest in adolescence, and that this sometimes is generalized against the adult society, particularly by lower class boys and girls who lack opportunities for achievement. These findings do not, however, advance us very far in working out reliable prediction systems.

The Ecology

Even before Clifford Shaw's (1929) pioneering study which showed official delinquency rates to be high in areas which are changing from residential to business, the association of high delinquency rates to other indices of social disorder was known. Juvenile delinquency correlates with family disruption, with adult crime, with poverty, with disease. If demographic census data are available, it is not difficult to predict which areas of a city will have the highest delinquency rates, as Lander has shown. Robison points out that these ecological studies, as well as the personality studies of the Gluecks, attribute causality to certain empirically established relationships. This level of analysis does not account for what may be more fundamental determinants, such as social role (Linton, 1936), social class (Cohen, 1955), and social structure (Whyte, 1955), as well as the many variables discussed in the sections above. Such criticism is justified in terms of developing useful definitions of delinquency, useful theories of etiology, useful programs of treatment and prevention, but not for developing useful methods of prediction. Using such data, we do not have workable systems of prediction, yet correlations do exist which appear to carry valid variance. The difficulty in adapting them to practical prediction situations resides sometimes in the lack of clarity of definitions, sometimes in the differential magnitudes of their variances, sometimes in interaction effects, and in the differential base rates of their occurrence, power, and importance.

The danger in using data of the types discussed here in making administrative decisions of the types which teachers, judges, personnel officers, and others must make is that these power figures may assume that, because they know—or have heard—that certain factors co-vary with known rates of delinquency, the appearance of these factors is then sufficient to predict *individual* delinquency.

METHODOLOGICAL ISSUES

There are no present systems for the prediction of delinquency. The discussion of definition in the first chapter indicated the difficulties in obtaining a uniform group which might be studied and which might yield a *system* (qua system) for prediction of delinquent behavior. The first issue in prediction is the identification of a set of phenomena that has a unity of origin on the one hand and a unity of identity or identifiability on the other. In the discussion in the first chapter, certain kinds of behavior were excluded from the definition of delinquency because of medical, social, or other primary links to bodies of knowledge or explanation. It seems likely that the definition of delinquency in behavioral terms is not possible to date. As yet, certain conditions have to be ruled out in order to label an event as delinquent rather than psychotic, subcultural, and so on. Most simply, one should understand that the conditions underlying delinquency in their simplest form are those which are *necessary* and *sufficient* for its occurrence, as is the case in understanding any other phenomena. Such knowledge would constitute an adequate theory of the origins of delinquency. There are incomplete theories constituting midpositions in the understanding of delinquency. A theory may remain incomplete insofar as it emphasizes concepts which are related to delinquency, but which are not encompassing of any definable whole or which do not meet the necessary and sufficient conditions for the prediction of delinquency.

In the present state of incomplete knowledge, there must be concern for both the necessary and sufficient conditions for delinquency and for the actual concept or definition of delinquency itself. Studies aiming at understanding and predicting delinquency must constantly readjust definitions of delinquency to better denote and surround behavior which yields to explanation.

First, let us consider the problems of the language systems in which the definition occurs. Delinquency may be viewed as behavior of an antisocial nature. It may be viewed as a crime rate in a sociological sense. It may be viewed as a condition relating to the conscious and unconscious motivational systems as these terms are used in psychiatry. It is possible for any one of these levels to surround and define a set of events that would be accessible to explanation.

There is, however, an interesting problem of parochialism which may be evident in such attempts. Sociological concepts are not reducible to behavioral definitions. Neither of these is reducible to intrapsychic definitions. Each of these approaches defines a separate set of events, to some degree, and at the level of events translation is not complete. This should not be disturbing if explanation in the system meets the strict standards we have indicated. The second problem in parochialism is more complicated. Occasional efforts are seen to utilize a definition drawn from one body of knowledge and traditions for use by another discipline. Thus, although there need be no necessarily unsatisfactory result, it is still the unfortunate fact that a hierarchy of reduction systems from one branch of the behavioral sciences to another does not exist. Therefore, psychiatric explanations of psychological phenomena have tended to be unsatisfactory both within the context of explanation itself and as stimuli for further investigation. Multidisciplinary approaches seem to gain their strength only insofar as joint and interreducible systems of linguistic structure are developed. Thus, when translation may be made between sociological and psychological concepts, economy in definition may permit and encourage the use of concepts drawn from both fields in an explanatory system. If such translation does not exist, it remains obvious that insofar as the broad fields are to contribute explanatory power, it is not possible to gain strength in explanation using definitions within one system and explanations within another.

A second aspect of the definition problem which bears particularly in the prediction sphere concerns the question of severity of delinquency. This problem originates where the definition of delinquency is concerned, in part, with the degree to which an act is antisocial. If certain minimal behaviors are to be excluded and others are to be accepted, then the definition of severity within the context of delinquency becomes necessary. Some delinquent acts are apparently more severe than other delinquent acts. Raters, in reviewing such acts, have little difficulty in rating severity. Yet, such judgments are a study of the opinions of the rater rather than of the act. It is important to obtain a measure of severity in order to obtain a measure of delinquency itself, which then becomes a proper designata for a predictive system. It seems likely that severity, as it is presently used, is analogous to the relationship between *apparent size* of an object (a psychological phenomena) and *mass* (a physical phenomena). In physics the large object is not necessarily the one with the greater mass. Newtonian physics does not deal with apparent sizes of objects, but with mass. Any predictive system, such as Newtonian physics, had to reject definitions imbedded in the observer in order to develop adequate predictive power. Similarly, definitions of the severity of antisocial behavior must relate to the intrinsic qualities of the behavior rather than qualities of the observer.

The focus of prediction may be the individual, the neighborhood, the family, or the entire culture. Similarly, a treatment program may be set up to have an impact on the rate of delinquency among narrow classes of individuals (such as boys with certain personality traits), upon a neighborhood which may be deteriorated, on a family that shows problems, or on the culture. It is not necessary to focus on individuals within certain predictive or treatment systems. This will depend upon the content of the prediction and treatment systems.

It has been shown (Wirt and Briggs, 1959) that judged severity of crimes committed by adolescents varies from age to age. Thus, one would wonder whether a prediction of delinquency must specify crimes at a particular time. Presumably the explanatory system relating prediction factors and the behavior to be predicted must be considered. If the explanatory system is to be in the language of behavior, then it is only reasonable to expect the definition to encompass the behavior rather than the view that others might take of such behavior. Again, at another level, if the explanatory system is to be in the language of intrapsychic events, then the definition of delinquency which will seem most adequate should be at the level of motivation. Similarly, sociological definitions and behavioristic definitions will not match appropriately.

The concern with definition naturally leads to a question of how encompassing that definition should be. Although desirable, it is not likely that all antisocial behavior can be explained within the same system. The homogeneity of the actual behaviors encompassed in delinquency is one approach to clarifying some of the questions arising in definition. Studies have examined the behavior that constituted a record of delinquency to discover the statistical properties. Nye and Short (1957) found seven topics that behaved as a Guttman-type scale. Quay and Blumen (1953) identified four types of offenses that seem factorially distinct. Each of these studies provides some ideas of how the concept of delinquency may have to be behaviorally defined in order to "cut nature at its joints."

In the foregoing discussions the emphasis has been placed on the fundamental likeness between prediction and explanation. Prediction seems to provide a forecast of what is to come, while explanation ties such a forecast to cognitive content and extends the material into broader avenues of understanding. Thus, a system of prediction and explanation may be viewed as a single system which serves two purposes. It is likely that systems of delinquency prediction and explanation will, therefore, emphasize either the prediction aspect or the explanatory aspect of the problem. Empirically derived item scales used in predicting delinquency contribute little at the explanatory level, at least unless they are further analyzed, and the complex psychiatric explanations contribute very little at the predictive level. Were either of the systems to be complete, more clarity would have to be developed so as to round out the prediction-explanation paradigm which we have emphasized.

The use of the prediction-explanation paradigm tends to make prediction studies more cognitive and tends to make explanatory or theoretical material more quantitatively oriented. A complete system, therefore, emphasizes the importance of definition of the variables, the measurement qualities of the variables, and the intervariable relationships.

In the development of a full-blown system including variables and an explanatory matrix which leads to prediction, the structure of the variables in question becomes an important theoretical issue. The test qualities of reliability and validity, emphasized by the test theorists and the intratest relationships, come to define the accuracy of the concepts within the theoretical structure. The sharpening of these concepts through the use of test construction technique and through the clarity of thinking provided by test theorists (Gullicksen, 1950; Loevinger, 1957) becomes a fundamental theoretical prerequisite of the system.

Emphasis on intervariable relationships becomes highly important elements in the understanding of delinquency: for instance, the relationships between delinquency and socioeconomic standing or between delinquency and achievements. The form taken by the relationship of the dependent variable, delinquency, and the other components in the system of explanation is ideally expressed in mathematical terms, such as those seen in the linear discriminate function and multiple regression. It is in this context that interreducibility between one level of concept and another is important. For this reason transferring concepts from a sociological context to a psychiatric context leaves sufficient slippage or low intercorrelation so as to make a theory relatively meaningless.

The relatively detailed standards that are developed for a theory of explanation and prediction, as we have noted above, tend to make one who is concerned with this enterprise turn to the methodological issues involved in good measurement, specific definition, and clearly stated intervariable relationships in order to shape a notion concerning the origins of juvenile delinquency.

Not only does the potential research worker find himself committed to looking for an explicit and connotative theory, but also the interim stages in formulating such a theory follow certain fairly well-defined steps. Therefore, if one believes that explanation and prediction are to be approached simultaneously, the first questions to be answered pertain to the measurement questions and the truth of certain hypothesized relationships between variables. In each such test one is concerned with the question of whether a particular variable, such as socioeconomic status or certain personality trends, can actually be measured and, if so, whether it relates in a hypothesized way to delinquency. At this level of examination there is no concern for the utility of the variables in question, since the initial attempt is one of trying to put together a set of reasonable concomitants or precursors of delinquency. Similar concern for the explanatory materials is seen in reviewing old theories or notions of the origins of delinquency. Scholarly efforts to reduce clinical observation, or institutional impressions, to measurement concepts and to test the actual relevance of these ideas to the concept of delinquency have served as a source for system construction.

Having found some factors that may reliably be associated with delinquency, the research worker then turns to shaping up the concept through emphasis upon measurement techniques and upon the kind of scale construction to be used. At this point, the focus is on the estimation of the true variance which will go into the theory through purification techniques and various subtleties of measurements. Factor analysis, item analysis, and so on become used as methods of obtaining increasingly accurate estimates of the real component. A measure of true delinquency is pursued through improved definition and selection of the items that go into such a measure. For example, socioeconomic status as a concept is subject to redefinition in order to integrate the data from education, from family background, and from the neighborhood. There is a tendency to move from clinical to statistical techniques in order to improve measurement (Meehl, 1954). Further, there is an attempt to move away from broad band survey techniques, such as the interview, which have relatively poor fidelity or reliability, into the narrow spectrum of specific techniques of the scale.

The general course taken by research study aiming at explanation and prediction includes emphasis on many cognitive factors which are not really necessary to a predictive system. For this reason it is wise to review the necessary factors involved in prediction to distinguish them from the enterprise of prediction and explanation. In form, a predictive system should be repeatable. This involves some preference for the use of objective techniques but does not make this necessary since reliable use may be made of ratings, judgments, and others. It is important that a kind of temporal stability about prediction be achieved. The second requirement is that the system yield definite predictions and that these predictions be evaluable at the time, or somewhat after, they have been developed. Unlike many elaborate theoretical systems, such as psychoanalysis, which does not yield definite predictions (but does emphasize the importance of certain motivational factors), the form of any predictive system must yield a definite A or not A classification or no answer. Repeatability and yield are the only formal requirements of the system, and it is within the context of these requirements that one sees predictive systems as tending to be empirical, to be statistical, and, in many senses, to become clerical in nature.

The second major requirement for a predictive system is that it have a certain degree of power. A predictive system should be gauged against certain criteria, of which four levels pertain. The weakest, and an insufficient, criterion is that the variables in question actually be related in a significant test sense to the prediction which the system is instituted to make. In a predictive system it is not sufficient to be able to show significant or reliable relationships between personality factors and delinquency. The second level of stringency involves the comparison of the predictions made by the system with comparable predictions resulting from knowledge of the population characteristics. If the base rate of the occurrence of delinquency within a population is .3 and a predictive system identifies delinquency with an accuracy of .4, then there is some question as to whether the system can, in fact, better predict delinquency than one can do without the system. Discussions of the base rate phenomena have been extensive, and in the paper by Meehl and Rosen (1955) the conditions for successful prediction are clearly developed. In this discussion the focus is upon the likelihood of being right, and the question tends to be how much error is introduced by the new system as opposed to errors made by predicting the most frequent class in the population. Thus, for instance, if 70 per cent of the population is nondelinquent and we have no predictive system, the best guess in each case is that an individual will be nondelinquent. If a predictive system raises the rate of delinquency within a subgroup to .4, or indeed anything less than .5, the best prediction for this subgroup is still nondelinquency. This prediction, however, is a best guess only in the sense of one's making the fewest errors in classification, and it does not consider the consequences of making an error.

The third level in evaluating the power of predictive systems is to consider the next best predictive system. It may be possible, for instance, to do a better job of predicting delinquency through the use of school achievement than it is to predict delinquency through the use of a delinquency test or a family evaluation. This may be the case even though a prediction of delinquency may be based upon theoretically relevant data. From an empirical point of view, this would be essentially superfluous if other systems were extant; thus, for instance, experienced workers in a field may think that they get as good an indication of whether a boy will be delinquent by looking at his address, or the record of his brothers and sisters, as can be obtained. If they are right, these data might well supplant a more complicated psychological or sociological evaluation of the situation.

The final level at which a predictive system must be evaluated is the relationship between power and cost. Power in prediction relates to the accuracy of the system. Cost relates to two factors; the first, the expense of the operation of the system, of testing and evaluation, clerical time, and other factors on the one hand, and the combined cost of error on the other hand. The cost of error is the expense of having an incorrectly predicted case which, in the context of delinquency (if there is an available treatment system), would be the difference between the cost of the individual becoming delinquent and the cost of providing treatment, i.e., the net cost of delinquency. An additional factor in the cost of error is that money is spent in providing treatment for an individual or group who would not be delinquent but has been mistakenly classified as predelinquent and, therefore, treated. The utility of a predictive system must be evaluated in terms of the context of its efficiency and accuracy on the one hand and the net savings, expenses, and losses provided through use of such a system on the other. There are certain obvious factors to be considered in this connection. Emphasis upon automatically administered screening approaches will reduce the cost of the operation of the system. Compare in this context, for instance, the cost of the broad screening approach used by Hathaway and Monachesi (1953) and the intensive screening approach used in the Glueck studies (1950, 1956). Unfortunately, in many instances the actual cost factors and figures are not available. These pertain in their most available form to many human values but are not, and have not, been translated into costs to society. Nonetheless, a relatively explicit balancing of these factors, at least in the minds of the administrators who must choose to use a predictive system, seem essential in developing an idea of whether the system has sufficient power to be useful.

A predictive system may be undertaken to meet certain goals that the investigator or institution may have. These goals actually develop a context of limits for the form of such a system. The first possible goal does not entail the prediction of delinquency per se, but rather the estimations of the true likelihood of delinquency within an individual. This is the narrowest form that we have indicated before, and is a form of variable estimation and is independent of most of the other issues in prediction.

Following a more broadly predictive context, we may secondly indicate that a predictive system may serve two functions: that of explanation and that of prediction. If one begins with the demand that a system follow along certain theoretical lines, then the predictive system largely serves both to predict and to test certain theoretical ideas. To follow more specifically the line of prediction as we have discussed it above, the third possible goal pertains to the use to be made of the prediction. We distinguish here giving information for personal use as opposed to using the information within institutional policies. This dichotomy is illustrated in the context of personal work where some information might be provided to a student as to his likelihood of finishing a particular course successfully. At the other extreme, if a management decision is to be made as to whether or not the individual is permitted to undertake the course, the same data might be used more arbitrarily and more consistently.

A fourth goal for a prediction system is set by the availability or nonavailability of dovetailing action systems that are consequent upon prediction. Is there a social treatment program which will be undertaken when delinquency has been predicted, or is the prediction for research purposes in which there will be a research program undertaken utilizing the material for the cases available? If either of these follows, then there is the possibility that there is a *quota* of individuals to be treated. One also needs to know how this quota is to be filled. It is possible, however, that a system used simply for classification of this kind might be desired for legal, administrative, or other purposes that did not entail immediate reference back to the system and for which the system is not to be altered in order to provide different rates of occurrence. The fifth and final goal pertains to the cost of the factors discussed above. A system is useful ideally at certain levels of cost or where certain costs have been minimized to a particular point. The cost of mistakes, or of making no prediction, or of following the best alternative system constitutes an issue that must be dealt with in making a specification as to cost in its grossest sense.

By omitting the question of connotative content within a system of prediction and emphasizing the goals for the systems as such, delinquency prediction comes to be a problem in decision theory (Cronbach and Gleser, 1957). Decision theory does not provide an over-all mathematical form but relies upon the explication of goals and of experience in prediction, utilizing particular variables and definitions. The history of delinquency prediction does not include the development of any system of prediction within the context of an organization which was itself trying to solve certain administrative decisions. For the most part, delinquency prediction has been undertaken by academicians who have tried to surpass base rate correctness. It is, therefore, necessary to evaluate these systems within the context of administrative problems in order to determine whether they are useful in institutional decision-making.

The availability of high speed electronic computational systems capable of solving multiple variable problems and of repeating these solutions for different structures of the problem makes it possible to approach delinquency prediction through the format of decision-making. It is actually feasible at this time to utilize estimates of the cost of no action program on the one hand, and the cost of predicting and then providing treatment with a certain success ratio on the other hand, to evaluate these costs against the power obtained by using particular variables in relationship to delinquency. In such a context, wholly apart from the systematic structure, the definitional qualities, and the theoretical implication, an administrator can, in fact, determine whether he is gaining and what amount of gain is being achieved through prediction and treatment.

Prediction studies of delinquency are largely inadequate. The reason for this appears to be that prediction and explanation have been the joint objects of investigation. There are no prediction studies for which particular administrative or decision-making criteria are stated. Furthermore, there is no attention to the problems of delinquent selection for a dovetailed program of treatment or isolation.

The Glueck Prediction Study; Description

The entire predictive investigation referred to in this section is reported in the volume, *Unraveling Juvenile Delinquency* (Glueck and Glueck, 1950). Here the authors defined delinquency as ". . . repeated acts of a kind, which when committed by persons beyond the statutory juvenile court age of 16 are punishable as crimes (either felonies or misdemeanors)—except for a few instances of persistent stubbornness, truancy, running away, associating with immoral persons, and the like . . ." (p. 13). In the study, delinquents and nondelinquents were viewed as unitary classes.

The subjects consisted of two groups of boys—500 delinquents and 500 nondelinquents between the ages of 11 and 17 with a mean age of 14.8 and 14.6, respectively. In order to have as sharp a contrast as possible between the two groups, only the more serious offenders were included in the delinquent group. This was accomplished by selecting boys who were committed to a state correctional school (predominantly from the Boston area). The nondelinquent group was selected from a public school population in Boston. Freedom from delinquent behavior was determined by a check of court files with a special investigation in doubtful situations as well as by a later verification of the history through the psychiatric interview which was part of the study.

The delinquent and nondelinquent boys were individually matched on four general variables. For every delinquent boy residing in an underprivileged area for at least two years prior to inclusion in the study, a nondelinquent living in the same kind of neighborhood was found. An underprivileged neighborhood in the city was defined as a deteriorating, low rent, urban area characterized by community conditions generally regarded as dubious to the wholesome environment of children. Usually it contained barrooms, pool halls, vice dens, hangouts, cheap commercialized recreation, railroad yards and tracks, alley ways, and dumps, and often lacked entirely in facilities of constructive recreation. By selecting both delinquents and nondelinquents from unwholesome neighborhoods, an attempt was made to find out why it was that even in regions of most adverse social conditions most children are not delinquents. The second matching factor was age. All ages were verified in the Massachusetts State Bureau of Vital Statistics. This variable was held constant because it is asserted that tendencies toward maladjustment and misbehavior vary with age. The third factor matched was national (ethnicoracial) origin. By holding ethnicoracial factors constant, it was thought possible to compare delinquents and nondelinquents in body morphology. The fourth variable held constant was general intelligence. Here there was an effort to neutralize the degree of behavior connected with intelligence as measured by standard tests.

The results of the efforts to match were as follows. Forty-nine of the delinquents and two of the nondelinquents had to be drawn from outside Boston proper, and, therefore, those areas could not be classified as to delinquency rates. In those areas which were classifiable, 5.8 per cent of the delinquents and 5.2 per cent of the nondelinquents were living in fair neighborhoods, areas in which there are no marked deleterious influences but there was an absence of opportunities for wholesome recreation. In regard to intelligence quotients, a difference of 10 points was allowed. In twenty-one cases—4.2 per cent—there was a difference of more than 10 points. As for age, up to twelve months' difference in age was allowed in matching the boys. In fourteen cases it was necessary to permit a month or two in age difference beyond the twelve-month limit. In the area of national origin almost complete success was achieved.

With these four variables controlled, study was then undertaken of the sociocultural, somatic, intellectual, and emotional-temperamental topics. This was done by (1) an interview with members of the family and any others who might be involved with the family: teachers, courts, and so on, (2) a photograph for classification into somatotype, (3) a 20-30 minute medical examination, (4) a Wechsler-Bellevue Intelligence Test, (5) Stanford Achievement Tests in reading and arithmetic, (6) a Rorschach Test, and (7) a psychiatric interview. Each segment of the investigation was explored independently of every other. As the reader may see, this provides an exceedingly broad spectrum of information from which a predictive matrix could be developed. The general approach in revealing the exceedingly numerous factors that have actually been tabulated in comparing the two sets of 500 cases was accomplished by using statistical tests to establish reliable differences between the two groups.

In terms of prediction, the authors felt that the three areas of *social background*, *character traits* as determined by the Rorschach, and *personality traits* as determined from the psychiatric interview might best differentiate between potential nondelinquents and delinquents at age 6, the age of school entrance. The Social Background Prediction Table consisted of five factors:

Social Factors	Weighted Failure Score
1. Discipline of Boy by Father:	
Overstrict or erratic	71.8
Lax	59.8
Firm but kindly	9.3
2. Supervision of Boy by Mother:	
Unsuitable	83.2
Fair	57.5
Suitable	9.9
3. Affection of Father for Boy:	
Indifferent or hostile	75.9
Warm (including overprotective)	33.8
4. Affection of Mother for Boy:	
Indifferent or hostile	86.2
Warm (including overprotective)	43.1
5. Cohesiveness of Family:	
Unintegrated	96.9
Some elements of cohesion	61.3
Cohesive	20.6

The percentage of delinquents in each subcategory of the rating of the factor constitutes the weighted failure score on each factor. By assigning to each delinquent and nondelinquent his score on each item (his rating), summating the scores, distributing the cases into seven class intervals, and translating the number of cases in each subcategory into a per cent of the total number, a prediction table was developed. The percentage overlap of the distribution was studied, and cutting scores were obtained to maximize the separation of the delinquent and nondelinquent groups. Similarly, from the Rorschach, five factors were isolated, and weighted failure scores were assigned to them to make up a final distribution. The factor topics were (1) social aggression, (2) defiance, (3) suspicion, (4) destructiveness, and (5) emotional lability. These factors are assumed to be well solidified by the sixth year. From the psychiatric personality interview, five factors were derived: (1) adventurous, (2) extraverted in action, (3) suggestibility, (4) stubbornness, and

(5) emotionally unstable. These factors also are presumed to be aspects of the personality that are available early in life.

The authors have presented their system of ratings and the accompanying weighted failure scores with the distributions of separation between delinquent and nondelinquent groups as a system of prediction. A comparison of the three scales shows that they are of approximately similar predictive range and indicate a similar incidence of chances of delinquency and nondelinquency. To ascertain the extent of agreement between the three scales, the authors compared the predictive values of the scales in the 424 cases with overlapping ratings. Using two class intervals, High chance of potential delinquency and Low chance of potential delinquency, the authors found that the Social Prediction Table and the Rorschach Prediction Table place 65.1 per cent of the 424 boys in the same predictive class; the Social and Psychiatric Prediction Tables place 67.9 per cent; and the Psychiatric and Rorschach places 69.8 per cent. All three tables place a boy in his proper predictive category in 49 per cent of the cases, while, in an additional 37.8 per cent, two of the three tables do so, making a total of 86.8 per cent of the boys in which two or all three of the tables are in correct agreement.

Criticism of the Glueck Studies

This study has a number of methodological weaknesses which pertain to the power of the predictive system which has been proposed. The first weakness was failure to incorporate true base rates into the predictive systems. Delinquents and nondelinquents were represented in equal numbers in the study; this is not true of the general population. The severe form of delinquency the Gluecks selected for study further restricts the generality of the results. Utilizing a very inclusive definition of delinquency in an unselected population nets at most a 35 per cent delinquency rate. The kind of delinquency selected for study by the Gluecks occur with less frequency than 35 per cent of the time in the general population and probably less frequently than 5 per cent of the time. By assuming the base rate to be a 50-50 ratio between delinquents and nondelinquents, the predictive system seems too powerful. The tables of weighted failure score predictors has been reanalyzed by Meehl and Rosen, who applied a 20 per cent base rate of delinquency. They show that the claimed high levels of accuracy in the prediction of delinquency may only be achieved by restricting prediction to the extremes of the distribution. Thus, the lowest acceptable hit rate, when predicting delinquency, is .67 correct predictions of delinquency, which incorporates only 18 per cent of the total population. Higher hit rates can be established but only by reducing selection ratios further. These authors conclude that the Glueck tables are apt to be misleading because of their expressive consideration of approximately equal base rates of delinquency and nondelinquency (Meehl and Rosen, 1955, p. 206).

Other evidence illustrating the concern with base rates may be found in the New York City Youth Board Research Department report (1961). There the authors of that report discuss the need to adjust the rate of occurrence of high weighted failure scores in order to correct for a tendency of these ratings to produce more delinquents than would be normally found within their population. Further concern with this problem is found in a study by the present authors (Briggs, Wirt, and Johnson, 1961) comparing the power of the weighted failure score distribution when equal frequencies of delinquency and nondelinquency and actual base rate data are utilized. Equal rates for the occurrence of delinquency and nondelinquency netted the correct identification of 68 per cent of the delinquents and 62 per cent of the nondelinquents utilizing the family pattern prediction table. When the personality items were utilized, 67 per cent of the delinquents and 69 per cent of the nondelinquents were correctly identified. After the population proportion for delinquents and nondelinquents had been corrected to the 23 per cent delinquent level, neither of the weighted failure score distributions (family items and personality items) was useful in prediction.

Rubin (1951) criticized the matching of cases drawn, in the Glueck study, from the delinquent and nondelinquent samples. Here he focused on the appropriateness of the variables used in the matching. This criticism and that of Reiss (1951) emphasize the importance of sociological theory. Such points are, of course, interesting, but not directly pertinent to the question of predictive power.

The third broad criticism that may be made of the Glueck study is that it is a retrospective study, since the individuals evaluated at the time the prediction system was developed were already known to be delinquent. Contamination and retrospective falsification are common problems to persons experienced with rating. The circumstances in which the rating of a boy was made transmit themselves to the rater's impression. Thus, boys interviewed in prisons or reform schools may have seemed different from boys interviewed in public schools simply because of the obvious criminal setting. The degree to which such circumstances alter a rating cannot be told; the only protection against this kind of contamination is to interview prior to the occurrence of a crime. A secondary aspect of the retrospective viewpoint is that the life pattern looks quite different in retrospect than do the events as they are occurring. The Gluecks suggest that their ratings are applicable to individuals at the sixth year (a time when they are entering school). They further suggest that this is the time delinquency predictions should be made.

There is but one study which actually did proceed from the 6-year-old group, utilized the Glueck ratings, and then waited for subsequent outcome. This study was undertaken by the New York City Youth Board. In 1952 the Youth Board (1957) embarked upon a program to test the validity of the Glueck Social Prediction Table. The progress report for October 1961 presents the experience of the Youth Board with two and three factor scales that were derived from the original five factor scales offered by the Gluecks.

The samples were drawn from high delinquency neighborhoods and consisted of 224 boys between the ages of 5½ and 6½. All boys entered the first-grade classes during the academic year 1952-1953 and were the entire populations of the two schools included in the study. The ethnic distribution of the boys varied considerably from those studies by the Gluecks. It consisted largely of a Negro group (58 per cent), white (23 per cent), and Puerto Rican (17 per cent). Because of the disparate representation of white boys in the sample, a second group consisting of seventy-six white boys who were non-Jewish was selected (thereby balancing somewhat the Negro group and the predominance of Jewish boys among the white boys in the first sampling). The final sample contained 42.6 per cent white boys, 43.2 per cent Negro boys, and 14.2 per cent Puerto Rican boys for an over-all sample of 303 boys.

The same caseworkers from the study served as home interviewers; the object of these interviews was to obtain ratings suggested by the Gluecks. A number of problems was immediately encountered in rating the cases. The major problem involved the nonapplicability of certain ratings because of the dependence of the ratings upon total family constellations. Thus, rating of cohesiveness and discipline by father seemed inappropriate because numerous families were fatherless. Adjustments were made in the meanings of the ratings, and shortened scales were developed to include three factors rather than five. The three factor scale and the two factor scales were thus derived. Other problems were encountered that pertained to the results obtained by the factors themselves. Delinquency was predicted at too high a rate when the Glueck weighted failure scores were used. This led the authors to re-examine the ratings made in the original context of five ratings and to alter the interpretation or the meaning of the rating so as to reduce the weighted failure scores of highly rated cases. Thus, we see some awareness of the importance of the rate of selection and of matching it to the true base rate.

The results presented to date include the ratings of the boys who are now 14½ to 15½ years of age on two and three factor scales. Utilizing the first sample of 223 boys (since the addition of the second sample of boys occurred a year later), there were thirty-six boys who were predicted to be delinquents: Nineteen (53 per cent) of the boys had already become persistent delinquents at the time of the report, and two additional boys (total of 58 per cent) were exhibiting serious predelinquent behavior. One hundred eighty-five boys were given less than a 50 per cent chance of becoming delinquents. Eleven of these boys are presently delinquent, and five are predelinquent. One hundred sixty-nine are showing no problems in delinquency. The authors suggest that part of the problem in misprediction starts from the large Negro group within the sample. However, an examination of the separate rates by the authors does not make this a very telling point.

Interpretation of these results is greatly hampered by the fact that the study is not completed at this time, and, further, that the study is made up of a very small sample. The rate of the occurrence of delinquency at the fourteenth year (about 17 per cent) is still on the rise, and it certainly is to be expected that a greater percentage of the cases will be delinquent as time goes on. It is impossible to say how new cases will be distributed over those predicted to be delinquent and those predicted to be nondelinquent. Yet, if the present trend continues, the results will be encouraging.

The Glueck study has been a starting point in the systematic prediction of delinquency. It has alerted workers in the field to the possibility of entering the schools, interviewing students, and making predictions. It has stimulated one study objectively, seeking to evaluate the predictive system that has been offered; but more than this, it has stimulated many workers to consider other problems: cost, base rate, and alternative systems.

An evaluation of the Glueck study as a whole suggests, first, that the predictive tables presented are of no actual utility at this time because of the failure to incorporate reasonable base rates. The factors themselves may be criticized because, in some cases, they are not discriminating regarding the difference of delinquents and nondelinquents, and, in other cases, they are unratable because of the frequent occurrence of broken homes among delinquent boys. From the level of prediction these are still weaknesses in the system. It is possible that the factors may be re-evaluated and reinterpreted as has been the aim of the Youth Board study. Unfortunately, that study will not provide much certainty since the evaluation of the factors has been contaminated by attempts to adjust them to the base rate. An additional validation study will be required. Besides this, the relatively small size of the samples in the Youth Board study is disappointing.

Two final issues must be brought out concerning the utility of the factors. The first is cost. The expense involved in fully investigating personality and family structure among 6-year-olds is, indeed, very high. Could cheaper data predictive of delinquency be found for the 6-year-old group? Gross demographic data is certainly cheaper. Further, some have questioned the appropriateness of surveying the 6-year-old group. Possibly, as Lively *et al.* (1962) have pointed out, the 12-year-old group is really a more reasonable focus for a treatment effort. The utility of prediction is additionally determined by the use for which it is intended. What is the age of effective treatment? If prediction at the brink of delinquency is adequate or useful, then it is clear that cheaper predictions are available and as powerful as the Glueck factor prediction. If treatment must proceed from the earlier years, then, possibly modification of the Glueck's factors may become useful. If control does not take the form of treatment but is a matter of police awareness, and so on, then other systems will certainly be employed.

The Kvaraceus Delinquency Proneness Scales

Three item sets are presented by Kvaraceus (1953) for the rating of delinquency proneness. "The KD Proneness Scale consists of 75 multiple choice items that have been composed around focal points of difference in personal makeup, in home and family backgrounds and in school experiences of delinquents and nondelinquents. . . . The 75 items have been analyzed and screened, in terms of their capacity to differentiate at a statistically significant pace, between delinquent and nondelinquent groups. . . . Separate keys are provided for girls and boys . . ." (Kvaraceus, 1956, p. 9).

A nonverbal revision of the proneness scale was later developed. This form contains sixty-two pictorially presented items which are choices between activities. Each item presents a typically delinquent, neutral, or nondelinquent choice. Scoring involves a single difference score between the number of delinquent and nondelinquent preferences. Sixty items are used in the actual scoring procedure.

"The checklist was assembled using the findings of the major research studies reporting significant differences between delinquent and nondelinquent samples. . . . All the items have been catalogued under the following three headings: personality factors, environmental factors—home and family and school factors" (Kvaraceus, 1956, p. 10). No validating work is presented for the check list.

The initial validating data and numerous subsequent studies of the power of the item set in the proneness scale are reported by Kvaraceus. There is little question that these items do differentiate between delinquents and nondelinquents. Unfortunately, all studies in the early reports were restricted to comparisons of mature delinquents and were not prediction studies. Therefore, the KD Proneness Scale was actually validated as an attitude scale.

The nonverbal form of the proneness scale (Kvaraceus, 1961) was evaluated by utilizing a sample of 1379 students from regular classes and 215 students from special classes. These students were followed for three years. The tests taken in the seventh, eighth, and ninth grades did not relate reliably to the subsequent history of delinquency. An incidental finding was that ratings made by teachers did show a reliable relationship to subsequent delinquency—albeit low. The net result appears to be the conclusion that interests at the age of delinquency, at least as they are tapped by a nonverbal measure, are not a part of the interest patterns of the earlier years.

The Hathaway and Monachesi Studies: Over-all Design

The third group of studies to be presented are those by Hathaway and Monachesi and include related works by different investigators, utilizing the same population (1963, 1953, 1957). The present discussion attends *only* to predictive issues. The basic components in the Hathaway and Monachesi work are large populations that were tested and subsequently followed. The test used was the Minnesota Multiphasic Personality Inventory (MMPI). This test is a set of 550 true-false questions that are answered on an answer sheet by the subject. Scoring involves the use of ten clinical scales. These scales were objectively derived from clinical adult populations and register the degree to which the subject uses certain neurotic or psychotic patterns of behavior. The use of the MMPI implies a theoretical orientation toward the etiology of delinquency which aligns it with personality and psychopathology. Readers interested in this instrument are referred to Welsh and Dahlstrom (1956). The testing was that of entire ninth-grade classes in the junior high schools in the state of Minnesota. The follow-up of these students was executed at different intervals in the ten years following testing.

The first ninth-grade MMPI testing program was initiated in the Minneapolis Public School System during the 1947-1948 school year. At the beginning of the school year there were 4572 ninth-graders registered in the sixteen Minneapolis public high schools. The MMPI was administered to 3971, or 87 per cent of this group (the Minneapolis sample). Most of the testing was done during March, April, and May of 1948. Two and four years after the testing (1950 and 1952), the files of the Hennepin County Probation Office and the Juvenile Division of the Minneapolis Police Department were searched for any record of those students included in the Minneapolis sample. An additional follow-up study was conducted by Wirt and Briggs (1959) from 1956 to 1958.

A second sample was gathered during the spring of 1954, when 11,329 additional ninth-graders were tested. This testing was done in ninety-two schools situated in eighty-six communities of forty-seven Minnesota counties. Sampling was actually broader than that suggested by the figures because Minnesota school district boundaries do not coincide with political or other subdivision boundaries. Many schools serve several communities, and frequently a school drew pupils from two or more counties. Schools were selected to include representation of Minnesota's diverse economic and geographic areas. The sample actually included 28 per cent of all of Minnesota's 1954 public school ninth-grade population, which would then be 36 per cent of all ninth-graders, exclusive of Minneapolis and St. Paul areas (not included in this 1954 sampling). Two Roman Catholic parochial schools were included in the sample. At the time of the state-wide MMPI testing, other data were collected from several sources: microfilms were made of school records, students filled out personal data sheets, and teachers filled out report forms on which they were asked to predict students considered likely to have legal and emotional difficulties. In 1956-1957, or two years after the testing of the state-wide sample, a student-by-student community follow-up survey was made, and police and court files were searched for names included in the 1954 sample. These data were used for ratings on delinquency. Ratings were also made from teachers' reports of school conduct and adjustment. In 1956-1957, a more intensive follow-up was also done of twelve schools which were representative of the state-wide sample. In these schools MMPI tests were again given, and further personal data were collected on each subject who was included in the 1954 sample. Normal school progress made this the twelfth-grade level for the students.

Net result of the testing and surveying efforts is extensive information available on somewhat over 15,000 Minnesota boys and girls. On each of these individuals information of the following kind has been obtained: chronological age, size of community from which the individual came, socioeconomic status, family status, intelligence ratings. On the state-wide sample, additional information has been obtained from the state-wide testing program, utilizing the Cooperative English Test Form Z, high school rank, the present school status, teacher predictions, and conduct and adjustment ratings made by the investigators during follow-up. Finally, a delinquency rating for all individuals in the samples was developed and updated with the addition of new information through the different follow-up periods.

The delinquency ratings and other demographic variables depicting the delinquency rates within particular standard population groups were presented in Chapter 1 of this volume. We will now present the data relevant to *prediction* of delinquency.

The discussion of these results depends to some extent upon an understanding of a method of clarifying MMPI results called *coding*. Test results are presented visually on a profile containing the ten clinical scales in standard score units. The most elevated scales are the most deviant, and are thought to signify the presence of pathology akin to the diagnostic labels that they carry. The coding process is a system of clarifying each profile by noting in descending order the scales that are elevated to give a high point code (e.g., from the pathological trait most deviant to the trait less deviant). For convenience, numbers are assigned which stand for the scales number. These number-name equivalents are 1—Hypochondriasis, 2—Depression, 3—Hysteria, 4—Psychopathic Deviancy, 5—Masculine-Feminine, 6—Paranoid, 7—Psychesthenia, 8—Schizophrenia, 9—Mania, 10—Social Introversion. Thus a code of 358 would stand for a profile in which the Hysteria scale deviation is the greatest, next the Masculine-Feminine, and next in elevation the Schizophrenia scale. In the following analysis the high point code is limited to the first two—the highest two scales.

The first attempts at relating MMPI results to delinquency were to examine the power of the *first two positions of the high point MMPI code*. The high point codes for all individuals in the population were distributed into a frequency distribution for all code types. At each code type, the percentage of delinquents and nondelinquents was calculated. This percentage was compared with the percentage for the over-all population (the base rate). Table 6-1 presents a portion of such a table. Certain code classifications have

TABLE 6-1. THE PERCENTAGES OF BOYS IN THE DIFFERENT CODE CLASSES WHO BECAME DELINQUENT *

	Number in Profile Type			Per Cent Delinquent		
Code Class	<70	≧70	Total	<70	≧70	Total
L>9			50			20
F>15			103			49
? invalid			8			0
0–	18	2	20	0	0	0
01	2	0.5	2.5	50	0	40
02	19.5	4	23.5	21	25	21
03	4	0	4	0	0	0
04	13	0	13	15	0	15
05	4	1	5	50	0	40
06	4.5	1.5	6	0	67	17
07	12.5	3	15.5	16	0	13
08	9.5	2.5	12	0	40	8
09	6	0	6	0	0	0
Total 0	93	14.5	107.5	12	21	13
27	6	3.5	9.5	17	14	16
–						
–						
–						
49	45	40	85	27	51	38

* From Hathaway and Monachesi. *Analyzing and Predicting Juvenile Delinquency with the MMPI.* Minneapolis, Minn.: Univer. of Minn. Press, 1953, pp. 128-129.

a rate of delinquency which reliably *exceeds* the base rate. A code reliably in excess of the delinquency base rate is the 49 code classification, where the delinquency rate is 38 per cent. Note also that certain codes such as the 27 code occur with a delinquency rate which is lower than that for the population.

This approach to prediction is not very powerful. Yet, within certain administrative contexts, a 10 per cent elevation in the rate of delinquency above the base rate might serve economic or experimental purposes. Yet, without a specific system of decision-making, no statement of the adequacy of code predictions can be made.

Secondly, Hathaway and Monachesi tried to develop a scale that would predict juvenile delinquency. Two forms of a scale were offered. The first scale contained thirty-three MMPI items selected after cross validation. A second scale was later offered as another attempt to develop a technique which would improve upon code prediction. Neither scale was successful. The authors state that their standard for comparison was derived from the data where it can be seen that code patterns with high delinquency rates separate delinquents from nondelinquents with higher accuracy than if the single scale were used. The reason for this probably lies in the multiple factors that contribute to the occurrence of delinquency. Apparently, delinquents cannot profitably be lumped together on the basis of a single index or scale. (A similar conclusion was drawn from examining the De scale derived by Gough and Peterson, 1952.)

Thirdly, teacher predictions were analyzed. When the original testing was done in the rural sample, the teachers were asked to name the children who seemed likely to get into trouble with the law or to develop emotional problems or both. No effort was made to provide the teachers with more explicit definition of terms. They could have interpreted "trouble with the law" to mean delinquency, crime, or minor difficulties. Although some children were named by several teachers, most of them were named only by one. All the pupils who were named once or more were placed in the "teacher prediction" groups. There were 790 boys and 283 girls in this delinquency prediction group, those who received predictions of delinquency or delinquency and emotional problems. These groups were, respectively, 13.9 and 5.0 per cent of the whole statewide samples of boys and girls.

In column I of Table 6-2 the teachers, in naming potential delinquents, selected 11.5 per cent of their boys from the day laborer socioeconomic status (SES) category and only 4.9 per cent from the professional and semiprofessional SES category. In column II these percentages are divided by the actual percentages of the total sample that are in each SES category. If the teachers had made a strictly proportional selection, the value in column II would be 1.00. For the day laborer group, the value 1.46 means that the teachers expected 46 per cent more boys from this group to be delinquent than would be expected on the basis of the proportion that this category is of the whole sample. For the professional and semiprofessional group the teacher selections were underrepresentative, with only 64 per cent of the proportional number.

Column III shows the teacher selection rates adjusted for actual delinquency rate. Since the delinquency rate is larger for the boys in the day laborer category, a good predictor of delinquency would, therefore, choose more of these boys, as was the case. Column III

TABLE 6-2. COMPARISON OF TEACHER PREDICTION OF DELINQUENCY WITH THE OCCURRENCE OF DELINQUENCY, HATHAWAY-MONACHESI STATEWIDE SAMPLE OF MALES AND FEMALES

Variable	I[a]		II[b]		III[c]		IV[d]	
	Males	Females	Males	Females	Males	Females	Males	Females
SES:								
Day laborer	11.5	13.6	1.46	1.79	1.04	1.13	45	53
Semi- and sl. skilled	47.2	51.5	1.13	1.23	1.03	.92	47	38
Farmer	19.5	20.1	.88	.89	1.18	1.82	30	26
Clerical	17.0	12.9	.83	.63	.75	.76	51	38
Prof. and semiprof.	4.9	1.9	.64	.25	.45	.27	54	20
Intelligence:								
1-15 %	19.7	20.4	1.54	1.89	1.13	1.85	44	35
16-39 %	29.3	31.5	1.17	1.39	1.13	1.05	38	40
40-68 %	31.2	34.1	1.09	1.16	1.04	1.31	50	40
69-90 %	15.0	11.5	.68	.47	.63	.46	47	39
91-100%	4.9	2.6	.43	.21	.54	.34	54	29
HSR:								
1-19 %	53.3	39.9	2.12	2.75	1.48	1.60	46	44
20-39 %	29.5	27.5	1.23	1.76	1.13	1.45	39	21
40-69 %	13.8	23.2	.47	.75	.55	.70	28	16
70-100%	3.4	9.4	.16	.24	.26	.41	29	15
Drop-out:	40.8	43.8	2.33	3.02	1.32	.95	52	51
Broken family:	10.7	17.3	1.67	2.70	1.07	1.33	54	39
Total sample:	13.9	5.0					45	38

[a] Percentage distribution of the teacher predicted group in the variable. Teacher expected sources of the delinquent group.

[b] Teacher predicted percentage divided by the total sample percentage in the category. Teacher expected rates by category.

[c] Teacher predicted percentage divided by the percentage of delinquency in the category. Teacher expected rates against real rates.

[d] The number of boys who were delinquent (omitting minor delinquents in male sample) in teacher prediction group divided by total number in teacher prediction group. Accuracy of the category predictions.

should show the value 1.00 when the rate of column II is in proper proportion to the observed delinquency rate for the category. As column III for the males, and especially for the females, shows, teachers choose too freely from the farmer group, even when corrections are made for the actual delinquency rate of the category. The teacher index is 18 per cent larger than it should be for boys and 82 per cent larger than it should be for girls. The most marked selection discrepancy for boys occurs at the high end of the SES series where the teachers underrate the delinquency of the professional group with an index of only .45. Only among the boys from day laborer and semi- and slightly-skilled homes is the index near 1.00, meaning that the prediction rate was comparable to the actual rate.

Column IV shows the accuracy of prediction made for each category of the variables. From the data in this column it can be seen that, when the teachers do select boys from the professional and semiprofessional group, they are 54 per cent accurate. In contrast, when they select from among farm boys, they have only a 30 per cent accuracy.

The remaining data of these tables interpret similarly. There are many points of interest to be found in the tables. The data on intelligence and on high school rank show striking contrasts. Teachers appear to be markedly influenced by high school rank (HSR) in their choice of boys and girls who appear likely to be delinquent. They are reluctant to predict delinquency for a child who makes good grades, and their predictions are inaccurate when they do choose one. In contract, 40.8 per cent of the boys chosen by teachers drop out of school and 10.7 per cent come from broken homes. Although the predictions of delinquency are quite accurate in picking drop-outs for boys and girls, the expected rates are greatly overestimated for boys; among the girls, however, this is not true, for the rate is near 1.00. Overestimation of rates for both boys and girls occurs for those from broken homes. For the girls, not only do the teachers select too infrequently from the professional category, but they are also more inaccurate than with the boys in prediction of delinquency. Intelligence seems to be more involved in teacher judgment of girls. Despite the fact that intelligence, as measured by the ACE or IQ, has little effect on the delinquency rate for boys and only a moderate effect for girls, and that fewer delinquent children came from the lowest intelligence group, teachers draw 20 per cent of their nominations from these groups. Their nominations are even more heavily loaded with children of low scholarship. Clearly, the teachers tend to relate poor school ability and achievement with delinquency.

Fourth, combined MMPI code predictions were examined. To provide some basis for judging the accuracy of teacher predictions, these predictions were compared with MMPI code predictions. Comparable MMPI groups were selected wherein cases were used with profiles known to relate to the frequency of delinquency in the Minneapolis study (49, 94, 49, 94, 48, 46, 48, 46, 64, 84, 4x9, 49x, 9x4, 94x, M; 770 on 46, 48, 49, 46, 48, 49, 64, 84, 94). To establish a cutting point comparable to teacher groups, the MMPI groups from the state-wide sample were made approximately equal in number to the teacher predicted groups. There were 795 boys and 253 girls who had valid profiles in any of the above 2-point codes. The data suggest that the teachers named the more severe delinquent cases in greater proportion than was representative of all delinquency levels for the total rated groups. The MMPI predictions are more accurate than teachers at the second level of delinquency because the rate was artificially regulated.

Table 6-3 shows the categorical data on the children selected by the MMPI. The columns are similar to those of the teacher prediction tables with which the data of these tables should be compared.

A general difference between the MMPI and teacher groups is that the MMPI tended to select predicted delinquents in proportion to the observed general base rates (see column II). Note that there is not a tendency to cluster predictions of delinquency within specific groups as occurred among the teachers. In this connection, the high delinquency rate for school drop-out children reflects the fact that some delinquents were encouraged or required to drop out by events related to their delinquency.

The general base rate of delinquency for girls was 10.4 per cent. Prediction for girls nets a rate for the teacher predicted group of 38 per cent and that of the MMPI predicted of 26 per cent, which is 68 per cent as accurate as the teacher predictions. Thus, for both boys and girls, teachers predicted with more over-all accuracy than did the MMPI, despite the fact that the MMPI selected groups in proportion to their contribution to the whole and was more accurate at level two. Teachers may have been able to heighten their accuracy from prior knowledge of delinquency of some of the children. This is suggested in the fact that their greatest accuracy was in selection of both boys and girls with ratings at a more severe level of delinquency. MMPI predictions were only slightly contaminated by such knowledge, even if the child had been in repeated trouble.

A fifth approach utilized two concepts: delinquency proneness

TABLE 6-3. COMPARISON OF MMPI PREDICTION OF DELINQUENCY WITH THE
OCCURRENCE OF DELINQUENCY AMONG STATEWIDE HATHAWAY-MONACHESI
SAMPLE OF MALES AND FEMALES

Variable	I[a]		II[b]		III[c]		IV[d]
	Males	Females	Males	Females	Males	Females	Males
SES:							
Day laborer	8.2	9.1	1.04	1.20	.75	.76	32
Semi- & sl. skilled	47.3	46.4	1.13	1.11	1.04	.83	41
Farmer	12.6	13.6	.57	.60	1.14	1.23	26
Clerical	24.4	26.0	1.19	1.27	1.06	1.53	37
Prof. & semiprof.	7.4	5.0	.96	.65	.93	1.25	35
Intelligence:							
1-15 %	9.0	12.5	.70	1.16	.60	1.14	46
16-39 %	19.4	26.1	.77	1.15	.88	.87	32
40-68 %	35.9	30.5	1.26	1.03	1.20	1.17	39
69-90 %	24.6	25.3	1.11	1.02	1.03	1.01	37
91-100%	11.0	10.1	.96	.82	1.22	1.26	31
HSR:							
1-19 %	24.7	17.3	.98	1.19	.69	.79	45
20-39 %	25.8	16.7	1.08	1.07	1.00	.88	36
40-69 %	31.9	32.0	1.09	1.04	1.27	.97	25
70-100%	17.6	33.9	.81	.87	1.35	1.47	23
Drop-out:	20.0	30.2	1.14	2.08	.65	.66	60
Broken family:	9.8	10.6	1.53	1.66	.98	.82	47
Total sample:	13.9	4.5					37

[a] Percentage distribution of the MMPI predicted group in the variable.

[b] MMPI predicted percentage divided by the total sample percentage in the category.

[c] MMPI predicted percentage divided by the percentage of delinquency in the category.

[d] The number of boys who were delinquent (omitting minor delinquents in male sample) in teacher prediction group divided by total number in teacher prediction group. Accuracy of the category predictions. Girls omitted because of small frequencies.

and delinquency resistance. The 0, 2, 5 scales (025) were identified as inhibitory or resistant to delinquency, and scales 4, 8, 9 (489) were identified as excitor or delinquency prone. A study by Briggs, Wirt, and Johnson (1961) developed a technique for the discovery and identification of delinquent boys using a random sample of these 13-year-old boys and including MMPI codes and social agency data. Two general approaches were used. In the first approach the group of boys was divided into those who had MMPI codes that were made up of the excitor scales 4, 8, and 9. Within this group, instances of severe diseases among family members were tallied. Using these two criteria—MMPI code and illness within the family—

it was possible to develop small subpopulations which were about 80 per cent saturated with predelinquent boys. The subpopulation, when compared with the general population, was approximately twice as dense with predelinquent cases (since the general population rate was about 40 per cent among the boys with 489 codes). The possibility of using this technique in the establishment of treatment programs where a small sample could be handled was pointed out. Such subpopulations would not be random samples of delinquents, but would be more homogeneous samples of delinquents than are usually obtained, which might suggest some treatment hypotheses. This particular study was presented without cross validation as an illustration of a *successive hurdles* approach to the identification of the predelinquent.

A secondary aspect of the study by Wirt and Briggs (1959) included an analysis of the frequency of delinquency among boys with delinquency-prone personality profiles on the MMPI and among boys with delinquency-resistance profiles on the MMPI. These two factors, in conjunction with the presence or absence of some social agency contact by members of the family preliminary to the occurrence of delinquency (not including the boys), netted interesting examples of delinquency concentration. When the family was not known to some social agency, the delinquency rate for 49 boys was only 23 per cent. But, in families with social agency records, the 489 cases had a delinquency rate of 42 per cent. The influence of code in this constellation of variables was also clear. The 025 boys with no family record of contact with agencies had a delinquency rate of 11 per cent, while it has increased 22 per cent for the 025 families known to social agencies.

Finally, a sixth approach, utilizing the information within the Hathaway-Monachesi project, was the Rempel (1958) one, which applied two multivariate analyses—the generalized distance function and the discriminate function—to the problem of predicting delinquency. Rempel found a particular combination of 1, 8, 5, and 4 capable of identifying 68 per cent of 175 delinquent boys in the original group and 70 per cent of the 176 in the cross validation sample. This level of accuracy in predicting the delinquency was achieved at the cost of misclassifying sixty of the 175 nondelinquents in the original sample (34 per cent), and seventy-two of the 175 nondelinquents in the second sample (41 per cent). Both of these methods improve upon the base rate classifications. Rempel then tried to incorporate non-MMPI variables in his prediction formulas. He included data on school attendance and grade achievement together with weights for MMPI scales 9, 8, 5, and 4. The net rate of correct identification was 70 per cent. Since the samples were not identical to those above in his first study, it is not possible to make correct comparisons.

Assessing these studies from the position of decision theory suggests that there are a number of factors unspecified. Essentially, these research workers have suggested items that relate to delinquency without taking part in the enterprise of prediction for purposes of control, treatment, and so on. This has left unspecified the actual level definition of delinquency that is intolerable, the rates of acceptable accuracy, the cost, and the capacity of a treatment program. These omissions have been our major criticism of the other studies.

Yet, there are many virtues to be noted in this family of studies. They are the size of the samples, 4000 in one study and 11,000 in another. These samples for the first time in delinquency research seem to be an adequate basis for prediction research. There was great care taken in definition of delinquency, involving levels of severity, rural and urban factors, and, of course, population-wide sampling. The use of longitudinal samples followed for the period of predelinquency through adolescence. The breadth of types of data examined ranged from test items to teacher ratings and family factors. Finally, there is the concern with cost factors in prediction and a search among predictors for those with the most power and the truest hit rates. No successful prediction program will be developed without all of these characteristics.

SUMMARY

We have noted that concern with delinquency control is an age-old enterprise. Society has long recognized its most vulnerable flank is its youth. Recently, behavioral sciences have offered some hope of understanding and controlling the criminal nonconformity of the adolescent group. This has been a multipurpose enterprise with three foci: understanding (theory), prediction, and treatment.

It has seemed that concentrating upon understanding delinquency has made the prediction enterprise more obscure. This has occurred for two reasons: (1) There has been a tendency to incorporate ideas from a number of different disciplines, e.g., sociology, psychoanalysis, criminology. These levels of study do not have intertranslation qualities. There are no reduction definitions from one language system to another. Thus, focusing upon understanding delinquency has fractionized efforts without providing a unitary theory. (2) Prediction involves attention to many factors that are largely utilitarian or functional. Examples of these points are the criterion of socially unacceptable delinquent behavior to be predicted, the cost of information relating to prediction, the use to be made of the prediction, acceptable rates of success, the cost of error in the prediction of a delinquent, and, finally, the costs of treatment and the availability of slots into which prospective treatment cases may be fitted. All prediction systems have left these factors unspecified, which leaves completely untold the value of such a system.

Major efforts to predict delinquency have been made. Historically, the first of these was proposed by the Gluecks in 1950. This study attempted to relate the occurrence of psychiatric, family, and personality factors to the occurrence of delinquency. The study was wholly empirical. But, unfortunately, the wrong rates of occurrence of delinquency were assumed. Further study of the factors proposed has shown the relatedness to delinquency of the factors proposed, but reiterated the inaccuracy of the rates. No careful prediction system has yet been developed.

The other major effort has been that of Hathaway and Monachesi and their co-workers. Utilizing samples of great size (15,000) and attending to the actual rates of antisocial behavior, many findings have been offered. The study is especially useful because the relative power of different prediction factors may be seen. Factors studied included special delinquency scale, personality test patterns, teacher ratings, ability, school success, family contact with social agencies—to name a few. As yet, these workers have not developed a prototype predictive system, although there appears to be enough data available to them to do this.

References

Aichorn, A. (1935) *Wayward youth.* New York: Viking.

Andry, R. G. (1960) *Delinquency and parental pathology.* London: Metheun.

Bennett, Ivy. (1960) *Delinquent and neurotic children.* New York: Basic Books.

Bettleheim, Bruno. (1950) *Love is not enough.* Glencoe, Ill.: Free Press.

Briggs, P. F., Wirt, R. D., & Johnson, Rochelle (1961) An application of prediction tables to the study of delinquency. *J. consult. Psychol.,* **25,** 46-50.

Briggs, P. F., Johnson, Rochelle, & Wirt, R. D. (1962) Achievement among delinquency prone adolescents. *J. clin. Psychol.,* **18,** 305-309.

Cleckley, H. (1941) *The mask of sanity.* St. Louis: Mosby.

Cloward, R., & Ohlin, L. (1960) *Delinquency and opportunity.* Glencoe, Ill.: Free Press.

Cohen, A. D. (1955) *Delinquent boys: the culture of the gang.* Glencoe, Ill.: Free Press.

Cronbach, L. J., & Gleser, Goldine (1957) *Psychological tests and personnel decisions.* Urbana, Ill.: Univer. of Ill. Press.

Dahlstrom, W. G., & Welsh, G. S. (1960) *An MMPI handbook: a guide to use in clinical practice and research.* Minneapolis: Univer. of Minn. Press.

Eissler, K. R. (ed.) (1949) *Searchlights on delinquency.* New York: Int. Univer. Press.

Friedlander, Kate (1945) Formation of the antisocial character. In *Psychoanalytic Study of the child.* New York: Int. Univer. Press.

Glueck, Eleanor T. (1960) Efforts to identify delinquency. *Fed. Probation,* **24,** 49-56.

Glueck, S., & Glueck, Eleanor T. (1950) *Unraveling juvenile delinquency.* New York: Commonwealth Fund.

Glueck, S., & Glueck, Eleanor T. (1956) *Physique and delinquency.* New York: Harper.

Goldfarb, W. (1945) Psychological privation in infancy and subsequent adjustment. *Amer. J. Orthopsychiat.,* **15,** 167.

Goring, C. (1919) *The English convict.* Abridged ed. London: HM's Stationery Office.

Gough, H. G., & Peterson, D. R. (1952) The identification and measurement of predispositional factors in crime and delinquency. *J. consult. Psychol.*, 16, 207-212.

Gullicksen, H. (1950) *Theory of mental tests.* New York: Wiley.

Hathaway, S. R., & Monachesi, E. D. (1953) *Analyzing and predicting juvenile delinquency with the MMPI.* Minneapolis: Univer. of Minn. Press.

Hathaway, S. R., & Monachesi, E. D. (1957) The personalities of predelinquent boys. *J. Crim. Law Criminol. police Sci.*, 48, 149-163.

Healy, W., & Bonner, Augusta (1936) *New light on delinquency and its treatment.* New Haven: Yale Univer. Press.

Henry, N. G. (ed.) (1948) *The Forty-seventh yearbook of the National Society for the Study of Education.* Part I: Juvenile delinquency and the schools. Chicago: Univer. of Chicago Press.

Herzog, Elizabeth (1960) Identifying potential delinquency. *Juvenile delinquency: facts and facets.* U. S. Department of Health, Education and Welfare.

Hooten, E. A. (1939) *The American criminal: an anthropological study.* Cambridge: Harvard Univer. Press.

Huxley, A. (1932) *Brave new world.* London: Chatoo & Windus.

Johnson, Adelaide M. (1949) Sanctions for superego Lacunae of adolescents. In K. R. Eissler (ed.), *Searchlights on delinquency.* New York: Int. Univer. Press.

Johnson Adelaide M., & Szurek, S. A. (1952) The genesis of antisocial acting out in children and adults. *Psychoanal. Quart.*, 21, 323-343.

Knott, J. R., & Gottlieb, J. S. (1943) The electroencephalograph in psychopathic personality. *Psychosom. Med.*, 5, 139-141.

Kvaraceus, W. C. (1953) *KD Proneness Scale and check list.* New York: World Book.

Kvaraceus, W. C. (1956) *Forecasting juvenile delinquency.* New York: World Book.

Kvaraceus, W. C. (1961) Forecasting delinquency: a three year experiment. *Except. Child.*, 27, 429-435.

Lander, B. (1954) *Toward an understanding of juvenile delinquency.* New York: Columbia Univer. Press.

Lindner, R. M. (1942-1943) Experimental studies in constitutional psychopathic inferiority. *J. crim. Psychopath.*, 4, 255-275, 484-504.

Linton, R. (1936) *The study of man.* New York: Appleton-Century.

Lively, E. L., Dinitz, S., & Reckless, W. C. (1962) Self concept as a predictor of juvenile delinquency. *Amer. J. Orthopsychiat.*, 32, 159-168.

Loevinger, Jane (1957) Objective tests as instruments of psychological theory. *Psychol. Rep.*, Monograph supplements, 9, 636-694.

Lombroso, C. (1918) *Crime, its causes and remedies.* Engl. transl. by Henry P. Horton. Boston: Little & Brown.

Lykken, D. T. (1957) A study of anxiety in the sociopathic personality. *J. abnorm. soc. Psychol.*, 55, 6-10.

*

McCord, W., & McCord, Joan (1956) *Psychopathy and delinquency.* New York: Grune & Stratton.

Meehl, P. E. (1954) *Clinical versus statistical prediction.* Minneapolis: Univer. of Minn. Press.

Meehl, P. E., & Rosen, A. (1955) Antecedent probability and the efficiency of psychometric signs, patterns or cutting scores. *Psychol. Bull.,* 52, 194-216.

Merrill, Maud A. (1947) *Problems of child delinquency.* Boston: Houghton Mifflin.

Merton, R. K. (1957) *Social theory and social structure.* Rev. & enl. ed. Glencoe, Ill.: Free Press.

Metfessel, M., & Lovell, Constance (1942) Recent literature on individual correlates of crime. *Psychol. Bull.,* 39, 133-164.

Miller, W. B. (September 1959) Implications of urban lower class culture to social work. *Soc. Ser. Rev.*

Mullins, C. (1945) *Why crime?* London: Metheun.

New York City Youth Board (July 1957) An experiment in the validation of the Glueck Prediction Scale, progress report from November 1952 to December 1956.

New York City Youth Board (October 1961) Delinquency prediction. A progress report.

Nye, F. I. (1958) *Family relationships and delinquent behavior.* New York: Wiley.

Nye, F. I., & Short, J. F., Jr. (1957) Scaling delinquent behavior. *Amer. sociol. Rev.,* 22, 327-331.

Orwell, G. (1949) *1984.* New York: Harcourt, Brace.

Ostrow, M., & Ostrow, Marian (1946) Bilateral synchronous paroxysmal slow activity in the encephalograms of non-epileptics. *J. nerv. ment. Dis.,* 103, 346-358.

Parsons, T. (1947) Certain primary sources and patterns of aggression in the social structure of the Western world. *Psychiat.,* 10, 172.

Quay, H. C., & Blumen, L. (1963) Dimensions of delinquent behavior. *J. soc. Psychol.,* 61, 273-277.

Reiss, A. J., Jr. (1951) An appraisal of the research methods. *Amer. J. Sociol.,* 57, 115-120.

Rempel, P. P. (1958) The use of multivariate statistical analysis of MMPI scores in the classification of delinquent and nondelinquent high school boys. *J. consult. Psychol.,* 22, 17-23.

Robison, Sophia M. (1960) *Juvenile delinquency.* New York: Holt.

Rogers, C. R., & Skinner, B. F. (1956) Some issues concerning the control of human behavior. *Science,* 124, 1057-1066.

Rubin, S. (1951) Illusions in a research project using matched pairs. *Amer. J. Sociol.,* 57, 104-114.

Scott, J. F. (1959) Two dimensions of delinquent behavior. *Amer. sociol. Rev.,* 24, 240-243.

Shaw, C. R. (1929) *Delinquency areas.* Chicago: Univer. of Chicago Press.

Sheldon, W. H., Hartl, E. M., & McDermott, E. (1949) *Varieties of delinquent behavior.* New York: Harper.

Smykal, A., & Thorne, F. C. (1951) Etiological studies of psychopathic personalities: II asocial type. *J. clin. Psychol.,* **7,** 299-316.

Stafford-Clark, D., & Ponds, D. (1951) The psychopath in prison: a preliminary report of a cooperative research. *Brit. J. Criminol.,* **2,** 117-129.

Szurek, S. (1942) Notes on genesis of psychopathic personality trends. *Psychiat.,* **5,** 1-6.

Thompson, R. E. (1952) A validation of the Glueck social prediction scale for proneness to delinquency. *J. Crim. Law Criminol. police Sci.,* **43,** 451-470.

Thompson, R. E. (1957) Further validation of the Glueck social prediction table for identifying potential delinquents. *J. Crim. Law Criminol. police Sci.,* **48,** 175-184.

Welsh, G. S., & Dahlstrom, W. G. (1956) *Basic readings on the MMPI in psychology and medicine.* Minneapolis: Univer. of Minn. Press.

Wirt, R. D., & Briggs, P. F. (1959) Personality and environmental factors in the development of delinquency. *Psychol. Monogr.,* **73** (Whole No. 485).

Wirt, R. D., & Briggs, P. F. (October 1960) Delinquency prone personalities. *Minn. Med.*

Whyte, W. F. (1955) *Street corner society: the social structure of an Italian slum.* Enl. ed. Chicago: Univer. of Chicago Press.

7

Delinquency and Community Action

WILLIAM C. RHODES

J*uvenile delinquency* can be viewed as a term used by communities to give focus to some of their generalized concerns about deviation and deviant behavior. Theorists and practitioners generally agree that lawbreaking behavior among juveniles is embedded in a tangled maze of social problems. This phenomenon is reported not only in the United States (Bernard, 1949; Wilensky and Lebeaux, 1958) but also throughout the world (Middendorff, 1960; Williamson, 1957). Investigators have associated delinquency with many other social problems, such as alcoholism, family disruption, economic dependency, illegitimacy, disability due to physical disease, high infant mortality rates, racial prejudices and discrimination, housing problems, crime and racketeering, population change, bad housing, mental disorder, desertion, and gross physical neglect.

All of these problems should be subsumed within any conceptual framework which focuses upon juvenile delinquency. It is impossible to give the term any degree of precision or clarity. Community action will necessarily be diffuse and varied in focus because of the present impossibility of clear definition and precise criteria for program effectiveness.

This chapter will be organized within the framework of a set of concepts embracing the many kinds of community problems and actions which delinquency represents. Delinquency will be considered in terms of community arousal, the behaviors which lead to such arousal, and the instruments of action which are forged from this interaction.

Juvenile delinquency is one of the many signals of community turbulence and discontent in our era. Historically, varying kinds of concern come to the front of community thinking and action at different time periods. In our time, a generalized concern about the human psyche and its behavioral correlates seems to be the major focus. This fermentation can be documented on an international, national, regional, and local level. It is evident in many of the structures of the World Health Organization. The avalanche of legislation and organizational efforts in the United States since World War II has included the National Mental Health Act, the President's Message on Mental Health and Mental Retardation, and program-creating legislation in such areas as special education, vocational rehabilitation, and child development. There has been the creation of the National Institute of Mental Health, the President's Committee on Mental Retardation, the proliferation of separate state mental health departments, and so on.

In the area of juvenile delinquency, this focus can be perceived in sessions on delinquency in the First United Nations Congress in 1955, in the 1960 Second United Nations Congress on the Prevention of Crime and Treatment of Offenders, and in the 1961 Juvenile Delinquency and Youth Offenses Control Act.

Behavioral sciences and mental health sciences have naturally been swept along in the avalanche. However, they are particularly inarticulate when they look within their body of knowledge for community constructs to weld together this kaleidoscope of behavioral concerns. We lack a language through which to recommend a systematic set of community actions. We lack construct systems which can relate to program action.

In this chapter, *juvenile delinquency* will refer to a set of behaviors, of legally defined juveniles, which are discordant with the expectations, sentiments, or codes of the community, and for which court action is indicated in that community. The boundaries of "community" will be defined by (1) the geographical jurisdiction of a court, and (2) the network of agencies, programs, and resources available to that court through formal and informal agreements.

The term *community concern* will refer to an arousal state in reaction to behaviors or potential behaviors which deviate from community codes. Some of the behaviors which lead to negative arousal states are suicide, alcoholism, mental disorder, perversion, drug addiction, and marital discord. Some of the behaviors which lead to positive arousal states are artistic triumphs, acts of heroism, unusual intellectual feats, educational accomplishments, and outstanding leadership.

Frequent or intense occurrences of such behaviors lead to community arousal and mobilization. This sequence of provocative behavior, community arousal, community mobilization, and instrumental action proceeds in the following typical fashion: there is an unusually provocative act committed, or the number of provocative acts are increased in frequency or intensity, or an increasing amount of publicity and mass media attention is given to the behavior. There is reverberation of concern within the community, and interaction among community members. Concern is aroused above the limen of action. The community members, through people in the power structure, demand that community resources and forces be brought to bear upon the specific provocative behavior. The power structure of the community engages professionals in the socializing systems, particularly those systems which are financed through governmental or semipolitical organizations of the community. The systems then mobilize their traditional operational patterns to bring their operations to bear upon the provocative behaviors.

Socializing Organizations

The organization which follows such community arousal includes forces, aspects of the environment, and current knowledge which can be interposed between the community and the arousing behavior. Community concern, in this way, becomes embodied in concrete structure. It can either be a newly created structure or mobilization of already existing structures. Such structures become intervening instruments between community concern and arousing behavior. They are not necessarily effective in coming to terms with the provoking behavior, but they are almost always effective in absorbing community concern about the behavior.

As we look at the kinds of institutions, agencies, and programs which serve this function in communities, we can categorize them into (1) socializing systems, (2) operational patterns, and (3) programs.

The socializing systems strive to reconcile community claims and individual claims. They form an interface which stands between deviant behavior and the community. Some of these systems form an interlock of psychosocial and political forces; others are less clearly tied to political forces. The systems to which this chapter will give major attention are those which form an interlock of psychosocial and political categories impressing the culture upon the individual. These are (1) the legal-correctional system, (2) the social welfare system, (3) the educational system, and (4) the medical system.

The other systems which are part of this interlock, but less clearly tied to governmental forces, are (1) the family system and (2) the religious system.

Historically, the legal-correctional and the social welfare systems have been assigned major responsibility in the area of juvenile delinquency. The educational and mental health systems, however, are now being legally required to assume increasing responsibility for delinquent behaviors.

The socializing systems themselves can be examined within the framework of organizational theories. Each can be conceptualized as an organizational complex consisting of (1) a basic orientation to human behavior which subsumes philosophy, assumptions, and beliefs; (2) a developed body of behavioral knowledge; (3) a set of socializing techniques and practices; and (4) a professional cadre indoctrinated in the philosophy, body of knowledge, and techniques which has official community sanction to practice these techniques (sanction can take the form of professional boards, certification, licensure, merit systems, and so on).

The socializing systems have developed standardized instruments or action forms through which the power of the community is brought to bear upon the provocative behavers. These instruments are actually patterns of operations developed by the systems to intercede in behalf of the community. The operational patterns incorporate all of the elements of the system listed above—behavioral orientation, knowledge, techniques, and professionals. In addition, they are the instruments of community power. They have a particular location in space, usually a brick-and-mortar structure in a particular geographical location. They have specific behavioral goals for their various operations. They might, for instance, aim at construction, reconstruction, and/or containment of behavior. And finally, they usually have a particular behavioral focus for their operations. Their focus can be upon interpersonal or intrapersonal antecedents of provocative behavior, upon the setting or situation which provides the ground for the behavior, or upon the specific provocative behavior itself.

The operational patterns themselves may have subunits, called programs. For instance, schools, as the major operational pattern of the educational system, frequently operate such behavioral programs as guidance, school social work, remedial reading, and special education.

Power is a very significant element in juvenile delinquency operational patterns and programs. The definition offered by Lippit, Polansky, Redl, and Rosen (1953, p. 463) is appropriate for the way in which the term is being used here: "Social power is (a) the potentiality (b) for inducing forces (c) in other persons (d) toward acting or changing in a given direction."

The community transmits social power to the operational pattern in the least two different ways. In the first place, it commissions the individual professional to use behavior-shaping knowledge and technique through such empowering mechanisms as certification, merit system ratings, boards, and licensing. In the second place, the community assures direction and control of the operational pattern through direct representation of power groups on the advisory, policy-making, or control boards of the operational patterns.

The current important power groups represented in this second source of community power include (1) governmental and nongovernmental fund-granting and fund-controlling agencies, (2) representatives of the socializing systems, and (3) the informal community power structure. It is through these power groups that the community is more likely to act and insure its continued action. The professional must recognize the importance of these groups and be fully conscious of his relationship to them. He should recognize that he is a mediator between culture and individual, and not merely an agent of society. He is as much responsible for transmitting and representing the claims of the individual as he is for reconciling the individual to the community. His most effective avenue of representation of the individual is through the community power structure. Through this structure he can institute reduction of community concern, redefinition of the nature of the provocation to which it is responding, and changes in community expectations and directions.

REPRESENTATIVE PATTERNS AND PROGRAMS

There are innumerable representative operational patterns and programs in each of the four-system categories discussed in this chapter. Only a few selected examples which have attracted recent attention, have departed slightly from traditional patterns, or can best illustrate the elements of the operational pattern and program will be discussed.

Cross-system Patterns

In the cross-system, coordinated pattern, there is usually representation from education, social welfare, legal-correction, and medicine or some combination of these. These units might be directly related to and participate in the power of governmental executive office, such as mayor (New York City Youth Board), commissions (Commissions Youth Council, Washington, D. C.), or governor (The California Youth Authority). On the other hand, the cross-system pattern might be independent of governmental relationships and participate in the informal power structure of the community. There are two relatively recent statutory stimulants to the proliferation of the cross-system patterns. One has already had considerable influence in the establishment of such operational patterns. The other should have equal or greater influence.

The oldest of these two is the Model Youth Authority Act, first promulgated in 1940 by the American Law Institute and revised by the same group in 1955. This act has stimulated cross-system patterns in California, Delaware, Illinois, Massachusetts, Minnesota, and Texas. Its influence can be seen in operational patterns of large cities, such as the Metropolitan Youth Commission in St. Louis, Missouri; the Commissioners' Youth Council in Washington, D. C.; the New York City Youth Board; and the Chicago Youth Commission.

This Youth Authority bill was aimed at youths under 21 but beyond juvenile court age. However, only the operational pattern in California has been applied to this target group. In spite of its influence, the bill has continued to arouse controversy (Tappan, 1959; Youngdahl, 1956; Bloch and Flynn, 1956, p. 487). It is widely discussed in the literature (Beck, 1951; McClosky, 1959; Robison, 1960, pp. 525-536; Newman, 1958, pp. 49-51; Bloch and Flynn, 1956).

The second source of probable influence is the Juvenile Delinquency Offenses Act of 1961 (Public Law 87-274, September, 1961). This act encourages "coordination" among agencies and places considerable power within such patterns. The act not only designates fund-granting responsibility to the Secretary of Health, Education and Welfare but also adds the following power source:

The Secretary shall consult with the President's Committee on Juvenile Delinquency and Youth Crime on matters of general policy and procedure arising in the administration of this Act, and shall consider the recommendations, if any, of such Committee on program applications submitted under section 3 or 4 and on proposed studies or other actions to be undertaken pursuant to section 5 (p. 3).

Cross-system patterns are based upon many different philosophies and assumptions. Their orientation may be influenced by the typical model of one of the major systems involved or it may incorporate a mélange of such models. However, every cross-system pattern gives tacit recognition to an "organization" model and organization constructs. In addition, each of these patterns seems to assume that a variety of behavior-shaping or educative approaches is necessary for community action in the area of juvenile delinquency.

The New York City Youth Board, for example, seems to lean heavily upon organization theory and orientation. It assumes that a multiple organization of socializing systems is necessary. It is based upon local evidence that juvenile delinquency is embedded in a matrix of social problems which must be tackled as a whole. Furthermore, it assumes that juvenile delinquency is associated with a failure of the family as a socializing system (Wheland, 1958).

The solution offered in New York is to mobilize socializing systems other than the family to perform this behavior-shaping task, and to provide stronger community supports and controls on behavior through "community organization."

The proposed Judge Baker Plan for Comprehensive Community Care of Juvenile Delinquents followed a combination medical and organizational model (Chap. 5, Appendix 1, N.I.M.H. Report to Congress, 1960). The medical assumptions, for instance, are evident in the theoretical statements of Dr. Elizabeth Makkay which conceptualizes the delinquent act as a symptom of a neurotic illness. The combined orientation is also evident in Dr. George Gardner's language, when he states that ". . . delinquency can be understood more and more as a complicated interplay among dynamic inner forces and social, economic, and cultural forces, all of which play important parts in the *etiology, pathology,* and self-perpetuation of this *disturbance* (p. 14).

The Mobilization for Youth Pattern, established to cope with the problem of delinquency in the Lower Eastside neighborhood in New York City, is another example of the cross-system pattern. One interpretation of the Mobilization for Youth Project conceptualizes the basic problem as ". . . the disintegration of the community and the

replacement of an organized society by a congeries of peoples"
(Appendix V, N.I.M.H. Report to Congress on Juvenile Delinquency, 1960, p. 3). The author of this statement sees the causes of
delinquency to be multiple, embedded in the fabric of the society,
and advocates an "integrated, interdisciplinary approach combining
community organization, treatment services and research" (p. 5).

Legal-correctional Patterns

The legal-correctional system has traditional operational patterns,
such as juvenile courts, juvenile bureaus, juvenile squads, probation
department, court-related diagnostic centers, youth study centers,
detention facilities, and training and correctional schools and institutions.

The basic orientation of this category of operational patterns is
quite confused. Its assumptions about human behavior, its body of
knowledge, and its methods are frequently in conflict. The problem
was adequately presented by Cressey (1957) in this statement:

In contemporary professional and academic penological circles it is not considered quite proper to talk about correctional agencies as places of punishment; it seems timely to call attention to the fact that our society expects them
to be punitive.

The issue comes out more clearly, however, in discussion of prisons
and institutions for juveniles. These agencies are expected to be
punitive but at the same time, they are expected to be treatment
organizations, like mental hospitals (Middendorff, p. 115).

Tappan (1952) argues that one of the consequences of this confusion is that children are deprived of their rights of "due process"
and "justice under the law." Among the deprivations which he sees
are the following:

(1) There are no clear and definite substantive norms for delinquency, thus the definition can be stretched to suit any purpose,
group, or individual having any type of jurisdiction over children.

(2) The child does not have legal counsel or legal representation
in court. The "social investigation" is the means of determining
whether the child be adjudicated delinquent and whether a problem
exists, such as to invite treatment. Tappan says that ". . . because of
the limitation in time and training of the staff there is altogether too
little cross-checking of information to assure the accuracy of factual
data. Surmise, opinion, gossip, scandal, hearsay, the distorted views

of prejudiced informants are too commonly accepted as the basis for subsequent court action" (p. 35).

(3) In most jurisdictions the child has no right to demand jury trial. He is not advised of his right to seek counsel or to seek witnesses in his behalf.

(4) In the vast majority of jurisdictions it is not required that there be proof beyond a reasonable doubt of the child's delinquency to support a finding of delinquency.

(5) In comparing the children's court to the criminal court, Tappan claims: "The most striking contrast in adjudication and disposition, however, is the far greater likelihood that the child coming to the juvenile court will be subjected to correctional measures than is true of adults accused of crime. . . . Next to this phenomena, the most striking feature of children's court operation is the relatively long periods of institutional treatment and—to a somewhat lesser extent—of probation supervision to which children are exposed for minor conduct problems, as compared to adult criminals" (p. 37).

This conflict of orientation extends through the total range of operational patterns in the legal-correctional category. It includes such occurrences as the youth authority and the juvenile police department in a large city maintaining separate gang files which are closed to each other. Another example consists of two units in a Youth Division of a major police department which are housed in the same building. The personnel of these two units have divergent orientations toward delinquent behavior. They were reported to have no contact with each other; and their unit commanders, with jurisdiction over the same territory, had not conferred or even met each other (Interim Report No. VII, Juvenile Delinquency Evaluation Project, 1957).

Some of the less traditional patterns and programs which are currently being widely discussed and written about include those described briefly below.

Forestry camps have become quite popular as an answer to the problem of delinquency (Stark, 1937; Holton, 1941; Close, 1945; Zuck, 1949; Breed, 1953). These camps possess a long history, having been established originally in the Forestry Department of Los Angeles by Karl Holton during the 1930's. This is actually the pattern of the CCC camps, prior to World War II, which has been copied in New York, California, Michigan, Wisconsin, Ohio, Minnesota, Illinois, and Tennessee.

In California, boys are referred by the Youth Authority after diagnostic screening and are grouped and placed under the supervision of a junior and senior counselor. Their various work assignments include trail building, road mending, telephone line maintenance, and pulpwood production. A camp contains fifty to seventy boys whose length of stay is no longer than six months. There are recreational, individual and group counseling, educational, and religious programs.

Another pattern embraces special institutions, such as Wiltwyck (McCord and McCord, 1956) and Highfields (Weeks, 1958). Highfields is a short-term, small, institutional pattern in New Jersey. Delinquents are received through the courts and a diagnostic center. Housed in the former Charles and Anne Lindbergh home, it consists of work groups of boys in supervised situations for 40 hours per week, guided group discussions five nights per week, and recreation and earned three-day furloughs.

The "half-way" pattern, such as probation homes and hostels in England, have received considerable attention recently. The probation hostel developed since World War I and is an integral part of the probation system in England (Spencer and Grygier, 1959). It is somewhat similar to an institutional program, but allows for some interesting variation. With the consent of the probationer, the judge or magistrate setting the probation terms can insert a condition of residence in a hostel up to twelve months. The probationers live in the hostel and work outside. France has a similar pattern in the foyers de semi-liberté (Arcadias, 1954).

Another English pattern is a "new" type of detention center. These centers, seemingly based upon a philosophy expressed by Grunhüt (1955), take juveniles from 14 to 21 years of age for a period of about three months. They are for treatment of a deliberately punitive character, "which is still acceptable from an educational point of view. . . ." This program, which has been called a "short sharp shock," was established in the Criminal Justice Act of 1958. The act provides for centers for two age groups—one for boys 14 to 17 years old and one for boys 14 to 21 years of age. In describing two of these for juniors, one at Oxford and one at Derbyshire, Wills (1962) says:

The regime is variously described as brisk, invigorating, disciplined, and there is no doubt that it is intended to make the inmates sit up and take notice. The day begins at 6:15 with P.T., and continues "at the double" until nine in the evening. The whole day is planned and there is no time for mooning and loafing. Boys of school age have normal lessons during the day, but also have jobs of work to do and activities to participate in during their spare time. The older boys work hard all day and have lessons or other activities in the evenings, with of course for both groups organized sport and religious observance at the week end. The hope is that the boys will learn to appreciate the pleasure to be derived from a good job well done, and the satisfaction to be found in "all out" physical effort (pp. 118, 119).

Still another pattern is the attendance centers in England. Here boys between 12 and 21 are ordered by the court to take part in a time-limited program while attending school or holding a job. They must attend a center for not more than 12 hours, in installments of not more than 3 hours at a time.

The Citizenship Training Group in Boston offers a similar plan (Maglio, 1959). Boys between 12 and 17 years of age placed on probation by the Boston Juvenile Court are required, as a condition of their probation, to attend the training program. Attendance is for twelve weeks, five days per week from 3:30 to 5:30 P.M. The program includes physical conditioning, crafts, and group discussions. The Pinehills Program located near the Brigham Young campus at Provo, Utah, is also very similar.

The United States Army has a program which bears some of the features of this pattern. Since World War II there have been screening and training procedures for soldiers who have been sentenced, which has made possible a more flexible program for administering a sentence. Offenders capable of potential restoration are either organized into special training units for a period of at least 20 hours per week, or they may be released to training units. If they are released to training units, they are expected to follow the training schedule of their own or similar units during normal training hours, returning to the stockade for custodial purposes during nonduty hours.

There are countless other operational patterns and program within the legal-correctional system. The sample given should be sufficient to provide referents, and an understanding of the orientation of the system.

Social Welfare Patterns

The social welfare system has been even more prolific than the other systems in developing patterns and programs. In addition to delinquency-focused programs within Public Welfare Departments and Family or Child Care Agencies, this system includes such patterns as settlement houses, community centers, area councils, recreation centers and other group-work agencies, homes for unwed mothers, youth employment programs, and summer camps.

Usually, a particular pattern or program is conceptually derived and conceptually bound to a specific kind of discordant behavior which is arousing community concern. Because of this direct relationship to the manifest behavior, the social welfare system seems to encompass a great diversity of operational patterns and programs.

Historically, these varied efforts within the social welfare category have grown out of the ecclesiastic programs and patterns dealing with poor relief. This relief effort, following the Reformation, became a direct community responsibility and was codified in the famous statute of the Poor Relief Act of 1601, and in the reforms of the Poor Law Amendment Act of 1834. It appears reasonable to say that a major portion of the social welfare patterns and programs are, even today, closely related to the concept of "poor relief," although the professionals within the system may reject this orientation.

An example of the responsiveness of the programs of this system to current behavioral concerns of the community can be seen in the programs of gang-work, street-corner group worker, or street-club work for gang control. This type of program has one of its roots in the Chicago Area Project, begun over twenty-five years ago under the influence of Clifford Shaw (Kobrin, 1959).

The Chicago project had three elements: recreation, community improvement, and direct work with gangs and individual boys. It is this third element which has recently become very popular in large urban areas. Some of the newer gang behavior programs which have been most frequently reported are the Roxbury, or Boston Special Youth Program (Miller, 1958, 1959); the Hyde Park Project in Chicago (Gandy, 1959); the Los Angeles Youth Project (Alston, 1951); the Street Clubs Program of the New York City Youth Board (Reaching the Fighting Gang, 1960); and the gang control operation of the Commissioners' Youth Council in Washington, D. C. (Trevvett, 1960). Gang work is not restricted to the United States. Father Borelli, "the urchin's priest," worked with gangs in Naples, Italy (West, 1957); and in France, the équipes d' amitié have made efforts similar to those in the United States (Parrot and Gueneau, 1959). Father Alan Cox, in Montreal, Canada, also carries on a similar program.

Gang theory has been elaborately developed in such works as Whyte (1943), Cohen (1955), Cloward and Ohlin (1961), Miller (1958), Bloch and Niederhoffer (1958), and Scott (1956).

Services to "multiproblem families" is another social welfare program which has become quite popular in recent years. The occurrence of multiproblem families has been dramatized by the studies of Buell *et al.* (Buell *et al.*, 1952; Buck, Buell, and Kandle, 1951). In their St. Paul study they reported about 6 per cent of the families were suffering from a combination of serious problems and were using 46 per cent of the community organized health services, 55 per cent of its adjustment services, and 68 per cent of its dependency services.

These findings have been supported in many other cities. In New York City, for instance, they have become a demographic fact upon which an important segment of the Youth Board's pattern has been founded. Ralph Wheland (1958) reported in a Senate subcommittee investigation: "In New York City, our research reveals, fewer than 1 per cent of the families make up the hard core responsible for some 75 per cent of the juvenile delinquency" (p. 85).

On this basis, the Youth Board has developed a program of "aggressive casework" to reach these families. In a quantitative analysis of a sample of 150 such families, the Youth Board categorized them on the basis of failure of functioning of the mother, the father, siblings, failure in marital adjustment, and economic deprivation. Of the 150 families, 87 per cent were failures in three or more areas, 35 per cent were failures in all five areas, 39 per cent in four areas, and only 13 per cent in less than three areas. Forty-five per cent of the fathers were separated from the families, and another 10 per cent were deceased. Over half of them were entirely financially dependent.

Another social welfare program focused upon the family as a unit constitutes the camps for asocial families which have been in operation in Holland since World War II. This program was recently recommended for inclusion in the programs of the Commissioners' Youth Council in Washington, D. C. (Trevvett, 1958).

The Ministry of Social Work in Holland operates twelve camps, with twelve to eighteen families, each located in a rural area three or four miles from the nearest town. The rehabilitation attempt not only concentrates on supplying housing, food, clothing, and so on, but also tries integrating the family into society. Referrals are made from local communities after intensive social, physical, and psychiatric screening. The objective is to retain family ties and develop adequate interpersonal relationships and a healthy family life.

Other social welfare patterns and programs will be mentioned briefly in the section which discusses operational goals and foci. A comprehensive catalogue of operational patterns and programs in the social welfare category would produce an even more voluminous document than that provided by the National Education Association in its published survey of principles and practices of education in the area of juvenile delinquency (Kvaraceus and Ulrich, 1959).

Educational Patterns

As the above-mentioned publications indicate, the educational system is very much involved in community concern over discordant child behavior. From the community point of view, the educational system shares equal, and maybe greater, responsibility than the family for the enculturation of children.

The community relies heavily upon the school and brings its power structure strongly to bear upon the educational system to develop children toward the cultural type. The school has the major responsibility for transforming the human nature of the child in such a way that he will become a "bearer of the culture" (Clarke, 1948).

The major orientation of education operational patterns and programs is, to paraphrase Rousseau, to reconcile the child's individual claims with the social claims. It is the major place in which the community attempts a synthesis of nature and nurture.

The educational system in the United States has developed only one operational pattern to accomplish this task. This is the school. Reports (e.g., Conant [1961]) raise questions concerning the appropriateness of the present pattern for the great American slums. Perhaps we need new patterns for this group. The teacher-learner transaction does not have to be carried on in this particular setting. Other settings might be devised which are more effective. The gang-worker, for instance, might be more clearly structured as a teacher. His role might be more carefully defined as an educational one.

Another possibility for education of this group might be a revival of the apprenticeship system in this country. It is still active in European countries (Kohler, 1960, p. 12). An apprentice-master relationship might accomplish as much for some of these children as our present school pattern. There is evidence that these schools are failing to teach the delinquency-prone child even such fundamentals as reading. There is no reason why reading could not be incorporated into an apprenticeship program.

The Kibbutzim program in Israel might also offer suggestions for new kinds of teaching-learning programs. Perhaps they could be used to teach the combined skills learned in family and school in our typical American community. They might be quite appropriate in disorganized neighborhoods made up of disintegrated family units.

The single stereotyped operational pattern of schools has occasionally been redesigned slightly to incorporate the child who is called delinquent. Typical of this is the Montefiore School in Chicago, and the pattern of the "600" schools in New York City. The "600" schools are administered by the Division of Child Welfare of the New York City school system. There are more than twenty such schools, falling into the categories of day schools, remand centers, institutions, and hospital schools. They "are composed of children who, in previous schools, have been unable to get along with adults or peers; and who, because of their extreme aggressiveness, could not be contained in a classroom or in the school" (Annual report—The "600" Schools, 1958-1959).

Most frequently, however, schools have attempted to graft on a multitude of special programs to deal with the problems of delinquency. In addition to the "600" school program, one of the most complex and complicated examples of a multitude of specialized programs can be found in the New York City school system, under the Division of Child Welfare of the Board of Education. This division, consisting of eleven different bureaus, offers samples of almost every kind of special school program that exists in this country. It has an elaborate special education program, a program of educational and vocational guidance, and probably one of the largest single systems of child guidance clinical services in any part of the world. Each of these semiautonomous units approaches discordant behavior in its own way and with its own specialists.

Still another education operational pattern offered by New York City is the All-Day Neighborhood School. These are nine regular elementary schools and are included in the "special service schools," a designation given by the Board of Education to about 25 per cent of the New York City elementary and junior high schools. The "special service schools" rank lowest according to such factors as mean reading grade and IQ and highest according to percentage of children getting free lunch, of pupil mobility, and of children having language handicap. Most of these schools have predominantly minority group children and classes of 30 per cent or more non-English speaking students (Interim Report No. XIII, Juvenile Delinquency Evaluation Project, December 1959). The All-Day Neighborhood schools have three goals: cultural enrichment, help to children with problems, and work with parents, citizens, and neighborhood.

Another example of a unique school program is Los Angeles

County Reception Center training program in which the teaching of vocational skills and prevocational skills and habits are carried on within the academic classroom. It is highly programmed, with a careful analysis of the important behaviors demanded in work situations.

A sequence of learning episodes for acquisition of new habits, understandings, purposes, goals, ideals, feelings, and attitudes are carefully prepared for each child. Each of these episodes is presented to the boys as a job rather than as an assignment. They are planned in terms of the individual's abilities, interest, academic skills, and underachievements. The level and number of jobs required are determined on the basis of achievement tests and mental age of mental ability expectancy levels. The teacher acts as foreman and provides conditions and opportunities for learning skills and vocational or on-the-job skills and behaviors (Los Angeles County Special Schools, Reception Center, 1959).

There are numerous other patterns and programs in the schools in the United States. The traditional ones include pupil-personnel services, school-psychology programs, school-social work programs, clinical programs, and others. A basic reference work for samples of such patterns throughout the country can be found in the already mentioned Kvaraceus and Ulrich (1959).

In other countries we also find a number of interesting educational patterns and programs oriented toward the problems associated with delinquency.

In England, for instance, there are a number of semi-independent schools for maladjusted children which are receiving support in connection with the 1944 Education Act, which gave approval and provided grant aid for schools for maladjusted children.

France and Canada have included the problems of the delinquent operationally in multiple uses of a special professional group known as *éducateurs*. France has a variety of special patterns and programs staffed with *éducateurs* which are devoted to work with delinquents. Of particular interest are the special homes which provide residential treatment-type programs for groups of thirty to forty children. The *éducateur* profession is newer in Canada, having been developed within the last eight or ten years, but it has an extremely interesting training program and a strong, cohesive professional organization. A special institution at Boscaville, near Montreal, works with delinquents, using the orientation and techniques of this group.

Medical Patterns

Medical patterns and programs are developed upon a concept of the genetically based social character of the human individual which unfolds in phases of epigenetic development. The clearest statements of this orientation have probably come from psychoanalysis. Examples of such theoretical constructions are contained in the works of Kate Friedlander (1947) and Erik Erikson (1950). In its direct application to special operational patterns, the writing of George Gardner and Elizabeth Makkay *et al.* (1960) spell out the structure and techniques of the system. This orientation is being criticized or questioned by theorists who prefer sociological and anthropological constructions (Hakeem, 1958; Cohen, 1955; Kobrin, 1959).

Within the medical construction, the discordant behavior of the delinquent is a symptom associated with an underlying pathology or an illness which can be diagnosed and treated and, perhaps, cured through clinical methods (Karpman, 1954; Makkay, 1960; Shields, 1962).

The medical orientation has considerable influence in communities concerned with discordant behavior. The professionals within the medical system are frequently called upon by members of the informal power structure. Usually, this professional person will suggest a child guidance clinic or a residential treatment center as a cure-all (in the same way that professionals in other systems usually recommend traditional operational patterns of their own systems).

These two patterns have proliferated, not only in child guidance and mental health clinics, but also within all of the other operational patterns. There are clinics in school, in courts or detention centers, in prisons, and in community centers. Many correctional institutions have shifted their operational pattern toward medical concepts and have become residential treatment centers.

The child guidance clinic pattern has been popular since the pioneering work of William Healy and Augusta Bronner (1936). The Judge Baker Child Guidance Center in Boston is an existing link with the work of these two pioneers in the treatment of juvenile delinquency. This is the same center that was the subject of the early Glueck and Glueck studies (1934).

One of the most publicized recent attempts to demonstrate residential treatment of children with extremely discordant behavior was the intensive effort of Dr. Fritz Redl and associates in the Child

Research Branch of the Clinical Center at the National Institute of
Mental Health in Bethesda, Maryland. This special project existed
from September 1953 until July 1959. The effort, although of great
heuristic value, pointed to some of the problems of treating delinquents within a hospital setting. An account of this project submitted in support of a report from N.I.M.H. to Congress on juvenile
delinquency (Vol. 6, Appendix IX, 1960) notes: "As things turned
out, the nature of the work demanded certain liberties of an administrative character that clashed painfully with the realities of normal
hospital management" (p. 19).

OPERATIONAL GOALS

The operational pattern has been conceptualized as the operational units of the professional socializing systems. These units include all of the elements of the system—a basic orientation to human
behavior, a body of knowledge, a set of socializing techniques, and
a group of professionals who have adopted the orientation and
learned the body of knowledge and techniques. In addition, the
action patterns of the socializing systems comprise institutionalized
community power, a structure, a geographical locus, a set of explicit
goals, and an explicit focus for their operations. The latter two elements, the goals and the foci, are particularly significant elements of
the patterns.

Although an operational pattern may not limit itself to a single
goal, one goal is usually predominant over the others. Furthermore,
there are goals which are more in harmony with the orientation of
certain socializing systems rather than with others.

These goals might be conceived of as growing out of the folklore
of society about ways of influencing human behavior, or they could
be conceived as social goals for the human organism.

Constraint and Control

Some operational patterns aim at repression, containment, control,
suppression, or extinction of discordant behavior. This goal is most
obvious in the case of the legal-correctional system in its detention
centers, remand centers, training school, and so on. However, it is
certainly involved to some extent in many other patterns, such as the
"treatment" structured institutions. Its involvement can be perceived
in an interim report of the Juvenile Delinquency Evaluation Project
of the City of New York which says of the "600" Day Schools (In-

terim Report, No. VI, December 1957): "Strictly in terms of a 'containing' function, the '600' day schools seem to be doing an admirable job."

Constraint patterns are not only those which exile the discordant from the community, but also some of them attempt to limit or control the behavior without removing the behaver. Furthermore, most socializing systems believe that external restraint is a prerequisite for the building of internal constraint.

Many behavioral theories contain constraining concepts. In the psychoanalytic construction of human behavior, the child begins as a small human being governed solely by his impulses, the satisfaction of which gives him pleasure. Friedlander (1947) states: "Deep down in the unconscious these old anti-social impulses which we have seen expressed in the toddler are still alive, and influence the thoughts and actions of the adult" (p. 14). They are handled in their mature edition through a variety of constraining or sublimating mechanisms.

The learning theorists also employ constraining concepts. Guthrie (1938) says: "All learning involves associative inhibition. Acquiring a tendency to respond in any manner whatsoever to a situation must involve losing other conflicting tendencies already established" (p. 54).

Some of the newer techniques of behavioral therapy may have considerable effect upon constraining and control patterns. Most of these involve extinction or suppression of old behaviors by supplanting them with new ones. Mary Cover Jones' well-known work with Peter (1924) in deconditioning fear behavior to a white rabbit is a classic forerunner of these methods. The techniques of reciprocal inhibition and desensitization developed by Joseph Wolpe (1958) could also have application to extinction or containment of delinquent behavior by direct control methods. The operant-interpersonal method used by King, Armitage, and Tilton (1960) offers another technique which could have utility in this category. The demonstration of learning principles in a psychiatric hospital by Ayllon and Michael (1959) is still another example. The present-day applications of Knight Dunlap's technique of negative practice by Leshan (1942) is another possibility.

One can see the constraint and control emphasis in the Chicago "school" of Burgess, Shaw, McKay, and Kobrin. Kobrin in talking about the Chicago Area Project (1959) says: "Disruption of cross-generation control produced the conditions for the emergence of a variant species of youth subculture in these communities marked by a tradition of sophisticated delinquency" (p. 21).

Nye (1958) says:

> It is our position, therefore, that in general behavior prescribed as delinquent or criminal need not be explained in any positive sense, since it usually results in quicker and easier achievement of goals than the normative behavior. The processes, agencies, and relationships which prevent it are the subject of social control as applied to delinquency (p. 5).

He says that his concept of control embraces four "not unrelated" clusters of attitudes and behavior patterns: (1) direct control from without, (2) internalized control through conscience, (3) indirect control through identification, and (4) availability of alternative means to goals and values.

Remediation and Re-formation

Any pattern or program whose techniques and operations have the goal of remediation, reinstatement, re-formation, reconstruction, or re-education would be classified within this category. Psychotherapy is a technique associated with this type of goal, as are remedial reading and rehabilitation programs. For the most part, the medical and social welfare patterns have this major behavioral goal.

This goal is built upon the assumption that there is a development within the individual (or sometimes, the situation) which has to be re-formed, or formed in a different fashion. The operations involved are aimed at either correction of a response pattern, or reorganization of the total personality of the individual. These operations assume a history of maldevelopment, disorganization, faulty learning, or pathology. They do not aim primarily at control of behavior or constraint of behavior, but upon a remolding of the incorrectly developed behavior.

Most frequently, these operations deny the significance of the specific behavior which arouses community concern. They assume that the manifest discordant behavior is relatively unimportant and cannot be attacked directly without other manifestations asserting themselves in the place of the behavior of concern.

An expression of this point of view can be found in some of the psychotherapeutically oriented theorists (Friedlander, 1947, p. 116; Healy and Bronner, 1936, p. 7; and Makkay, 1960, p. 79). Friedlander, for instance, says:

> A neurotic symptom is the outcome of an unconscious mental conflict, and unless the unconscious material is revealed the symptom appears to the person

afflicted with it and to the onlooker to be entirely meaningless. In the same way certain delinquent acts can be understood only if their unconscious motivation is unearthed. It has been found that there is no fundamental difference between unconscious conflicts underlying neurotic symptoms formation and unconscious conflicts causing those delinquent actions which we might call "delinquent symptoms" (p. 116).

Construction or Formation

The third category of goals of operational patterns is construction, formation, or development. This is a goal which is more common to the operational patterns of the system of education. The term *prevention* has gained widespread popularity among people concerned with juvenile delinquency, but there are very few patterns devoted to prevention in terms of its specific operations.

The concept of prevention is dependent upon historical tracing of antecedents of juvenile delinquents' behaviors. However, there is little unanimity among historically oriented theorists and practitioners socializing with respect to the crucial antecedents of discordant behavior. Therefore, there are few specific "preventive" techniques and few patterns of operations specifically dedicated to prevention.

The operational patterns of education might be conceptualized as constructive or developmental. The kinds of operations which the other socializing systems have developed assume that the behavior has gone awry and intervention is necessary to reinstate more normal or concordant behavior. The system of education within its operational goals and its techniques, however, is devoted to construction or formation of the person into the cultural type. This end has been stated for education by sociologists (Mannheim, 1950), educational philosophers (Clarke, 1948), and psychologists (James, 1946).

The Educational Policies Commission (1938) said: "The general end of education in America at the present time is the fullest possible development of the individual within the framework of our present industrialized society" (p. 41). This commission has declared that educational purposes are a form of social policy, a program of social action based on an accepted scale of values.

The system of education, in addition, appears to be the major socializing system to which the community, through its power structure, turns when it is inspired by contributory constructive or creative behavior of its community members. When such positive concern is aroused and the community wishes to assure that such behaviors will continue and will be replicated, the school is given the task of acting in the community's behalf.

The operational goals of education, therefore, can be perceived primarily as "construction" rather than "reconstruction" or "constraint"; and the techniques of education can be applied in behalf of either community negative concern, aroused by discordant behavior, or community positive concern, when aroused by contributory behavior.

Schools, of course, are not the only socializing system devoted to constructive goals. This subsidiary goal can also be found in the operational patterns of the social welfare system, the legal-correctional system, and the medical system. The area approach, for instance, as exemplified in the Chicago Area Project, has not only the goal of reorganization of neighborhoods to control discordant behavior, but also the development of an organization which will stimulate the positive and creative forces of leadership within the area.

A clear statement of constructive operational goals is contained in one of the presentations of the Mobilization for Youth project. This presentation associates the project with a set of theoretical statements which attempt to integrate and reconceptualize the cultural transmission and differential association tradition in sociological approaches to delinquency. The reconceptualization is contained in the theory of Richard Cloward and Lloyd Ohlin (1961). In the view of these authors, ". . . pressures toward the formation of delinquent subcultures originate in marked discrepancies between culturally induced aspirations among lower-class youth and the possibilities of achieving them by legitimate means" (p. 78).

These authors advocate that, in addition to re-establishing mechanisms for "control" in disorganized slum communities, we also develop structures through which the lower class child can achieve the culturally induced aspirations: "Slum neighborhoods appear to us to be undergoing progressive disintegration. The old structures, which provided social control and avenues of social ascent, are breaking down. Legitimate but functional substitutes for these traditional structures must be developed if we are to stem the trend toward violence and retreatism among adolescents in urban slums" (p. 211).

Summary

In summary, a logical analysis of the apparent goals of the operations in the operational patterns of the legally commissioned professional educative systems suggests the following goal categories: (1)

constraint and control, (2) remediation and re-formation, and (3) construction or formation. The techniques which are derived from the basic philosophy or orientation of the socializing systems seem to be directly related to these behavior-shaping goals. Although no system relies exclusively upon a single goal in their operational patterns and programs, there is a major emphasis upon one or the other. The three systems of medicine, legal-correctional, and social welfare appear to emphasize constraining or re-forming goals. The system of education has a single operational pattern of school which seems to orient its techniques and forces toward the forming or construction of the child.

The Operational Foci

In addition to operational goals, the patterns usually have specific foci for their operations. It is a rare pattern or program which has a single focus. However, as in the case of operational goals, a particular pattern or program usually has a primary focus which is reflected in the kinds of techniques utilized to shape behavior. As we examine the operations and techniques of various operational patterns, we can divide the foci into:

(1) Interpersonal or intrapersonal factors believed to be associated with the discordant behavior.

(2) The setting or situation within which the behavior recurs.

(3) The specific pattern of discordant behavior which is arousing the concern of the community.

As indicated in a previous paragraph, the focus can be deducted from a study of the major operations or techniques employed within the operational pattern. When a community empowers the educative agents of a particular professional educative system to practice their techniques directly upon provocative behavers and their behaviors, it frequently specifies that particular techniques are the property of the particular system. One of the major recent controversies between professionals over legal right to practice a technique has been between psychiatry and psychology. The new licensing or certification laws for psychologists have been battlegrounds upon which the ownership of psychotherapy has been bitterly contested. This quarrel reflects not only the whims of the two professional groups involved, but also the gravity with which communities legally approve and empower the use of specific techniques aimed at specific human factors.

Personal Factors

The operational patterns which focus upon interpersonal and intrapersonal factors in juvenile delinquency currently favor the techniques of (1) diagnosis and (2) psychotherapy. The techniques of diagnosis and therapy, of course, are derived from a medical conception of human behavior. The problem of "diagnosis" in the delinquency area is a particularly difficult one for the clinically oriented professional. In the first place, although there is usually a verbal recognition of a distinction between the psychopath or sociopath and the delinquent, this distinction is not always evident in the thinking or writing of clinicians.

The first Round Table of the American Orthopsychiatric Association (Karpman, 1950) which concentrated upon the delinquency area was entitled *The Psychopathic Delinquent Child*. It was not until the discussion period of the second Round Table that there was an attempt to make a distinction between the psychopathic and the delinquent child. In either case, whether merging or differentiating these two concepts, the diagnostic approach admits considerable confusion. Karpman (1950) said: "There is no nosological condition in the entire field of psychiatry on which there is so little agreement, and which is subject to so much misunderstanding and equivocation, as that of psychopathy and psychopathic personality" (p. 223). Peck, in another Round Table (1955), said: "Let us be clear then, that whatever else delinquency is, it is not a diagnostic category" (p. 266).

Bender, in the same Round Table quoted above, took a different point of view and said that any delinquent child falls in some psychiatric classification (p. 274). She adds that she cannot understand what is meant by "normal" delinquency. Kanner (1955), on the other hand, presents two cases of delinquency and says that they should suffice to demonstrate the futility of trying to find a common denominator for all childhood delinquency.

Part of the problem lies in the divergent theorizing about antecedent factors. Although most clinicians agree that there are multiple causes or antecedents, and that criminal behavior of the same type may mean quite different things from individual to individual, this is not always so clear in their discussions. Louis Lurie (1951, 1953) seems to assume a constitutional basis for discordant behavior. Others believe that extreme examples of discordant behavior may not be explained primarily upon a constitutional basis; however, once the condition has progressed to a certain point, there is a formed substratum which is unalterable. Still others accept the possibility of predetermining organic or psychogenic factors but lay heavy emphasis on the kinds of early relationship experience the child has had (Allen, 1950; Rabinovitch, 1952).

As further evidence of the difficulty involved in the diagnostic approach, several studies have shown that the major portion of adjudicated delinquents either cannot be placed in a clinical category or that there is very little reliability of diagnosis (Reiss, 1952; Overholser, 1944, p. 156; Hakeem, 1958, pp. 79-112).

The technique of psychotherapy as applied to interpersonal and intrapersonal factors offers the same problems. Stella Chess says: "The problem of delinquency as a whole is not likely to be answered by individual psychotherapy. It requires epidemiological and sociological approaches" (p. 5). John Rose opened a 1952 symposium of the American Orthopsychiatric Association by saying that the problem remains that many of these cases are simply not accessible to psychotherapy. Robinson (1959, p. 224) observes that the delinquent child is notoriously hard to reach in psychotherapy or indeed in any type of personal relationship. Cleckley (1962) agrees with Hakeem that there is no scientific evidence for a specific medical or psychiatric treatment for delinquency.

On the other hand, there has developed an elaborate body of literature on such treatment (Aichhorn, 1959; Friedlander, 1947; Schmideberg, 1935; Noshpitz, 1957). A recent innovation by Charles Slack (1960) has the "therapist" playing the "patient" and assuming the role of student to the delinquent teacher who is the expert on delinquency. Slack uses the terms "experimenter" for therapist and "subject" for patient. The author of this chapter had the interesting and unique experience of discussing Dr. Slack's work with him, through the interpolated comments and interpretations of one of these consultant delinquents.

The Setting or Situation

Some operational patterns, instead of focusing their techniques and specific operations on personal factors and the organism, give major emphasis to the setting or situation out of which discordant behavior arises. The two major techniques with this focus are (1) milieu therapy and (2) community organization.

Milieu therapy has been conceived of either directly within the medical paradigm, or has been structured more closely to the social welfare or the educational paradigm. Rioch and Stanton (1953) define milieu therapy within the medical paradigm as: ". . . procedures directed toward the modification of the environmental part of the patient-environment process with a view to facilitating more satisfactory patterns of interaction . . ." (p. 65). In the area of discordant behavior, such people as Redl (1957), Jones (1953), and Bettleheim (1950) have attempted to spell out the operations of milieu therapy. In the educational or social welfare orientation, milieu therapy has been practiced and described by Homer Lane (1928), Makarenko (1955), and Wills (1941).

Community organization operations were originally developed and applied to delinquent populations by the Chicago Area Project (Kobrin, 1959). The basic procedure is the development of local welfare organization among residents of the high delinquency rate neighborhoods. This involves identifying the residents holding key positions of influence and arousal of their interest in youth welfare activities.

Thelen and Sarchet (1954) published a manual for community leaders called *Neighbors in Action,* which describes the block organization approach which has resulted in some 200 blocks organized in Chicago to promote physical maintenance of property and prevent deterioration, solve problems of social relations, and organize community-wide projects. This type of operation has become extremely popular and can be found in most of the patterns and programs based upon the Model Youth Authority Act. It has been sponsored by state departments, community councils, universities, civic organizations, and many others.

One of the interesting community organization approaches is the effort of the National Probation and Parole Association Citizen Action Program, which is financed through a Ford Foundation grant. This program involves a loose federation of state councils related to a national chairman. The state councils consist of members who have power and influence in the state. They are prominent leaders in business, industry, law, labor, religion, agriculture, finance, publishing, and education. The responsibility of the state council is to inform itself about the state's facilities and services for dealing with juvenile and youthful offenders from first contact to disposition and final treatment. The council then informs the public and attempts to get action on the problem. There are councils in such states as Texas, Michigan, Washington, Ohio, Montana, Indiana, Oklahoma, and West Virginia.

Specific Behavior

There are a number of operational patterns and programs which focus upon specific discordant behaviors associated with juvenile delinquency. Examples of this focus are programs aimed at drug addiction and alcoholism, and those concerned with the by-product of sexual promiscuity in teen-agers, such as venereal disease programs and homes for unwed mothers. There are also numerous programs focused on job behavior and job-getting.

Another focus on specific behaviors can be found in the operations aimed at fighting behavior in gangs. This is one of the current areas of greatest effort in delinquency programs of large urban areas. The New York City Youth Board publication, *Reaching the Fighting Gang* (1960), gives a detailed account of the operations used in this effort. The rather formal procedures worked out by the New York City group for a mediation meeting between two gangs could provide very effective pointers to United Nations mediators.

Another operation which focuses upon the problem of juvenile delinquency through a specific behavior is the remedial reading approach advocated by Melvin Roman (1957). Since early school drop-out and extreme underachievement in reading are correlated with adjudication, Roman advocates using a specialized remedial reading program that he developed as an approach to this problem. Reading programs are beginning to attract the attention of several juvenile delinquency programs. It is quite probable that this particular approach will spread.

Of all aspects of the operational pattern, the most important are the techniques. It is through the techniques that the power of a pattern is focused. The impact of a clearly defined, carefully timed, and specifically focused technique can be seen in a dramatic experience described by A. S. Makarenko (1955). He had the task of taking charge of the disorganized, corrupted, chaotic, hostile Kuryazh colony of 300 delinquent youths with a detachment of 100 children from the highly organized and cohesive Gorky colony. Makarenko says: "In my preparations for the struggle with Kuryazh I kept before me the idea of a single lightning stroke—the Kuryazhites must be taken by storm. The slightest delay, any hopes of evolution, of 'gradual infiltration,' would jeopardize the outcome of our operations" (p. 11).

Much later in this third volume of his narrative, Makarenko describes how he accomplished the "conversion" of the Kuryazhites in a matter of hours. His method seemed to consist of building up a high level of emotionality; presenting a sharp, dramatic model of highly organized behavior contrasting quite dramatically with that of the Kuryazhites; and opening this model for easy and rapid adoption by the Kuryazhites. If Makarenko's recounting is accurate, one could contrast before and after characteristics of the Kuryazh colony and show dramatic results within the situation over a period of a few hours.

Although there are limitations in using the public health model as an analogy to delinquency patterns, it is reasonable to say that, as we examine the various operational patterns and programs contained in public health activity, it becomes evident that specific technology is the most important aspect of the success of individual programs. The social-political-administrative gestalt in such programs is, of course, of vital importance. However, without specific control devices, without specific agents, acting upon specific physical or other interaction systems and producing more or less specific effects, the rest of the pattern cannot be very efficient.

In the area of juvenile delinquency there is a proliferation of both theory and operational patterns. What is lacking is a well-developed and empirically established technology, a technology which offers specific operations for each of the three separate foci: (1) personal and intrapersonal factors, (2) the setting or situations, and (3) specific discordant behaviors.

ASSESSMENT OF OPERATIONAL PATTERNS

A review of existing reports of research, investigations, and evaluative studies of various operational patterns is very discouraging if one is looking for specific information about program effectiveness. Actually, however, the community does not demand or weigh such evidence in the same way that professionals do. The kind of evidence the community accepts, the purpose for which such information or evidence is sought, the particular importance of the power person who is weighing the evidence and drawing conclusions, and the felt-need of the community at the time—all will affect the utility and influence of the facts provided.

These statements are not attempts to undervalue the process of assessment. They merely point to the fact that evaluation has one meaning for the professional social system and another for the community at large. The current emphasis upon evaluation of operational patterns within the professional educative systems themselves is evident in two recent publications dealing with this process. One is the N.I.M.H. publication on *Evaluation in Mental Health* (Green-hill, Ford, Olson, Ryan, Whitman, and Skeels, 1955), and the other is a Children's Bureau publication, *Some Guidelines for Evaluative Research* (Herzog, 1959).

The value which the professional social systems place upon the gathering of information and evidence about operational patterns is, however, gradually being transmitted to power structures and is affecting their decisions and actions. One of the major aims of the Juvenile Delinquency Offenses Control Act of 1961, for instance, is evaluation of the actions which it will stimulate: ". . . The Secretary of Health Education and Welfare is authorized to make grants for projects for the *evaluation,* or demonstration of the effectiveness of techniques which in the Secretary's opinion hold promise."

Need

One of the important pieces of information gathered by the professional systems which communities seem also to value is the extent of the problem. From the point of reference used in this chapter, "need" is a complex concept. It can be defined by expressed concern which has been transmitted by community to power groups, or it can be defined in terms of the number of instances of discordant behavior and/or the intensity of the acts themselves. Need is also defined by the frequency of use of a particular operational pattern. (In the case of delinquency, it is defined by frequency of use of the courts; when exploring mental illness, it could be defined by the extent of use of mental hospitals.)

No matter what the definition of need is, information regarding the extent of discordant episodes is more complete in the area of juvenile delinquency than it is in any other area of discordant behavior. Although there is no universal definition of juvenile delinquency, there is consensual validation within each of the individual legal jurisdictional areas as to what constitutes instances of discordance requiring court action; and in each jurisdiction there are methods of counting instances of such discordance. Available reports of delinquency statistics have been incomplete in ways unrepresentative of the population of reporting areas (Perlman, 1957). Studies of nonapprehended delinquency in the population at large indicate extensive "underreporting" (Murphy, Shirley, and Witmer, 1946; Wallerstein and Wyle, 1947; Short, 1954; Short and Nye, 1958). Nevertheless, the periodic reports of Juvenile Court Statistics by the Children's Bureau and the Uniform Crime Reports compiled by the

Federal Bureau of Investigation provide one of the best statements of numbers of instances of discordant behavior that exists in any of the many behavioral areas which are referred to the socializing systems.

Accomplishment or Effectiveness of Delinquency Operational Patterns

The assessment of accomplishment of operational patterns and programs in the area of juvenile delinquency offers very little clear-cut evidence which could help decide their effectiveness. It is very doubtful, however, that the community will really ever demand that a particular operational pattern present unequivocal evidence that it reduces or eliminates episodes of the discordant behaviors which arouses community concern.

Communities have continued to support existing delinquency operational patterns and programs in every socializing system even though delinquency trend lines have been continually upward (Glaser, 1958; Middendorff, 1960, Chap. 1; Perlman, 1960). This is true, of course, for community action in all of the areas of discordant behavior, and not just in delinquency. From a psychological point of view, it would seem that when community concern is aroused, all that it asks is that this concern be reduced. The creation of a new operational pattern or a new program appears to serve the function of reducing anxiety or concern to the point where the community can relax. These operational patterns seem to perform the same external, concrete functions for shared concern in communities that defense mechanisms do for individual anxiety. Even if there is continued increase in numbers or intensity of discordant behaviors, the community will rarely discard an operational pattern as ineffective and wasteful. The most usual reaction is either to further fortify the existing operational pattern, or add new patterns and programs to the existing ones.

Whether the professional person is scornful of the community for this attitude, or is defensive and supporting of the community depends upon what part of the system gets his major attention. If he is involved in further development and explication of the philosophy, orientation, and body of knowledge, he is scornful; if he is more directly involved in the actions of the operational pattern, he is supportive.

No matter what attitude is taken toward evaluation, the present literature offers very little direct evidence that any single operational pattern has effectively reduced occurrences of any discordant behavior, and, more specifically, that it has effectively reduced occurrences of delinquency. Two professional people weighing the same evidence will frequently come to opposed conclusions regarding effectiveness. A brief review of evaluative studies in each socializing system will give some idea of how true this is.

Legal Correctional Patterns

Institutions. Studies of Highfields in New Jersey (McCorkle, Elias, and Bixby, 1958) and studies of Wiltwyck School near Poughkeepsie, New York (McCord and McCord, 1944; 1956) report the results of the influence of nontraditional institutional operational patterns. These studies, although containing many methodological inadequacies, are unique in their inclusion of comparison or "control" institutions. The conclusions of both reports support the belief that the use of re-forming operations will bring greater accomplishment than institutional patterns emphasizing control and constraint.

Nevertheless, the Juvenile Delinquency Evaluation Project of the City of New York (Interim Report No. XI) states:

For Wiltwyck, a study completed May, 1954 by New York School of Social Work students and based on the records of 393 out of 450 boys discharged during the sixteen years up to 1953, showed that at some time after their discharge six per cent were readmitted to Wiltwyck, 34 per cent were placed in penal or correctional institutions, and 12 per cent were placed in various other institutions. . . . Excluding those who were subsequently committed to mental institutions or to institutions for dependent children, we reach a recidivism rate of about 45 per cent (p. 3).

This same report offers a standard or base rate for comparison. It claims that in New York State the recivitism rate for the large institutions for juvenile delinquents "ranges broadly from 40 to possibly 60 per cent" (p. 4).

This latter stated rate does not agree with other figures presented by Hershel Alt in the case of Hawthorne School in New York State (Hearing before the Subcommittee to Investigate Juvenile Delinquency of the Committee of the Judiciary, 1958): "In 1950 our agency made a follow-up study of the progress of 100 boys discharged from our Hawthorne Cedar Knolls School. It was found that over 70 per cent have made good adjustments 5 years after their release" (p. 150).

Schreiber (1960) reports on a number of older studies:

A number of older studies dating back to the 1930's and 1940's have been in the files of the Children's Bureau. Success rates in these studies range from a low of 6 per cent to a high of 74 per cent. A majority shows a failure rate of from 35 per cent to 50 per cent. The follow-up phases cover various periods of time, ranging from 6 months to 15 years after release. And these studies, like the other reviewed, differ considerably in the groups studied and the classifications used for rating outcome (partial failure, temporary success, good adjustment, etc.) (p. 11).

Polsky conducted a somewhat different and very revealing study of the impact of institutional programs on delinquent children. As a participant observer, he attempted to evaluate what was happening in the treatment process. His report (1962) clearly indicates that the professional's concept of what is going on within the treatment institution has very little to do with reality. He shows rather dramatically how the culture of the streets is carried into the institution and very effectively excludes and nullifies the pitiful impotence of the intended therapy.

Probation

There have been a number of studies of the effectiveness of probation patterns. Again, there is considerable disagreement with respect to accomplishment. Evaluation reports range from almost complete failure to phenomenal success. For instance, MacCormick (1948) claims:

Based on actual performance over a term of years, a good juvenile court and probation service, operating in a community with adequate social resources and utilizing them fully, can put as high as 90 per cent of its juvenile delinquents on probation the first time around and 50 to 75 per cent the second or third time around, and get as high as 75 to 80 per cent successes (p. 88).

In England, a follow-up study of probationers (Radzinowicz, 1958, p. 52) reports on 5020 boys and girls between 8 and 17 who were put on probation, which terminated during 1948-1950. Of the total, 78.5 per cent were not reconvicted within three years and 21.5 per cent were reconvicted within three years.

Teeters and Reinemann (1950) report:

Wide discrepancies are recorded in all attempts to evaluate probation success statistically. The gap ranges from a failure rate of 84.6 per cent reported by the Gluecks, to a success average of 75 per cent mentioned by Sutherland. An analysis of case records of 500 children (400 boys and 100 girls) studied at the Judge Baker Guidance Clinic and placed on probation in the Juvenile Court of Boston revealed that among the boys permanent success was recorded in 43 per cent of the cases, temporary success in 34 per cent, and failure in 21 per cent of the cases; in 2 per cent the outcome was undetermined. The permanent success rate for the girls was 75 per cent; temporary success, 12 per cent; and failure 12 per cent. The study was undertaken at a time when five to seven years had elapsed after termination of probation (p. 427).

In the Children's Bureau publication, already mentioned, Paul Schreiber (1960) reviews studies of probation and concludes:

Two important points about the studies just listed have been made by two of their authors: (1) "The extent of recidivism will vary with the definition of recidivism" and (2) "Until there are satisfactory statistics with an agreed-upon basis for uniform reporting, it is not feasible to make generalizations." A third point is also important, however, although we cannot generalize about actual recidivism rates, we can report the range of rates revealed by a variety of studies, using different methods and dealing with different groups of boys under different kinds of treatment.

We have seen that the failure rates during supervision ranged from 15 per cent to 22 per cent, according to the studies under review. We now see that the post-probation rates, although they vary widely, tend to show higher failure and lower success rates. This is hardly surprising. Nevertheless, it is a generalization that can be made on the basis of admittedly inadequate data, and one that would be merely an untested assumption without supporting data. In the post-probation studies we have found success rates as low as 43 per cent and failure rates as high as 43 per cent; and more success rates under than over 70 per cent (pp. 8, 9).

Educational Patterns

Special Schools. Among the most visible samples of this operational pattern are the Montefiore Schools in Chicago and the "600" Schools in New York City.

Stullken (1956) says approximately half of the pupils of Montefiore leave school at 16 years of age. He claims that studies of these students show that approximately 60 per cent keep out of difficulty after they leave the special school, and 70 per cent make good records in the schools to which they are returned.

Although there are many differences between the Montefiore and the "600" Schools, the reported Montefiore percentage who stay out of trouble after leaving is slightly higher than tentative figures from the "600" Schools. A report on the "600" Schools by the Evaluation Project of the City of New York (Interim Report, No. VI, December 1957) shows there were 1005 students in the schools in November-December 1956 and 217 graduates of the years 1954, 1955, and 1956. Over one-third transferred or discharged from these schools during this period were sent to institutions. In the same report, the 1955 and 1956 figures indicated that only seven boys of each 100 transferred or discharged from these schools are transferred back to the regular schools.

However, eight out of ten "600" boys are rated by their teachers as "good" or "fair" in their social adjustment. The authors say that in this context the "containing" function of these schools seems adequately fulfilled. On the positive side, they also report that seven out of ten pupils show "normal" or better reading progress in these schools. This is particularly significant since the modal retardation in reading of boys referred to the "600" Schools is four years. Stullken (1956) reports that the elementary school pupils in Montefiore are retarded in reading almost five years below their chronological age, and the high schools groups show reading retardation to be three years and two months, as based upon chronological age.

Other special school studies include those of the M. Gertrude Godwin School of Boston, and the All-Day Neighborhood Schools in New York City.

Handy (1955) reports that of 6000 boys sent to the M. Gertrude Godwin School over the past twenty years because they were pronounced unmanageable or had been truant again and again, 84 per cent are living normal lives as responsible citizens.

In the All-Day Neighborhood Schools (Franklin, 1959; Juvenile Delinquency Evaluation Project of the City of New York, Interim Report XIII; Gold and Winter, 1961), an evaluation was also carried on during the demonstration period under the direction of Dr. J. Wayne Wrightstone. The program included interviews with representatives of various social agencies and questionnaires given to parents and teachers. There were two matched control schools. Insofar as regular class procedures and accomplishments were concerned, the control and ADNS schools were similar. However, the ADNS program resulted in gains in interpersonal relationships among pupils and between pupils and teachers. Franklin (1959) says: "Statistics show there is a conspicuous lack of truancy and a minimum of vandalism in the schools and the delinquency rate declines."

Special Programs in Schools. Bowman (1959) reports on The Community Youth Development Project, Quincy, Illinois. He traces the history of the project and the varied approaches used within it. This was not designed as a study of delinquency, but rather as a study of the range of maladjustment and talent in children. After trying a variety of approaches, the project staff decided to concentrate its efforts in the school program. All of the children were in the eighth grade who were "doing poorly" in school and were the discipline problems of the school. Forty-one per cent had police or court records. This group was divided randomly into three smaller groups. One continued in the regular class as a control group, but the other two groups were placed in special classes. In general, in these classes: "The efforts of the teachers were aimed at making school a pleasant experience; helping pupils learn the basic skills of reading, writing, and arithmetic; helping them learn the practical things they would use in their daily lives; and providing experiences in which they could find some success."

Bowman (1959) reports that over a period of two years the experimental groups showed greater interest in school than ever before as measured by their attendance record. In the eighth grade, the control groups averaged twenty-two days of absences and the experimental group averaged twelve days. In the ninth grade, the control group averaged twenty-nine and one-half days and the experimental groups averaged eleven days. Delinquency rate was reported to have "more than tripled" in the control group, and the experimental group delinquency rate decreased by one-third. Bowman states: "The numbers here are too small for generalization and the data are incomplete, but the trend is clear."

This approach has been extended to other groups. Bowman believes that the data on the class of slow learners at the first-grade level "are even clearer" and supports this with some information.

Medical Patterns

The typical medical pattern is the child guidance clinic. This pattern has changed very little since the early days of William Healy, whose work stimulated the National Committee for Mental Hygiene and the Commonwealth Fund to establish demonstration child guidance clinics. These clinics were to develop the psychiatric study of difficult predelinquent and delinquent children in schools and juvenile courts and to develop sound methods of treatment based on such study. They were the forerunners of the present, widely adopted child guidance pattern.

These early efforts resulted in a number of interesting assessment efforts which were published during the 1930's. Sheldon and Eleanor Glueck (1934) reported a study of the Judge Baker Guidance Center in Boston which reviewed the subsequent court records of 1000 boys five years after study at the Judge Baker Center. The Judge Baker approach at that time consisted largely of study, diagnosis, and recommendations to the court for appropriate social interventions. The Gluecks found that 88 per cent of the boys had continued their misconduct, 70 per cent had been convicted of serious offenses, and one-third had been arrested four or more times. The Glueck study concluded that guidance services such as those provided by the Boston Juvenile Court were ineffectual in reducing recidivism.

The Judge Baker research staff conducted its own study in which it examined the records of a comparison group of 1000 boys who had come before the court in the same years, but who had not been seen in the guidance center. These researchers also concluded that the study and recommendation method of their services as a method of delinquency prevention was ineffective (Healy, Bronner, and Shimberg, 1935).

In the widely known study reported by Healy and Bronner (1936), clinics in Boston, New Haven, and Detroit functioned during a period of three years to apply a "treatment" approach to juvenile delinquents. Their final personality data were based upon their clinic findings of 105 delinquents paired with their 105 nondelinquent siblings. Their treatment group comprised 163 delinquents, divided into three different categories. There was a follow-up based on personality and social factors over varying periods of time ranging from two to four years. It is not clear at what point in the study the three groupings were made. Group I consisted of "all those delinquents who cannot be considered hopeful for treatment under even ordinarily good conditions of family and community life" (p. 161).

The descriptions of this group are subjective, and there are no data on the reliability of grouping. Twenty-six cases were placed in this category, and only one individual at the end of the treatment period had overcome his delinquent tendencies.

Group II were "all those cases in which the social pathology, particularly as involving human relationships within and outside the family circle, appears to weigh so heavily against the possibility of successful treatment of the delinquent in his family environment that the given situation seems largely hopeless" (p. 166). Fifty cases were placed in this category. The results in this group were as follows: "The final report is that 19 cases (38 per cent) of the group have not been delinquent during a period of two or more years" (p. 168).

Group III consisted of 67 cases "whose personality or internal difficulties did not show extreme deviation and they came from conditions where the social pathology did not give evidences of greatly weighing against chances of successful treatment" (p. 169).

As a result of treatment, this was noted: "During the follow-up period of two years or more, 48 cases (72 per cent) of Group III have not been delinquent" (p. 170).

Hakeem (1958) offers a number of criticisms of the Healy and Bronner study. Among the most cogent of these criticisms are the following:

It does not fulfill one of the most imperative dictates of scientific methodology, namely, the presentation of the research data and operations in such a way that the study could be replicated by other investigators. . . . Nothing is said as to the methods followed in making judgments as to the presence, kind, degree, duration and meaning of emotional disturbance. It is not even indicated who made the final judgments. . . . To give one final shortcoming among many others that could be mentioned, the study lacks a test of reliability (pp. 93, 94).

Healy, himself, in another publication (1934) says: "As it stands at present in most large communities, it is impossible for child guidance clinics, through their work with individual cases, to be playing any very important part in the prevention of delinquent and criminal careers" (p. 15).

Adamson and Dunham (1956) compared delinquents in Detroit who received psychiatric treatment in a court-affiliated clinic with a group not receiving such treatment. The outcomes were almost identical for the two groups. Although there was some evidence that those receiving intensive treatment engaged in crime to a lesser extent, the authors say: "This suggests that recidivism at the juvenile level is often a forerunner of later registration with police, irrespective of any kind of relationship therapy" (p. 319).

The present Judge Baker—Newton, Massachusetts, Public Schools project has radically departed from the concept of psychotherapy as a specific technique for "cure" of delinquency. It is a multioperational pattern approach with the family as the unit of focus. The next few years should give some indications of the effectiveness of this generalized approach.

Social Welfare Patterns

Community organization in area councils or community councils is one of the social welfare patterns which is proliferating throughout the country (Beam, 1957, p. 234).

Although reduction in rate of delinquency can be shown in area projects (Sutherland, 1955), it is difficult to clearly demonstrate the relationship between specific programs in the project and the through-time changes in delinquency statistics. According to Kobrin (1959):

At bottom this difficulty rests on the fact that such programs, as efforts to intervene in the life of a person, a group, or a community, cannot by their very nature constitute more than a subsidiary element in changing the fundamental and sweeping forces which create the problems of groups and of persons or which shape human personality (p. 20).

The St. Paul's experiment in child welfare (Stone, Castendyck, and Hanson, 1946) gives staff judgments of the effectiveness of individual service. According to subjective judgment of the staff involved in the rendering of these services, 18 per cent showed major improvement or profit, 65 per cent showed some improvement, and 17 per cent showed no improvement. There were no controls in this study. Donald Cook (1960) points out that these subjective estimates are similar to values reported for untreated controls in studies of psychotherapy with children (Levitt, 1957).

Group work patterns, such as the YMCA and Boy Scouts, frequently screen out or do not serve the significant population of discordants. Reed (1948) reports a study of such agencies in Cincinnati and says:

Group work agencies were shown to be serving to an important extent a different group from that represented by the juvenile court youths. Group work youths were less concentrated in the economically underprivileged areas of the city and their families were less frequently known to casework and relief agencies. They were a younger group than juvenile court youths, and had smaller percentage of boys and Negroes in their membership (p. 347).

In connection with the Reed claim, this author found a YMCA program in a highly disorganized area of a major American city refusing admission to gang members from that neighborhood who were being worked with by a gang-worker from the central YMCA office. It was felt that the behavior of the gang boys was too disrupting for their program.

Some of the more careful evaluations of the group work pattern are those of Shanas and Dunning (1942), Thrasher (1936), and Brown and Dodson (1959). In the Brown and Dodson data the delinquency rate for the Club Area decreased rather steadily from 1 in 19 boys when the Boys' Club opened in 1946, to 1 in 39 in 1954. For the city (Louisville) as a whole, the rates for the comparison areas in Louisville increased. In Area B, it went from 1 in 44 boys in 1946, and to 1 in 16 in 1954. In Area C, the increase was from

1 in 28 to 1 in 21 in the same period. Thrasher, Brown, and Dodson seem to conclude that Boys' Clubs do have an effect in reducing delinquency. Brown and Dodson, however, point out that the difference in delinquency rates over the period of study of the neighborhood with the Boys' Clubs and the "control" neighborhoods could be due to other factors which made for "social stability in the Club Areas and social instability in the other areas" (p. 52). Furthermore, they felt: "Another interpretation, however, might be that the social forces in the community that led to the establishment and expansion of the Boys' Club were lacking in the other areas" (p. 52).

Witmer and Tufts (1954) seem to feel rather strongly that these studies have not offered evidence of the effectiveness of this pattern: "In other words, important as the provision of adequate and well-staffed recreational and group work facilities is for the well-being of children generally, it is by no means established that delinquency will decline if good facilities are provided" (p. 48).

Another carefully evaluated social welfare pattern was the Cambridge-Somerville Project. It was a well-designed demonstration, with matched pairs of boys in a study group and a control group. According to Witmer and Tufts (1954), the project differed in three ways from the usual casework agency. First, unlike the typical casework agency, boys and their families were sought out and urged to accept help. Work with each boy was continued until late adolescence. Second, cases were not to be closed at a "maximum benefit" point, but work was to continue with each boy until late adolescence. Third, "friendship" rather than the usual "casework relationship" was to be the basis of the counselor's influence.

At the end of the Study's service program, the police and court records of the treatment and control groups were compared. The two groups had almost identical records, whether the comparison was based on the number of boys appearing in juvenile court and frequency of juvenile court, on police department appearances, or on commitments to the correctional institutions.

Cook (1960, Vol. 2, Chap. VI, p. 9) points out that in spite of the negative results of this study it gives us very important knowledge. For one thing, the similar results in the treatment and control groups make one question the positive results reported in programs without control groups. A second finding which can be of significance to the professional and the community is that there was a general tendency of the staff to overpredict criminality. As each child entered the project, a committee of judges assigned him a "delinquency-proneness prognosis," and the social workers and psychologists who examined the child each made their predictions. Approximately sixteen years after the judgments were made, only 59 per cent of the total 129 children from both groups who were given ratings of high probability of later delinquency became criminal.

As an interesting aside, McCord, McCord, and Zola (1959) demonstrate that ". . . equally accurate and more specific predictions could have been made solely from certain factors in the child's environment, without any knowledge of the child himself. . . ."

A third area of information provided by this study is related to the significance of the criterion measure of success.

When the counselors and the boys themselves evaluated the results, the program appeared to be a decided success. Powers (1949) says that counselors reported that two-thirds of the treatment group had "substantially benefited" from their contact with the study, and half of this group were "outstanding" with respect to benefits received. Sixty-two per cent of the boys themselves judged that the program had been of value to them. These judgments were not validated by outcomes in adjudicated delinquency.

Another social welfare program which had been evaluated is the demonstration known as Maximum Benefits Project of the Commissioners' Youth Council of Washington, D. C., which involved four years of work with problem children in elementary schools. Like a similar project in Passaic, New Jersey (Kvaraceus, 1945), it attempted to utilize total community services and was not a school program involving educational techniques.

It was located in a typical large city's disorganized neighborhood with rates of discordant behaviors of all types. Although the neighborhood had only 7 per cent of the city's population of the juvenile court age group, it contributed 16.6 per cent of the children referred to courts for juvenile delinquency. The special project provided a control and treatment group. Social casework, including financial aid, was the treatment recommendation most frequently made, occurring in 157 cases. Recommendations for special handling in the school situation were made in 103 instances. Psychotherapy for child or parent was recommended in thirty-three instances. Removal from home was recommended for seventeen children. Other recommendations were legal aid, health services, group activities, more adequate housing, and the total array of welfare services.

The project began in 1954. In 1956 and again in 1958, surveys determined each child's behavioral and academic performance in school and police or juvenile court contacts.

The 1956 follow-up in school showed much better behavior for the treated than the untreated group. The 1958 follow-up, however, showed negligible differences between the two groups. According to a report of the project (Trevvett, 1958):

The court and police results speak rather eloquently. At the time of the follow-up nine of the 37 treated children (first year group of 73) had already become known to these official agencies as opposed to six of the 32 untreated. Five of these boys (two treated, two untreated, and one mixed) had been placed in institutions because of delinquent behavior. Four more had been placed at least temporarily because of some combinations of delinquency or neglect (p. 8).

Miller's (1962) report on the "total community," multiple-impact approach of the Midcity Project in Boston also gives negative results for a tremendous amount of effort and activity. Without going into details, we can quote Miller on his findings:

"Was there a significant measurable inhibition of law-violating or morally-disapproved behavior as a consequence of Project efforts?" The answer, with little necessary qualification, is "No." All major measures of violative behavior-disapproved actions, illegal actions, during-contact court appearances, before-during-after appearances, and Project-Control group appearances provide consistent support for a finding of "negligible impact."

PROGRAM PLANNING INFORMATION

One area of information or assessment which is very important to the professional involved in community action is current knowledge of the who, where, what, and why of delinquency. The community will take action irrespective of the status of existing knowledge. Much of the action demonstrates the considerable social lag between the gathering of information and its utilization in action. The professional, as a behavioral scientist, should know the precision or lack of precision and the level of sophistication of information regarding the who, what, where, and why of delinquency. However, he must utilize the inexact information currently available and try to influence changes or shifts in operational patterns as new knowledge becomes available.

All of our current information must be presented with elaborate qualifiers, the most cogent of which is the awareness that today's information may be tomorrow's myth. But action will be taken by the community with or without information.

The question of what constitutes delinquency has been discussed frequently, with some agreement among authors (Middendorff, 1960, Chap. 1; Tappan, 1952, Section 1; Cook, 1960, Chap. 1; Glaser, 1958). The definition is usually a legal one.

The question of who the delinquents are is a particularly involved and interesting one. Before any operational pattern can begin to approach the problem of juvenile delinquency, it must know who the discordants are. These data are contained in the FBI Uniform Crime Reports and the Children's Bureau statistical series. Evidence to date seems to indicate that the delinquent is more likely to be a boy than a girl. In the United States, chances are 5 to 1 that the delinquent is a male.

To some extent, the age depends upon legal definitions. Although there are some differences throughout the world, age as pointed out in the European report (*The Comparative Survey of Juvenile Delinquency*, Part II, 1952) is the common element of the definition. In Europe, as pointed out in the above reference, the legal age range is from 8 or 9 years to 16, 17, or 18. In Asia and the Far East (*Comparative Survey of Juvenile Delinquency*, Part IV, 1952) the age range is from 7 to 18 or 20. In the United States, the majority of the states set 18 as the upper age limit, although in California it ranges up to 21 years of age (Glaser, 1958). In a Children's Bureau Pamphlet on *Facts and Facets of Juvenile Delinquency* (No. 4, 1960, p. 3), the vulnerable age group in the United States is reported to be between 10 and 17 years of age.

The ethnic group producing the greater number of delinquents has varied from time to time. Today, the major legal and administrative problem is within the Negro group (Barron, 1959; Douglass, 1959; Johnson, 1951). Douglass (1959) reports the problem as follows:

Such information as is now available (for example, data on arrests, referrals to courts, and commitments to state or Federal institutions), reveals that on an over-all basis the Negro group as a whole continues to manifest a highly disproportionate share of criminal and other forms of anti-social behavior as related to its proportion in the total population. These rates ordinarily exceed those of the general population, as well as those of other minority groups such as Puerto Ricans, Mexican-Americans, Chinese, and American Indians (p. 226).

Douglass and others (Robison, 1960; Johnson, 1951; Axelrad, 1952) point out the kinds of reservations which must be stated in reporting a disproportionately higher incidence of juvenile delinquency and crime among Negroes in the United States. Among the reservations, for instance, is the fact that in institutionalized delinquents (1) Negro children are committed at a younger age, (2) for less serious offenses, (3) with fewer previous court appearances, and (4) with less prior institutionalization than white children (Axelrad, 1952).

With regard to the "where" of juvenile delinquency, there are several consensually validated pieces of tentative information. The delinquent is more likely to be located in the lower socioeconomic strata, in the urban socially disorganized and deteriorated neighborhoods (Shaw and McKay, 1942; Lander, 1954; Polk, 1957). This is true for the greater proportion of apprehended delinquents, although delinquency also exists in other social situations (Bandura and Walters, 1959; Reiss, 1952). Research indicates that the neighborhoods which produce delinquency also produce a higher prevalence of other discordant behaviors. This seems to apply to mental illness (Faris and Dunham, 1959; Schroeder, 1942), suicide (Cavan, 1928; Gillin, 1946; Sainsbury, 1955), alcoholic psychosis, and drug addiction (Faris and Dunham, 1939).

In the "where" of juvenile delinquency we can also include the particular kinds of families dubbed the "hard core," "multiproblem," or "hard-to-reach" in the disorganized neighborhoods which contribute more than their proportionate share (Buck, Buell, and Kandle, 1951; Buell, Beissler, and Wedemeyer, 1958; Trevvett, 1960). Another group of studies which supports the family-centeredness of the problem provides clinically oriented data (McCord, McCord, and Zola, 1959; Glueck, 1934).

For the "how" of juvenile delinquency, one must turn primarily to theoretical points of view rather than data. One can look to Freudian psychoanalytic theory (Friedlander, 1947; Eissler, 1949; Aichhorn, 1939) or to the theory of identity diffusion and psychosocial moratorium (Erikson, 1959), of "anomie" and "status deprivation" (Merton, 1949; Lander, 1954; Cloward and Ohlin, 1961), of differential association (Sutherland, 1955), of cultural conflict (Kobrin, 1959), of cultural transmission (Cohen, 1955), of "lower class culture" (Miller, 1958), or of "age-grading" (Eisenstadt, 1956).

The professional, called upon for program advice by the community power structure, must have assimilated the kinds of information offered above, provided his own synthesis and conclusions, and attempted to translate such conclusions into recommendations for operational patterns and programs. He can now keep current on significant information through the National Research and Information Center on Crime and Delinquency.

SUMMARY

We have attempted to review juvenile delinquency as one kind of discordant behavior which arouses community concern and results in community action. The approach has presented an organized system of concepts and constructs which maintain the community as a central referent. It discusses organized community effort to deal with the problem of juvenile delinquency as a part of a total pattern of cultural mechanisms, systems, and agents having responsibility for reconciling the inner nature of the individual with the demands of a particular culture. These systems have been described as "socializing" or "behavior-shaping" systems which perform the function of transforming the individual from an organism with potentials and capacities into a bearer of a particular culture.

The set of constructs offered here begins with the assumption that, in the short run, most of the socializing systems have developed behavior-shaping operational patterns in response to the community's demand to interpose defensive or protective external mechanisms between its concern and the discordant behaver who provokes that concern. These patterns and the subsequent efforts of the professional represent community power and community sanction to shape behavior in directions consonant with either positive or negative concern which has been aroused in the community by individuals whose behavior deviates from the cultural type.

The socializing systems which have legal sanction from the community to perform these behavior-shaping and concern-reducing operations have been categorized into the following groups: (1) the legal-correctional system, (2) the medical system, (3) the social welfare system, and (4) the education system.

The socializing systems were conceptualized as an organization of the following significant elements:

1. A basic orientation toward and philosophy of human nature, with a developing body of knowledge derived from and related to the orientation.
2. A set of operations and techniques derived from or related to the basic orientation, philosophy, and body of knowledge.
3. A group of professionals who have learned the techniques, body of knowledge, and orientation.
4. A set of operational patterns through which the above are brought to bear upon individuals or individual behavior with which the community is concerned.

The operational patterns and subpatterns, which have been called programs, are conceived of as organization of all of the above elements, plus the following:

1. Power attributed by the community to shape behavior in directions concordant with its expectations. This power is conferred in

many ways to the operational pattern. It is particularly represented in the sanction of the community to the individual professional for the practice of his techniques. This sanction takes the form of merit system ratings, professional boards, licensing, certification, and so on.

2. A structure of formal and informal communication and administration networks.

3. A place or a plant within which the operations are carried out.

4. A particular focus, or set of foci, for the operations of the pattern.

5. A set of goals toward which the behavior-shaping operations are directed.

A discussion of the existing behavior-shaping operational patterns and programs discussed a logical taxonomy of operational goals and foci. The behavioral goals were categorized as follows: (1) constraint and control, (2) reconstruction and re-formation, and (3) construction and formation.

The foci of the operations of the behavior-shaping patterns and programs were classified as concentrating primarily upon one or the other of the following foci: (1) the interpersonal and intrapersonal factors, (2) the setting or situation out of which behavior arises, and (3) the specific behavior which is arousing community concern.

A community action conceptualization of the problem of juvenile delinquency must necessarily take into account all of the elements of the socializing systems and the operational patterns. Professional effort must be distributed in the areas of furthering of knowledge, development of effective techniques, training of personnel, and the development of new operational patterns or more effective use of existing patterns. Furthermore, each of the behavioral goals which have been conceptualized refer to real community efforts to effect human behavior in particular ways. These goals, in spite of a particular professional preference, have been pursued historically by societies attempting the enculturation of its members. They will probably continue to be pursued. It is a responsibility of the behavioral scientist to study these more extensively and offer whatever knowledge he can generate in each of the goal areas. The culture will probably never concentrate its enculturation forces on any single locus of effort. It is appropriate, therefore, that the socializing systems and their professionals diversify their focus of interest and technology.

Finally, any professional or system working in the area of juvenile delinquency must, for the present time, encompass many problems of discordant behavior. The multifaceted nature of the problem, the wide range of forces and factors, the multivarying sources of institutional power, the confusing array of patterns and programs—all coalesce to push the practitioner and the theorist into many areas of human life that he would otherwise never explore.

References

Adamson, L., & Dunham, H. W. (1956) Clinical treatment of male delinquents. A case study in effort and result. *Amer. Sociol. Rev.,* **21,** 312-320.

Aichhorn, A. (1935) *Wayward youth.* New York: Viking.

Allen, F. (1950) Psychopathic behavior—fact or project. In B. Karpman (chm.), The psychopathic delinquent child. *Amer. J. Orthopsychiat.,* **20,** 223-265.

Alston, Estelle (1951) Group work with hard-to-reach teen-agers. *The Social Welfare Forum, Official proceedings of the National Conference of Social Work.* New York: Columbia Univ. Press.

Alt, H. (1958) Statement: *Juvenile delinquency.* Hearing before the Subcommittee to Investigate Juvenile Delinquency of the Committee on the Judiciary, United States Senate. Dec. 4, 1957, p. 145. Washington, D. C.: U.S. Govt. Printing Office.

Arcadias, Y. (November-December 1954) Homes et foyers de semi-liberté. *Re-education.* 60/61: 1-45.

Axelrad, S. (1952) Negro and white male institutionalized delinquents. *Amer. J. Sociol.,* **57,** 569-574.

Ayllon, T., & Michael, J. (1959) The psychiatric nurse as a behavioral engineer. *J. expl. anal. Behav.,* **2,** 323-334.

Bandura, A., & Walters, R. (1959) *Adolescent aggression.* New York: Ronald.

Barron, M. L. (1959) *The juvenile in delinquent society.* New York: Knopf.

Beam, K. S. (1957) Organization of the community for delinquency prevention. In F. Cohen (ed.), *Youth and crime.* New York: Int. Univer. Press.

Beck, B. (1951) Five states: *A study of the Youth Authority Program as promulgated by the American Law Institute.* Philadelphia: The Amer. Law Institute.

Bender, Lauretta (1955) Further contributions. In B. Karpman (chm.), Psychodynamics of child delinquency (summarization). *Amer. J. Orthopsychiat.,* 25, 238-282.

Bender, Lauretta (1947) Psychopathic conduct disorders in children. In R. M. Lindner (ed.), *A Handbook of correctional psychology.* New York: Philosophical Library.

Bernard, Jessie (1949) *American community behavior.* New York: Dryden.

Bettleheim, B. (1950) *Love is not enough.* Glencoe, Ill.: Free Press.

Bloch, H., & Flynn, F. (1956) *Delinquency. The juvenile offender in America today.* New York: Random House.

Bloch, H. A., & Niederhoffer, A. (1958) *The gang. A study in adolescent behavior.* New York: Philosophical Library.

Bowman, P. (1959) Effects of a revised school program on potential delinquents. *Ann. Amer. Acad. Pol. Soc. Sci.,* 322, 53-61.

Breed, A. F. (1953) California youth authority forestry camp program. *Fed. Probation,* 17, 37-43.

Brown, R. C., Jr., & Dodson, D. W. (1959) The effectiveness of a Boys' Club in reducing delinquency. *Ann. Amer. Acad. Pol. Soc. Sci.,* 322, 47-52.

Buck, C. E., Buell, B., & Kandle, R. P. (1951) Family health in tomorrow's community. *Amer. J. Publ. Hlth.,* 41, 1258-1262.

Buell, B., Beissler, P. T., & Wedemeyer, J. M. (1958) Reorganizing to prevent and control disordered behavior. *Ment. Hyg.,* 42, 155-194.

Buell, B., et al. (1952) *Community planning for human services.* New York: Columbia Univer. Press.

Cavan, R. S. (1928) *Suicide.* Chicago: Univer. of Chicago Press.

Chess, Stella (1953) The social factors in delinquency. In B. Karpman (chm.), Psychodynamics of child delinquency. *Amer. J. Orthopsychiat.,* 23, 1-5.

Children's Bureau (1961) *Juvenile court statistics—1960.* No. 65. Washington, D. C.: U. S. Dept. Health, Education and Welfare.

Clarke, F. (1948) *Freedom in the educative society.* London: Univer. of London Press.

Cleckley, H. M. (1962) Psychiatry: science, art, and scientism. In H. Schoeck and J. W. Wiggins (ed.), *Psychiatry and responsibility.* Princeton, N. J.: D. Van Nostrand, 83-116.

Close, O. H. (1945) California camps for delinquents. *Yearb. Nat. Prob. Assoc.,* 136.

Cloward, R. A., & Ohlin, L. E. (1961) *Delinquency and opportunity.* Glencoe, Ill.: Fress Press.

Cohen, A. K. (1955) *Delinquent boys: the culture of the gang.* Glencoe, Ill.: Free Press.

Conant, J. B. (1961) *Slums and suburbs.* New York: McGraw-Hill.

Cook, D. (January 1960) An assessment of current mental health and social science knowledge concerning juvenile delinquency. National Institute of Mental Health. *Report to the Congress on Juvenile Delinquency.* Vol. 2, Appendix II.

Cressey, D. R. (Spring and Summer 1957) Rehabilitation theory and reality. *Calif. Youth Authority Quart.*

Douglass, J. H. (1959) The extent and characteristics of juvenile delinquency among Negroes in the United States. *Yearb. J. Negro Educ.*, 28, 214-229.

Eisenstadt, S. N. (1956) *From generation to generation: age groups and social structure.* Glencoe, Ill.: Free Press.

Eissler, K. R. (1949) *Searchlights on delinquency.* New York: Int. Univer. Press.

Erikson, Erik H. (1959) *Childhood and society.* New York: Norton.

Erikson, Erik H. (1959) *Identity and the life cycle, selected papers.* New York: Int. Univer. Press.

Faris, R. E., & Dunham, H. W. (1939) *Mental disorders in urban areas.* Chicago: Univer. of Chicago Press.

Franklin, Adele (1959) The all-day neighborhood services. *Ann. Amer. Acad. Pol. Soc. Sci.*, 322, 62-68.

Friedlander, K. (1947) *The psychoanalytical approach to juvenile delinquency.* New York: Int. Univer. Press.

Gandy, J. M. (1959) Preventive work with street-corner groups: Hyde Park Youth Project, Chicago. *Ann. Amer. Acad. Pol. Soc. Sci.*, 322, 107-116.

Gardner, G. E., Makkay, E., Schwaab, E., & Fleming, A. (January 1960) Comprehensive community care of the juvenile delinquent. National Institute of Mental Health. *Report to the Congress on Juvenile Delinquency.* Vol. 1, Appendix I.

Gillin, J. L. (1946) *The Wisconsin prisoner: studies in crimogenesis.* Madison: Univer. of Wisc. Press.

Glaser, D. (1958) Dimensions of the problem. In J. S. Roucek (ed.), *Juvenile delinquency.* New York: Philosophical Library.

Glueck, S., & Glueck, Eleanor T. (1934) *One thousand juvenile delinquents, their treatment by court and clinic.* Cambridge: Harvard Univer. Press.

Gold, M., & Winter, J. A. (1961) *A selective review of community based programs for preventing delinquency.* Institute for Social Research. Ann Arbor: Univer., of Mich. Press.

Greenhill, M., Ford, L., Olson, W., Ryan, W., Whitman, S., & Skeels, H. (1955) *Evaluation in mental health.* U. S. Dept. of Health, Education and Welfare, Public Health Service, N.I.M.H. Washington, D. C.: U. S. Govt. Print. Office.

Grünhut, M. (1955) Juvenile delinquents under punitive detention. *Brit. J. Delinq.*, 3, 191-209.

Guthrie, E. R. (1938) *The psychology of human conflict: the clash of motives within the individual.* New York: Harper.

Hakeem, M. (1958) Critique of the psychiatric approach. In J. S. Roucek (ed.), *Juvenile delinquency.* New York: Philosophical Library.

Handy, Mary (December 1955) Willing to school. *Nat. Educ. Assn. J.,* 544-545.

Healy, W. (1934) Twenty-five years of child guidance. *Institute for Juvenile Research,* Series C., No. 256. Ill. Dept. of Public Welfare, p. 15.

Healy, W., & Bronner, A. (1936) *New light on delinquency and its treatment.* New Haven: Yale Univer. Press.

Healy, W., Bronner, A., & Shimberg, Myra E. (1935) The close of another chapter in criminology. *Ment. Hyg.,* 19, 208-222.

Herzog, Elizabeth (1959) *Some guide lines for evaluative research.* U.S. Dept. of Health, Education and Welfare, Social Security Adm., Children's Bureau. Washington, D.C.: U.S. Govt. Print. Office.

Holton, K., & Morrison, D. (1941) Forestry camps for delinquent boys. *Probation,* 19, 97-116.

James, W. (1946) *Talks to teachers.* New York: Holt.

Johnson, G. B. (1951) The Negro and crime. In A. Rose (ed.), *Race prejudice and discrimination.* New York: Knopf.

Jones, M. (1953) *The therapeutic community.* New York: Basic Books.

Jones, Mary C. (1924) A laboratory study of fear. The case of Peter. *Pedag. Seminary (J. Genet. Psychol.),* 31, 308-315.

Juvenile Delinquency, Subcommittee on (1957) Report of the Committee on the Judiciary, U. S. Senate, 85th Congress, 1st Session. *Juvenile Delinquency.* No. 130. Washington, D. C.: U. S. Govt. Print. Office, 189-198.

Kanner, L. (1955) In B. Karpman (chm.), Psychodynamics of child delinquency: further contributions. *Amer. J. Orthopsychiat.,* 25, 238-282.

Karpman, B. (1950) The psychopathic delinquent child. *Amer. J. Orthopsychiat.,* 20, 223-265.

Karpman, B. (1954) *The sexual offender and his offenses.* New York: Julian Press.

King, G. F., Armitage, S. G., & Tilton, J. R. (1960) A therapeutic approach to schizophrenics of extreme pathology: an operant-interpersonal method. *J. Abnorm. Soc. Psychol.,* 61, 276-286.

Kobrin, S. (1959) The Chicago Area Project—a 25-year assessment. *Ann. Amer. Acad. Pol. Soc. Sci.,* 322, 19-29.

Kohler, Mary C. (January 1960) An American views some European approaches to juvenile delinquency. National Institute of Mental Health. *Report to the Congress on Juvenile Delinquency.* Vol. 5, Appendix VI.

Kohler, Mary C. (1956) The courts for handling youth. *Nat. Prob. Parole Assn. J.,* 2, 123-141.

Kvaraceus, W. C., & Ulrich, W. E. (1959) *Delinquent behavior: principles and practices*. Washington, D. C.: National Education Association.

Kvaraceus, W. C. (1945) *Juvenile delinquency and the school*. Yonkers-on-Hudson, N. Y.: World Book Co.

Lander, B. (1954) *Toward an understanding of juvenile delinquency*. New York: Columbia Univer. Press.

Lane, H. T. (1928) *Talks to parents and teachers*. London: Allen & Unwin.

Leshan, L. (1942) The breaking of a habit by suggestion during sleep. *J. Abnorm. Soc. Psychol.*, **37**, 406-408.

Levitt, E. E. (1957) The results of psychotherapy with children: an evaluation. *J. Consult. Psychol.*, **21**, 189-196.

Lippitt, R., Polansky, N., Redl, F., & Rosen, S. (1953) The dynamics of power. In D. Cartwright and A. Zander (eds.) *Group dynamics*. Evanston, Ill.: Row, Peterson.

Los Angeles County Special Schools Reception Center (1959) *Teaching of vocational skills in academic classes for emotionally disturbed children*. Los Angeles: The Center.

Lurie, L. A. (1951) Psychopathic behavior of little known or idiopathic origins. In B. Karpman (ed.), Psychopathic behavior in infants and children: a critical survey of the existing concepts. *Amer. J. Orthopsychiat.*, **21**, 224-226.

Lurie, L. A. (1953) The role of endocrine factors in delinquency. In B. Karpman (chm.), Psychodynamics of child delinquency. *Amer. J. Orthopsychiat.*, **23**, 21-30.

McClosky, M. (1959) State and municipal youth authorities (or commissions) and their role in juvenile delinquency prevention. *J. Negro Educ.*, **28**, 339-350.

McCord, W., & McCord, Joan (1956) *Psychopathy and delinquency*. New York: Grune & Stratton.

McCord W., & McCord, Joan (November-December 1953) Two approaches to the cure of delinquents. *J. Crim. Law. Criminol. Police Sci.*

McCord, W., McCord, Joan, & Zola, I. (1959) *Origins of crime: a new evaluation of the Cambridge-Somerville youth study*. New York: Columbia Univer. Press.

McCorkle, L., Elias, A., & Bixby, F. L. (1958) *The Highfields story: a unique experiment in the treatment of juvenile delinquency*. New York: Holt.

MacCormick, A. (1948) The community and the correctional process. *Focus*, **27**, 65-89.

Maglio, L. G. (1959) The citizenship training program of the Boston juvenile court. In S. Glueck (ed.), *The problem of delinquency*. Boston: Houghton Mifflin.

Makarenko, A. S. (1955) *The road to life.* Part III. (Translated by Ivy & Tatiana Litvinov). Moscow: Foreign Languages Publishing House.

Makkay, Elizabeth (January 1960) Further consideration (psychoanalytic) of the delinquent act as a symptom of antisocial character disorder and delinquency-proneness in children. National Institute of Mental Health. *Report to the Congress on Juvenile Delinquency.* Vol. 1, Appendix I.

Mannheim, K. (1950) *Freedom, power and democratic planning.* New York: Oxford Univer. Press.

Merton, R. K. (1949) *Social theory and social structure.* Glencoe, Ill.: Free Press.

Middendorff, W. (1960) *New forms of juvenile delinquency: their origin, prevention and treatment.* General report to second United Nations Congress on the prevention of crime and the treatment of offenders. New York: United Nations, Dept. of Economic and Social Affairs.

Miller, W. B. (1958) Lower class culture as a generation milieu of gang delinquency. *J. Soc. Issues,* 14, 5-19.

Miller, W. B. (1959) Preventive work with street-corner groups: Boston delinquency project. *Ann. Amer. Acad. Pol. Soc. Sci.,* 322, 97-106.

Miller, W. B. (1962) The impact of a "total-community" delinquency control project. *Soc. Probl.,* 10, 168-191.

Murphy, F. J., Shirley, Mary, & Witmer, Helen L. (1946) The incidence of hidden delinquency. *Amer. J. Orthopsychiat.,* 16, 686-696.

National Council on Crime and Delinquency (1962-1963) Current Projects in the Prevention, Control, and Treatment of Crime and Delinquency, New York.

National Institute of Mental Health (January 1960) Mobilization for youth: the Lower East Side, New York. *Report to Congress on Juvenile Delinquency.* Vol. 4, Appendix V.

National Institute of Mental Health. (January 1960) National Institute of Mental Health programs related to juvenile delinquency. *Report to Congress on Juvenile Delinquency.* Vol. 6, Appendix IX.

Newman, D. J. (1958) Legal aspects of juvenile delinquency. In J. S. Roucek (ed.), *Juvenile delinquency.* New York: Philosophical Library.

New York, Juvenile Delinquency Evaluation Project of the City of (December 1957) *Students and their progress in the "600" day schools.* Interim Report No. VI. Mimeo.

New York, Juvenile Delinquency Evaluation Project of the City of (December 1957) *The police department: one year later.* Interim Report No. VII. Mimeo.

New York, Juvenile Delinquency Evaluation Project of the City of (December 1958) *The institutionalization of young delinquents.* Interim Report No. XI. Mimeo.

New York, Juvenile Delinquency Evaluation Project of the City of (De-

cember 1959) *The All-Day Neighborhood Schools.* Interim Report
No. XIII. Mimeo.

New York City Board of Education (1958-1959) Annual Report. *The
"600" Schools.* Mimeo.

New York City Youth Board (1954) *Reaching teen-agers through group
work and recreation programs.* Monogr. No. 1.

New York City Youth Board (1960) *Reaching the fighting gang.*

Noshpitz, J. (1957) Opening phase in the psychotherapy of adolescents
with character disorders. *Bull. Menninger Clinic,* **21**, 153-164.

Nye, F. I. (1958) *Family relationships and delinquent behavior.* New
York: Wiley.

Overholser, Winfred (1944) Who are the juvenile delinquents? *J. Soc.
Hyg.,* **30**, 304-308.

Parrot, P., & Gueneau, M. (1959) *Les gangs d'adolescents.* Paris: Presses
Universitaires.

Peck, H. P. (1955) In B. Karpman (chm.), Psycho-dynamics of child
delinquency. *Amer. J. Orthopsychiat.,* **25**, 238-282.

Perlman, I. R. (1960) Delinquency prevention: the size of the problem.
Juvenile delinquency facts-facets. No. 4. Washington, D. C.: Children's Bureau.

Polk, K. (1957-1958) Juvenile delinquency and social areas. *Soc. Probl.,*
5, 214-217.

Polsky, H. W. (1962) *Cottage six—the social system of delinquent boys in
residential treatment.* New York: Russell Sage Fdn.

Powers, E. (1949) An experiment in prevention of delinquency. *Ann.
Amer. Acad. Pol. Soc. Sci.,* **261**, 77-88.

Rabinovitch, R. D. (1952) Observations on the differential study of
severely disturbed children. In B. Karpman (chm.), A differential
study of psychopathic behavior in infants and children. *Amer. J.
Orthopsychiat.,* **22**, 230-236.

Radzinowicz, L. (ed.) (1958) *The results of probation; a report of the
Cambridge department of criminal science.* London: Macmillan.

Redl, F. (1957) The meaning of "therapeutic milieu." In *Symposium on
preventive and social psychiatry.* Washington, D. C.: U. S. Govt.
Print. Office, 503-515.

Reed, E. F. (1948) How effective are group work agencies in preventing
delinquency? *Soc. Serv. Rev.,* **22**, 340-348.

Reiss, A. J. (1952) Social correlates of psychological types of delinquency.
Amer. Sociol. Rev., **17**, 710-719.

Rioch, D. McK., & Stanton, A. H. (1953) Milieu therapy. *Psychiatry,* **16**,
65-72.

Robinson, J. F., Statement of (1959) In B. Karpman (ed.), *Symposia on
child and juvenile delinquency.* American Orthopsychiatric Assn.
Roundtable Five. Emotional Factors in Delinquency, p. 244. Washington, D. C.: Psychodynamics Monograph Series.

Robison, Sophia M. (1936) *Can delinquency be measured?* New York: Columbia Univer. Press.

Robison, Sophia M. (1960) *Juvenile delinquency.* New York: Holt.

Roman, M. (1957) *Reaching delinquents through reading.* Springfield, Ill.: Charles C. Thomas.

Sainsbury, P. (1955) *Suicide in London: an ecological study.* London: Chapman & Hall.

Schmideberg, Melitta. (1935) The analysis of asocial children and adolescents. *Int. J. Psycho-Anal.,* XVI.

Schreiber, P. (1960) How effective are services for the treatment of delinquents? *Juvenile delinquency facts-facets.* No. 9. Washington, D. C.: Children's Bureau.

Schroeder, C. W. (1942) Mental disorders in cities. *Amer. J. Sociol.,* **48,** 40-47.

Scott, P. (1956) Gangs and delinquent groups in London. *Brit. J. Delinq.,* **1,** 4-26.

Shanas, Ethel, & Dunning, Catherine E. (1942) *Recreation and delinquency.* Committee on Recreation and Juvenile Delinquency, Univer. of Chicago. Chicago: Clarke McElroy Co.

Shaw, C. R. & McKay, H. D. (1942) *Juvenile delinquency and urban areas.* Chicago: Univer. of Chicago Press.

Shields, R. (1962) *A cure of delinquents.* London: Heinemann.

Short, J. F., Jr. (1954) A report on the incidence of criminal behavior, arrests and convictions in selected groups. *Proc. of the Pacific Sociol. Soc.,* **22,** 110-118.

Short, J. F., Jr., & Nye, F. (1958) Extent of unrecorded juvenile delinquency, tentative conclusions. *J. Crim. Law Criminol. and Police Sci.,* **49,** 296-302.

Slack, C. W. (1960) Experimenter-subject psychotherapy: a new method of introducing intensive office treatment for unreachable cases. *Ment. Hyg.,* **44,** 238-256

Spencer, J. C., & Grygier, T. (1959) The probation hostel in England. In S. Glueck (ed.), *The problem of delinquency.* Boston: Houghton Mifflin.

Stark, H. G. (1937) Forestry Camps for Delinquent Boys. *Yearb. Nat. Prob. Par. Assn.,* 357-361.

Stone, S. A., Castendyck, E., & Hanson, H. B. (1946) Children in the community. *The St. Paul Experiment in Child Welfare.* Children's Bureau, No. 317. Washington, D.C.: U.S. Govt. Print. Office.

Stullken, E. (1956) Chicago's special school for social adjustment. *Fed. Probation,* **20,** 31-36.

Sutherland, E. H. (1955) *Principles of criminology.* 5th ed. Philadelphia: Lippincott.

Tappan, P. W. (1952) *Comparative survey on juvenile delinquency, Part I, North America.* United Nations Dept. of Social Affairs, Div. of Social Welfare, New York.

Tappan, P. W. (1959) Young adults under the youth authority. In S. Glueck (ed.), *The problem of delinquency*. Boston: Houghton Mifflin.

Teeters, N., & Reinemann, J. (1950) *The challenge of delinquency: causation, treatment and prevention of juvenile delinquency*. Englewood Cliffs, N. J.: Prentice-Hall.

Thelen, H. A., & Sarchet, B. B. (1954) *Neighbors in action*. Human Dynamics Lab., Dept. of Educ., Univer. of Chicago.

Thrasher, F. M. (1936) The Boys' Club and juvenile delinquency. *Amer. J. Sociol.*, 42, 66-80.

Trevvett, Nina B. (1958) Maximum Benefits Project of the Commissioners' Youth Council—four years of work with problem children in elementary schools. Mimeo.

Trevvett, Nina B. (1960) Annual report of the Executive Director, Commissioners' Youth Council. Mimeo.

Trevvett, Nina B. (March 1960) Paper delivered to state and municipal youth commission, Children's Bureau.

Wallerstein, J. S., & Wyle, C. J. (1947) Our law-abiding lawbreakers. *Probation*, 25, 102-112, 118.

Weeks, H. A. (1958) *Youthful offenders at Highfields*. Ann Arbor: Univer. of Mich. Press.

West, M. (1957) *Children of the sun*. London: Heinemann.

Wheland, R., Statement of (1958) Report of the Committee on the Judiciary, United States Senate, 85th Congress, 1st Session. *Juvenile delinquency*. No. 130, 84-88. Washington, D. C.: U. S. Govt. Print. Office.

Whyte, W. F. (1943) *Street corner society*. Chicago: Univer. of Chicago press.

Wilensky, H., & Lebeaux, C. N. (1958) *Industrial society and social welfare*. New York: Russell Sage Fnd., 1958.

Williamson, R. (1957) Crime in South Africa. Some aspects of causes and treatment. *J. Crim. Law Criminol. Police Sci.*, 48, 187-189.

Wills, W. D. (1962) *Common sense about young offenders*. London: Victor Gollancz.

Wills, W. D. (1941) *The Hawkspur experiment: an informal account of the training of wayward adolescents*. London: Allen & Unwin.

Witmer, H. L., & Tufts, Edith (1954) *The effectiveness of delinquency prevention programs*. U. S. Dept. Health, Education and Welfare, Social Security Administration, Children's Bureau, Pub. No. 350. Washington: Govt. Print. Office.

Wolpe, J. (1958) *Psychotherapy by reciprocal inhibition*. Stanford, Cal.: Stanford Univer. Press.

Youngdahl, L. W. (1956) Give the youth corrections program a chance. *Fed. Probation*, 20, 3-8.

Zuck, J. M. (1949) The junior probation camps of Los Angeles County. *Yearb. Nat. Prob. Par. Assn.*, 76-89.

Delinquency Treatment
In An Institutional Setting

J. Douglas Grant

The Problem

How does one intervene (treat) in an institution setting, so that those institutionalized become less apt to commit delinquent acts when returned to the community?

Delinquent-prone youths are viewed in many ways, and from each there follows a more-or-less explicit proposed treatment: he is sick—give him treatment (a psychoanalytic equivalent), he is socially deprived—give him a job, he is lazy—motivate him, or he is bad—lock him up.

It looks as if one is free to take any position one wants concerning the nature of delinquency and the appropriate treatment for it. One suspects that there must be little evidence to support one alternative over any other. This chapter will show that our ignorance is almost this bad, but not quite. Galileo is reported to have said that the goal of science is not to prove infinite wisdom but to set some limits on infinite error. By this definition, we have the beginnings of a delinquency-treatment science. First, we can support strongly the view that the problem is complex, not simple. Second, there are several empirical studies which demonstrate scientific methods of proceeding and at least raise more sophisticated questions than were being asked when the studies were initiated. We will consider now the evidence for complexity.

CONSIDERATIONS IN TREATMENT

A very plausible case has been made for the influence of the following variables on treatment outcome. It appears that any treatment rationale and study would have to account for these possible effects.

Social class affects psychiatric treatment. Hollingshead and Redlich (1960) have dramatically demonstrated a relationship between social class and the way psychiatrists and patients view each other. Middle class people accept the notion that they may be psychiatrically sick, and are oriented toward a psychiatric-type game played by doctor and patient to cope with the illness. Psychiatrists apparently also view middle class people as diagnosable in psychiatric terms and capable of playing psychoanalytic-type games. Lower class people, however, do not see themselves, their relatives, or anyone else as psychiatrically sick, nor do they deem playing psychiatric-type games to be at all appropriate for themselves or anyone else. When psychiatric concepts are applied to treatment of lower class delinquents, it would appear that social class variables should be given consideration in predicting the behavior not only of the clients but of the doctors as well.

Peer relationships must be considered in efforts to change delinquent activity. Ohlin and Lawrence (1951) among many have emphasized that, in determining attitudes and behavior, what goes on among delinquents is more important than what goes on between staff and delinquents. Cloward (1955) has shown that attitudes toward postinstitutional behavior are determined by an interaction of peer group relationships and discrepancies between staff promised and provided opportunities.

Fiedler, Hutchins, and Dodge (1959) speak of quasi-therapeutic relationships and show that what goes on among people in regular living group relationships predictably affects attitude change and personality development. Dorothy Kipnis (1961) has demonstrated predictable changes in self-concepts as related to perceptions of others. We not only know that relationships with one's peers can bring about change, but we are also starting to learn something about the dynamics of these changes.

Personality differences affect efforts to modify delinquent attitudes and behavior. Richard Jenkins (1955) has made the plausible argument that delinquent actions are either goal motivated, adaptive responses, or responses to frustration. He has demonstrated that personality structures prone to frustration-reaction delinquencies differ from those prone to adaptive delinquencies. Further, different treatments are emphasized for the maladaptive as opposed to the adaptive delinquent. With adaptive delinquency, the first emphasis must be upon thwarting delinquent activities. With maladaptive delinquency, the emphasis must be upon reducing frustration responsible for the maladaptive behavior.

Two studies presented later in this chapter strongly suggest that different treatment strategies are appropriate for different kinds of delinquents. In the Pilot Intensive Counseling Organization study (Adams, 1961), subjects classified as amenable to treatment responded significantly better on parole when given psychiatric casework treatment before release than did a nontreated amenable control group. However, the treated nonamenables did worse on parole than either the nontreated amenables or the nontreated nonamenables. In the Grants' (1959) study of military offenders, interaction was found between kind of supervision and kind of delinquent in a milieu therapy program. Michael Argyle (1961) has made a case for four classifications of delinquent-prone personalities. He has presented plausible arguments for the appropriate kinds of treatment for each of the four personality classifications. This statement warrants careful review by the serious student; it is the most scholarly effort to date to develop appropriate treatment models for identifiable kinds of personality classifications.

Staff characteristics affect delinquent treatment. A study of military offenders (Grant and Grant, 1960) suggested that different staff personalities are needed for the treatment of different kinds of delinquents.

Institution climates must be considered. Studies by Mannheim and Wilkins (1955) and the California Youth Authority (Beverly and Guttmann, 1962) support the position that open treatment-oriented programs improve postinstitutional success.

Recent studies of universities and colleges (Freedman, 1962; Pace and Stern, 1958; Webster, Freedman, and Heist, 1962) have shown that meaningful changes in atttitudes, values, and behavior can take place in 17- to 22-year-old students, and strongly suggest that the classroom and college social environment influence student learning. Data support an interaction between kinds of school environments and kinds of personalities.

Vinter and Janowitz (1961) found that distance between staff and inmates was greater in custody-oriented institutions than in milieu therapy-oriented institutions, and this effect was even more marked in the inmate leaders than among their peers.

It does appear that rehabilitation needs to be viewed in terms of who is affected, how, by what, and in which social-cultural context. With this statement of the problem and its complexities, let us now turn to some empirical studies of delinquency treatment in an institutional setting.

THE BORSTAL STUDIES

England's institutional approach to delinquency is a kind of training school which attempts to develop moral character. The essential instrument for this character development is a House of not more than fifty inmates. Each House is considered a separate corporate entity, with a housemaster or housemistress, who, in turn, reports to the school's governor. These schools, called Borstals because the first one was established in the town of Borstal, vary in size from two to five Houses. There is further variation from school to school in kind of inmate, kind of program, and degree of "openness"—i.e., how restricting its physical characteristics and rules are.

The use of prediction methods in studying British Borstal training is an impressive example for empirical studies of delinquency treatment (Mannheim and Wilkins, 1955). As we will see, the Borstal Studies did not set up experimental designs which systematically varied kinds of treatments. Rather, they analyzed the variation which naturally existed over the total Borstal program. The analysis of existing differences in a program provides a procedure for isolating the areas where much more expensive experimental designs, calling for systematic variation of program, can be most effectively utilized. Only the section of the study specifically related to treatment effects will be presented here. Any serious student of delinquency treatment should review the entire Borstal Studies.

The treatment rationale for Borstal systems emphasizes character training. Good character is seen as developing through practicing the choosing of right over wrong and the rewarding of good choices. The treatment must offer opportunities for right and wrong choices to be made and for appropriate rewards to be administered. These rewards are seen as resulting from formal actions as well as through the informal standard setting, motivating, and appraising which comes from peer and staff relationships in personal influence and the corporate spirit of the House.

The program varies among institutions as to training content, but all have the essential ingredients of the House as the living unit and of promotional grades with increasing responsibilities and privileges which ultimately lead to release from the institution. At the time of this study (1954), there were twelve of these training schools in England; six were classified as "open" and six as "closed." They varied as to the maturity of the inmates, as well as to their previous confinement, escape risk, intellectual ability, and educational achievement. The institutions also varied in the trade each conducted, although there was increasing emphasis on training as opposed to production in the workshops and on the farms. The institutions varied among and within themselves regarding time served. The shortest discharge was in nine months, and the longest two years and three months, with an average of approximately eighteen months.

It can be seen why there is interest in whether the open Borstals are more effective than the closed Borstals. All the newer ones have been open institutions, which offer more opportunity for individual initiative and learning self-responsibility. They also, incidentally, cost less to maintain. The research design attempted through an analysis of natural variation to determine whether the open institutions were in fact providing a favorable treatment effect over the closed institutions.

The research design analyzed natural variance over three components: the input, the program, and the output. The input was measured by developing a posttreatment prediction formula from information available in each subject's case record. Seven hundred twenty case records were studied for information available prior to the Borstal training which might be related to whether the subject would be returned to confinement within a year after release from the training (output). These coded bits of information were then analyzed in terms of their relationship to the output and their relationships with each other. From this a formula was developed which allowed output success to be predicted from input information. The outcome after considerable exploratory work was measured by the per cent returned to confinement within one year after release from training. Preliminary explorations showed this measure of outcome to be as effective as many more complicated ones over longer periods of time. Program variation was determined by whether the subject took part in open or closed Borstal training.

The test of program effect consisted in seeing whether the program difference (being in an open or closed Borstal), when combined with input information, increased the ability to predict output over the prediction which could be made from the formula based on input information only.

The findings showed that program variance did improve the outcome prediction over that obtained from input information only. Analysis of the 720 case records produced the formula given in Table 8-1.

TABLE 8-1. THE PREDICTION EQUATION

Factor	Add
If evidence of drunkenness	24
If any prior offense(s) resulted in fine	9
If any prior offense(s) resulted in committal to prison or to approved school	8
If any prior offense(s) resulted in term or probation	4
If not living with parent or parents	7.5
If home is in industrial area	8
If longest period in any one job was:	
Less than 1 month	11.7
Over 4 weeks up to 6 weeks	10.4
Over 6 weeks up to 2 months	9.1
Over 2 months up to 3 months	7.8
Over 3 months up to 4 months	6.5
Over 4 months up to 6 months	5.2
Over 6 months up to 9 months	3.9
Over 9 months up to 12 months	2.6
Over 1 year up to 18 months	1.3
Over 18 months	0

SOURCE: From Mannheim and Wilkins (1955), p. 145.

For every factor which applies, count the number shown against the item. Add together. The result is basic score. From these scores the success categories found in Table 8-2 were obtained.

TABLE 8-2. THE FAILURE SCORE ANALYZED BY SUCCESS AND FAILURE

	Score	Successes	Failures	Total	Per Cent Successful
A	0-9.9	47	7	54	87
B	10.0-14.9	48	24	72	67
X	15.0-23.9	96	65	161	60
C	24.0-39.9	28	54	82	34
D	40.0 and over	2	14	16	13
		221	164	385	57

$$r\phi = 0.46 \ {}^*$$

SOURCE: From Mannheim & Wilkins (1955), p. 146.

* This is a measure of the relationship between the prediction score and the outcome which indicates that the input information could account for approximately 20 per cent of the beyond chance variance for this sample.

Table 8-3 shows the per cent not reconvicted within a year after

TABLE 8-3. A COMPARISON OF SAMPLE WITH TOTAL FIGURES
OF SUCCESS AND FAILURE

		No. Discharged	Not Reconvicted	Per Cent Not Reconvicted	Per Cent of 720 Sample Study
Open:					
Howell Grange		156	120		
Gringley	(1947-1949)	(?)	(?)	63	70
Hollesley Bay		1,069	649		
Hunterscombe		237	169		
Lowdham Grange	(1946-1949)	906	455	56	60
Gaynes Hall		179	114		
North Sea Camp		534	317		
	(1947-1949)			57	43
Usk		727	408		
All "open"		3,808	2,232	59	58
Closed:					
Feltham		700	309		
Camp Hill		443	207	45	45
Portland		1,323	395		
Borstal		989	308	32	30
Nottingham		927	344		
All "closed"		4,382	1,563	36	36

SOURCE: From Mannheim & Wilkins (1955) p. 110.

release from Borstal training, both in total releases and in the sample of 720 used in the prediction study. The similarities, as you will see, are most reassuring. Without considering input information, there was a 23 per cent difference in favor of the open Borstals. Is there any difference in favor of the open Borstals when predicted success from input is held constant? Table 8-4, based on the 385

TABLE 8-4. PROGNOSIS OF TYPE OF TREATMENT
ANALYZED BY CRITERION

	Type of Institution					
Prognosis	Open			Closed		
	Success	Failure	Per Cent Successful	Success	Failure	Per Cent Successful
Good AB	73	21	78	22	11	67
Average X	55	35	61	39	30	57
Poor CD	15	24	38	17	43	28
Total	143	80		78	84	

SOURCE: From Mannheim & Wilkins (1955), p. 112.

cases of the 720 study samples for which all information was available, shows that input identified much but not all of the accountable variance. An analysis of variance indicated that the program variance contributed significantly more to accounting for success variance than could be done from input information alone.

While no further studies have been reported on the Borstal institutions which replicate these findings, studies of California Youth Authority programs appear to support the positive effect of "openness" in treatment. The Youth Authority (Beverly and Guttmann, 1962) has analyzed its programs with an input base expectancy design comparable to that employed in the Borstal Studies. It found that wards assigned to the more open programs did significantly better on parole than expected from their base expectancies. "Open" programs included camps, release to parole within a month after reception, and institutionalization at Soledad, North Branch, which emphasizes milieu therapy and considerable freedom among inmates, as well as between staff and inmates. The more closed programs within the Youth Authority did not show this better-than-expected phenomenon. The Highfields Study (see below) also supports the positive effect of "openness" on treatment.

Significant as these studies are in suggesting that we should look within the nature of "openness" for the dynamics of effective delinquency treatment, this is not their major contribution. The major contribution is the demonstration of pay off to be derived from systematic study of the natural variance in existing programs. These demonstrations make it a crime against the taxpayer (Grant, 1962) not to build operations accounting as well as fiscal accounting into any program. Fiscal accounting only checks whether funds have been spent in accord with some agreed-upon budget category. Without studies to evaluate the program (operations accounting) there is no guarantee that the public would not be better off if the program were not in operation.

The Highfields Study

Highfields is a specialized facility for short-term commitments for first offenders 16 and 17 years of age, featuring a community therapy program with guided group sessions, minimum security, and work projects. Housing not more than twenty-one boys, the facility is the former home of Charles and Anne Lindbergh, which had been deeded to the state of New Jersey. Highfields, which was the name of the estate, consists of 390 acres and was opened in 1950.

The study of youthful offenders at Highfields (Weeks, 1958) was an effort to apply the analysis of natural variance to a short term "open" residential program. As will be seen, the research design was not as tight as that in the Borstal Studies. The original Highfields proposal called for random assignments to three treatment alternatives, but judicial and administrative demands reduced the study to one of natural variance. Fortunately, for future studies of delinquency treatment, precedents are developing (California Department of Corrections, 1956, 1958; Havel and Sulka, 1962; California Youth Authority, 1962; Empey and Rabow, 1960) for judicial and administrative cooperation with designs which call for random assignments over decision alternatives.

The treatment rationale for Highfields can be traced from the efforts of Aichhorn (1935) to establish residential treatment for problem youths in Vienna about 1920. Aichhorn (1935), Redl and Wineman (1952), and Bettelheim (1950) have tried to use the dynamics of interpersonal relationships in living units as a way of bringing about behavior change. In contrast with the rewarding of good normal habits in Borstal training, these therapists were concerned with allowing the "bad" to be expressed and "worked through." Delinquent acts were seen as symptomatic, immature, and defensive behavior. Treatment was focused on personality growth and fostering controls from within. Highfield's treatment assumes that three conditions are necessary for therapy to take place:

First, the environment must be such as to aid the individual to discover and solve his difficulties. Second, there must be a supportive relationship and a therapeutic situation wherein an individual, although he may repeatedly fail to make his faulty perceptions and modes of behavior work, may be given encouragement and support so that in failure he will not look upon himself as worthless or helpless. Third, the therapeutic situation must provide opportunities whereby more effective modes of perceiving and behaving can be learned, tested, and established by the individual because he becomes aware that the newer modes are more satisfactory and rewarding than his older ways of behaving (Weeks, 1958, p. 14).

The treatment program had four characteristic features: (1) informal and intimate staff-inmate living for a short period (approximately four months), in a small group of about twenty in a noncustodial residential center; (2) the experience of a regular routine of work under supervision; (3) evening sessions of guided group interaction designed to give the boys insight into the motivations for their conduct and incentives to change their attitudes; and (4) continuing group discussions outside these sessions during their leisure time. The program was limited to older male youths, although the wife and family of the superintendent lived in the residence.

The research design analyzed the natural variance in parole performance of input samples from two New Jersey institutions. Two hundred twenty-nine Highfield boys were followed through their approximately four months of treatment and at least twelve months on parole. One hundred sixteen Annandale [1] boys were followed through their average of twelve months institutional stay and at least eight months of parole. Formulas were developed for these samples to predict parole success from input (pretreatment) information. Analyses then were made to see if the institution accounted for any of the parole success variance beyond that which was predictable from intake information.

The findings demonstrated the Highfields boys as doing better on parole than Annandale subjects. The data suggested that the Highfields superior parole success could be entirely accounted for by input variations. Further, it appeared that any Highfields effect beyond that attributable to input was occurring among the Negro boys but not among the non-Negroes in the study.

The following Table 8-5 and Table 8-6 for Negroes and non-Negroes compare the parole success of Highfields and Annandale

TABLE 8-5. SUCCESSFUL OUTCOME BY NUMBER OF ADVERSE
BACKGROUND VARIABLES FOR ALL WHITE BOYS SENT
TO HIGHFIELDS OR ANNANDALE

Number Adverse Background Variables	Highfields Per Cent Success Outcome	Annandale Per Cent Success Outcome
0	100	
1	90	67
2	90	63
3	75	82
4	62	78
5	42	38
6	19	33
7		
8		
Total	64	59

SOURCE: From Weeks (1958) p. 68.

[1] Annandale is a state reformatory in New Jersey for juvenile delinquents 15 to 21 years of age. Annandale opened in 1929 and has a normal capacity of 518 young men.

TABLE 8-6. SUCCESSFUL OUTCOME BY NUMBER OF ADVERSE
BACKGROUND VARIABLES FOR ALL NEGRO BOYS SENT
TO HIGHFIELDS OR ANNANDALE

Number Adverse Background Variables	Highfields Per Cent Success Outcome	Annandale Per Cent Success Outcome
0	50	100
1	71	80
2	75	33
3	42	21
4		17
Total	59	33

SOURCE: From Weeks (1958) p. 73.

subjects for each input prediction score (number of adverse background variables [2]).

The study concluded from these tables that "there is no reason to believe, so far as these distributions indicate, that the higher proportion of successful outcomes for the Highfields Negro boys is accounted for by the fact that they have better backgrounds" (Weeks, 1958, p. 73).

PILOT INTENSIVE COUNSELING ORGANIZATION (PICO)

Thus far we have discussed studies of natural variance in treatment programs. A much more expensive and difficult-to-operate design is one utilizing experimental variance—where subjects are assigned systematically to different conditions of the study. As will be seen, experimentally induced variance allows more rigorous, though more costly and administratively inconvenient, tests of treatment hypotheses.

The PICO project is a study of individual-oriented casework with institutionalized older delinquent youths. The treatment rationale for casework counseling is to help the client become aware of and work out ways to handle his needs in the social world with which he must react. Help is provided on a continuum extending from superficial, easily verbalized problems, to those of a deeper and more elusive nature. For example: (1) An inmate may be assisted in formulating an educational-vocational program. (2) Subsequently, he may

[2] Number of prior delinquencies, amount of education, number of jobs held, duration of jobs, number of cities lived in, number of associates in present delinquency, kind of delinquency, and county of commitment.

require reassurance and support if he is to be able to maintain his socially acceptable drives toward self-improvement. (3) As the relationship develops, and identification proceeds, attitudinal changes may become evident as the inmate's ambivalence surfaces, and he begins to alter his concept of himself and others. (4) In some instances, an inmate may finally derive some insights into his own personality dynamics, as he works through emotionally laden experiences and developmentally significant problems (California Department of Corrections, 1958a).

The program consisted of four specially selected correctional counselors, each with caseloads of approximately twenty-five inmates, and qualified by at least two years of graduate training in the social sciences. This training usually includes field placement under the graduate school's supervision. In addition, trained supervision and psychiatric consultation were provided the PICO counselors throughout the study.

Each inmate was seen by the caseworker for a minimum of one interview hour per week. Group counseling was used selectively as an adjunct to individual treatment. This experimental casework was in addition to regular institution programming. Control subjects were assigned to a 200-inmate caseload of a regular correctional counselor.

The research design called for identifying the eligible wards during intake at the reception-guidance center; classifying the eligibles as amenable or nonamenable to treatment; randomly assigning eligibles to treatment and control status; administering intensive casework to the treatment assignees; and evaluating the postrelease behavior of the four categories of subjects. Eligibility for the experiment was established by screening out at intake wards with any of the following "unwanted" characteristics: (1) commitment of less than six months' duration, (2) probable out-of-state parole, (3) psychosis, (4) gross mental deficiency, (5) non-English-speaking, and (6) serious reading difficulty. Altogether, about 1600 wards were identified as eligibles during the period 1955-1960, the first phase of the project.

Amenability to treatment was ascertained through pooled clinical judgments by a team that studied wards at intake into the reception-guidance center. During the period covered by intake, the ratio of amenable to nonamenable judgments was approximately 50-50. Although the most salient ingredient of amenability appeared to be the quality of anxiety, the typical amenable ward might be more fully described as "bright, verbal, and anxious." In addition to these primary characteristics, the judgment of amenability was also influenced by evidence of "awareness of problems," "insight," "desire to change," and "acceptance of treatment." The treatment averaged about nine months for both the treated amenables and the treated nonamenables.

The principal criterion of performance was "return to custody" or "lockup" in facilities of the Departments of Corrections (principal recipient of the returns), Youth Authority, and Mental Hygiene. This criterion has the statistical virtues of a linear scale. It lends itself to the development of a weighted index based on qualitative differences implied in confinement in different institutions. Finally, it yields a realistic estimate of the economic gains or losses in a particular treatment process.

Findings to date consist of the analysis of the first 100 paroled subjects in each of the four cohort groups: treated amenables, control amenables, treated nonamenables, and control nonamenables. Parole performance of over thirty-three months in parole is presented by months of reconfinement time spent in California custody and actual lockup time as a percentage of total possible lockup time for each cohort for a given time on parole. (See Table 8-7.)

TABLE 8-7. CUMULATIVE RETURN TO STATE CUSTODY FOLLOWING
RELEASE FROM PICO: FOUR PICO COHORTS
(N = 100 per Cohort)

Post-release Time in Months	Months of Time Spent in Return to Custody				Maximum Months of Lockup Possible	Actual Lockup As a Percentage of Possible Lockup			
	TA*	CA	CN	TN	Per Cohort**	TA	CA	CN	TN
6		8	14	15	600		1.3	2.3	2.5
12	6	77	79	92	1,200	.5	6.4	6.6	7.7
18	45	162	171	211	1,800	2.5	9.0	9.5	11.7
24	100	281	287	346	2,400	4.2	11.7	12.0	14.4
30	167	414	418	479	3,000	5.6	13.8	13.9	16.0
33	206+	480+	481	550	3,300	6.2	14.5	14.6	16.7

SOURCE: From Adams (1961).

* Treated amenable, control amenable, and so on.
** Maximum months of lockup possible is the product of postrelease time in months and the number of wards in a cohort.
+ The difference between means is significant at .01 by t-test.

These data disclose a number of features of interest. First, they indicate that the treated amenables were decidedly superior to the control amenables in avoiding return to state custody. This superiority is statistically significant at the .01 level by t-test of the difference between lockup mean. Since only a minority of either the treateds or controls was locked up, the distribution of lockup time was strongly skewed, but the t-test was deemed applicable, nevertheless. (For a discussion of this point, see Boneau [1960].) As presented in the original report (Adams, 1961) the difference in general performance, as well as the difference in lockup performance between treated and control amenables, also was found to be statistically significant.

A second point of interest in the table is the continuous growth of the difference in lockup time. At 18 months, the mean difference is 1.17 months; at 24 months, it is 1.81; at 30 months, it is 2.47; at 33 months, it is 2.74. These figures signify that the lockup differential between treated and control amenables is a growing quantity, and it appears that only a follow-up of indefinite length will disclose the ultimate extent of its growth.

A third point of interest is that there appears to be no relation between amenability and parole performance, judging by the virtually identical rates of lockup among the control amenables and control nonamenables. This is a surprising finding, particularly in view of the qualities that are supposedly the marks of nonamenability—lack of insight, no desire for change, denial of problems, and so on. The interpretation of this finding is difficult, especially because in a later section it will be observed that on some criteria there is an apparent relationship between amenability and performance among untreated wards.

A fourth point of interest is the relatively poor performance of the treated nonamenables as compared with the control nonamenables. Although the difference in lockup means at thirty-three months is not statistically significant, the lockup differential grows continuously with time, as in the case of the treated and control amenables. It does not appear likely, however, that the magnitude of the difference between these two cohorts will ever approach that of the two corresponding amenable cohorts.

Further analysis of these cohorts, as well as successive replications on additional cohorts, will be forthcoming from the PICO project. Present findings, however, provide caseworkers with a powerful argument for their use in the treatment of older male youths. It should be carefully noted that the advantages of casework appear to be selective. The treated amenables have less reconfinement time, but the data strongly suggest that nonamenables *not* be assigned to intensive, individual-oriented casework counseling while institutionalized.

THE CAMP ELLIOTT STUDY

Camp Elliott was one of several Navy institutions for the confinement and retraining of court-martialed sailors and marines. The Camp Elliott population consisted of approximately 1000 men, confined for offenses ranging from absence without leave (about 85 per cent) to murder. The average period of confinement was about four months, with 55 to 60 per cent of the men being restored to military duty at the termination of their confinement. The institution was one of the first to allow systematic variation of its program for research purposes.

Delinquency treatment evaluation, as in all efforts to apply scientific methods, needs to state clearly a generalizable rationale. This can be thought of as the "why" statement. Hopefully, it can be logically tight enough to qualify as a theory or model. The rationale must be able to generate testable questions. These questions become the hypotheses which state that if the rationale is right, certain relationships will be observed. If these relationships cannot be found, modification will have to be made in the rationale. Observations can be made through the analysis of existing phenomena, or through the analysis of experimentally created variance.

The Camp Elliott experiment warrants study, not because it is a good example of efforts to apply the scientific method to institutional treatment of delinquency, but only because it is one of the best efforts available to date. A treatment rationale was developed. Specific hypotheses were derived. These hypotheses predicted relationships between treatment variables defined by the rationale. The variables were then experimentally varied as part of the process to improve the rationale. The experiment has been run, the rationale is being modified, and further research has been stimulated.

The treatment rationale for this study developed from an awareness of the pessimism being expressed regarding the possibility of curing delinquents with traditional methods of psychotherapy. Traditionally, psychotherapy was aimed at helping the neurotic whose conflicts are internalized, who carries his guilt and anxiety with him. This kind of neurotic tends to know that he is upset or uncomfortable. He may, for example, feel afraid, have bad dreams, or not be able to speak in groups. In contrast, the acting-out personality tends to dissipate his anxiety before he feels it by running away, striking at someone, or having an affair. Since the acting-out personality resolves his uncomfortableness, he abates any felt-need for personality change. Traditional psychotherapeutic methods are not nearly as appropriate for this kind of personality, since he feels no need to change and since he most certainly would run away from any therapy relationship which made him feel anxious.

Since a majority of delinquents are acting-out personalities, the task in treatment becomes one of putting the offender in a nonpanic-producing correctional situation, which keeps him concerned about and facing his problems, in an attempt to bring about personality change in him. Acceptance of a need to change or grow results from a challenging uncomfortableness. Since this prerequisite for personality change—this uncomfortableness—is absent or easily dissipated, it needs to be created or maintained for the acting-out person. However, intense anxiety leads to rigidifying panic where no personality change can occur. Therefore, the goal of the treatment program is to maintain a situation which would produce in the subjects a challenging uncomfortableness without rigidifying panic.

The program called for research subjects to be placed for six or nine weeks in groups of twenty in small closed communities called "Living Groups" (Grant and Grant, 1959). The twenty men, with three supervisors, lived together in the same barracks, ate together, worked on a farm as a unit, held classes together, and participated as a team in recreational activities. The group was "closed," not only in the sense that no new members were admitted or old members dismissed, but also in the sense that great effort was made to eliminate interpersonal dealings with anyone outside the group. The attempt was made to establish close, continuing interpersonal relationships within the group—with no way out. Ordinarily in confinement institutions there is much opportunity for running away even while staying within the fence by getting transferred from job to job or from one living unit to another or running from therapist to therapist. To as great an extent as possible, all chances for this kind of acting-out or running away from anxiety were eliminated.

These groups may be seen as the primary family situation revisited. Group therapy, has often been likened to a family constellation with the therapist representing a parent and other group members the siblings. In the Camp Elliott Living Groups two additional factors were present which contributed to the analogy: being together for 24 hours a day and maintaining the "closedness" of the group. One of the characteristics of the family situation for the young child is that it is a closed system—he is trapped in it, and he has no other resources. In our closed Living Groups, the men also could not escape. There is the possibility that interpersonal problems which for some reason could not be worked out in the original closed group—the family—may be worked through on such a return trip, especially with a parent figure who is perhaps more able to be supportive.

Three supervisors were assigned to each Living Group. These were Marine noncommissioned officers who volunteered for the program. They were on a two-day-out-of-three duty schedule. Two of the three supervisors were with the men on the job for half of each day; they held discussion classes with the men for the other half day. During free time and evening hours, one of the three supervisors was in the barracks available to the men for individual or small group "bull sessions." A psychologist was available to the confinees and supervisors for individual conferences, although every effort was made to keep as much as possible of the interpersonal relationship for group discussion. Each consultant's main function was to conduct 90-minute, five-days-a-week group therapy sessions attended by the twenty men and the supervisors. These sessions were the heart of the attempt to encourage social maturing by "forced" working through of the anxiety provided by the close, continuing interpersonal relationships. The psychologist's job was to prevent the challenging uncomfortableness from turning into rigidifying panic, yet not to allow subjects to flee the group. The focus in the group discussions was the interpersonal interactions within the group. An attempt was made to create a self-study atmosphere in which group members were encouraged to notice some interpersonal dealing of self with others, or among others—to notice this interaction and to bring it to the group for discussion.

The research design called for twenty-seven Living Groups to be run over a two-year period with three operating simultaneously most of the time. Four major variables were studied:

1. Kinds of offenders.

Before entering the experiment, research subjects were classified on the basis of clinical interviews as high or low on a scale of interpersonal maturity (Ives and Grant, 1956). Maturity level was found to be uncorrelated with education and intelligence. Low maturity subjects were described as concerned primarily with rules of how to get along and frequently manipulated their relationships, responded to threats of external punishment rather than to inner controls, tended to deny anxiety, and showed a general resistance to looking inside themselves.

High maturity subjects showed a more differentiated perception of other people and some capacity for empathy and identification; they tended to be anxious, either openly or symptomatically; they felt guilt, regret, and remorse; they showed some capacity for reflection. It was predicted that men classified as high maturity would respond more favorably to the treatment program than men classified as low maturity.

2. Kinds of Supervisors.

The three supervisory teams were ranked by two psychologists in terms of their predicted effectiveness in bringing about attitude change. Primary considerations were the maturity and flexibility of the individual supervisors.

3. Kinds of Living Groups.

Six of the groups were composed of high maturity, and another six of low maturity, subjects. The remaining fifteen groups included both maturity levels. Because of scheduling difficulties, nine of the mixed groups operated for six weeks rather than the usual nine weeks.

4. Duration of the Supervisor-Group Relationship.

Eighteen of the groups were exposed to only one supervisory team. The other nine changed supervisors and consultants every three weeks.

Many interpersonal rating scales were used, and throughout the duration of the experiment peer evaluations, supervisor-confinee, consultant-confinee, and consultant-supervisor evaluations were systematically obtained. Effects of treatment were evaluated by success of the offender on restoration to service, defined as six months free from further disciplinary action.

The findings were as follows:

(1) Kinds of groups, whether all high maturity, all low maturity, or a combination of the two maturity levels did not effect restoration success. High and low maturity subjects in mixed groups did as well as those in groups where all were high or all were low.

(2) When their entire treatment time had been spent with one of the two supervisory teams which had been predicted first or second in effectiveness, high and low maturity subjects showed a

marked difference in restoration success. This difference, in favor of the high maturity group, could have happened by chance alone less than one time in 100. (See Table 8-8.)

(3) When their entire time had been spent in the supervisory team which had been predicted least effective, high and low maturity subjects did not differ in restoration success.

(4) The high and low maturity subjects reacted differently to the three kinds of supervision. The high maturity subjects had the greatest success with supervision ranked first and second in effectiveness, slightly higher under the second ranking team. Restoration success was less after experience with the third ranking team. Low maturity subjects, on the other hand, had the least restoration success under the team ranked as most effective. They improved noticeably under the second ranking team and did best of all under the team ranked as least effective.

(5) The differences described were found only when subjects were supervised by the same team throughout the Living Group experience. When supervision was changed every three weeks, differences between high and low maturity offenders disappeared. Under changing supervision, only when the last six weeks were spent with the predicted most and next most effective teams did some relationship begin to emerge.

This interaction pattern between kinds of supervision, kinds of confinees, and restoration success was impressively consistent over several breakdowns in the data. The maturity classification system appears valueless without an effectiveness of supervision classification, and an effectiveness of supervision classification appears valueless without a maturity classification. Pre- and posttreatment differences on a delinquency attitude scale supported the posttreatment findings (Table 8-8). These findings are consistent with the amenable, nonamenable treatment interaction found in the PICO study.

Since supervision affected the relationship between maturity level and restoration success, an important question concerns the nature of differences among supervisory teams (Havel, 1959). The nine supervisors and the three consulting psychologists were asked to describe themselves and each other on a series of sociometric items, on an adjective check list, and on a group of role descriptions. The score of each supervisory team was the sum of scores of its members. Differences among the teams were significant at the 5 per cent confidence level.

The members of the third ranking team—predicted least effective

TABLE 8-8. RESULTS OF CAMP ELLIOTT LIVING GROUP EXPERIENCE

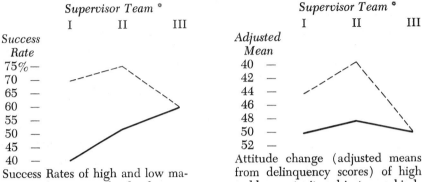

Success Rates of high and low maturity subjects over kinds of supervision (N = 335).

Attitude change (adjusted means from delinquency scores) of high and low maturity subjects over kinds of supervision (all-high groups and all-low groups only) (N = 103).

* Supervisory Team I, predicted to be most effective; Supervisory Team II, predicted second most effective; and Supervisory Team III, predicted least effective.

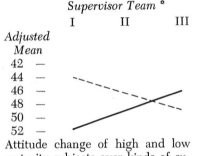

Attitude change of high and low maturity subjects over kinds of supervision (all nine-week groups) (N = 161).

Attitude change of high and low maturity subjects over kinds of supervision (all six-week groups) (N = 173).

* Supervisory Team I, predicted to be most effective; Supervisory Team II, predicted second most effective; and Supervisory Team III, predicted least effective.

in changing delinquency attitudes, and the one that proved actually to be the most effective with low maturity subjects—were described by their peers as follows: "They stay away from retrainees, act superior, and think retrainees are bad actors; they act as if they should get a medal for doing what everyone has to do; they are lone wolves, anxious to be seen as not contaminated by research or by other ship's company personnel; they are good Marines, but should never have been given an assignment in a research company." They were described as not understanding the retrainee's point of view, unable to sacrifice self-interest for that of others, not concerned with having the retrainees like them, closed to new ideas, disliking to take chances, not friendly, not relaxed, undemocratic, and not resentful of authority people. The roles of dictator and maximum security guard were assigned to them significantly more often than to members of other teams. These items give a picture of men who are conforming, status-oriented, concerned with self-aggrandizement and in maintaining the status quo, socially rather isolated and, perhaps, potentially emotionally explosive. They were described as the most strict with retrainees, the least socially mature, but as the most effective Marine non-commissioned officers. Consistent with the prior ranking by research staff, they were considered the least effective in changing delinquency attitudes among retrainees.

The team predicted second in effectiveness was actually as effective with high maturity subjects and somewhat more effective with low maturity men than was the team ranked first in effectiveness. These team members were described as impulsive, enjoying taking chances, close to cracking up, anxious to have retrainees like them, tending to lean on others and to be sorry for themselves, acting like one of the boys, knowing how to work all the angles, open to new ideas, irresponsible, not superior, and not able to get much work out of retrainees. The roles assigned them were playboy, athletic coach, cracker-barrel philosopher, lawyer, shoeshine boy, valet, and retrainee. The picture here is one of emotional lability, social anxiety with a high degree of interaction, absence of concern with status distinctions, and probably a lack of concern with rules in general. This team was described as the least strict and least effective as Marine noncommissioned officers.

The team predicted to be the most effective generally held higher status among their peers, as indicated by their selection as the best research men, the most socially mature, the best for retrainee morale, and the best in changing delinquency attitudes. They were in fact effective with high maturity subjects, but low maturity subjects did significantly worse under their supervision. These team members were described as sincere, helpful, honest, able to get the most work out of retrainees, most able to sacrifice self-interest for that of others, and rejecting of other research company staff members. The picture seems to be one of stern dedication to the task of changing retrainee personality—with both supervisor and retrainee driven hard to accomplish this goal. Seen as more poised and somehow grown-up than the other teams, they were also seen as somewhat aloof.

The first and second ranking teams were seen as alike in some ways, however. In contrast to the team ranked least effective, they were both more often described as accepting and understanding of trainees, democratic, and showing a general resentment of authority figures. They were significantly more often assigned roles of research psychologist and counselor. The two higher ranking teams can thus be regarded as more closely in tune with the therapeutic orientation of the Living Group program (and of psychological consultants), while the third ranking team comes closer to representing the traditional officer-enlisted man approach to the supervisor-retrainee relationship.

The retrainees were asked to describe their supervisors on a sociometric scale of similar content. In general, high maturity subjects gave more differentiated descriptions than lows, and were more likely to see through show-offish, con-type behavior. Where highs criticized supervisors for not being close enough to the retrainees, low maturity subjects saw the same supervisors as helpful and understanding. Differences were greatest when highs and lows described the supervisors rated least effective. Low maturity subjects described them more favorably, referring more often to their nurturant qualities; highs, when they responded favorably, more often referred to their leadership qualities.

High maturity delinquent subjects, in trouble and concerned about it, reacted favorably to a therapeutic community experience which was in sharp contrast to the military setting. They did not react well to the community experience within a more traditionally military, authoritarian structure.

The low maturity delinquent persons responded to more therapy-oriented group experience with increased acting-out behavior. One can infer that the appeal of self-reflection and interchange was actually met with a poorly tolerated increase in anxiety. Lows did best under supervision that marked the least departure from a known rule-oriented experience.

One interpretation of these data might be that highs had a successful experience playing the psychologist's game with therapy-oriented supervisors, while lows had another failure experience, intensifying out-group and military rejection failures. With the more authoritarian supervisory team, the lows had more success playing the "good Marine" game.

CURRENT TRENDS

Thus far some of the complexities of delinquency treatment have been presented. Social class, peer relationships, personality differences, staff characteristics, and institution climates must all be considered in efforts to modify delinquent behavior in an institution setting. Further, examples of specific treatment evaluations have been reviewed. The Borstal and Highfields studies demonstrated analyses of natural-variance approaches to treatment evaluation. PICO and Camp Elliott researches illustrated experimental variation in evaluation.

Where are institution-oriented approaches to delinquency going from here? Three trends currently are emerging. The first is methodological. Institution treatment agencies are developing experimental and agency-study strategies. Rather than promoting *the* treatment for delinquency, agencies are encouraging innovation and evaluation.

The second trend follows from leads in studies supporting "open" approaches to treatment. Therapeutic culture development is under study, and pilot programs are expanding institution treatment into the community.

The third trend follows from observations of inmates in therapeutic communities. Peers are being seen as potential forces in anti-delinquency programs. The question now is becoming: how much use can be made of the products of a social problem in coping with the problem?

EXPERIMENTATION

Experimental strategies are being built into delinquency control agencies. There is a shift from "We know how to treat but cannot because of insufficient budget" to "The control of delinquency is a complicated and changing problem which requires an agency continually to innovate and evaluate."

It is becoming recognized [3] that agency management must deal

---

[3] Although the most extensive applications of research methods to delinquency treatment have been developed by California's Youth Authority, certainly they are not alone with this trend. Both the United States federal and British systems are committed to research approaches to crime and delinquency. New York State has a Division for Youth entirely devoted to experimentation. New Jersey, Wisconsin, Minnesota, and Massachusetts have established research programs. Many other states have individual projects and integrated research proposals for legislative action. New York City as well as Los Angeles and Alameda have research built into their delinquency treatment efforts.

with uncertainties and probabilities. No one knows what will happen next year or how effective a given delinquency treatment program will be, but management must budget, plan, and put into operation next year's program this year. It must operate from its best guesses and probabilities.

From this point of view all management is experimentation. It becomes good management or scientific management. The scientific method is the best rationale approach yet devised to approach uncertainties. The scientific method allows systematic use of past experience in optimizing the chance of being right with future decisions.

Good management and good science both require:

1. Stated objectives—what are we trying to do?
2. Explicit rationales, theories, or models for obtaining these objectives—why are we doing it?
3. Detailed programs to expedite the rationales—what are we doing?
4. Effective monitoring to assure that programs are performed as planned—are we doing what we think we are doing?
6. Continued revisions of programs, rationales, and objectives based upon the evaluations: Systematic use of past experience is making decisions for the future.
5. Continuous program-evaluation—are we accomplishing our objectives as expected?

In order to develop continued evaluation systems, agencies are integrating four methodical approaches to the study of treatment programs and operation. First is population movement. They must know how many of which kinds of inmates go into a given program, how long they stay there, and what happens to them after being moved out of the program. The second is expected-to-observed analyses of natural variance. Besides knowing how many of which kinds were assigned in a given program, the agency must know how many it expected to assign to the program. The agency must know how many of which kinds were returned from a given parole district compared to its expected return. This expected-to-observed strategy allows a continual evaluation of the agencies' operations. Does the expected account for the observed variance, or is something going on which management did not expect?

When unaccounted variance is discovered, the agency has an opportunity to increase its knowledge and potential effectiveness. If the outcome from program or a routine operation varies significantly from the expected, something is happening beyond what management already knows. Then, it calls upon its third methodology. Experimental variation is introduced to test hypotheses concerning the nature of the departure from the expected. The fourth methodology is the cohort interview, and observation of the treatment process itself. Process studies help provide the hypotheses and ideas for treatment rationales which are then tested through the analyses of natural and/or experimental variance.

This total evaluation system requires continual measurement development. Measures are needed of the objectives (criteria), the expectancies (base expectancy formulas), the clients (classification), and the program characteristics (staff, institution climate, performance).

The California Department of Corrections (Grant, 1962) has had an early example of the potential value inherent in this rationale-improvement approach to agency development. The top 15 per cent of good parole risks, as determined by base expectancy rates, were placed under minimum parole supervision. The "good risks" performed as well as they were expected to do under regular supervision. At the same time, the middle range (55 per cent), as determined by base expectancy rates, performed better than expected when experimentally placed under reduced caseload supervision. The "good risks," however, only performed as expected under reduced caseload supervision. Further, process studies showed that "good risks" received more than their 15 per cent share of parole agent time under regular supervision.

"Open" Treatment

Open approaches to treatment are being expanded through the development of therapeutic cultures and through the extension of institution treatment into the community.

The Fricot Ranch Study (Jesness, 1962) exemplifies research in therapeutic culture development. Under Rosenberg Foundation sponsorship, 8- to 14-year-old delinquents are assigned experimentally to either a twenty-boy or a fifty-boy living unit. Efforts are being made to develop therapeutic cultures in both. Data also are being kept on the post institutional behavior of both samples. Major process differences can be summarized as follows:

1. Control-punishment versus permissiveness-reward.
It is perhaps obvious that in a fifty-boy lodge, the supervisory

staff must impose stricter limitations on behavior, both for the preservation of the staff member's sanity and for the protection of one boy from another. In the small unit, there is virtually no marching and almost no use of military formation. In the fifty-boy unit, on the other hand, control is a major preoccupation. It is necessary to call the boys into formation, or otherwise use standardized group procedures for almost all routine tasks, such as showers and bathroom call.

Concomitant with the need for more rigid control in the fifty-boy lodge is the greater use of punishment. Possibly for lack of time to deal with problems on an individual basis, and greater insecurity, punishment is frequently likely to be harsh and arbitrary. In the experimental unit, punishment is less frequent and is usually administered individually. "Correction" often takes the form of reasoning. With few exceptions, individual infractions are not handled by group punishment. However, in the large unit the use of group techniques, such as being on "silence," standing for periods at attention, or loss of privileges for the entire group, is routine, occurring almost daily, and sometimes more frequently.

It is reasonable to expect that this frequent, harsh punishment in rigidly structured situations will lead to failure of development of inner control, greater externalization of responsibility, a more negative attitude toward authority, and a negative perception of self. In the smaller unit, the more permissive situation allows for a greater self-direction, initiative, and autonomy necessary if the boy is to learn from his own experience. Consequently, the experimental boys may be expected to develop greater inner control and use better judgment in unstructured situations.

2. Authoritarianism-equalitarianism.

Because of the tighter controls and large-group techniques, the supervisor in the large unit must routinely act in the authoritarian role. He must maintain a marked social distance, and commonly assumes a harsh, threatening tone of voice. He can neither show his total personality nor take account of the feelings of the boys. When the supervisor must assume the authoritarian role for such a large part of the day, it is unreasonable to expect him to switch easily into the role of counselor or friend. Warm, informal relations appear to become difficult. Moreover, time is rarely available for individual informal contacts.

In this situation, feedback from boy to staff is difficult. There is little opportunity for a boy to express his opinions, show disagreement with supervisors, or to have a voice in the operation of the unit. Here, the effects may be reflected by the development of negative attitudes toward authority, and identification with the authoritarian element of the supervisory role.

Dependency on staff is discouraged. The supervisor cannot intervene in every quarrel, cannot listen to every boy who wants to confide, cannot respond to every request. It is common to see five or six boys surrounding a supervisor, competing for his attention. Boys who persist in seeking attention are considered bothersome, and a supervisor soon learns to discourage inmates from seeking help in small matters.

Over a period of several months, the research staff made a count of the time spent talking or counseling informally with from one to five boys at a time. It was shown that a boy in the small experimental unit can expect at least four times as much informal staff attention as can a boy in the large unit. Thus the boys' attempts at relating are frustrated, and they become increasingly dependent on the peer groups for status and on peer norms as guides to conduct. Boys in the larger unit appear to become increasingly aggressive and superficially self-sufficient. The tendency to deny feelings of dependency may be further reinforced by the large lodge's structure. The implications here are many since close, adequate interpersonal relationships are seen to be crucial in leading to identification, which in turn is considered essential to the development of inner controls. Some suggest that an awareness of concern, interest, or personal liking by others is the most important element in any treatment process.

There are many other differences. There is little privacy in the larger lodge, while boys in the smaller unit are given the option of privacy several times during the day. Greater privacy and informality promote an atmosphere of greater trust and respect by staff toward the inmates. There is in the small unit much less evidence of the occupational habit, apparently found in widely different kinds of institutions, of talking to wards in a disparaging, even hostile tone of voice—a factor which although difficult to document may be quite crucial in its effects.

In addition to the staff-inmate interaction variables are others associated with differences in the inmate subculture. An understanding of the influence of the peer group requires an intimate acquaintance with the boy's world. The very least that could be said is that the experience of a boy with higher peer status is quite different from that of a boy with low status. Among the many hypotheses which can and will be tested are those relating peer status to official status and length of institutional stay. The central proposition here is that in a larger unit, tractability (conformity, and apparent adjustment to program) is in part dependent upon high status, which is in turn more dependent upon aggressive, manipulative skills than upon the absence of antisocial attitudes. Thus, the tractability criterion of improvement in the larger unit may prove to be unrelated to parole success or measures of attitude change. The smaller unit, with less staff-boy social distance, should allow greater upward mobility of low status boys or of disturbed boys. Differences in status should also be less apparent. The peer subculture in general should interfere less with the accomplishment of relevant rehabilitative goals in the smaller unit, where less staff-boy social distance prevails and the boys can be more dependent on staff for a close relationship.

Although this study will run for two more years, its preliminary postinstitution performance findings are of interest.

Considering only the shorter exposure periods, it is clear that up to this time the twenty-boy unit graduates have been more successful than those of the fifty-boy unit. After nine months on parole, for example, approximately 39 per cent of the fifty-unit have had parole revoked, compared with 18 per cent of the twenty-unit. The differences in rate at twelve and eighteen months are also significant and unlikely to be accountable on a chance basis. (See Table 8-9.)

TABLE 8-9. REVOCATIONS FROM PAROLE STATUS

Months Since Release	N	Fifty-Boy Unit Number Revoked	Per Cent Revoked	N	Twenty-Boy Unit Number Revoked	Per Cent Revoked
3	59	2	3.4	46	0	0
6	58	7	12.1	46	3	6.5
9	57	22	38.6	40	7	17.5 *
12	44	22	50.0	37	10	27.0 *
18	28	18	64.3	27	7	26.0 *
24	24	16	66.7	21	9	42.9
36	13	10	77.0	11	8	72.7

Source: From Jesness (1962).
* Chi-square significant beyond .05 level.

Further expressions of the openness trend is the using of institutions as bases for community-oriented treatment programs consisting of community job placements during the day with night and week-end confinement. Another development is the Halfway House of the federal system (McDannell, 1963). Programs for the narcotic-addicted (Burkhart and Sathmary, 1963) have emphasized early detection and short-time-institution return treatment units as part of a continuing treatment-control program.

The best illustration of institution-based community treatment is the Community Treatment Project (Grant, Warren, and Turner, 1963) of the California Youth Authority. This is a study where community versus institution treatment is experimentally varied.

All first commitment wards sent to the Youth Authority from the juvenile courts covering the greater urban areas of Sacramento and Stockton are eligible for this study, with the following excluded categories:

1. Wards whose most appropriate placement is outside metropolitan Sacramento and Stockton.
2. Wards requiring transfer to the Department of Mental Hygiene.
3. Wards who will likely move from metropolitan Sacramento and Stockton within six months after release to the project.
4. Cases of murder second degree, robbery first degree, forcible rape, manslaughter, vicious assault, and other serious offenses.
5. Cases involving intense community reaction.

In the first nine months of operation, 173 juvenile court commitments (155 boys, 18 girls) from the defined geographic areas were screened for possible inclusion in the project. Forty-two boys (27 per cent) and no girls were declared ineligible. Of the forty-two ineligibles, 64 per cent were excluded on the basis of offense or offense history. Most other cases were eliminated because of serious emotional disorder or community reaction to the ward's negative influence on peers. In personal characteristics, the ineligible group differed from the eligible group in having a higher proportion of Negroes and, of course, in having more commitments for assaultive offenses.

From the pool of eligibles, cases were randomly assigned to experimental and control groups, the proportion varying somewhat over time in relation to workload requirements in the experimental unit. Forty-one boys and nine girls have gone into the experimental group, and seventy-two boys and nine girls have gone into the control group.

The treatment-supervision program is divided into three stages, each providing a different level of service, proceeding from intensive programming to a more routine parole program. Stage A is the

intensive contact period into which all wards enter upon release from
the Reception Center. Intensive contact is defined as from two to
five contacts per week and may involve partial or full-day programming for the ward. Cases remain in this stage until they appear to
be capable of adjusting to the community with less supervision and
support from the project. In length, this stage varies according to
the ward's needs, but, for the unit, approximates the average institutional stay (eight months).

Stage B is a transitional period when the treatment goal is to help
the ward work through any difficulties arising from the agent. Case
contacts average one per week.

Stage C is a minimum supervision period, when treatment of experimental cases is comparable to treatment accorded to regular
parolees in the Youth Authority. Case contacts average one per
month.

The use of temporary detention in the institution has emerged as
an important intervention strategy. Five kinds of usage have been
identified:

1. To enforce rules and limits;
2. To prevent acting out in reactions to internal or situational
   stress;
3. To focus the ward's attention on the therapeutic relationship
   with the community agent;
4. To impress the ward with his responsibilities to the project;
5. And to hold the ward in custody pending important decisions
   regarding his status.

Thus far, twenty-five wards have been placed in detention, a total
of forty-one times, with an average of 6.8 days per situation stay.

As Table 8-10 shows, this project already has demonstrated the

TABLE 8-10. EXPOSURE TIME IN COMMUNITY FOR
THE EXPERIMENTAL CASES

Months in Community Program	Number of Wards	Cummulative Percentage
More than 7 months	5	12
More than 6 months	11	40
More than 5 months	3	48
More than 4 months	3	55
More than 3 months	8	75
More than 2 months	7	92
More than 1 month	1	95
Less than 1 month	2	100

Source: From Grant, Warren, and Turner (1963).

feasibility of community-oriented treatment for a large segment of the California Youth Authority wards. It remains to be seen how much ultimate treatment success can be achieved for dollars spent under the two programs. Five experimental cases, not included in these figures, have been revoked as project failures after periods of exposure ranging from two to six months. The five revoked wards were sent to institutions for law violations or failure to adjust to project demands. The total exposure time in the community for all experimental wards is 197 months.

Using Delinquents to Cope with Delinquency

It is a challenging specific in a general development to use the products of a social problem in coping with the problem. Therapeutic culture (Weeks, 1958; California Youth Authority, 1962; Polsky, 1962) and institution organization studies (Ohlin and Lawrence, 1951; Cloward, 1955; Vinter and Janowitz, 1961) strongly suggest that delinquency-involved peers not only affect the delinquent behavior of others, but that they can also assert antidelinquency influences.

The trend now is to see how far systematic use of the delinquent-involved and ex-involved can be developed in coping with crime and delinquency. Already there are several indications that major contributions can come from their use. The role of the ex-alcoholic in the Alcoholics Anonymous program is impressive. Short (1962) has been using older delinquency-involved youths as remedial instructors for younger potential school drop-outs and delinquents. Lippitt (1962) has a project devoted to maximizing the feelings of meaningfulness and purpose of delinquency-prone groups in their work with the community. Schwitzgebel (1960) and Slack (1963) have used delinquents as paid subjects and experimenters in delinquency research. Leary (1962) has parolees stand periodic 24-hour duty sessions with Harvard graduate students to help keep fellow parolees from returning to prison. The Hausers (1960) were one of the first to demonstrate the potential in the products of a culture's problems to aid in coping with the problems.

The Navy's program at Camp Elliott (Grant, 1957) utilized thirty-five confinees in antidelinquency efforts. The California Department of Corrections now has twenty inmates and four parolees actively engaged in correctional research. In addition, it is using inmates as social therapists in therapeutic culture programs.

Volkman and Cressey (1963) have documented the value of ex-addicts and criminals in treating addicted criminals in the Synanon program. Impressive as the Synanon program is, the Volkman-Cressey paper's major contribution is its demonstration of Cressey's (1955) principles for delinquency treatment. These principles warrant careful study. As Cressey (1955, p. 118-119) has written:

If criminals are to be changed, they must be assimilated into groups which emphasize values conducive to law-abiding behavior and, concurrently, alienated from groups emphasizing values conducive to criminality. Since our experience has been that the majority of criminals experience great difficulty in securing intimate contacts in ordinary groups, special groups whose major common goal is the reformation of criminals must be created.

The more relevant the common purpose of the group to the reformation of criminals, the greater will be its influence on the criminal members' attitudes and values. Just as a labor union exerts strong influence over its members' attitudes toward management but less influence on their attitudes toward say, Negroes, so a group organized for recreation or welfare purposes will have less success in influencing criminalistic attitudes and values than will one whose explicit purpose is to change criminals.

The more cohesive the group, the greater the members' readiness to influence others and the more relevant the problem of conformity to group norms. The criminals who are to be reformed and the persons expected to effect the change must, then, have a strong sense of belonging to one group: between them there must be a genuine "we" feeling. The reformers, consequently, should not be identifiable as correctional workers, probation or parole officers, or social workers.

Both reformers and those to be reformed must achieve status within the group by exhibition of "pro-reform" or anti-criminal values and behavior patterns. As a novitiate . . . he is a therapeutic parasite and not actually a member until he accepts the group's own system for assigning status.

The most effective mechanism for exerting group pressure on members will be found in groups so organized that criminals are induced to join with non-criminals for the purpose of changing other criminals. A group in which criminal A joins with some non-criminals to change criminal B is probably most effective in changing criminal A, not B: in order to change criminal B, criminal A must necessarily share the values of the anti-criminal members.

SUMMARY

Delinquency treatment needs to be viewed in terms of who is affected, how, by what, and in which social-cultural context. Social class, peer relationships, personality differences, staff characteristics, and institutional climates have been identified as influences to be considered in delinquency treatment.

Studies of the natural variance in treatments were exemplified by the Borstal and Highfields evaluations. These researches tested whether variations in treatment contributed anything to predicting posttreatment behavior, beyond predictions based only on prior-to-treatment information. Both studies support the contention that open treatment-oriented programs improve postinstitutional success.

Studies which experimentally varied treatments were illustrated with the California Pilot Intensive Counseling and the U.S. Navy Camp Elliott projects. Both studies strongly suggest that treatments which are appropriate for some personality classifications are inappropriate for others.

Three trends in institution treatment research are apparent: (1) institutions are building innovation and evaluation into their administrations, (2) open approaches to treatment are being expanded into the community, and (3) offenders and ex-offenders are being used in coping with delinquency problems. The latter is part of a general development in the use of the products of social problems in coping with the problem.

References

Adams, S. (1961) Effectiveness of interview therapy with older youth authority wards: an interim assessment of the PICO project. *Research Report No. 20*, California Youth Authority, Division of Research.

Adams, S. (July 1961a) Interaction between individual interview therapy and treatment amenability in older youth authority wards. *Monograph No. 2*, California Board of Corrections, 27-44.

Aichhorn, A. (1935) *Wayward youth*. New York: Viking Press.

Argyle, M. (July 1961) A new approach to the classification of delinquents with implications for treatment. *Monograph No. 2*, California Board of Corrections, 15-26.

Bettelheim, B. (1950) *Love is not enough: the treatment of emotionally disturbed children*. Glencoe, Ill.: Free Press.

Beverly, R. F., & Guttmann, Evelyn S. (November 1962) An analysis of parole performance by institution of release. *Research Report No. 31*, California Youth Authority, Division of Research.

Boneau, C. A. (1960) The effects of violations of assumptions underlying the *t*-test. *Psychol. Bull.*, **57**, 49-64.

Burkhart, W. R., & Sathmary, A. (May 1963) Narcotic treatment-control project, phases I and II. *Research Report No. 19*, California Department of Corrections.

California Department of Corrections (November 1956) Special intensive parole unit, phase I: Fifteen-man caseload study. Division of Adult Paroles, Adult Authority. Mimeo.

California Department of Corrections (December 1958) Special intensive parole unit, phase II: Thirty-man caseload study. Division of Adult Paroles. Mimeo.

California Department of Corrections (January 1958a) A measure of casework in corrections.

Cloward, R. (1955) Remarks on a study in ideology formation in a delinquent subculture. In Helen L. Witmer & Ruth Kotinsky (eds.), *New perspectives for research on juvenile delinquency.* U. S. Department of Health, Education and Welfare. Washington, D. C.: U. S. Government Printing Office, 80-91.

Cressey, D. R. (1955) Changing criminals: the applications of the theory of differential association. *Amer. J. Sociol.*, **61**, 116-120.

Empey, L. T., & Rabow, J. (1960) The Provo experiment in delinquency rehabilitation. Paper read at the 90th annual Congress of Correction, Denver, August 28–September 2, 1960.

Fiedler, F. E., Hutchins, E. B., & Dodge, Joan S. (1959) Quasi-therapeutic relations in small colleges and military groups. *Psychol. Monogr.*, **73** (Whole No. 473).

Freedman, M. B. (1962) Studies of college alumni. In R. Nevitt Sanford (ed.), *The American college.* New York: Wiley.

Grant, J. D. (1957) The use of correctional institutions as self-study communities in social research. *Brit. J. Delinqu.*, **7**, 301-307.

Grant, J. D. (1962) Its time to start counting. *Crime & Delinqu.*, 259-264.

Grant, J. D., & Grant, Marguerite Q. (1959) A group dynamics approach to the treatment of nonconformists in the Navy. *Ann. Amer. Acad. Pol. Soc. Sci.*, **322**, 126-135.

Grant, Marguerite Q., Warren, M., & Turner, J. K. (August 1963) Community treatment project: an evaluation of community treatment for delinquents. *CTP Research Report No. 3*, California Youth Authority, Division of Research.

Hauser, R. (1960) Rehabilitation work in prison. Institute for Group and Social Development. London, England. Mimeo.

Havel, Joan (April 1959) Factors responsible for treatment interaction between staff and inmate. Presented at the Western Psychological Association Meeting, San Diego.

Havel, Joan, & Sulka, Elaine (March 1962) Special intensive parole unit: phase III. California Department of Corrections.

Hollingshead, A. B., & Redlich, F. C. (1960) Social stratification and psychiatric disorders. *Amer. soc. Rev.*, **18**, 163-169.

Ives, Virginia, & Grant, Marguerite Q. (1956) Initial steps in the measurement of interpersonal maturity. Sixth technical report, Rehabilitation Research, U. S. Naval retraining command, Camp Elliott, San Diego.

Jenkins, R. L. (1955) Adaptive and maladaptive delinquency. Nerv. Child, 2, 9-11.

Jesness, C. F. (August 1962) The Fricot Ranch School study: an analysis of a training school experience. Fricot Progress Report No. 3, California Youth Authority, Division of Research.

Kipnis, Dorothy M. (1961) Changes in self concepts in relation to perceptions of others. J. Pers., 29, 449-465.

Leary, T. (November 1962) How to change behavior. Paper presented at symposium with California Department of Corrections, Research Division, San Francisco.

Lippitt, R. (October 1962) Dissemination of project results. Paper presented at proceedings of Idellwild Conference on Crime and Delinquency, and Youth Studies Center, Los Angeles.

Mannheim, H., & Wilkins, L. T. (1955) Prediction methods in relation to Borstal training. London: HM's Stationery Office.

McDannell, K. A. (1963) The federal government pre-release guidance program for juvenile delinquents. Unpublished. Mimeo.

Ohlin, L. E., & Lawrence, W. C. (April 1951) Social interaction among clients as a treatment problem. Soc. Work.

Pace, C. R., & Stern, G. G. (1958) An approach to the measurement of psychological characteristics of college environment. J. educ. Psychol., 49, 269-277.

Polsky, H. W. (1962) Cottage six. New York: Russell Sage Foundation.

Redl, F., & Wineman, D. (1952) Controls from within: techniques for the treatment of the aggressive child. Glencoe, Ill.: Free Press.

Schwitzgebel, R. (1960) A new approach to understanding delinquency. Fed. Probation, 24, 31-35.

Short, J. (October 1962) Treatment evaluation. Paper presented at proceedings of Idellwild Conference on Crime and Delinquency, and Youth Studies Center, Los Angeles.

Slack, C. W. (July 1963) SCORE—a description. Paper presented at Proceedings of Social Development Conference, California Rehabilitation Center, Norco, California.

Vinter, R. D., & Janowitz, J. (December 1961) Comparative studies of juvenile correctional institutions: a research report. Ann Arbor: Univer. of Mich. School of Social Work.

Volkman, Rita, & Cressey, D. R. (1963) Differential association and the rehabilitation of drug addicts. Amer. J. Sociol., 49, 129-142.

Webster, H., Freedman, M. B., & Heist, P. (1962) Personality changes in college students. In R. Nevitt Sanford (ed.), The American college. New York: Wiley.

Weeks, H. A. (1958) Youthful offenders at Highfield. Ann Arbor: Univer. of Mich. Press.

9

Delinquency and the Educational System

John R. Eichorn

A consideration of the role of the school in the area of juvenile delinquency poses a number of questions. First, is prevention and control of juvenile delinquency a responsibility of public schools? If it is, are the schools equipped to handle their part of the task? It also raises the questions as to how the schools see their role and how their personnel can prepare for the task. The answers to these raise the questions as to what the schools are doing in this area and how successful their programs are.

America has always held education in high esteem. No other people have demanded so much of education as have Americans (Commager, 1956). Since early colonial times the value and need of education have been recognized. Originally viewed as the privilege of a few, education has become the opportunity for all. As Crow and Crow (1950, p. 3) state, "The philosophy that underlies modern educational theory has evolved slowly but surely as political, social, and economic philosophies have changed." Schools are no longer for the able and willing alone, for many children who at one time would have been excluded because of economic status, limited intelligence, physical limitation, or emotional maladjustment are now accepted. Present-day education is a far cry from that of 100 years ago or even twenty or thirty. The three R's are essential but not sufficient for our modern society. The educational programs of American schools have gradually expanded to include concern for health, personal and emotional adjustment, vocational preparation, and civic training. The concern is for the individual in a modern, ever-changing society.

Commager (1956) suggests that America has been served better by its schools and educators than has any other country. And yet, everyone is aware of the periodic criticism of American educators and educational systems. This is to be expected and welcomed; constructive criticism is to be encouraged in an ever-changing society if progress is desired. A former United States Commissioner of Education believes that we can be proud of the diversity and strength of our schools, but he suggests that until their weaknesses are eliminated the task of educating our youth will not be complete (Derthick, 1962).

It must be appreciated that no matter how well the schools are serving America they do have limitations. Thus a question might be raised as to how well modern schools can perform the broad and generous goals set for them. Are such goals too ambitious? This could lead to the question concerning the relation of the schools to the problem of juvenile delinquency and ways of helping to prevent and control the problem. Brownell (Moore, 1958, p. 51), also a former Commissioner of Education, has said that delinquency is related to the school in three ways: "Schools may produce delinquency. Schools may help prevent delinquency. Schools may help with delinquency through curriculum and program of activities."

Significance of the School's Role

Actually, the school occupies a key position in the community's program for the prevention and control of juvenile delinquency. There is no complete agreement as to what this role is, but most child workers do recognize the strategic position of the school. Some tend to minimize this role. Bloch and Flynn (1950, p. 198) maintain that the function of the school is to provide education in the restricted sense. They believe that the school imparts knowledge and intellectual and reasoning skills which enable the children to make practical adjustments to the type of world and community in which they will live. Educators would agree with this in part, but they would suggest that readying a child for his place in the world goes beyond the task of "imparting knowledge and intellectual and reasoning skills." They would be more inclined to agree with Stullken (1959, p. 155), who believes that schools were established to help youth to realize their potentialities and to develop into wholesome personalities and useful citizens, and that education is "a process by which the behavior of people is improved that they may think, feel, and act differently than they ever did before." He adds the fact that the schools must aim to develop young people physically, spiritually, and morally as well as intellectually. Thus, he concludes, the schools are concerned with all problems of life including juvenile delinquency.

Educators over the years have stated and revised the objectives of education as they see them. Four objectives often quoted (Crow and Crow, 1950) are: (1) self-realization, (2) human relationships, (3) economic efficiency, and (4) civic responsibility.

It is on the basis of objectives that school curriculums are developed. Those who ascribe to these and similar lists of objectives set forth by outstanding leaders in their own profession must agree that such objectives do incorporate, in principle, some responsibility for the prevention and control of juvenile delinquency.

Sheldon and Eleanor Glueck (1959) believe that the school is the second social institutional circle of influences to which a child is subjected. The rearing of children is the responsibility of the home, and yet in this rapidly changing world the home has recognized it needs the help of many community agencies. Robison (1960) suggests that one of the major institutions to which the home turns for assistance is the school. In this institution parents recognize a force which, theoretically, is aimed at the betterment of all who come under its influence. This includes all children except the few who cannot profit from its services but who can benefit only by the help of medicine or a related discipline.

EFFECTIVENESS OF THE SCHOOL

But how effective can the schools be in helping to prevent and control juvenile delinquency? Bloch and Flynn (1950) suggest that, by the time a child has reached school age, his basic personality traits have been formed and many of the incipient and active tendencies toward delinquency and waywardness have been established. Even if one were in complete accord with this, does it suggest that traits cannot be altered or reversed? Neumeyer (1961) believes the school has an excellent opportunity to help prevent juvenile delinquency. He predicates his belief on the fact that the school sees almost all the children at an early stage of development and teachers who have the pupils for several hours a day are able to observe them closely. Therefore, as the Gluecks (1959, p. 1070) suggest, the schools are in a position to reach children before maladjusted behavior expresses itself overtly or becomes too deeply rooted. But recognize that "the school affects the formation of personal controls insofar as its personnel represent acceptable models of authority and provide rational guides for behavior" (Reiss, 1952, p. 711). The school is not alone a physical plant of walls, windows, and class-rooms, but an institution composed of trained personnel, each charged with specific duties but all responsible for contributing cooperatively to the welfare of the children.

This does not suggest that the school has the sole or chief responsibility for juvenile delinquency. Delinquent behavior is seldom the product of the school alone. Also it must be appreciated that the school cannot solve the juvenile delinquency problem by itself (Kvaraceus and Miller, 1959). And there is much the school cannot and should not be expected to do, for actually the school functions within the orbit of societal, financial, and personnel limitations (Yoshino, 1959). There are occasions when the locus of the problem rests with the school, but more frequently it is elsewhere and the school must cooperate with other agencies in seeking information that will help all to better understand deviant children.

Educators' Awareness of the School's Role

It is important that school personnel be aware of the role the school must play in helping to prevent and control juvenile delinquency. Educators are conscious of the magnitude of the problem—they are confronted daily, through various communication media, with reports of the delinquent behavior of youth. But educators must appreciate the fact that the subjects of these reports are "their" children. They are children whom teachers and other school personnel have seen grow up from "ordinary" 6-year-olds to socially maladjusted adolescents. Certainly these educators must at times wonder whether the school could have failed—failed as one of the community agencies responsible for the welfare of these youth. Are educators aware of their responsibility in helping to prevent children from becoming delinquent? Currently, considerable attention is being focused upon the educational problems of exceptional children, particularly the gifted and the mentally retarded. But often juvenile delinquents are considered the bane of society—a fact which is reflected in the community's schools. Kvaraceus (1960, p. 381) has said that "no deviate child among exceptional children suffers more in the way of retaliatory and rejecting attitudes on the part of those around him than does the delinquent youngster." He reports, in a study of youth workers (including teachers), that, of all types of exceptional children, the delinquent child is the one with which they like least to deal.

This does not suggest that educators fail to appreciate that the school has a role to play in the prevention and control of juvenile delinquency. Horace Mann and many other educators since have been proclaiming that the schools must help deviant youth. Evidence of the schools' concern is reflected in the work and publications of their various professional organizations. The oldest and largest of these, the National Education Association (NEA), has published many articles and other writings on delinquency. A discussion of some aspects of the problem can be found in the 1907 annual proceedings of this organization (Bache, 1907). Some years later the NEA published a research bulletin which discussed crime prevention through education. More recently, an NEA study of juvenile delinquency, conducted under the direction of Kvaraceus, included a series of interdisciplinary seminars which considered the school's role in the prevention and control of juvenile delinquency. The result of these meetings was two publications aimed at helping teachers and school administrators with problems associated with the understanding and treatment of juvenile delinquency (Kvaraceus and Miller, 1959; Kvaraceus and Ulrich, 1959).

Somewhat earlier, the Association for Supervision and Curriculum Development (Moore, 1958) published a booklet which provided information of value to schools attempting to determine their role in helping to solve the problem of juvenile delinquency. Moore, with the help of a study-discussion group, compiled a concise but informative review of much of the more significant writings and research in the area.

The National Society for the Study of Education (1948) focused considerable attention on the problem in 1948. And for many years the Council for Exceptional Children has attempted to bring to its members some understanding of the problem through professional meetings and through its official journal. A number of other organizations of educators have also concerned themselves with this problem.

EDUCATORS' PREPAREDNESS

It has been said that the school cannot be everything to everyone. School personnel do have particular functions to fulfill. But actually these functions cannot be accomplished individually; therefore, educators must have a broad background that permits them to understand their task in relation to the work of other child workers. Professional training for teachers involves work in many fields and should provide them with an understanding of children—their growth and development in our modern society. It should permit them to work more effectively with children and to sensitize them to problems of the extreme deviates. Also it should permit educators to recognize their own limitations as well as their strengths and the value and need of working with other youth-serving agencies.

How well are teachers prepared to understand children, and how effectively can they recognize the problems of children? Sharp (1942) feels the teacher's main task is to carry the children through the curriculum, and for this reason her evaluation of each child centers on his activity relative to the curriculum. But, as indicated earlier, educators feel that teachers must concern themselves with many aspects of the development and adjustment of children as these have a direct bearing on how they learn. Therefore it is essential that teachers recognize behavior which is indicative of maladjustment. In 1928 Wickman reported research findings which raised considerable doubt as to the ability of teachers to recognize symptoms of serious behavior problems. But since that time schools have raised the professional requirements for teachers. Today, more states demand that their teachers have a bachelor's degree, and in some the current trend is toward a five-year teacher training program. Also, teachers' license requirements today include more work in those fields which will help educators to work more effectively with children. However, it must be recognized that the critical shortage of teachers has necessitated the hiring of some teachers without the desirable background, and some small communities, and some not so small, have had to settle for teachers with bare minimum license requirements because they were unable to meet the financial competition for the more qualified teacher. In addition, there are some teachers who were licensed before the stringent requirements were imposed. This does not imply that the meeting of state certification standards will of itself guarantee that a teacher will possess the ability to recognize severe behavior problems. Conant (1963) in his study of the education of American teachers has challenged the patterns of certification of teachers in this country. It is his opinion that none of the present methods of certification assure the public of competent and adequately prepared teachers.

To understand the deviant, teachers must first understand the "average" child. How well does teacher training prepare educators to do this? The quality of training varies considerably from one institution of higher learning to another (Conant, 1963), but Long and Newman (1961) believe the majority of teacher training institutions are such that beginning teachers find their attempts to transfer their educational beliefs and methods into an educational program unsuccessful. A more recent publication lends some support to this claim (Sarason, Davidson, and Blatt, 1962). It is essential that we be concerned with this problem, for, as Brownell (Moore, 1958) suggests, even in combination the home, school, church, and other community groups have not been able to prevent more and more youth from becoming delinquent.

The majority of teachers are reasonably healthy, capable people who attempt to do the best they can (Long and Newman, 1961). Despite the ever-present criticism of their work, the condition of our country and its people evidences that most school teachers are doing their part. This is true despite our seemingly limited knowledge of children and their behavior. But to do a good job, teachers, as Morse (1958) suggests, should know what children do and what motivates them to do it. It is in this direction that the formal training of the educator is aimed—to know what children do and their motivation for doing it. It would seem that teachers with this training would recognize significant behavior problems.

But Wickman (1928) seemed to demonstrate that teachers are concerned about the types of behavior regarded by mental hygienists as least likely to result in behavior disorders. Teachers are still being indicted on the basis of the Wickman study (Clinard, 1959), and yet there have been later studies which tend to refute or modify these earlier findings. In one study, made in 1951, it was found that the attitudes of the 119 teachers and thirty-seven mental hygienists studied were in much greater agreement with the criterion attitudes established by the clinicians than were those of the teachers of the Wickman study (Schrupp and Gjerde, 1955). In another study reported several years earlier, an attempt was made to measure teacher insight into child behavior. The teachers surveyed recognized constructive measures for dealing with child behavior (Stendler, 1955). Gronlund (1950) and Gage and Suci (1951) found that the ability to judge the behavior of pupils accurately is correlated positively with the teachers' effectiveness with them.

In their study, Amos and Washington (1960) reported that teachers recognize fewer problems in junior high school pupils than the pupils themselves recognize. Harris' (1952) study seems to lend some credence to these findings. In his study, teachers were asked to select "normal" children. Those selected were taken to clinics where they were studied extensively as "problem" children usually are. Harris found large discrepancies between the findings of the teachers and those of the clinicians. The latter classified as problem cases one in four of those selected by the teachers as normal. But Klein's (1956) interesting discussion of this study raises the question as to whether what appeared to be on the surface is so, that is, whether the teachers could have been more nearly correct in their appraisals than were the clinicians. Klein's discussion of Luft's (1950) investigation also helps to remind us to analyze carefully the reported results of such studies.

Mitchell (1942) found in his study that mental hygienists had changed their ratings on some of the traits in the Wickman study in the conservative direction. And, he reports, teachers were somewhat closer to the mental hygienists, especially in their ratings of non-aggressive traits. On the basis of his study of 308 elementary and secondary school teachers in New Orleans, Hunter (1963) suggests that today's teachers are definitely showing more concern about non-aggressive traits and behavior suggesting mental problems than did the teachers involved in the Wickman study. One of his findings also agrees with that of Sparks (1952) that teachers with training beyond the bachelor degree evaluate problems more nearly like mental hygienists than do those with less education.

Despite the greater emphasis of teacher training on what children do and what motivates them to do it, too few educators gain any great degree of understanding of juvenile delinquents through course work. Evidence of this may be noted in a recent study of 260 educators enrolled in graduate courses. Of these, eight had taken college courses entitled "Juvenile Delinquency" while seventy-five had had in their graduate or undergraduate studies courses in which a specific segment had been devoted to the problem. About half had had only courses which devoted no more than one or two class hours to the problem. The remaining had had no classes in which consideration was given to the problem (Eichorn, 1962).

The writer's experience with graduate students taking courses in the area of exceptional children suggests that most of them tend to have a somewhat more sophisticated background than the average well-read lay person. For example, they appreciate that there is more than one causal factor and that no one discipline alone can be expected to prevent or to control delinquency. But these same educators are too prone to generalize and to have set and positive ideas which research does not bear out. Frequently, they accepted as truisms the very same common misconceptions of delinquency listed in the recent NEA study (Kvaraceus and Miller, 1959).

EVIDENCE OF DELINQUENCY IN THE SCHOOLS

The idea that the school is an agency which can contribute to juvenile delinquency is not new. Over 100 years ago Pierce (1854) presented an evidently controversial essay in which he stressed the lack of moral training in American schools and its relationship to crime. But a decade ago Clinard (1959, p. 188) made this statement: "It is a curious commentary on our modern world, which emphasizes education, that the school is a large contributing factor in juvenile delinquency." More recently, the challenging question was raised as to why, in the minds of so many, should the schools, which along with mass media should be a force of good, help to breed evil as well as good (Robison, 1960).

It is not a simple matter to pinpoint those factors within the realm of the school which help to cause juvenile delinquency. Although their actions often belie it, educators are generally cognizant of the fact that the elements which contribute to any one case of delinquency are numerous and varied. As the schools, in periodical revisions of the curriculums, began to focus attention on the individual, some educators became aware of this fact and attempted to uncover ways in which the schools contribute to the problem of juvenile delinquency. It is difficult to stipulate, with any degree of certainty, that a particular condition or circumstance in the school contributes to the problem. In many instances, according to Sullinger (1929, p. 23), "the determiners of delinquency in the schools are acts of omission rather than of commission."

Smith (1958) lists twenty-seven conditions which he believes are among those factors which bring about conditions contributing to delinquency either directly or indirectly. A great many of these are conditions which well-informed educators have been militating against for years. These include (1) lack of trained teachers, (2) poor school facilities, (3) lack of consideration for individual needs, (4) pupil discrimination, (5) lack of concern for leisure time pursuits, (6) inadequate counseling and guidance services, and (7) lack of needed specialized personnel.

There is no agreement as to how significant these factors are. The jurist, the sociologist, the psychologist, and the psychiatrist have widely divergent approaches to the issues of delinquency (Ausubel, 1954). Although members of the disciplines which these individuals represent might agree that the aforementioned are contributing factors, they probably place different values on each. This is quite understandable when it is recognized that those in the various disciplines differ in their opinions as to causal factors. The jurist is concerned with the ability of the individual to know right from wrong and to appreciate the nature and quality of his act, while the sociologist puts the greatest weight upon social disorganization and conditions of socioeconomic deprivation. The psychologist and psychiatrist tend to consider delinquency a problem of disordered personality development arising from unfortunate relations between the child and significant persons in his psychological field rather than to consider a manifestation of disturbance in grosser patterns of social organization (Ausubel, 1954). Appreciating the existence of these divergent beliefs, the educator may find it difficult to decide for himself which are the most important factors. Rather than to pretend to be able to do so, he may take a positive approach and attempt to ameliorate all which might tend to cause problems. Document Number 2 of the NEA 1959 study (Kvaraceus and Ulrich) can serve as a very helpful stimulant for those who recognize the need for improving conditions which might possibly contribute to the problem of delinquency.

There are a number of signals which can serve to warn the school that a child may become a juvenile delinquent. Not all those who evidence such behavior will become delinquent; some who commit delinquent acts will, without special assistance, grow up to be good law-abiding citizens. And yet schools should be alert to such signals and afford whatever services are within their power to counteract the seemingly inevitable happenstance which results for many. The importance of these early signs may be appreciated when one reads such statements as that of the superintendent of schools who suggested that the public schools had a record on the guilty youth which could have predicted the crime for practically every major crime case in his locale (Fine, 1959). These signs generally include school absenteeism, academic failure, and/or behavioral problems.

ABSENTEEISM

Compulsory education demands that children attend school daily. Yet for various reasons there are a number of children who are absent from school each day. On any given day in New York City in 1948, from 80,000 to 90,000 children were absent from the public schools (Lash and Kahn, 1949). Today similar figures, but on a lesser scale, are found in many other school communities across the nation. The absences are often for legitimate reasons, such as cases of measles, heavy snow blocking transportation, or death in the family, but in some instances the children are truants who are absent with no "acceptable" excuse. There are also those whose absence may be considered legitimate and yet who should be investigated, for the very legitimate reason which excuses them may indicate that they need special attention.

Truancy

The chief concern with truancy is that it is frequently a forerunner of delinquency. Shulman (1961) suggests that most truants do not become delinquent, although studies indicate that severe delinquency is usually preceded by chronic truancy (Robison, 1960; Abrahamsen, 1960). This can be misleading, for chronic truancy as of itself is generally classified as delinquency.

Definitions of truancy are not uniform, and communities often interpret regulations to suit local situations. In 1930 New York City defined truancy as absence for three consecutive days without a satisfactory explanation. The only change made by 1947 was to raise the number of days to five (Robison, 1960). The California Education Code defines a truant as "any child between the ages of 8 and 15 (inclusive) who has been absent from school without valid cause for more than three days or tardy more than three days" (Neumeyer, 1961, p. 233). A child reported as truant three or more times is regarded as a habitual truant. In a discussion of truancy by a class of graduate students in education, a number expressed the opinion that the important thing is not the length or continuity of absences, but rather the causes. Several suggested that a legitimate cause for absence in their rural community is the fact the child is needed at home to help with farmwork. The question was raised as to how different this type of case is from that in which the child in the urban center is kept home to take care of younger children while both parents go to work. In a 1930 study Robison (1960) reports that only about one-third of 20,000 of the absences were wilful truancy. More recently it has been reported that nearly 80 per cent of the cases of absenteeism are due to legitimate reasons (Culbertson, 1960).

Although the educator's chief concern for school truancy may stem from a sincere wish to have children benefit from a good educational program, the concern of some appears to be due to the fear of losing some state financial aid. In New York City the decrease in attendance of only one per cent in 1948 meant the loss of almost $750,-000. Today's figures are, of course, moumental. Those interested in the financial side of the problem will be concerned chiefly with the legal aspects of school attendance. One writer (Culbertsen, 1960) reports that, in about 1915, schools were for the first time beginning to be aware of the nonlegal aspects of truancy. It was the beginning of the idea of doing something *for* rather than *to* the absentees. Studies dealing with general student populations have uncovered the fact that illness is the most frequent cause of absence, while, among the nonmedical reasons, work is the most frequent cause (especially in rural areas), with travel running second (Culbertsen, 1960).

In the 1920's students of delinquency and crime became interested in truancy. There has been a considerable number of studies of truancy since, but very few have considered causal factors (Neumeyer, 1956). Nor have there been any studies which give evidence of the causal relationship between truancy and subsequent other types of delinquency (Robison, 1960).

For the average child, school is (as Hurlock [1955] says of the average adolescent) a pleasant, or at least a tolerable, experience, and yet each school year brings children problems of adjustment, of learning, and of give-and-take with others (Goldberg, 1948). These are normal in the process of growing up. But for a few, school is neither a pleasant place nor does it afford a tolerable experience. Some youths resolve this problem through truancy (National Congress of Parents and Teachers, 1957). Truancy may be related to such school problems as academic failure, ill-suited curriculum, or inability to adjust to school routine. On close examination the truant may be a bright normal child best served by a more stimulating school program, or he may be a schizophrenic needing hospitalization (Kahn, 1953). Truancy per se may not be the real problem but, rather, it may be a warning of one. In some cases these problems may be school-centered, but they often have their roots in the home or the basic structure of the personality of the child.

Studies of truants show that, as a group, they have more personal and family problems than do other children. Neumeyer (1961) reports two studies that help bear this out. Abrahamsen (1960) suggests that, with 60 per cent of all offenders starting their criminal careers as truants, it is essential that truancy be investigated as to its start, its frequency, and its relation to the offender's home and school atmosphere, to the possible influence of his companions, and to his parents' reactions. Some schools attempt to do this, but Cavan (1955) believes that the occasional truant is tracked and punished for his actions with no attempt to understand why he does not want to go to school. The occasional as well as the habitual truant may need special attention. If a child has problems related only to the school, would he become a truant? One study concludes that most children will go to school when they are well and when their parents want them to go and cooperate in assuring attendance.

Chronic Absenteeism

Smith (1958) believes that chronic absenteeism is more of a problem than truancy. He labels as "chronic absenteeism" those cases which are not wilful truancy. He reports that the factors which are responsible for this type of absence are (1) periodic or seasonal migration of many families; (2) child labor; (3) failure to enforce school attendance laws among some families in urban slum areas; (4) failure to enforce attendance laws in backward and isolated places; (5) nonenforcement of attendance laws among Negroes, especially in parts of the rural South; and (6) the need for the child's help at home because of a combination of parental illness, unemployment, and extreme poverty. Such absences prevent these children from acquiring the education which would permit them to obtain adult employment other than unskilled and menial types of jobs. With such limited choice of occupations, Smith (1958) suggests it is easy for these individuals to follow the line of least resistance and to drift into a career of delinquency and crime.

Drop-outs

Not classified as delinquency but often evidence that the school is failing to meet its avowed objectives is the problem of drop-outs. A study of 31,000 Michigan high school students reveals that fully one-third of those who enter school fail to finish (Smith, 1958). This represents an enormous social loss, as many of the early drop-outs do not gain the type of preparation which would permit them to make the contribution to society which an adequate education would permit. As Conant (1961) suggests, youth who have dropped out of school and never have had a full-time job are not likely to become constructive citizens. They are more apt to be frustrated individuals who become antisocial and rebellious, and as a result may well become juvenile delinquents. This is indeed cause for concern when it is appreciated that in June 1961 the unemployment rate in the United States was 7 per cent for all age brackets, while unemployment among youth under twenty-one years of age was about 17 per cent (Conant, 1961).

School Phobia

In some cases school phobia may appear to be truancy. A closer study of the facts reveals that this behavior would be better classified under "emotional problems." Unlike truants, these children generally remain at home, and, as Talbot (1957) suggests, those who do arrive at school frequently flee, dashing straight home to mother.

School phobia refers to an anxiety about going to school. Actually this concern is an assumed cloak which hides the real source of anxiety (Levison, 1962). The anxiety generally has to do with a concern for being separated from the home. Invariably the child so disposed evidences psychosomatic symptoms. Typical is the child who vomits his breakfast and uses this device to remain at home (Robison, 1960).

As the school has increased its concern for the *why* of absenteeism the number of cases of phobia has appeared to increase. Eisenberg (1962) reports that, in a survey of 4,000 clinical admissions over a period of eight years, the incidence of school phobia has risen from three cases per 1,000 to seventeen cases per 1,000. No longer can we treat these children as truants, but rather we must recognize that they are children who frequently need special attention, often from sources outside of the school.

School Failure

The first recognizable symptom of delinquency noted in many youths has been school failure. Actually academic failure is a perennial problem which has plagued the schools since their conception. For years schools have been trying to cope with this problem, and a number of studies to determine causal factors have been conducted. Although many children who are academically retarded are not delinquent, there is considerable evidence that delinquents are generally academically retarded (Roman, 1957; Glueck & Glueck, 1950; Louttit, 1957).

Kvaraceus (1945) reports that about all the delinquents served by the Passaic Children's Bureau receive failing or just passing grades.

As academic achievement is directly related to one's reading ability, it is interesting to discover that one study revealed 84 per cent of the cases at the treatment center of a New York children's court had reading disabilities. The investigator defines a reading disability as "reading retardation in excess of two years below what might be expected of a child's intellectual capacity as indicated by psychological tests" (Roman, 1957, p. 5). This writer reports another study of the incidence of reading disability. The findings reveal an incidence of 10 per cent in a school sample but of 83 per cent in a sample of predelinquent and delinquent children.

The relationship between delinquency and school failure is not understood too well. Causes of academic failure are varied, and no one cause can account for any individual case. Causes enumerated by educators include low intelligence, poor health, irregularity of attendance, cultural and economic deprivation, poor attitudes toward education by home and/or community, and poor quality of instruction. In discussing the subjects in their study the Gluecks (1959) have suggested some of the possible reasons why the delinquents are more educationally retarded than the nondelinquents. They include the greater moving of the delinquents from one place to another with their families, their placement in foster homes after disruption of the parental home, and commitments to correctional institutions. But as these experimenters attest, these were not the only possible reasons. Although it is not clear as to what specific causes we can attribute to academic failure, Roman's observation is interesting. He says that "in retracing the development of an individual's delinquent behavior, it is not unusual to find the triad: reading retardation-truancy-delinquency" (Roman, 1957, p. 4). This, he adds, is not to suggest that failure in reading is the basic causal factor of delinquency in such cases.

BEHAVIORAL PROBLEMS

Although not all children who misbehave in school become delinquent, a review of case studies reveals that a great many delinquents were behavioral problems in school beginning at an early age (Hurlock, 1958). Delinquency in youth is evidenced generally in early adolescence, but Ausubel (1957) says that two-thirds of adolescent delinquents begin their delinquent behavior in preadolescence. In the Gluecks' (1950) study almost one-third of the delinquents, compared to one-twelfth of the nondelinquents, misbehaved before the age of 8. Eighty-six of the nondelinquents compared to 478 of the

500 delinquents persistently or seriously misconducted themselves at school. In the Passaic study it is reported that more than half of the children referred to the Children's Bureau came from the 6-to-10 year level (Kvaraceus, 1945).

J. Edgar Hoover (1960) believes that the school stands as the symbol of law and order for many boys and girls. But to some the school is an intolerable place where they have encountered many unpleasant tasks and unsympathetic adults. There are studies which report that a great number of delinquents have expressed their decided distaste for school and its offerings. With such attitudes, misbehavior and other difficulties are bound to develop. Young (1952) states that uncongenial schools and educational tasks that are distasteful have resulted in emotional scars and waste of human talent.

Misbehavior of school children is a universal problem—a problem which has existed since early times. American history reveals this when it tells us of the colonial schoolmaster and his rule by the rod. Although ideas of discipline have changed since those early days, modern professional books in the field of education reveal that discipline is still a major problem. Class control is a challenge to the experienced teacher as well as to the novice. According to Cutts and Moseley (1957) almost every teacher has one child or more in his class whom he finds difficult to control. The secondary school teachers in this study were practically unanimous in their opinion that the problem is greater today than it ever was.

School misdemeanors can be attributed to a great many youth who are not delinquent or predelinquent. The behavior of the delinquent or predelinquent is generally similar to that of other youth, except that it is of a more serious and persistent nature (Hurlock, 1958). For example, Hurlock (1958) believes that most adolescents engage in minor pilfering or occasional truancy, but she states that the juvenile delinquent steals consistently or spends more time away from school than in school. But it must be appreciated also that some children who could be labeled delinquents are not reported to public agencies as such because of reasons of chance or social, religious, or ethnic background, economic status, or availability of special resources (Kahn, 1953). Short and Nye (1958) report that only a portion of delinquent behavior is followed by arrest and conviction. Their study included comparisons of unrecorded delinquency with recorded delinquency. One of their findings suggested that the noninstitutionalized students experienced arrests in a far smaller proportion of offenses which they reported they committed than did the training school students.

Why do delinquents (or predelinquents) misbehave in school? Young (1952) suggests that many of the so-called problem children were probably problems before they entered school. And yet misbehavior in school can result from curriculums which do not fit the interest or the needs of children or it can result from an unwholesome classroom climate. Schools which attempt to have every child fit a single prescribed curriculum foster behavioral problems. They also force many to drop out of school who, because of lack of employment and other possible contributing factors, eventually may become juvenile delinquents. Programs which fail to challenge children and provide for the slow learner, and which make special provisions for the handicapped, breed malcontent. In addition, some teachers with adjustment problems of their own can do much to create problems among the children. Neumeyer (1961, p. 381) puts it quite forcefully when he states that "social deviation may be the result of a situation in which the atmosphere in the classroom is austere and antagonistic, the children's interests and abilities are not fully recognized, teachers do not understand the needs and personality weakness of their pupils, inadequate testing devices are used to ascertain the accomplishments and deficiencies of pupils, counseling and adjustment techniques are applied too late or not at all, and the school experience as a whole is not satisfactory."

Behavioral problems can be created by teachers without adequate training or experience. Most teachers come from middle class homes (Warner et al., 1954; Rich, 1963; Robison, 1960), and in addition most have the type of training which equips them to teach in suburbia but not in the slums or the fringe areas. With such a background are these teachers able to understand that children in slum areas are apt to look upon a "policy king" or other person who has achieved success through illegitimate means as their hero (Cloward & Ohlin, 1962)? Or can they appreciate that lower class children are often hurt by the contrast that they see between their homes and those portrayed in their every-day school books (Kaplan, 1959)? And can they appreciate the significance of the theories of subcultures in the lower class milieu as discussed by Cohen (1962), Miller (1958), and others? Or can they understand why these children are more prone to settle disagreement by violence or to use speech which is considered offensive at school? Kaplan (1959) suggests that few teachers are able to project themselves into the lives of lower class children. He suggests that they lack insight into the ways of these children, and as a result they are not equipped to handle many of the problems of the classroom. He reports that teachers have been found to favor upper class status children and to handle lower class children with more directness and less regard for their feelings or their educational welfare. The significance of this statement can be appreciated when one reads that 85 per cent of the delinquent youth population comes from the lower class (Kvaraceus and Miller, 1959). This same NEA research project report emphasizes the problem of middle class teachers working with lower class children. This report provides guidelines to help teachers in working with children and suggests that these contain many implications for teacher training. Special courses, practicum, and in-service programs must be considered for the student preparing to teach and for the teacher already employed.

School behavioral problems are sometimes symptomatic of emotional problems. Many children revealing these symptoms will not be delinquent because their behavior seldom violates legal or social norms. According to Miller (Kvaraceus and Miller, 1959), juvenile delinquents who demonstrate emotional disturbances make up but 25 per cent of the delinquent population. The remaining 75 per cent have little or no emotional disturbances. In a study of 1110 male juvenile delinquent probationers, 730 were classified as relatively integrated delinquents (the type which in all probability will become a mature independent adult). An approximate 25 per cent (245) had relatively weak ego control and were generally viewed as highly insecure persons with low esteem or as highly aggressive and hostile persons. The remaining 135 consisted of those with morally defective superego controls not having internalized the social controls of the middle class and who experience little sense of guilt for their delinquent acts (Reiss, 1952). However, Abrahamsen (1960) believes that, while most delinquents do not suffer from well-defined psychiatric or neurological conditions, many are neurotic and all are emotionally undeveloped.

PREVENTION AND CONTROL

There appears to be considerable agreement that the school can help to prevent and control juvenile delinquency. Educators, especially classroom teachers, are the logical ones to observe deviant behavior (Massachusetts Child Council, 1940). They see almost all children and have the opportunity to observe the type of behavior which is frequently indicative of predelinquency. This includes truancy, school failure, and behavioral problems. This information, coupled with an understanding of home and community problems, can help to locate children who are delinquent-prone. It can also help educators to recognize some of the school situations which fester the delinquency cancer. In the latter categories, the school can play a major role in prevention, but often the school's responsibility is to supply information to another agency, better equipped to handle particular problems.

In order to play a positive role in the prevention and control of delinquency, the school must have personnel with an understanding of the problem, curriculums which meet the educational needs of all children, special services for those who need special attention, and a working relationship with other child-serving agencies. It must be recognized that schools so prepared will not only help to prevent many cases of juvenile delinquency but also will help to improve the lot of a great many nondelinquents.

School Staff

Schools that expect to play a role in the prevention and control of juvenile delinquency cannot overlook the need for qualified personnel. Qualified school personnel should be able to recognize behavior which suggests the possibility of predelinquency. They should have the knowledge which permits them to help discover why children are truant, why they fail in school, and why they become serious behavior problems. They must be able to recognize which of these problems may need special services—either through the school or some other agency. Therefore, the schools must be very selective in hiring their personnel. Special consideration must be given to the personal attributes and professional training of the classroom teachers for, as Mouley (1960) says, in the final analysis it will be the teachers who do most for the vast majority of children in the development of effective behavior.

Schools should certainly consider the academic training of the teacher, but equally important is her mental health. There are teachers who have the professional training which would help them to recognize and understand the predelinquent but who are not emotionally equipped to work with them. Kaplan (1959) reports studies which reveal the problems of teachers whose influences are devastating to children's emotional health. The emotional climate of the classroom of these teachers could help to foster rather than prevent behavioral problems.

Many communities attempt to select teachers without giving due consideration to mental health. Teacher shortages play a role, but another aspect of the problem is the lack of good screening techniques and counseling services in many teacher training institutions. Generally, in order to take the teacher preparatory curriculum, a student must be of college level intellectually, be free of severe physical defects which might affect his teaching, and obtain passing grades, but no consideration is given to mental health problems. There are school systems and colleges which do consider the problem of mental health, and some provide counseling services for those who need it (Abrahamsen, 1960). However, more colleges and more school administrators should be aware of the need for considering the mental health of teachers. If colleges and schools hiring their products could work together more closely, better teachers would be available.

Mental health is not something which one has or does not have. Mental hygienists suggest it is difficult to define, but Cutts and Moseley (1957, p. 154) state that mental health is "the ability to adjust satisfactorily to the various strains of life." Any individual's ability to adjust is affected by many circumstances and situations including those on the job. These will not affect all the same way. School administrators must be aware of conditions which help to create problems for teachers as well as for pupils. These include heavy teaching loads, crowded classrooms, lack of special services for children who need them, poor physical facilities, lack of supplies and equipment, and inadequate supervision.

All schools are concerned to some degree with the problem of preventing juvenile delinquency; therefore, all teachers will be confronted with the task of aiding in prevention and control. Some teachers, especially in areas where conditions and circumstances seem to help foster delinquency, will be charged with a greater responsibility. While it is not yet possible to predict all delinquency with sufficient accuracy, they must be well aware of behavior which appears to be very strongly indicative of predelinquency. They should be very concerned with the "whys" of behavior. Which students will hold teaching positions in such areas is not generally known during their initial training period. Therefore, it is essential that teacher training programs include for all teachers some consideration of the problems of children who deviate from the "average." As noted earlier, some schools and colleges of education allot time to problems of delinquency in courses in psychology, sociology, and/or education, but the amount of time so allotted is unfortunately not enough.

Moreover, most education students pursuing such courses being more concerned with "average" children may tend to disregard exceptional children (including juvenile delinquents).

As Eliot (1960) suggests, a program of prevention will not be sufficient in itself. Consideration must be given to the child already well into the throes of delinquency. In areas where there are a number of such children, teachers should be selected with care. At present too many ill-equipped teachers have been assigned to "difficult" schools. Sometimes such assignments have been made as administrative punishment, with good teachers being rewarded by placement in schools with few behavioral problems. Teachers with qualities suggested by Mackie, Kvaraceus, and Williams (1957) should be offered time and financial assistance to prepare themselves to teach in "difficult" schools.

The teachers of these classes need a different kind of training. They must be able to work in or near slums and to work with children, many of whom are not only poor but without roots. The turnover in some "slum schools" is 100 per cent in one year (Hechinger, 1962). One attempt to prepare teachers for such a setting was made in New York City. The City University was asked to staff one of the most difficult junior high schools. Students were asked to volunteeer to become student teachers, with the expectation that they would be placed as regular teachers after passing the regular examinations. The university promised to provide them help even after graduation. This proved so successful that other schools were included in the plan (Hechinger, 1962).

Although, as Long and Newman (1961) suggest, the challenge of teaching how to transfer educational beliefs and methods into an educational program is primarily the task of teacher training institutions, in-service training programs do help and school administrators use this approach quite frequently. This approach can be used to help teachers to understand better the problems of juvenile delinquency. Another way in which administrators can help teachers to increase their knowledge in this area is by making certain that the school's professional library contains pertinent and recent literature of value. Both of these approaches can be of value to the school administrators themselves, for they should certainly have a good understanding of the problem.

It is not a simple task to compile a reading list that will help teachers understand juvenile delinquency from the point of view of the schools. This is not due to a dearth of literature in the area of juvenile delinquency, for actually there are many excellent books and other publications devoted to this problem. Although many do include the school as a concern, a great many generalities are made where the school's role is considered. This leaves unanswered a number of questions which haunt the educator. As a result, he must read the broad works of the psychologist, the psychiatrist, the sociologist, and the criminologist and must distill the information in order to get some answers to his questions. He wants to know the effect of a child's socioeconomic status on adjustment and learning. He would like to know whether the youth in his school today are like the youth of the Elmtowns and the Midtowns. He wants to learn the effect of forcing middle class standards on children of lower levels. He would like to understand the effect that family structure, social mobility, and other factors have on a child as a student. He would like to learn the role that self-concept, vocational aspirations, and vocational opportunities play in deciding how successful a child will be. Some of the knowledges he has regarding these problems he gets from his formal professional training and experience, but a great deal must come from his individual reading and professional meetings.

CURRICULUM ADJUSTMENT

"Don't attempt to adjust the child to the curriculum, but rather adjust the curriculum to the child." This statement, in many areas, has degenerated into a cliché. But schools not adhering to this principle fail to provide a practical curriculum for those whose intellectual status does not permit them to benefit from the usual school program. There are educators who still feel that the same curriculum can fit all children. Their idea of curriculum adjustment is to offer the same course content at a slower pace. This, perhaps, accounts for attempts to compare certain academic-skill levels of retarded children in the regular grades with those of retarded children in special classes. The curriculum for those children should reflect their needs and not be merely a "watered down" version of one suited to the needs of children of average ability. Special educators do attempt to plan programs with adjusted curriculums. However, one recent report raises the question as to how well these programs are meeting their avowed purposes (Johnson, 1962).

Mentally retarded children or slow learners who are forced to spend hours attempting to achieve beyond their capacity are quite likely to seek an escape; this can result in juvenile delinquency. One method of providing for the mentally retarded so that they may have a curriculum more commensurate with their need and abilities is to establish special classes.

Although we do not really know what the needs of the mentally retarded are in terms of a method or a curriculum (Quay, 1963), we do have the help and the guidance of a number of people who have had considerable experience in teaching these children (Kirk and Johnson, 1951; Ingram, 1962; Garton, 1961). Their publications have helped many special class teachers plan programs which, although it may be difficult to demonstrate through controlled research, appear to have met the needs of a number of retarded children. However, special classes are no panacea. To benefit from such a program, it is advocated that the retarded be placed in special classes as early as discovery will permit. Equally important, those classes must be special in more than name only. Also it is essential that special class teachers have the professional background as well as those personal attributes necessary for successful work with retarded children.

Slow learners also need an adjusted curriculum. In the elementary grades, this can be accomplished through grouping within the classes. As these children move into secondary school they must be provided with a curriculum that is of interest and value to them. When they are confronted with a program too challenging or too dull, or when they fail to appreciate the values of the prescribed work, there is likely to be revolt and truancy. As one school does, stress could be placed on practical courses in home management or in shopwork of a general nature where there will be some transition to the semiskilled and unskilled type of employment. For those individuals who are more capable, courses in barbering, hairdressing, auto mechanics, and so on are being offered (Indianapolis Public School, 1957). If the dignity of labor is stressed from the early school years, these students might appreciate the importance of the various jobs within their capacities. Coupled with the above program, opportunities for part-time employment can be provided. Pupils can be employed during or after school hours. The cooperating employers can report areas in which the pupil requires additional training. The school program could then be geared to help pupils overcome their reported deficiencies. Havighurst (1960) suggests that, unless the slow learner is given a simplified academic program with some out-of-school experience, school administrators and school boards had better plan to move in the direction of modifying child labor laws. He suggests that, as school is now conducted, a considerable number of social misfits would be better off out of school than in school. Conant's (1961) work has also emphasized the need for providing a curriculum which fits the needs of this 20 per cent of the school-age population.

Although some studies indicate that the mean intelligence for adjudicated delinquents is slightly below that for the average population, the difference is not large, and as many of these youth are average or above in intelligence as measured by standardized tests as are nondelinquents. (See Chapter 4.) In addition, there are a number of unadjudicated delinquents (those who were handled by agencies other than the courts and those who were not apprehended) who are in the average or above average class. As indicated earlier, a large number of delinquents are educationally retarded. These children, whether or not they are mentally retarded or slow learners, need special consideration. Special consideration should be given to all educational retardates in an effort to provide them the education to which they are entitled.

To what extent educational retardation can cause delinquency (including truancy) is not readily understood. However, Behrmann (1963) reports that 85 per cent of 1500 children referred to the St. Louis Diocesean reading clinic for reading disabilites had developed emotional disturbances only after they had failed to learn to read. These disturbances he suggests may become so aggravated that they blossom into truancy and delinquency.

To determine if the school years could be made a profitable rather than a defeating experience for the delinquents, a special program was developed in one small Midwestern city. Early findings report that at the junior high school level the interests, attitudes, and aggressive behavior were more favorably influenced than academic achievement or personality patterns (Bowman, 1959). Although not evaluated on experimental bases, there are a number of special programs which seem to be beneficial to children with special learning problems (Kvaraceus and Ulrich, 1959).

SPECIAL SERVICES

With the ever-growing complexity of our modern society, schools have learned that regular classroom teachers and administrators cannot do all the work necessary to help insure a successful school experience for all children. They recognize that there is a need for specialists, such as visiting teachers, guidance workers, school psychologists, itinerant teachers, and special class teachers. A decade ago, Young (1959) suggested that the services available in any given school vary widely from a sporadic attention by an individual teacher to a complex and well-integrated system of social services and clinical psychotherapy. Although more and more communities have expanded and improved their services, this is still true today. Also many with seemingly well-integrated programs could improve greatly. Even the country's largest school system has seen the need to improve its services during the past several years (Kahn, 1963).

Large cities have need for very extensive special services. Also, it is expected that these communities can afford to expend the monies necessary to employ the special personnel needed for these services. But neither the extent of the services nor the monies expended by themselves determine the quality of services. Kahn (1963) discusses the special services provided by New York City. He suggests some of the problems involved in providing these special services, emphasizing the fact that creativity, large-scale investment, and dedication is not enough. He believes that roles must be defined, services integrated, and the total pattern coordinated. The value of coordinating all services for youth in New York City is stressed by the report of the Juvenile Delinquency Evaluation Project (MacIver, 1961). The NEA (1959) recommends that all schools join other community agencies in a coordinated effort to assist all children who need help.

Many special services are for the purpose of providing better service to all children, not merely to the relatively small per cent who are delinquent, predelinquent, or emotionally disturbed. Guidance workers, many special class teachers, itinerant teachers, and some therapists in particular serve a great many who are not severe or potentially severe behavior problems. However, some of these services may work chiefly with the behavior deviates.

Visiting Teachers

One special service aimed at prevention and treatment of behavior disorders is the visiting teacher program. Visiting teachers are individuals trained to assist regular classroom teachers to better understand children with problems which are interfering or may interfere with their learning and to assist the childen who are experiencing difficulties. They work cooperatively with other members of the school team. Some school systems classify a person with such duties as school social workers. The Michigan County Directors of Special Education suggest that visiting teachers are concerned with pupils having difficulty in personal and social adjustment in school and/or home and community. They state that "it is the purpose of the Visiting Teacher program to help pupils understand themselves and aid them in their environment as well as to assist parents and teachers to understand and help the children" (Michigan County Directors of Special Education, 1960).

This type of personnel is generally found in the larger school community. With the type of training which is expected of them in some communities, these workers are a natural link between the school and other agencies. The Michigan County Special Education Administrative Manual (1960) indicates that the training of visiting teachers includes skills and content areas work in dynamics of behavior and some medical, psychiatric, and psychological information. As well-trained professional people, they should function as a member of the school team. It is essential that they recognize their role as such and equally as important that they be accepted by teachers and school administrators as a vital link in a school program aimed at serving all children.

Special Classes

Special classes are provided for many types of exceptional children. Most common are those for the mentally retarded and the physically handicapped. There are also communities which provide special classes for the gifted, the deaf, the blind, the partially sighted, and/or the emotionally disturbed. During the past decade there has been a rapid growth in the number of special classes. This growth has been far more rapid than America's population explosion would have predicted (Mackie and Robbins, 1961). Despite this decided increase, educators believe far too few exceptional children who might benefit from special class placement are in the special classes. As indicated earlier, special classes are no panacea. The mere setting up of such classes solves little except perhaps to provide relief for the regular classroom. To be beneficial, the class should include (1) the children who can benefit from and who need such placement, (2) a teacher equipped emotionally and professionally, (3) a program flexible enough to provide for the interest and needs of all in attendance, and (4) adequate equipment and supplies. It should have also the understanding, help, and guidance of the school's administration and teaching personnel as well as of the community at large. Helpful guides are available which suggest the qualifications of teachers of exceptional children as well as the standards which the various states have set up for licenses in the field (Mackie, Kvaraceus, and Williams, 1957).

Emotionally disturbed children have been for many years the most neglected group among those generally classified as "exceptional." Because of the great number of such children, educators should be aware of the immensity of this problem. In a study of two and three-quarter million public and private school children, Abrahamsen (1960) found ten per cent of the public school population emotionally disturbed. In the past, the common solution to the problem of severely disturbed children in many public schools was to exclude all those who were disrupting the class. In other schools these children were either tolerated in the regular classrooms or, in cases when they were severely educationally retarded and had received low scores on intelligence tests, relegated to special classes for mentally retarded children. Those who were placed in special classes or schools for the disturbed often could not be afforded all the special services they needed. One reason for not supplying these services was the lack of trained personnel. One study suggests that ideally there should be available one psychiatrist for every 8,000 children—there is now one for every 50,000; one psychologist for 2,000 children —there is now one for every 10,964; and one psychiatric social worker for every 3,000 children—there is now one for every 38,461 (Abrahamsen, 1960).

Special classes and schools have been established for truants, delinquents, and those whose behavior might designate them as predelinquents. Chicago, Detroit, New York, and other cities have for some time provided such special services. Kirk (1962) gives a good description of some of these programs. In establishing such classes Kirk suggests that some of the factors considered are (1) size of class (ten to fifteen for predelinquents), (2) curriculum adjustment, (3) special teachers willing and able to work with this type of children, and (4) needs and interests of the children.

Such factors were considered in a program in Gary, Indiana, where 100 such youth were provided with a special school setting. No more than fifteen were enrolled in a class. Attendance was not compulsory, and sessions were for a half day. Although reading and writing were taught, other types of activities were also emphasized. Casework counseling was provided for the parents. After two years, truancy was no problem and the majority of parents commented on the improved behavior of their children (Robison, 1960).

Among the best known classes for these children are New York City's "600" schools (cf. Chapter 7). Since 1940 New York has provided for boys under 12 who have had contact with the courts. In 1949 the "600" schools were established for disturbed, disruptive, and delinquent children (Smith, 1959). These classes were to provide the special services which the children needed. One of their assets is the fact that they do relieve the regular classroom teachers of the responsibility of their severest behavior problems. It is also beneficial to the children of the regular class, for no longer do they have to contend with the disturbances which most likely have been a disrupting influence affecting their learning. Abrahamsen (1960) recognized these factors as assets, and he reports the benefits as more one of isolation than of correction. He states that between 10 and 15 per cent of the children sent to these schools are so disturbed that they need a type of treatment and setting not afforded at the schools, owing to the lack of qualified personnel and facilities. He also criticizes the method of selecting the children for placement in these schools. He believes the Bureau of Child Guidance rather than the principals should select the children who are to be assigned to these classes. Whether or not this is the practice, the initial recommendation for study generally emanates from the school through the principal, who should be familiar with all aspects of the problem. The writer believes that the principal should have the professional training which will permit him to assist in the decision as to which children can benefit by a special program. This means, of course, that he will be one voice in the coordinated effort of the various disciplines who can help to select those who can benefit from the special school program.

After new outbreaks of juvenile delinquency in 1957, New York City established its "700" schools. These were to serve pupils who manifested consistent and even more serious problems in school, including those who have been convicted in court but returned because of lack of room in appropriate institutions and those who have been charged with violence and insubordination (Abrahamsen, 1960). Abrahamsen believes that the same criticisms of these classes can be made as he made of the "600" schools.

Chicago's Montefiore and Mosley schools are as well known for their work as are the "600" schools. These serve boys, but each has a branch for girls. The children come from school districts throughout the city. In addition to the regular school offerings, special courses and services are provided, including remedial education, speech correction, and psychiatric and social services. "These schools serve an intermediate function between the regular school and the residential school for those requiring twenty-four hour management" (Kirk, 1962, p. 358). Again, one very real function which these schools serve is the "relief factor," removing the "problems" from the regular schools.

Most programs of this type are found in the larger communities. Actually, only a very small fraction of the norm-violating cases cannot be helped within the limits of the regular classroom. Thus the number of cases which need this type of special service is so low that the establishment of a special class in a smaller community may be difficult or uneconomical (Kvaraceus and Ulrich, 1959).

Guidance Workers

The role that guidance workers play in combating juvenile delinquency depends upon their professional training and experience. The backgrounds of those classified as school guidance counselors vary considerably. One source states that their basic professional preparation is in the field of education but that they will have acquired certain techniques of professions related to education, such as clinical psychology and social work, through course work and/or experience (Kitch and McCreary, 1959). They work with both staff and students, their chief responsibility being to assist individuals in solving their various personal adjustment problems. According to McDaniel *et al.* (1959) they are concerned with problems of teaching and administration and study and social services, as well as, in many instances, with serving as school psychometrists and therapists. It must be appreciated that their effectiveness in the various duties ascribed to them depends not only upon the quality and extent of their background and experience, but also upon their possessing the personal attributes necessary for such work.

The guidance worker's personal philosophy and the breadth of the task as he sees it will also affect his role in helping control and prevent juvenile delinquency. A review of basic texts in guidance raises the question as to whether or not guidance workers feel that this is one of their responsibilities. However, Williams (1959, p. 238) in discussing counseling and discipline states the belief that, in addition to acting as consultants in explaining deeper motivations underlying misbehavior, they should, through counseling, be involved in the active rehabilitation of misbehaving offenders, aid in the prevention of misbehavior, and aid students "to accept that external authority which influences inner development and modifies unbridled individualism."

School Psychologists

School psychologists also differ greatly in terms of training and duties. In one state an individual must have a Ph.D. in psychology, or its equivalent, while in other states he must have certain prescribed courses or courses which fulfill requirements in certain required content areas. Bower (1959) says that school psychologists are relatively new on the school staff. At first, they were primarily intelligence testers, but their area of responsibility has expanded. There is no complete agreement as to their functions and as to where their duties complement or overlap those of other disciplines. Bower lists the duties which most psychologists perform to some degree and suggests additional duties some have to perform. Among the latter, he includes work with children with serious behavior problems. His original list of duties includes that of helping school personnel "to understand the causes underlying various kinds of behavior and methods of helping each child to develop desirable behavioral patterns" (Bower, 1959, p. 41).

Other Special Services

Some schools provide speech therapy for children who have speech problems so severe and so complex as to require special services which the regular classroom teacher is not equipped to give. These problems and their concomitant causes require the services of a well-trained therapist and sometimes the help of other disciplines. Although there is an ever-increasing number of speech therapists, there are not enough to serve all the children who need help. For this reason too few children with severe speech problems are receiving the therapy which they need. In addition, some schools are hiring individuals to do this type of work who have qualifications far below those suggested by the American Speech and Hearing Association. It is not known whether any speech-handicapped children who are not being helped by a speech therapist avoid school, become truant, and then become involved in other delinquent acts.

Occupational therapy and/or physical therapy is provided for physically handicapped children in some schools. Some states give financial assistance to schools that provide these services, much as they do for communities that set up special classes.

There are educators who are well aware of the value and need of special services. Where there is the understanding and cooperation of responsible school communities and community leaders, schools are able to afford the salary and other benefits necessary to employ the types of persons needed for these special programs. Some schools have to settle for much less than "the ideal," providing whatever services they can with available financial support and personnel. But there are educators who are not interested enough and some school board members as well as some responsible community leaders who are not far sighted enough to provide all the services needed. They fail to see that these services not only help to stem the tide of delinquency but also improve education for a great many youths.

Early Identification

Quay and Peterson (1960) have said that "over the long-range period the only satisfactory treatment of delinquency will be the prevention of delinquency through the understanding of the psychological and sociological causes of delinquent behavior and through early identification of the delinquent-prone." Early recognition of the delinquent-prone permits attempts to establish preventive measures tailored to meet individual needs.

As we have seen in Chapter 6 the prediction problem is knotty and by no means solved. Nevertheless, the pressure of sudden increases in the delinquency rate and/or the pressure of public concern sometimes forces schools to initiate programs which it is hoped will have some immediate return. In some locals, this may be the establishment of special classes, which often become a dumping ground for behavioral problems. Or it may be the employment of special personnel to work with certain cases which have become severe behavioral problems. These approaches serve more to control than to prevent the problem. This suggests not that schools should not establish programs aimed at rehabilitating those who are known to be problems but rather that the approaches used be more than appeasement measures designed to relieve the pressures exerted by concerned citizens. But the schools must recognize that, although immediate returns may not be evident, early recognition can be the most productive method of preventing delinquency. As Abrahamsen (1960) says, "The earlier we discover antisocial signs and mental or emotional difficulties, the better chance we have combating them."

Kvaraceus (1960, p. 382) states that early identification and referral of predelinquent and delinquent children must be done systematically. He suggests that prevention cannot be achieved unless efforts are made to identify early "those children whose deviations in home, family, school, and neighborhood promise future hazards or difficulties in personal adjustment." He lists a number of significant deviations reported in controlled studies of delinquents and nondelinquents. Among the deviations in the school he has included truancy, intent to leave school early, motivational problem, and others. As an aid to the trained professional worker, Kvaraceus (1959) has recommended the use of several prediction tools and devices which he says "have been especially prepared for the purpose of early identification and delinquency-prone, vulnerable, susceptible, or exposed children." He indicates that none of them is fool-proof or predicts with 100 per cent accuracy, but each has shown to be valid enough for the trained worker to use.

Tait and Hodges (1962) recommend another way of using teacher observations which they feel would be less tiring for the already overburdened teacher. Rather than having teachers complete rating scales on children, they would have teachers call for special assistance to help work with problem children. Thus, they feel children would be referred in the natural course of daily school life and would not be singled out for special services before they presented serious behavior problems. This leaves the actual burden of identifying the predelinquent in the hands of the specialists. Also, it assumes that schools are able and willing to hire the necessary special personnel or that they have access to the services of other agencies which can do the job.

The school must exercise precautions if its staff is to be involved in helping to locate the delinquent-prone. Any special method employed to assist in locating such youth should be administered by those prepared to use them. In discussing the available prediction tools, Kvaraceus and Ulrich (1959) have suggested that some assume the availability of specialized personnel not presently found in our schools. Steps should be taken so that children who are identified as appearing to be delinquent-prone are not labeled by teachers who lack adequate understanding of such problems. Also, if the school does participate in attempts to identify the predelinquent, it should be concerned with the problem of rehabilitation. It is futile to locate such youth if nothing constructive is done for them.

The role teachers can play in the early identification of the delinquent-prone will vary in accordance with their professional knowledges and experiences. Generally, they will be aware of certain types of significant behavior which suggest that a child should be observed more closely and/or referred to the person in the school who is charged with the task of taking a closer look at children. But even with a fair amount of understanding of psychology and sociology, teachers can use help in determining the significant behavior patterns or conditions with which to be concerned. One guide some teachers find of value is the check list which accompanies the KD Proneness Scale (Kvaraceus, 1953).

Nationwide, there are school communities that have attempted to cope with the problem of juvenile delinquency in their own way. Some of these approaches involve the need for early identification, but many consist of special services ranging from special educational provisions to special extracurricular programs. Although it is difficult to evaluate these programs, many communities feel confident that they do help. Some of these were reported in the 1959 NEA study. Many were aired and discussed at the various meetings which Kvaraceus operated during the study itself. These are worthwhile reading for communities looking for ideas. In no case can they be superimposed on another, as the circumstances involved for two communities are likely to be very different.

RESEARCH

Like any problem in the area of human behavior a great deal more research in the area of juvenile delinquency is needed before it can be said that there is any real understanding of prevention or control. Research in this area is not new. Sociologists, psychologists, criminologists, and educators have tackled certain aspects of the problem. Of particular interest to educators are those that help them (1) to better understand how children behave and why they deviate in their behavior, (2) to locate at an early age children who will need special attention, and (3) to evaluate school programs which are most effective in helping to prevent and control juvenile delinquency.

Many studies designed to differentiate between delinquents and nondelinquents have been completed over the years. Kvaraceus (1959) reports the results of a number of those in which some forms of evaluative techniques have been used. There also have been some later reports of such studies. Although the investigators have appreciated that there are shades of delinquency—that it is not a matter of all white or all black—the results frequently have revealed significant differences among the two criterion groups in such areas as academic achievement, personal adjustment, physical structure, and socioeconomic factors. The located differences have been also the basis for such predictive devices as those devised by Sheldon and Eleanor Glueck (1950) and William Kvaraceus (1953). These studies can and are being used to better understand some of the conditions that affect the behavior and adjustment of the child in school. Used discreetly, this information can help schools in their plans for curriculums adjustment and special services. It also helps to provide some clues as to which children are vulnerable.

School personnel should not only be aware of completed and ongoing research projects of value and interest to them, but, when feasible, they should be involved in certain types of projects. These may be studies in which an educator is the chief investigator, or they may be those made in conjunction with others wherein the educator plays a minor but significant role. In discussing his proposed Institute of Research idea, Abrahamsen (1960) stated that one of the questions he thought should be tackled was, "How can schools contribute further in helping to deal with misbehavior in children?" More specifically, educators should conduct more research in the area of understanding just how schools contribute to delinquency. This should include research into causes of truancy and other forms of "school delinquency," the relationship of school failure to delinquent behavior, and the effect of teachers on the behavior and adjustment of children. Just as important is the fact that this research should be carefully evaluated and should be shared widely with all educators, including those concerned with teacher training and with other disciplines concerned with the welfare of children.

Kvaraceus' (1959) summary statement regarding research over a six-year period is still valid today: "In spite of the mythology and folklore that persists in approaches to delinquency in most communities, there are now discernible a number of promising practices aimed to prevent and control norm-violating behavior—practices which appear to be relevant to the factors which germinate and cause such behavior."

SUMMARY

Authorities in fields concerned with the welfare of children agree that the school can play an important role in the prevention and control of juvenile delinquency. Educators are evidently aware of the school's responsibility, and yet there is some question as to whether all teachers are equally well prepared to understand the problem.

Some studies seem to indicate that teachers are not capable of recognizing problems which will become significant, while others suggest that teachers today are better equipped to do so than formerly.

Some authorities believe schools help to cause juvenile delinquency. This is evidenced frequently by certain types of behavior. This same behavior may indicate delinquency resulting from factors not in the realm of the school. Chronic truancy is generally considered as a forerunner of serious delinquency. Others forms of absenteeism may be indicative of maladjustment. School failure may result from a misfitted curriculum or from some seemingly quite unrelated factor. Behavioral problems may also reflect school conditions or conditions of the home environment. Although not all children who misbehave in school become delinquent, delinquents generally misconduct themselves in school.

Teachers are in a logical position to help in the recognition of delinquent or delinquent-prone youth. They also have to play an important part in the schools' role of prevention and control. For this reason, schools should select teachers who are not only prepared professionally, but are also well adjusted and capable of working with this type of youth. The hiring of qualified teachers will lessen the chance that schools are aiding and abetting juvenile delinquency.

One way in which schools help to cause juvenile delinquency is by placing improper academic demands on children. Thus, curriculums should be adjusted to meet individual needs. In addition, some children need special services. Schools endeavoring to help to prevent juvenile delinquency and/or rehabilitate the delinquent provide many types of special services. These include such items as visiting teachers, special classes, guidance workers, psychologists, and school psychiatrists. These services are of benefit to many besides the delinquent and potential delinquent.

Educators can help to identify the predelinquent. Information and prediction devices are available that can aid in the identification of such youth. But care must be exercised in order to prevent the misuse of any information. Educators should be well aware of the limitations as well as the strengths of these devices.

There is too little research in the area of delinquency, as it relates to the school. Although it is recognized that some data gathered by other disciplines can be used by the educator, there is still a real need for him to become involved in research pertaining to problems related to delinquency.

References

Abrahamsen, D. (1960) *The psychology of crime.* New York: Columbia Univer. Press.

Amos, R. T., & Washington, R. (1960) Comparison of pupil and teacher perceptions of pupil's problems. *J. educ. Psychol.,* **51,** 255-258.

Ausubel, D. P. (1954) *Theory and problems of adolescent development.* New York: Grune & Stratton.

Bache, J. (1907) Delinquency and the responsibility of the school. *Annual proceedings of the National Education Association.*

Behrmann, E. H. (1963) Educational administrative procedures to promote pupil mental health. In L. Crow & Alice Crow (eds.), *Mental hygiene for teachers.* New York: Macmillan, 1963.

Bloch, H. A., & Flynn, F. T. (1950) *Delinquency: the juvenile offender in America today.* New York: Random House.

Bower, E. M. (1959) The school psychologist. In H. B. McDaniel, J. E. Lallas, J. A. Saum, & J. L. Gilmore (eds.), *Readings in guidance.* New York: Holt.

Bowman, P. (1959) Effects of a revised school program on potential delinquents. *Ann. Amer. Acad. Pol. Soc. Sci.,* **322,** 53-61.

Cavan, Ruth S. (1955) *Criminology.* New York: Crowell.

Clinard, M. B. (1959) Secondary community influences and juvenile delinquency. In S. Glueck (ed.), *The problem of delinquency.* Boston: Houghton Mifflin.

Cloward, R. A., & Ohlin, L. E. (1962) Illegitimate means and delinquent subcultures. In M. E. Wolfgang, L. Savitz, & N. Johnston (eds.), *The sociology of crime and delinquency.* New York: Wiley.

Cohen, A. (1962) The content of the delinquent subculture. In M. E. Wolfgang, L. Savitz, & N. Johnston (eds.), *The sociology of crime and delinquency.* New York: Wiley.

Commager, H. S. (1956) Our schools have kept us free. In L. D. Haskew (ed.), *This is teaching.* Chicago: Scott, Foresman.

Conant, J. B. (1961) *Slums and suburbs.* New York: McGraw-Hill.

Conant, J. B. (1963) *The education of American teachers.* New York: McGraw-Hill.

Crow, L. D., & Crow, Alice (1950) *Introduction to education.* New York: World Book.

Culbertson, J. (1960) Attendance. *Encyclopedia of educational research.* New York: Macmillan.

Cutts, Norma E., & Moseley, N. (1957) *Teaching the disorderly pupil in elementary and secondary school.* New York: Longmans, Green.

Derthick, L. E. (1962) Fundamental issues in American education. In L. D. Haskew (ed.), *This is teaching.* Chicago: Scott, Foresman.

Eichorn, J. R. (1962) Do teachers study juvenile delinquency? Unpublished paper.

Eisenberg, L. (1962) School phobia: a study in the communication of anxiety. In E. P. Trapp & P. Himmelstein (eds.), *Readings on the exceptional child.* New York: Appleton-Century-Crofts.

Eliot, Martha M. (1960) The family today: its needs and opportunities. *Soc. casework,* 34, 47-54.

Fine, B. (1959) *A million delinquents.* New York: World Publ.

Gage, N. L. & Suci, G. (1951) Social perception and teacher-pupil relations. *J. educ. Psychol.,* 42, 144-152.

Garton, Malinda D. (1961) *Teaching the educable mentally retarded.* Springfield, Ill.: Chas. Thomas.

Glueck, S., & Glueck, Eleanor (1950) *Unravelling juvenile delinquency.* New York: Commonwealth Fund.

Glueck, S., & Glueck, Eleanor (1959) *The problem of delinquency.* Boston. Houghton Mifflin.

Goldberg, Harriet L. (1948) *Child offenders.* New York: Grune & Stratton.

Gronlund, N. E. (1950) The accuracy of teachers judgments concerning the sociometric status of sixth grade pupils. *Sociometry,* 13, 197-225, 329-353.

Harris, A. J. (1952) What is a "normal" child? *J. teacher educ.,* 3, 58-61.

Havighurst, R. J. (1960) Dealing with problem youth. In J. F. Magary & J. R. Eichorn (eds.), *Exceptional children.* New York: Holt.

Hechinger, F. M. (1962) City emergency. *The New York Times,* October 14, 1962.

Hoover, J. E. (1960) The school and juvenile delinquency. *The educ. Forum,* 25, 19-20.

Hunter, C. E. (1963) Changes in teacher's attitudes toward children's behavior over the last thirty years. In L. Crow & Alice Crow (eds.), *Mental hygiene for teachers.* New York: Macmillan.

Hurlock, Elizabeth B. (1955) *Adolescent development.* New York: McGraw-Hill.

Hurlock, Elizabeth B. (1959) *Developmental psychology.* New York: McGraw-Hill.

Indianapolis Public Schools (1957) The Wood High School. Indianapolis.

Ingram, Christine (1962) *Education of the slow-learning child.* New York: Ronald.

Johnson, G. O. (1962) Special education for the mentally handicapped —a paradox. *Except. child.,* 15, 62-65.

Kahn, A. J. (1953) *A court for children.* New York: Columbia Univer. Press.

Kahn, A. J. (1963) *Planning community services for children in trouble.* New York: Columbia Univer. Press.

Kaplan, L. (1959) *Mental health and human relations in education.* New York: Harper.

Kirk, S. A. (1962) *Educating exceptional children.* Boston: Houghton Mifflin.

Kirk, S. A., & Johnson, G. O. (1951) *Educating the retarded child.* Boston: Houghton Mifflin.

Kitch, D. E., & McCreary, W. H. (1959) The school counselor: his work and training. In H. B. McDaniel, J. E. Lallas, J. A. Saum, & J. L. Gilmore (eds.), *Readings in guidance.* New York: Holt.

Klein, D. B. (1956) *Mental hygiene.* New York: Holt.

Kvaraceus, W. C. (1945) *Juvenile delinquency and the school.* New York: World Book.

Kvaraceus, W. C. (1953) *KD proneness scale and check list.* New York: World Book.

Kvaraceus, W. C. (1954) *The community and the delinquent.* New York: World Book.

Kvaraceus, W. C. (1959) The delinquent. *Rev. educ. res.,* **29,** 545-552.

Kvaraceus, W. C. (1960) What the school and community can do to prevent juvenile delinquency. In J. Magary & J. R. Eichorn (eds.), *Exceptional children.* New York: Holt.

Kvaraceus, W. C., & Miller, W. B. (1959) *Delinquent behavior: culture and the individual.* Washington, D. C.: National Education Association.

Kvaraceus, W. C., & Ulrich, W. E. (1959) *Delinquent behavior: principles and practices.* Washington, D. C.: National Education Association.

Lash, Trude, & Kahn, A. J. (1949) Children absent from school. Citizens Committee for Children of New York City, Inc.

Levison, Beatrice (1962) Understanding the child with school phobia. *Except. child.,* **28,** 393-397.

Long, N., & Newman, Ruth G. (1961) The teacher's handling of children in conflict. *Bulletin of the School of Education, Indiana University,* **37,** 4.

Luft, J. (1950) Implicit hypotheses and clinical predictions. *J. abnorm. soc. Psychol.,* **45,** 756-759.

Louttit, C. M. (1957) *Clinical psychology of exceptional children.* New York: Harper.

MacIver, R. M. (February 1961) The planning of delinquency prevention and control. Final report No. 1, juvenile delinquency project of the City of New York, City College, N. Y.

Mackie, R. P., Kvaraceus, W. C., & Williams, H. M. (1957) Teachers of children who are socially and emotionally maladjusted. Washington: U. S. Office of Education.

Mackie, R. P., & Robbins, Patricia P. (1961) Exceptional children and youth. A chart book of special education enrollments in public schools. Washington: U. S. Office of Education.

Massachusetts Child Council (1940) Responsibilities of the schools in relation to delinquency. Boston.

McDaniel, H. B., Lallas, J. E., Saum, J. A., & Gilmore, J. L. (eds.) (1959), *Readings in guidance.* New York: Holt.

Michigan County Directors of Special Education (1960) (C. Nange, ed.). Special Education Administration Manual. Kalamazoo, Mich.

Miller, W. B. (1958) Lower class culture as a generating milieu of gang and delinquency. *J. soc. Issues,* **14,** 5-19.

Mitchell, J. C. (1942) A study of teachers' and mental hygienists' ratings of certain behavioral problems of children. *J. educ. Res.,* **36,** 292-307.

Moore, Bernice M. (1958) *Juvenile delinquency.* Washington: Association for supervision and curriculum development.

Mouley, G. J. (1960) *Psychology for effective teaching.* New York: Holt.

Morse, W. C. (1958) The education of socially maladjusted and emotionally disturbed children. In W. M. Cruickshank & G. O. Johnson (eds.), *Education of exceptional children and youth.* Englewood Cliffs, N. J.: Prentice-Hall.

National Congress of Parents and Teachers (1957) What PTA members should know about delinquency. Chicago.

National Education Association Bulletin (1959) Crime prevention through education, **10,** 4.

National Society for the Study of Education (1948) *Juvenile delinquency and the schools.* (The forty-seventh yearbook.) Chicago: Univer. of Chicago Press.

Neumeyer, M. H. (1961) *Juvenile delinquency in modern society.* Princeton, N. J.: Van Nostrand.

Pierce, C. (1854) *Crime: its cause and cure.* Boston: Crosby, Nicholas.

Quay, H. C. (1963) Some basic considerations in the education of emotionally disturbed children. *Except. Child.,* **30,** 27-31.

Quay, H. C., & Peterson, D. R. (1960) Personality factors in the study of juvenile delinquency. *Except. Child.,* **26,** 472-477.

Reiss, A. (1952) Social correlates of psychological types of delinquency. *Amer. sociol. Rev.,* **17,** 710-718.

Rich, J. M. (1963) How social class values affect teacher-pupil relationship. In L. Crow & Alice Crow (eds.), *Mental hygiene for teachers.* New York: Macmillan.

Robison, Sophia (1960) *Juvenile delinquency.* New York: Holt.

Roman, M. (1957) *Reaching delinquents through reading.* Springfield, Ill.: Charles C. Thomas.

Sarason, S. B., Davidson, K. S., & Blatt, B. (1962) *The preparation of teachers.* New York: Wiley.

Schrupp, M., & Gjerde, C. M. (1955) Teacher growth in attitudes toward behavior problems of children. In A. P. Coladarci (ed.), *Educational psychology.* New York: Dryden.

Sharp, G. B. (1942) Ignorance and the teacher's situation. *J. Educ. Psychol.*, **33**, 61-66.

Short, J. F., & Nye, F. I. (1958) Extent of unrecorded juvenile delinquency: tentative conclusions. *J. crim. Law, Criminol. Police Sci.* **49**, 296-302.

Shulman, H. M. (1961) *Juvenile delinquency in American schools.* New York: Harper.

Smith, Carol C. (1959) The "600" schools. *Educ. J.*, **80**, 215-218.

Smith, P. M. (1958) The school as a factor in juvenile delinquency. In J. S. Roucek (ed.), *Juvenile delinquency.* New York: Philosophical Library.

Sparks, J. N. (1952) Teachers' attitudes toward the behavior problems in children. *J. Educ. Psychol.*, **43**, 28-291.

Stendler, Celia B. (1955) How well do elementary school teachers understand child behavior? In A. P. Coladarci (ed.), *Educational psychology.* New York: Dryden.

Stullken, E. H. (1959) The school and the delinquency problem. In S. Glueck (ed.), *The problem of delinquency.* Boston: Houghton Mifflin.

Sullenger, T. E. (1929) Social determinants in juvenile delinquency. Unpublished doctoral dissertation, University of Missouri.

Tait, C. D., Jr., & Hodges, E. F. (1962) *Delinquents—their families and the community.* Springfield, Ill.: Charles C. Thomas.

Talbot, Mira (1957) Panic in school phobia. *Amer. J. Orthopsychiat.*, **27**, 286-295.

Warner, W. L., Havighurst, R. J., & Loeb, M. B. (1954) *Who shall be educated?* New York: Harper.

Wickman, E. K. (1928) *Children's behavior and teacher's attitudes.* New York: Commonwealth Fund.

Williams, E. G. (1959) The fusion of discipline and counseling in the educative process. In H. B. McDaniel, J. E. Lallas, J. A. Saum, & J. L. Gilmore (eds.), *Readings in guidance.* New York: Holt.

Yoshino, R. (1959) Classroom teacher and the pre-delinquent. *Educ. sociol.*, **33**, 124-130.

Young, Paulina (1952) *Social treatment in probation and delinquency.* New York: McGraw-Hill.

Editor's Epilogue

One cannot read this book and not be impressed by the complexities involved in researching and theorizing about juvenile delinquency. In the midst of this complexity, some promising directions emerge. It is gratifying that research is becoming more sophisticated in the application of scientific methods of study. One thing seems certain: the trend toward conceptual refinement in what is meant by "the delinquent" must continue and this refinement must be accompanied by an increased awareness of methodological requirements.

We also seem to have arrived at the point at which studies of the individual and studies of the culture must be conducted jointly. Neither the individual nor the culture can continue to be considered separately if research results of maximum meaningfulness are to occur. We need more research in which individual differences in response to cultural pressures are studied. At the same time the studies of subcultures and ecology need to pay a great deal more heed to the nature of the persons who belong to the gang or live in the urban deteriorated area. Juvenile delinquency has both cultural and personal correlates; the time has arrived to find out how these interact.

Current theorists also need to attend to the lessons of the past relative to the formalities of theory construction. Theory is most valuable when it has been tested; next most valuable when it can be tested. Our currently popular theories are often based on untested assumptions rather than on empirical propositions. They frequently fail to generate specific and testable hypotheses which can be either confirmed or rejected. Too often the implicit assumption that delinquency is a unitary phenomenon gives rise to unwarranted generalizations, whereas theory may be appropriate only in regard to a specific kind of delinquent or delinquency.

338

There has been an unfortunate tendency for research and theory to be unrelated. Little of the mass of research accomplished in recent years has been generated by current theory or bears directly upon it. Part of this situation seems to be due to the relative lack of operationality in some current theorizing. Empirical research is still most frequently accomplished by those interested in individual differences or the influence of family factors, while the broader conceptualizations have been contributed by those with less predilection for controlled inquiry.

Name Index

Abrahamsen, D., 308, 309, 315, 317, 324, 325, 328, 331
Ackerly, S., 106
Adams, S., 264, 275, 276
Adamson, L., 245
Adams, J., 11
Aichorn, A., 173, 174, 233, 251, 271
Allen, F., 233
Alston, E., 220
Alt, H., 239
Altus, W. D., 112
Amos, R. T., 304
Anderson, A. C., 143
Andry, R. G., 71, 72, 74, 78, 80, 81, 88, 174
Arcadias, Y., 218
Argyle, M., 265
Armitage, S. G., 227
Atkinson, J. W., 20
Austin, O. L., 104
Ausubel, D. P., 306, 307, 312
Axelrod, S., 154, 155, 250
Ayllon, T., 227

Babcock, M. E., 109
Bach, G. R., 81
Bache, J., 302
Baker, B. O., 133, 134
Baker, H. J., 105
Balistrieri, J. J., 148, 149
Bandura, A., 20, 78, 81, 83, 85, 86, 87, 88, 95, 251
Barndt, R. J., 140
Barron, M. L., 124, 250
Beam, K. S., 245
Beane, J. C., 104
Beccaria, C. B., 13
Beck, B., 214
Becker, W. C., 85, 86, 87, 166
Behrmann, E. H., 321
Beissler, P. T., 251
Bender, L., 232

Bennett, I., 19, 70, 72, 84, 85, 173, 174
Bernard, J., 209
Bernstein, R., 112
Bettelheim, B., 173, 174, 234, 271
Beverly, R. F., 265, 270
Bijou, S. W., 109
Binet, A., 102
Bixby, F. L., 239
Blank, L., 113
Blatt, B., 304
Bloch, H., 44, 45, 57, 106, 214, 220, 299, 300
Blumen, L., 149, 179
Bohlke, R., 42, 57
Boneau, C. A., 276
Bordua, D., 34, 35
Borelli, Father, 220
Bowen, T. W., 165
Bower, E. M., 327
Bowlby, J., 70, 75, 93
Bowman, P., 242, 243, 321
Bradford, J., 20
Breed, A. F., 217
Bremer, G., 81
Briggs, P. F., 17, 20, 125, 145, 175, 178, 189, 194, 201, 202
Bronfenbrenner, U., 66
Bronner, A., 75, 82, 106, 225, 228, 244, 245
Brown, A. W., 105
Brown, R. C., 246, 247
Buck, C. E., 221, 251
Buell, B., 221, 251
Burgess, E., 30, 64, 227
Burke, E. C., 98
Burkhart, W. R., 291
Burt, C., 68, 69, 70, 75, 82, 85, 105

Cabot, P. S. DeQ., 103
Cameron, G. R., 125, 158, 164
Cameron, N., 55

340

Subject Index